LITERARY CRITICISM

A SHORT HISTORY

WILLIAM K. WIMSATT, JR.
& CLEANTH BROOKS

LITERARY CRITICISM

A SHORT HISTORY

1: Classical and Neo-Classical Criticism

The University of Chicago Press
Chicago and London

TO RENÉ WELLEK

The University of Chicago Press, Chicago 60637
The University of Chicago Press, Ltd., London

© 1957 by William K. Wimsatt, Jr., and Cleanth Brooks
All rights reserved. Published 1957
Phoenix Edition 1978
Printed in the United States of America

82 81 80 79 78   987654321

ISBN: 0-226-90173-4
LCN: 78-55046

CONTENTS

Contents

PART III

PART IV

PART V

INTRODUCTION

IT IS NOT LIKELY THAT A PERSON WHO ENTERTAINS EVEN A MODEST prejudice against the kind of history writing which appears in this book will have his mind changed by introductory apologetics. Still some preliminary advertisement of aims may be only fair—and may even be generally helpful to a receptive reading. The first principle on which we would insist is that of continuity and intelligibility in the history of literary argument. Plato has a bearing on Croce and Freud, and vice versa. Or, all three of these theorists are engaged with a common reality and hence engage one another through the medium of that reality and either come to terms or disagree. Literary problems occur not just because history produces them, but because literature is a thing of such and such a sort, showing such and such a relation to the rest of human experience. True, languages and cultures, times and places, differ widely. The literary historian will always do well to nurse a certain skepticism about the thoroughness with which he may be penetrating the secret of his documents. But then he has to worry too about an opposite danger of being merely and overly skeptical. There are techniques of caution and neutrality which put the historian somewhat in the position of the student who, having his difficulties with a Latin or German reading examination, is content to put down a translation that does not make sense. He writes as if he is not convinced that the foreign language does make sense. Our own notion of how to write a history of literary ideas is just the opposite of that. The history is bound to be an interpretation, in part even a translation. In part it will even be built on reasonable guesses. The least it can do is make sense.

And that connects closely with a second of our main notions about method; namely, that a history of literary ideas can scarcely escape being written from a point of view. It seems to us that on a strictly neutral plan there can be in fact no history of literary ideas at all, nor, for that matter, any direct history of literature. At least not any history that hangs together. This book, we hope and believe, both grows out of and illustrates and contributes to a certain distinct point of view. It is the history of one kind of thinking about values, and hence it could not have been written relativistically, or indifferently, or at random. It contains much praise and blame, both implicit and explicit. There are even senses, complimentary we believe, in which it could be called "polemic" or "argumentative." It is nevertheless, we contend, a true history. Call it *An Argumentative History of Literary Argument in the West.*

The reader will now readily conceive yet another of our notions: namely, that in a history of this sort the critical *idea* has priority over all other kinds of material. The present "short" history does not attempt a grand assemblage of information (though information of the right kind and in the right amount, we believe, is here). Neither encyclopedism nor the Saintsburyan gigantically conversational range has been our purpose, but a series of narrative focusses precisely on ideas. In some chapters, especially in those concerning the neo-classic age, the argument runs directly along thematic lines. Other chapters, especially those concerning classical antiquity, are developed around certain heroic figures—Plato, or Aristotle, or Longinus. Still even in these chapters, the idea, not the hero, is always paramount. Hence it happens that we have attempted no complete account of any one philosopher or literary man (much less any complete survey of disciples or other minor figures). We have used the little figures, and even the great figures, as they came in handy to our narrative. Hence also we have been little interested in proving the consistency, we have been little dismayed by the frequent inconsistencies, of our great literary theorists. Where we have here and there noticed inconsistencies (as, let us say, in Addison's account of imagination, or in Arnold's account of classic grandeur and the "touchstones"), the point has been made not so much against the author as against a collection of ideas which have often been credited with more coherence than they actually exhibit. Or it has been made simply for the sake of gaining the expository advantage of contrast. By and large, as notably with Plato in the first chapter, we have preferred the idea in full bloom and have made no attempt to harmonize the smaller contradictions, real or apparent, which are always to be found in the canon of a prolific author. When the main ideas of an author have been leveled off or averaged in with all the marginal variations, the result is not a story with parts, contours, accents, climaxes, but a dead level of neutrality—the melted wax doll. The principle applies with equal force to themes and eras in intellectual history. Statistical scrupulosity in the study of "ideas" tends of course toward a smudge. This truth was never more clearly betrayed than in the following recommendation of minute history by a late distinguished American scholar:

> One of the surest evidences of a better understanding of an individual or a period is that sharp lines disappear, strong lights and shadows are modified, uniqueness and isolation melt away, the man is seen to be more like other men, the age like other ages.[1]

The present writers, despite their confidence in the continuity and real community of human experience through the ages,[2] are confident also

[1] R. D. Havens, "Changing Taste in the Eighteenth Century," *PMLA*, XLIV (June, 1929), 534-5.

[2] Some variations on the theme of the "universal" perhaps relevant to the present paradox are to be found near the end of Chapter 15.

of differences—of levels, depressions, and eminences—of the difference between Elizabethan England and Augustan Rome, of that between Chaucer and Pope, and of that between Pope and Blackmore, Dryden and Rymer.

The examples just mentioned invite allusion to one further methodological notion and one which is perhaps not very immediately entailed by what we have so far been saying. We have finally to confess what may seem to some of our more severely idealist friends a principle of distinct impurity in our method. Our book is not a history of general aesthetics (though a few quite limited excursions into the aesthetic ambient have been ventured). On the other hand, it is not a history of literary technicalities or techniques, of prosody or grammar. Yet if we had had to make a choice between a more markedly aesthetic direction and a more grammatical, it is the latter (in the full classical sense of the term "grammatical") which we should have chosen. That is, we have written a history of ideas about verbal art and about its elucidation and criticism. The ultimate object of our regard then, though seen at a remove, through the eyes of the critic and the theorist of criticism, has been poetry or literature. So much literary criticism and theory and so much of the best has been written by the men of letters. Often, whether consciously or not, they have written their general theories as a comment on their own best performances in poetry, and on the *kinds* of poetry which were most dear to them. The theory, furthermore, has been both stated and exemplified by the poems, and undoubtedly both poetry and theory have interacted in several ways. To show that the history of literary theory has been no more than a series of temporary explanations directed toward poetic vogues of the moment and hence that the name of "poetry" enjoys only a long record of equivocality, would be the final triumph of the neutrally and pluralistically minded investigator. Such (need it be said?) has scarcely been our aspiration. On the other hand, to show that through all the ambiguous weave and dialectical play of the successive concrete situations which make the history of poems and theory, the sustaining truth continues and may be discerned and its history written—this would seem to be an appropriate enough goal for the historian who believes that he has in fact a coherent, a real and unequivocal subject matter. To tell the story pure, as a series of internally driven developments of ideas or patterns of abstractly significant oppositions and resolutions, will have advantages for the philosopher. But to tell it more or less impurely, bringing in the colors of the literary milieu and allowing critical episodes to take shape out of the milieu, will have some advantages for the student of literature. In a few sentences of the Epilogue which concludes this book we have tried to sketch a view of how the several literary genre conceptions dominant in several ages—dramatic, epistolary, heroic, burlesque, and lyric—will if studied carefully open up not so many diverse views into multiplicity and chaos but so many complementary insights into the one deeply rooted and perennial human truth which is the poetic principle.

As our chapter titles will suggest, the substance of the book includes Greek and Roman classicism, Renaissance, Augustan, romantic, and Victorian English criticism, and 20th-century English and American. In addition, there are excursions or inter-chapters or sections of chapters dealing with the Middle Ages and with main episodes in modern Italian, French, German, and Russian criticism. The book tries to follow the main lines of the critical heritage and then draw in the story toward the end to the immediate arena of the modern English-speaking world.

Any history of any subject has to begin somewhere—a matter perhaps of some embarrassment. Where it begins will be determined not only by the availability of certain documents but by the views of the author concerning the real nature of his subject. The present history might have lingered longer near its beginning than it actually does with certain proto-glimpses of literary critical consciousness in the Western tradition—invocations by the early Greek poets Homer and Hesiod to the Muses and assertions of an aim to teach or to charm, phrases of some pith and relevance concerning craft and genius or the fate of man, from early and all but lost lyric poets, from law-givers, dramatists, and pre-Socratic philosophers. The history as it actually begins, in our first chapter, plunges immediately, with only a few preliminary words, into an early Platonic dialogue, the *Ion*. This is the earliest extant Western writing that addresses itself deliberately, formally, and exclusively to the general matter of literary criticism. Furthermore this dialogue treats the topic of literary criticism in a way which the present writers conceive to be the correct way—that is, by asking a difficult question about the kind of knowledge which a criticism of a poem, or a poem itself, can lay claim to. What does a poem say that is worth listening to? What does criticism say? The entire course of literary theory and criticism, from the time of Plato to the present, has in effect been occupied with producing more or less acute versions of those questions and more or less accurate and telling answers. Plato's *Ion* is a thoroughgoing, radically naive, inquiry into the nature of poetic composition as a department of verbal meaning and power. It has also the advantage to the historian that it is a dialogue—that is, its arguments are put not purely and schematically but in dramatic form. There are two speakers and at least two points of view. The historian of critical ideas who takes such ideas in any degree tentatively, yet seriously, could scarcely find himself beginning on more congenial ground.

The supplementary passages which appear after most of the chapters in the book are intended to supply in part historical and theoretical dimensions which could not be conveniently handled in the narrative and in part illustrations or problems (some of them comic) which the meditative reader may enjoy placing for himself in relation to the themes of the narrative. Passages following a given chapter may stand either in harmony with one another or in opposition, and in various relations to the content of the chapter.

Quotations from Greek and Latin and from modern foreign languages appear for the most part in already available translations, which are appropriately acknowledged. But here and there the authors have for one reason or another attempted their own, perhaps rather free, translations. These appear for the most part without further advertisement.

This book would perhaps never have been begun except for a suggestion made to the authors a few years back by two friends, George W. Stewart and John Nerber. The authors wish to record their debt and express their gratitude.

The whole work has been written by a method of fairly close collaboration not only in the general plan but in the execution of each part. The authors have read and criticized each other's work closely and repeatedly at various stages. The substantial responsibility for the chapters is, however, to be divided as follows: Chapters 1–24, and 32, W. K. Wimsatt, Jr.; Chapters 25–31, Cleanth Brooks.

The parts of the book by W. K. Wimsatt, Jr., owe an obvious large debt to a Yale graduate English seminar, Theories of Poetry, inaugurated many years ago by Albert S. Cook, and conducted subsequently by F. A. Pottle and T. W. Copeland. To those founders, and especially to F. A. Pottle, and to the students in the course since 1942 and to those in its more recent undergraduate parallel, Introduction to Criticism, the author makes a grateful acknowledgement.

Cleanth Brooks did part of his work on the book while holding a Fellowship of The John Simon Guggenheim Memorial Foundation. He wishes to acknowledge the kindness of the Foundation and to express his thanks.

For various kinds of assistance in research and preparation of typescript, the authors express their thanks to Robert B. Brown, Richard J. Browne, James Cook, Harold Cogger, Mrs. D. W. Gordon, John Oates, Michael Pertschuk, Mrs. David Underdown, and Donald Wheeler.

A more or less pervasive debt in several chapters to a manuscript book by H. M. McLuhan concerning the ancient war between dialecticians and rhetoricians is here gratefully acknowledged and is underscored by the quotation, following Chapter 4, of two substantial excerpts from published essays by Mr. McLuhan.

To their colleagues Bernard Knox, Maynard Mack, John Palmer,

John Smith, and René Wellek, the authors are indebted for reading and criticism of various chapters in early drafts, and to Charles Feidelson, Charles C. Walcutt, and Father Walter J. Ong, S.J., for various kinds of critical advice. More than to any other single scholar, they are indebted for general theoretical and historical help to René Wellek. Not only his published but his yet unpublished works and his advice in conversation have done much to promote the writing of the modern chapters.

To Margaret and Tinkum, for labors expert, various, and unremitting, the authors join in affectionate expression of gratitude.

To Marshall Waingrow the authors owe special thanks for a skillful reading of the entire page proof. Alfred Stiernotte made the index.

Two fairly extended passages of Chapter 32, the Epilogue, follow an essay "Criticism Today: A Report from America," published by W. K. Wimsatt, Jr., in *Essays in Criticism*, VI (January, 1956), 1–21. Our thanks are due to F. W. Bateson, the editor.

ANNOTATIONS AND SOURCES

This book is annotated lightly. The notes aim at giving a guide to verifying our treatment of sources and a minimal clue to further reading. Certain works which have general relevance for the whole book or for major sections of it are brought together in the following list. At various places in the annotation, some of these works are cited by abbreviated titles or simply by names of their authors. The reader will easily understand such references on consulting the list.

Meyer H. Abrams, *The Mirror and the Lamp*. New York: Oxford University Press, 1953

Raymond M. Alden, ed., *Critical Essays of the Early Nineteenth Century*. New York: Charles Scribner's Sons, 1921

J. W. H. Atkins, *English Literary Criticism*. I, *The Medieval Phase*. Cambridge: At the University Press, 1943; II, *The Renascence*. London: Methuen & Co. 1947; III, *The Seventeenth and Eighteenth Centuries*. London: Methuen & Co., 1951

J. W. H. Atkins, *Literary Criticism in Antiquity*, vols. I and II. Cambridge: At the University Press, 1934

Charles S. Baldwin, *Ancient Rhetoric and Poetic*. New York: The Macmillan Company, 1924

Medieval Rhetoric and Poetic. New York: The Macmillan Company, 1928

Renaissance Literary Theory and Practice. New York: Columbia University Press, 1939

Walter J. Bate, *From Classic to Romantic, Premises of Taste in Eighteenth-Century England*. Cambridge, Mass.: Harvard University Press, 1946

Walter J. Bate, ed., *Criticism: The Major Texts*. New York: Harcourt, Brace and Company, 1948

Albert C. Baugh, *A History of the English Language*. New York: D. Appleton-Century Company, 1935

Albert C. Baugh et al., *A Literary History of England*. New York: Appleton-Century-Crofts, 1948

Bernard Bosanquet, *A History of Aesthetic*. London: Swan Sonnenschein & Co.; New York: Macmillan & Co., 1892

Aisso Bosker, *Literary Criticism in the Age of Johnson*. Groningen: J. B. Wolters' Uitgevers-Maatschappij, 1930; revised edition, 1953

René Bray, *La Formation de la doctrine classique en France*. Dijon: Maurice Darantière, 1927

Edgar de Bruyne, *Etudes d'esthétique médiévale*, vols. I, II, III. Brugge (België): "De Tempel," 1946

E. F. Carritt, *Philosophies of Beauty from Socrates to Robert Bridges*. Oxford: Oxford University Press, 1931

Alexander F. B. Clark, *Boileau and the French Classical Critics in England (1660–1830)*. Paris: Librairie Ancienne Édouard Champion, 1925

Ronald S. Crane et al., *Critics and Criticism Ancient and Modern*. Chicago: The University of Chicago Press, 1952

Benedetto Croce, *Aesthetic as Science of Expression and General Linguistic*, trans. Douglas Ainslie, 2nd ed. London: Macmillan and Co., 1922

John F. D'Alton, *Roman Literary Theory and Criticism*. London and New York: Longmans, Green and Co., 1931

Willard H. Durham, ed., *Critical Essays of the Eighteenth Century*. New Haven: Yale University Press, 1915

T. S. Eliot, *The Use of Poetry and the Use of Criticism, Studies in the Relation of Criticism to Poetry in England*. Cambridge, Mass.: Harvard University Press, 1933

Allan H. Gilbert, ed., *Literary Criticism Plato to Dryden*. New York: American Book Company, 1940

Katharine E. Gilbert and Helmut Kuhn, *A History of Esthetics*. New York: The Macmillan Company, 1939; Bloomington: Indiana University Press, 1953

Theodore M. Greene, *The Arts and the Art of Criticism*, 2nd ed. Princeton: Princeton University Press, 1947

Werner Jaeger, *Paideia: The Ideals of Greek Culture*, trans. Gilbert Highet, vols. I, II, III. New York: Oxford University Press, 1939–44

Leah Jonas, *The Divine Science, The Aesthetic of Some Representative Seventeenth-Century English Poets*. New York: Columbia University Press, 1940

Thomas Munro, *The Arts and Their Interrelations*. New York: The Liberal Arts Press, 1949

William V. O'Connor, *An Age of Criticism 1900–1950*. Chicago: Henry Regnery Company, 1952

Melvin Rader, ed., *A Modern Book of Esthetics, An Anthology*. New York: Henry Holt and Company, 1935, 1952

William Rhys Roberts, *Greek Rhetoric and Literary Theory*. New York: Longmans, Green and Co., 1928

George Saintsbury, *A History of Criticism and Literary Taste in Europe*, vols. I, II, III, 4th ed. Edinburgh and London: William Blackwood & Sons, 1949

Mark Schorer *et al.*, eds., *Criticism: The Foundations of Modern Literary Judgment*. New York: Harcourt, Brace and Company, 1948

Joseph T. Shipley, ed., *Dictionary of World Literature: Criticism—Forms—Technique*. New York: The Philosophical Library, 1943

G. Gregory Smith, ed., *Elizabethan Critical Essays*, vols. I and II. Oxford: Oxford University Press, 1937

James H. Smith and Edd W. Parks, eds., *The Great Critics, An Anthology of Literary Criticism*. New York: W. W. Norton & Company, 1951

Joel E. Spingarn, ed., *Critical Essays of the Seventeenth Century*, vols. I, II, III. Oxford: At the Clarendon Press, 1908–9

Joel E. Spingarn, *A History of Literary Criticism in the Renaissance*. New York: Columbia University Press, 1899

Robert W. Stallman, *Critiques and Essays in Criticism, 1920–1948, Representing the Achievement of Modern British and American Critics*. New York: The Ronald Press Company, 1949

Alba H. Warren, Jr., *English Poetic Theory, 1825–1865*. Princeton: Princeton University Press, 1950

René Wellek, *A History of Modern Criticism: 1750–1950*. I, *The Later Eighteenth Century*; II, *The Romantic Age*. New Haven: Yale University Press, 1955

René Wellek, *The Rise of English Literary History*. Chapel Hill: The University of North Carolina Press, 1941

René Wellek and Austin Warren, *Theory of Literature*. New York: Harcourt, Brace and Company, 1949

Morton D. Zabel, ed., *Literary Opinion in America*. New York: Harper & Brothers, 1951

Titles of learned and critical journals are sometimes abbreviated in the notes, as follows:

AJP *The American Journal of Philology*
ELH *ELH: A Journal of English Literary History*
JEGP *The Journal of English and Germanic Philology*
JHI *Journal of the History of Ideas*

MLN   *Modern Language Notes*
MLQ   *Modern Language Quarterly*
MLR   *The Modern Language Review*
MP   *Modern Philology*
PQ   *Philological Quarterly*
SP   *Studies in Philology*
PMLA   *Publications of the Modern Language Association of America*
RES   *The Review of English Studies*
TLS   *The Times Literary Supplement*

LITERARY CRITICISM:
A SHORT HISTORY

PART ONE

CHAPTER I

SOCRATES AND THE RHAPSODE

BECAUSE POETS HAVE A STRONG TENDENCY TO FORM OPINIONS ABOUT THEIR craft and to use these opinions as part of the message of their poems, we are likely to find literary theory of a sort as far back as we can find poems. When Homer begins his epics with an invocation to the muse, he is uttering a theory about his poems—namely, that they are written, or had better be written, with the help of divine inspiration—and this is an idea which has played a considerable role in the sub-

3

sequent history of poetics. During the several centuries that elapse between Homer and Plato, the first philosopher of literature whose ideas we shall examine with any care, other Greek writers, Hesiod, Solon, Simonides, Pindar and the rhetoricians and dramatists of the fifth century, made various critical remarks—that poetry is charming, that poetry is instructive, that it comes natural to a genius, that it has to be learned by art, that it is like painting, that it consists in a clever use of words-—and to these opinions we shall here and there have occasion to allude in retrospect.

In Athens towards the close of the fifth century, after the great Periclean age, the comic dramatists, who made satirical criticism of life in general their business, had some sharp things to say about literature. Especially Aristophanes, and his special literary target was the modernist tragic dramatist Euripides. The earliest piece of extended literary criticism which survives from classical antiquity is an agon or debate in the *Frogs* of Aristophanes (405 B.C.), where Dionysus, patron and god of the theater festivals, has descended into Hades for the purpose of bringing back to earth the recently departed Euripides, but in the end actually makes the award to the good old-fashioned writer Aeschylus. The announced standards of criticism are "skill in the art" and "wise counsel for the state." The latter of these is perhaps the more important, but the actual decision of Dionysus seems to rest not so much on an appeal to either standard as on the fact that Aeschylus is the poet who takes his fancy. Some specific poetic traits are amusingly criticized—the wild and whirling magniloquence of Aeschylus (his "hippalectors" [1] and "trage-laphs" [2]), the sentimental fondness of Euripides for lame beggars as heroes. But the thing that a critically inclined person may remember most vividly is a certain directness in the form of argument. Scales are brought out, and the poets are weighed against each other line for line.

DIONYSUS:	Now, then, each repeat a verse.
EURIPIDES:	"I wish that Argo with her woven wings."
AESCHYLUS:	"O streams of Spercheius, and ye pastured plains."
DIONYSUS:	Let go!—See now—this scale outweighs that other. Very considerably.

—lines 1381–5 [3]

Although this is a parody of critical procedure, one might take it as a symbol of what is often most refreshing in early critical documents—a certain frontal naiveté, an immediate shrewdness of inquiry which the inheritors of criticism have long since, and by necessity, obscured in their more sophisticated formulations. To be able to speak about

---

[1] Horse-cocks, gryphons.
[2] Goat-stags, fantastic animals such as were known on Eastern carpets.
[3] Translation of J. Hookham Frere.

Homer's epics, not as the remote and venerable source of a classical tradition 3,000 years old, but as heroic poetry currently recited at popular festivals, and to be able to speak about tragedy and comedy as social and religious forms of art which had developed only within a preceding half century of Athenian prosperity—these were great advantages to the free-lance speculator on general problems of human existence who is the central figure in the next critical work which we are to consider.

<h2 style="text-align:center">II</h2>

PLATO's *Ion* was written sometime in the first decade of the fourth century, a few years later than the death of his master Socrates in 399. Like the agon in the *Frogs* of Aristophanes, this piece of criticism takes the dramatic form. It is a philosophic dialogue, the scene being at Athens a short time before the close of the Peloponnesian war and the temporary eclipse of Athenian democracy. The interlocutors are Socrates and the rhapsode Ion, the latter just returned from Epidaurus, where he has won first prize at a festival in honor of Asclepius. A rhapsode (as we conceive him, and indeed largely on the evidence of this dialogue) was a person who might be described, in terms of our own culture, as a sort of combined actor and college teacher of literature. He gave public recitations from the *Iliad* and the *Odyssey*, especially of the more exciting passages; and he undertook to deliver critical and moral lectures. He must have drawn large audiences (even if we take the 20,000 mentioned in the dialogue as a great exaggeration), and he sometimes succeeded in moving these audiences very deeply, even to tears. He appeared in rich attire, perhaps wearing a golden crown, and he received a handsome pecuniary reward. He is representative of the older, literary, and unsystematic Greek education (*paideia*).

Socrates as he confronts Ion in this dialogue may be taken as representing a spirit of criticism which was increasing with the sad experiences of the city state. A mere sophist in the *Clouds* of Aristophanes, as he appears in his *phrontistērion* or "thinkery," corrupting a youth to turn against his father, Socrates is transformed into a subtle philosopher and relentless enemy of ignorance as he appears in the dialogues of Plato. In a friendly and restrained yet insistent way, Socrates, as if seeking to know something of our literary professor's trade secrets, succeeds in asking him some uncomfortable questions and in eliciting some unfortunate answers. Ion admits, for instance, that although there are many poets, and although they speak often on the same topics, he himself is skilled only in reading Homer, and he is interested only in Homer. He drops off into a doze when somebody talks about any other poet. Enough comes out to make it appear that anything Ion has to say about Homer is scarcely said with the help of what Socrates would call art and knowledge (*technē kai epistēmē*). Ion has no rational technique, for a technique or art is a unified thing (*holon*). Or, as we might say, the term "poetry" if it means anything intelligible is a univocal term, not a quibble. Anybody who can criticize one poet ought to be able to criticize another.[4]

A general tendency of the Socratic argument to thrust at the poet himself through his punier representative the rhapsode [5] culminates midway of the dialogue in a celebrated speech which likens the poet to a magnet radiating a kind of divine power (*theia dunamis*) out through a chain of iron rings, the rhapsode and his audience. Both poets and rhapsodes utter what they do by a divine dispensation, a form of madness.

> For the poet is a light and winged and holy thing, and there is no invention in him until he has been inspired and is out of his senses, and the mind is no longer in him: when he has not attained to this state, he is powerless and unable to utter his oracles.—534 [6]

This passage has, during later centuries, sometimes been used for the purpose of invoking Plato as a witness in the cause of poetry. Shelley, for instance, translated the *Ion* and in his own *Defense of Poetry* echoed this passage. Yet it is perhaps worth noting that Ion himself is reluctant to accept this version of his talents.

> That is good, Socrates; and yet I doubt whether you will ever have eloquence enough to persuade me that I praise Homer only when I am mad and possessed; and if you could hear me speak of him I am sure you would never think this to be the case.—536

And in fact the heavy reiteration by Socrates of the idea that the poet is out of his mind or senses—not acting by art, not his own master—does not seem an unequivocal compliment. One might easily come away with the impression that this is a lame alternative to the rational explanations

---

[4] At the end of Plato's *Symposium*, Socrates, having outlasted all the other guests in an all-night drinking party, is seated, as dawn breaks, with the tragic poet Agathon on one hand and the comic poet Aristophanes on the other, forcing them to admit, drowsily, that since poetry is *one* art, a comic poet should be able to write tragedies, and a tragic poet comedies. Despite literal interpretation by the Platonists, this looks like an ironic counterpart of the argument from fact to theory in the *Ion*. In the *Symposium*, Socrates, starting with a theory, urges it against the well-known contrary fact: that poets do *not* work by a scientific technique.

[5] Craig LaDrière, "The Problem of Plato's Ion," *Journal of Aesthetics and Art Criticism*, X (September, 1951), 26–34, elaborates the view that the dialogue is aimed not at poetry itself but only at the art of criticism.

[6] Quotations from Plato's *Dialogues* in this chapter are in the translation of Benjamin Jowett, the third edition, revised, first published in 1892. The Fourth Edition of the *Dialogues*, revised by order of the Jowett Copyright Trustees, 4 vols., Oxford, 1953, does not make substantial changes in any of the passages which we quote.

which Socrates has apparently tried so hard to elicit. A second series of questions, leading to the conclusion of the dialogue, is not calculated to minimize such an impression.

SOCRATES: Then which will be a better judge of the lines which you were reciting from Homer, you or the charioteer?

ION: The charioteer.

SOCRATES: Why, yes, because you are a rhapsode and not a charioteer.

ION: Yes.

SOCRATES: And the art of the rhapsode is different from that of the charioteer?

ION: Yes.

SOCRATES: And if a different knowledge, then a knowledge of different matters?

ION: True.

SOCRATES: You know the passage in which Hecamede, the concubine of Nestor, is described as giving to the wounded Machaon a posset, as he says,

"Made with Pramnian wine; and she grated cheese of goat's milk with a grater of bronze, and at his side placed an onion which gives a relish to drink." [*Iliad* XI, 639–40]

Now would you say that the art of the rhapsode or the art of medicine was better able to judge of the propriety of these lines?

ION: The art of medicine.—538

Socrates drives the inquiry along for some time in this manner, obtaining admissions about the rhapsode's incompetence in one art after another, until at length he is in a good position to raise the question whether any art at all remains the peculiar possession of the rhapsode himself.

SOCRATES: . . . Do you, who know Homer so much better than I do, Ion, select for me passages which relate to the rhapsode and the rhapsode's art, and which the rhapsode ought to examine and judge of better than other men.

ION: All passages, I should say, Socrates.

SOCRATES: Not all, Ion, surely. Have you already forgotten what you were saying? A rhapsode ought to have a better memory.

ION: Why, what am I forgetting?

SOCRATES: Do you not remember that you declared the art of the rhapsode to be different from the art of the char-ioteer?

ION: Yes, I remember.

SOCRATES: And you admitted that being different they would have different subjects of knowledge?

ION: Yes.

SOCRATES: Then upon your own showing the rhapsode, and the art of the rhapsode, will not know everything?

ION: I should exclude certain things, Socrates.

SOCRATES: You mean to say that you would exclude pretty much the subjects of the other arts. As he does not know all of them, which of them will he know?

ION: He will know what a man and what a woman ought to say, and what a freeman and what a slave ought to say, and what a ruler and what a subject.

SOCRATES: Do you mean that a rhapsode will know better than the pilot what the ruler of a sea-tossed vessel ought to say?—539–40

So the argument swings back to where it was before. We observe that a momentary attempt by Ion to move into an area which we might call something like "general human nature" is quickly checked by Socrates with a question which insists on the technical or scientific. At the conclusion of the dialogue Ion is reduced to the comic position of maintaining that his being rhapsode implies at least that he would be also a good general—perhaps because, as Plato explains in Book X of the *Republic*, the reading of Homer was traditionally supposed to have something to do with the art of warfare.

In the starkest and least reducible sense the questions put to Ion amount to these: What does poetry tell us? What is the source of the poet's power? And, though this is left more obscurely implicit: What is the relation between the poet's source and the nature of what he actually says? At the beginning of his *Theogony* the poet Hesiod had qualified the traditional appeal to the Muses with a voucher for their veracity. The Muses had actually appeared to him and said:

> Many feigned things (*pseudea*) like to the truth we know how to tell; yet we know how, when we are willing, to tell what is true.—*Theogony*, 27 ff.[7]

By a kind of joke or sleight of argument Socrates combines a partly negative answer (poetry and rhapsody—in their own right and as such

[7] Cf. W. C. Greene, "The Greek Criticism of Poetry, a Reconsideration," in *Perspectives of Criticism*, ed. Harry Levin (Cambridge, Mass., 1950), p. 21.

—do not tell us anything scientific) with a positive answer about the divine origin of poetry and rhapsody. One of the traditionally respectable accounts of poetry (Not only had Homer and the other poets invoked the Muses, but Pindar, for instance, had maintained that poetry proceeds from genius, *phua*, rather than art, *technē*) is put in such a context as to suggest a certain emptiness. Either Ion has been teasing, Socrates implies, and deceitfully refusing to reveal his rationally understood professional secrets, or else there is nothing rational for him to reveal. He is either dishonest or divinely mad. The cross-examination has carefully kept out of sight whatever may be the rhapsode's type of actual professional discourse, the external manifestation of his "madness" —though from the start Ion has been eager to give an exhibition of that. Overlooking a degree of unfairness in the procedure of Socrates, we may say that we are invited by this dialogue to consider at least two principles which are not on the face of the matter absurd: 1. Being able to compose poetry is not the same as being able to give a rationale of it; 2. poetry is not concerned with making scientific statements.

III

IT IS possible to point out places in the dialogues of Plato where he seems to treat poetic inspiration very respectfully. In the *Meno* (98–99), for instance, a useful kind of "right opinion" (rather than "knowledge") is conceded to statesmen, interpreters of oracles, seers, and "all poetic persons"—and all these are divinely inspired. And in the *Phaedrus*, although poets rank only sixth in a hierarchy of the elite (248), and although the chief aim of the dialogue is to assert the philosophic or dialectical responsibility of rhetoricians, there is more than one hint that a philosopher is the better for a dash of madness. As for the poet, the *Phaedrus* contains a very strong statement of his dependence on divine madness—in a passage (245) which may be looked on as reversing the ironic emphasis of the parallel passage in the *Ion*.[8] But a history of arguments about poetry will have to claim some license to look rather for ideas in full bloom than for the person behind the ideas. It is another kind of job to try to harmonize all the statements in the dialogues of Plato.

After the *Ion*, the place where we find Plato's mistrust of poetry

[8] See R. G. Collingwood, *The Principles of Art* (Oxford, 1938), pp. 46–7, for a good instance of the argument that Plato was really a friend of the arts. We proceed here on the assumption that the student of poetry need not be really much concerned to enlist Plato on the side of poetry, nor much discomfited to believe that on the whole Plato disapproved of poetry. Plato may conveniently be taken as the representative of an impressive and fairly coherent system of anti-poetic. From early times, the attack upon poetry has often enough been made in his name.

expressed in the simplest and most practical terms is the passage on the "musical" education of the "Guardians" in Books II and III of the *Republic*, a work, be it remembered, of Plato's mid-career and maturity. Here, and again in Book X of the *Republic*, in a more metaphysical context, and in the *Laws*, the compromise *Republic* of Plato's old age, we encounter his well-known objection to the moral effects of poetry. Poetry "feeds and waters the passions," creating division and unsteadiness in the heart, or frivolous laughter, and producing the opposite of civic virtue. The Guardians of the Republic will in fact have the duty of showing poets the gate.

> And therefore when any one of these pantomimic gentlemen . . . comes to us, and makes a proposal to exhibit himself and his poetry, we will fall down and worship him as a sweet and holy and wonderful being; but we must also inform him that in our State such as he are not permitted to exist; the law will not allow them. And so when we have anointed him with myrrh, and set a garland of wool upon his head, we shall send him away to another city. For we mean to employ for our souls' health the rougher and severer poet or story-teller, who will imitate the style of the virtuous only, and will follow those models which we prescribed at first when we began the education of our soldiers.—III, 398

A passage of similar tenor in the *Laws* speaks of an ideal, civic-minded poet, a man "more than fifty years old," a safe one for composing patriotic songs. But such a one was not to be found among the actual poets—Homer, the tragedians, the writers of comedy.

> We are ready to acknowledge that Homer is the greatest of poets and first of tragedy writers; but we must remain firm in our conviction that hymns to the gods and praises of famous men are the only poetry which ought to be admitted into our State. For if you go beyond this and allow the honeyed muse to enter, either in epic or lyric verse, not law and the reason of mankind, which by common consent have ever been deemed best, but pleasure and pain will be the rulers in our State. . . . But that she may not impute to us any harshness or want of politeness, let us tell her that there is an ancient quarrel between philosophy and poetry.—*Republic* X, 607

The quarrel between the poet and the philosopher is the deep end of the quarrel between the poet and the moralist. If poetry produces immoral results, this happens not without certain causes in the nature of poetry itself—one of these, for instance, is the very fact that poetry deals with a variety of motives and feelings, the good and the bad, pleasure and pain. In Books II and III of the *Republic* it appears that poetry is engaged in fictions—often, moreover, in wicked fictions—wicked lies. Homer and Hesiod and the dramatists, instead of representing God as good and the source of all good (instead of telling the truth about which Hesiod's Muses boasted), give us an anthropomorphic, wrangling, deceitful, and revengeful crowd of deities. These poets show heroes as emotional and cowardly, wicked men as prosperous, and just men as wretched. Earlier exegetes, forsooth, had invented a pretty way of defending these impieties by saying that they were "allegorical." They were supposed to conceal an acceptable message at a more abstract level.

At this stage of the argument appears the incidental concept of "imitation" (*mimēsis*)—which, with a certain modification, becomes in later passages the center of Plato's poetics. Certain poems, he observes in Book III, simply tell what happened; others actually imitate what happened—dramas, of course—and these are the most dangerous ones, because the most contagious. A man who is to play a serious part in life cannot afford to imitate any other kind of part. (Let the slaves and hired strangers, he says in *Laws* VII, 817, act our comedies for us.) It is needless to try to guess how consciously Plato's view had developed by the time he wrote his second discussion of poetry in the *Republic*, that of Book X (it was written perhaps some years after Books II and III). In any case the concept of imitation [9] has now become markedly more pejorative and is furthermore now applied to poetry as if it were inseparable.

> Speaking in confidence, for I should not like to have my words repeated to the tragedians and the rest of the imitative tribe—but I do not mind saying to you, that all poetical imitations are ruinous to the understanding of the hearers, and that the knowledge of their true nature is the only antidote to them.—595

The reasoning is made clearer in a very explicit analogy between a poet and an illusionist painter of a bed.

> And the painter too is, as I conceive. . . . a creator of appearances, is he not?

> Of course.

> But then I suppose you will say that what he creates is untrue.
> And yet there is a sense in which the painter also creates a bed?

> Yes, he said, but not a real bed.

[9] Richard McKeon's exposition of the analogical series of meanings enjoyed by the term *mimēsis* in Plato's works ("Literary Criticism and the Concept of Imitation in Antiquity", MP, XXXIV, August, 1936, 1–35) tends to soften the application of the term to poetry in these contexts, but the pejorative implications can scarcely be dismissed.

And what of the maker of the bed? were you not saying that he too makes, not the idea which, according to our view, is the essence of the bed, but only a particular bed?

Yes, I did.

Then if he does not make that which exists he cannot make true existence, but only some semblance of existence; and if any one were to say that the work of the maker of the bed, or of any other workman, has real existence, he could hardly be supposed to be speaking the truth.

Beds, then, are of three kinds, and there are three artists who superintend them: God, the maker of the bed, and the painter?

Yes, there are three of them.

God, whether from choice or from necessity, made one bed in nature and one only; two or more such ideal beds neither ever have been nor ever will be made by God.

And what shall we say of the carpenter—is he not also the maker of the bed?

Yes.

But would you call the painter a creator and maker?

Certainly not.

Yet if he is not the maker, what is he in relation to the bed?

I think, he said, that we may fairly designate him as the imitator of that which the others make.

Good, I said; then you call him who is second[1] in the descent from nature an imitator?

Certainly, he said.

And the tragic poet is an imitator, and therefore, like all other imitators, he is twice removed from the king and from the truth?

That appears to be so.—596-7

With the allusion to the ideal bed, the work of God, we are involved in the Platonic metaphysics of transcendental reality, a system of ideas which needs to be clarified by reference to two passages which inter-

[1] The words in Plato's text are actually "third" and "thrice," but their meaning depends on the classical or inclusive method of counting.

vene in the *Republic* between the discussion of poetry in Books II–III
and that in Book X. One is the allegory in Book VII of the cinematic
cave in which men sitting on a bench with their backs to an opening
and a great fire beyond, see only the shadows of a sort of passing puppet
show cast on the wall before them. Such is our own experience of what
we think to be reality. The other passage is the more technically instructive figure of the "line," in Book VI, with its four ascending phases
of knowledge: the lowest *eikasia*, or sensory imaging (of the surface of
things and their shadows—the aspects of the bed which can be painted);
the second, *pistis* (faith), a kind of trustful apprehension of the solid yet
mutable things of our world (beds and horses); the third, on the upper
side of a major central division, *dianoia*, discursive understanding of
mathematicals or geometric figures; and at the top, *noēsis*, intuitive and
true knowledge of permanent beings, the forms or ideas (*eidē*).[2] For
the moment let us not attempt to say more precisely what these last are.

IV

PLATO's doctrine of ideas is perhaps most often known in its rather vague
relation to the "beautiful" (*to kalon*) and to love (*erōs*), and in this relation chiefly through three other dialogues, the *Phaedo*, the *Symposium*
and the *Phaedrus*. In the first of these, the conversation on immortality
held by Socrates with his friends on the day he is to drink the hemlock,
we find the doctrine of *anamnēsis*[3] (Wordsworthian otherworldly recollection) as an explanation of how we come to be possessed at all of ideas
more perfect than the things of our worldly experience. As for beautiful
things, they are indeed beautiful "by reason of beauty"—that is, by participating in the beautiful—but beauty is named only as one among other
kinds of perfection (75a–d; 100c–e). The discourse is ascetic rather than
aesthetic, stressing preparation for immortality by philosophic discipline.
But in the *Symposium* and the *Phaedrus*, the preparation, or approach,
is that of the lover, by way of mortal beauty. The lover graduates, in
the *Symposium* (210–12), from single beautiful bodies to all beautiful
bodies, from bodies to forms, and from forms to practices and notions,
until he contemplates "the vast sea of beauty"; and in the *Phaedrus* (249,
265–6, 277), he graduates from bodily beauty not only to ideal beauty
but to "wisdom, goodness, and the like," all the hierarchy of ideas. The
lover becomes in effect the philosopher.

[2] Both *dianoia* and *noēsis* come under the generic head of *epistēmē* (knowledge), what Socrates found wanting in Homer and Ion. Both *eikasia* (the awareness
of images, *eikones*) and *pistis* come under the generic head of *doxa* (mere opinion)
and both refer to the world of becoming, *ta gignomena*.

[3] See too the *Meno*, 82–5, where Socrates elicits geometrical reasoning from
a slave boy.

An honest reading of these and other passages in Plato can scarcely blink the fact that the bodily beauty alluded to is that of the boy lover. (*Orthōs paiderastein* reads one phrase of the *Symposium*, 211, rendered by an eminent Victorian translator as "true love.") Pederasty was a Spartan cult, supposed to induce military virtue, and, as the first two speeches of the *Symposium* and the temptation of Socrates described in the same dialogue by Alcibiades make sufficiently clear, it had a vogue among Athenian intellectuals during Plato's boyhood. "Love is of generation," says the *Symposium* (206), "of birth in beauty." "Souls which are pregnant conceive wisdom and virtue" (209). The beautiful notions begotten through this love make a clear enough contrast to the results of heterosexual love.[4] Without wholly endorsing the charge of one writer on this theme,[5] that these dialogues have been the "sulphurous breviary" of homosexual literary cults in all succeeding ages, we incline to say that the general warmth and color of the dialogues, the brilliant use of allegorical imagery like that of the soul as charioteer and the higher and lower passions as his pair of horses in the *Phaedrus*, and the vivacious drama of the conversationalists at the banquet—Aristophanes, Agathon, Alcibiades, Socrates—on the attractive theme of love, have helped a great deal to make the aspect of Platonism that relates to "love" and "beauty" best known and best liked among literary students during every Renaissance. Yet these topics have furnished not so much a workable theory about the nature of poetry as inspirational subject matter for literary treatment—the "Ideas on hie . . . which Plato so admyred" in Spenser's *Hymne of Heavenly Beautie* or the conception of Platonic pure love in the Fourth Book of Castiglione's *Courtier*.

The term "beauty" (*to kalon*) is used in the Platonic dialogues to refer rather loosely to a wide range of natural objects, artifacts, institutions, and ideas. In the *Philebus* (64e) we have the relatively helpful concept of beauty as measure and proportion (*metriotēs kai summetria*) and the distinction (51c) between the beautiful in itself and the relatively beautiful. In the *Memorabilia* of Xenophon (III, 8; IV, 6) Socrates produces the concept of the beautiful as the convenient (i.e. the "functional"—a dung basket, if well made, is beautiful; a golden shield, if not well made, is ugly). And the dubiously Platonic *Greater Hippias* presents him in his most sustained effort to face the difficult problem. He disposes easily of such too concrete suggestions by the sophist as that a beautiful horse or a beautiful maiden may be adduced to define the

---

[4] In the *Phaedo*, as Socrates prepares for the draught of hemlock, the women of his family are admitted to see him, but briefly and grudgingly toward the close of the day.

[5] John Jay Chapman, *Lucian, Plato, and Greek Morals* (Boston, 1931), p. 133. Cf. the more sober account by Warner Fite, *The Platonic Legend* (New York, 1934), Chap. VIII, "Platonic Love." Plato censures this kind of *eros* in *Republic* III, 403 and *Laws*, 636.

concept of the beautiful (*parthenos kalē kalon*), or that whatever is gold is beautiful. (What about the chryselephantine statue of Athena? says Socrates. Why didn't Phidias make it all gold?) Canvassing the problems of the convenient, the appropriate, and the useful—in fact, the whole difficult problem of terminal and instrumental values—he arrives at the tentative (and far from ridiculous) conclusion that the beautiful may be that which is beneficially pleasurable (*hēdonēn ōphelimon*) through the senses of sight and hearing (303E). But the idea of the "beneficial" persists in betraying the instrumentalism of the concept. The conclusion is that the discourse has been useless. And even these efforts at definition are not very precisely reflected in the *Symposium* or in the other classic places where Plato discusses beauty and love.

V

LET us turn back, toward a colder side of Plato's theory of ideas which we have already hinted. The presence of the hypothetical *mathēmatika*, the geometric forms, at the third level of the scale of knowledge in Book VI of the *Republic* might lead one to wonder whether any more purified element of the mathematical is implicit in the highest level, that of the pure forms. A pronounced attention to mathematics and geometry as one stage of the Guardian's education, in Book V of the *Republic*, might suggest the same speculation. Students of the Platonic text and of other evidence about Plato's thought, especially the criticisms of Aristotle, do in fact distinguish two strains in his theory of ideas. One is the Socratic or logical, the argument that our use of general terms and class conceptions entails the existence of real and transcendent unities corresponding to these conceptions. It is an argument which receives heavy criticism, apparently from Plato himself, in the *Parmenides* and other late dialogues. The second is a more subtle ontological attempt to get at the permanent and necessary structure of reality, a development of Pythagorean number theory in which Plato distinguishes between the continuous and boundless stuff of our sensory experience, the indeterminate world of becoming, and a real or rational world of limit, that is, of *ratios* between both unit numbers and geometric lines. The word for the rational principle is *logos*—the same word that appears in the crucial definition of geometric ratio in the Fifth Book of Euclid. At the level of *mathematicals* or geometric figures, one may have, let us say, a multiplicity of isosceles triangles, all of different sizes and hence participating in the diversity and indefiniteness of material extension. The final oneness, or what they have in common, is their ratio, something intelligible though unimaginable. As Aristotle was to put it:

> Further, besides sensible things and Forms he says there are the
> objects of mathematics, which occupy an intermediate position,
> differing from sensible things in being eternal and unchange-
> able, from Forms in that there are many alike, while the Form
> itself is in each case unique.—*Metaphysics* I (A), 6.[6]

What may be difficult for us to conceive is that the theory posits
such a number or ratio as the real idea behind each of the ordinary and
immediately concrete names which we give to objects. As a modern interpreter has put it:

> The idea of man is not the general term which designates all
> perceived men. The idea of myself is not what I sense when I
> consider myself introspectively. The idea of fire is not the gen-
> eral term (or any notion in the mind of which the general term is
> a symbol) referring to all cases of perceived fire. Nor is the idea
> of fire that notion given by a definition which distinguishes fire
> from all other factors in the universe, in terms of perceived prop-
> erties. All the so-called concepts which we use in ordinary dis-
> course, and which most modern philosophers have in mind when
> they refer to Plato's theory of ideas,—all such notions are not
> ideas, in the Platonic meaning of the term. They are merely
> nominalistic terms referring to factors in "the class of the mixed."
> Ideas are purely in the class of the limit and they cannot be il-
> lustrated by pointing to anything immediately sensed. . . .
> "ideas," whether they be the idea of the fire, the idea of myself,
> or the idea of the good, are ratios which only an analytical math-
> ematical symbolism can express and only the pure scientific intel-
> lect can grasp.[7]

Perhaps the most easily grasped evidence that Plato really thought this
way is to be found in his late cosmological dialogue the *Timaeus*,
(53–6), where, taking advantage of the fact that there are five, and only
five, kinds of regular polyhedra, he assigns a basic structure, the real
idea, to each of what were then supposed to be the four primary elements: fire, earth, air, water, and to a fifth imagined element, "ether."
Fire, as we might guess from its volatility and sharpness, has for its
mathematical the regular pyramid or tetrahedron, and for its "idea" the
ratio of magnitudes which defines the tetrahedron. Earth, as the most
solid and least movable element, has the cube or hexahedron; and so
forth with perhaps less plausibility, according to the lightness and number of faces of the octahedron (air), the icosahedron (water), and the

[6] See *post* Chapter 2, p. 22, n. 1.
[7] F. S. C. Northrop, "The Mathematical Background and Content of Greek
Philosophy," in *Philosophical Essays for Alfred North Whitehead* (New York, 1936),
pp. 32–3. By permission of Longmans, Green & Co., Inc.

dodecahedron (ether).[8] Until very recent times the five regular solids were known as the Platonic bodies. The better part of the soul, Plato said in *Republic* X (602), trusts to measure and calculation. He is said to have inscribed over the entrance to his school: "Let no one ignorant of geometry enter" (*Ageōmetrētos mēdeis eisitō*).[9]

One will be perhaps likely to think that this side of Plato's theory, hyperintellectual and even frigid, must have seemed even to him far less relevant to the nature of literature than the more visionary conceptions which we have described somewhat earlier. It is possible, however, that through another group of arts which were highly cultivated in Greece during Plato's time—the visual—at least a remote kind of relevance may be inferred. One of Plato's later dialogues, the *Philebus*, is a discussion of pleasure and knowledge in which he attempts for one thing to distinguish what he calls mixed pleasures (those that follow on pain or are somehow dependent on it—and here he puts the pleasures of tragedy and comedy) from certain kinds which he considers more pure and hence more nearly related to the good. One passage of this dialogue has often been produced in our day as a charter from antiquity for theorists of "significant form" in the visual arts.

> I do not mean by beauty of form such beauty as that of animals or pictures, which the many would suppose to be my meaning; but, says the argument, understand me to mean straight lines and circles, and the plane or solid figures which are formed out of them by turning-lathes and rulers and measures of angles; for these I affirm to be not only relatively beautiful, like other things, but they are eternally and absolutely beautiful, and they have peculiar pleasures, quite unlike the pleasures of scratching. And there are colours which are of the same character, and have similar pleasures.—51[1]

Let us place in conjunction with this a tabular view of the imitative arts digested from several places in another late dialogue, the *Sophist* (219, 235, 264, 266). The sophist himself, viewed by Plato as a special kind of

---

[8] *Timaeus*, 53c–56c. Francis M. Cornford, *Plato's Cosmology, The Timaeus of Plato Translated with a Running Commentary* (London, 1937), pp. 210–22. The assignment of the dodecahedron to ether is not explicit in Plato but was apparently made so in early Platonic commentary. See the quotation from Plutarch's *On the E at Delphi* (XI) in Cornford, p. 220; Paul Shorey, *What Plato Said* (Chicago, 1933), p. 408; *Epinomis* 981, 984.

[9] Adolph Busse, ed., *Commentaria in Aristotelem Graeca*, XVIII (Berlin, 1900), 118, the commentary of Elias. Cf. Aristotle: "Mathematics has been turned by our present day thinkers into the whole of philosophy" (*Metaphysics*, I, 9).

[1] Cf. E. F. Carritt, in *Philosophies of Beauty* (Oxford, 1931), pp. 29–30; Herbert Read, *Art Now* (New York, 1933), p. 101; R. H. Wilenski, *The Meaning of Modern Sculpture* (London, 1933).

imitator or deceiver, is the object of definition, but some incidental light
is cast in another direction.

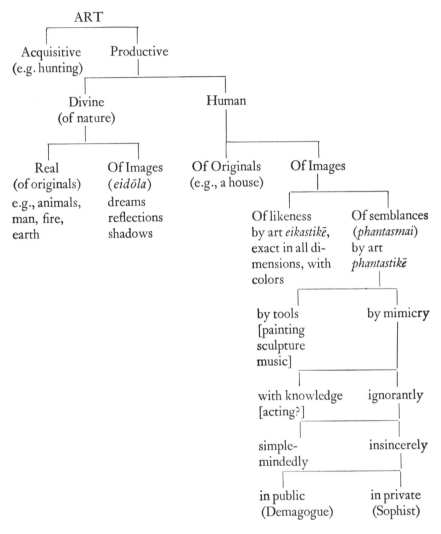

The part of the table which specially concerns us is the division between
eikastic (or realistic) images and phantastic (or imaginative). Here Plato
seems to be attempting to deal, though perhaps not very decisively, with
a question which is prominent in ancient theory of art, that of illusion.
There is a passage in the *Iliad* of Homer—often quoted by historians of
literary theory—where the shield made by Hephaestus for Achilles is described with great admiration—the images with which it was adorned
were so life-like that the furrows of a ploughed field, though wrought

from the gold, seemed black. During the lifetime of Plato himself Greek visual art seems to have been moving rapidly in the direction of naturalism and illusionism. Art historians of the formalist school like to tell us that even the Great Period of Greek sculpture (that of the pediments of the Temple of Zeus at Olympia, for instance, or the Periclean Parthenon at Athens) is a degeneration from a more formal (and Egyptian) antiquity. Visual art was already tending toward the Rogers-ware style of Hellenistic narrative and genre sculpture (the dying Gaul, the old market woman). Later documents of antiquity, especially the *Natural History* of Pliny the Elder, record such instances of illusionist virtuosity in Plato's day as that of Zeuxis, who painted grapes so well that they attracted birds,[2] or that of Parrhasius, who painted drapery that appeared to move. These achievements seem to have arisen out of one of the chief developments during the fifth century in theatrical design, that of *skiagraphia* (shaded painting) or perspective scenery. At the same time the formal and geometrical element of visual art continued very prominently in the architecture by which Plato was surrounded. Modern investigation has fairly well demonstrated that the art of Greek vases and temple architecture was based on the principle of "dynamic symmetry"—the commensurability of area rather than of line and above all the commensurability generated by extreme and mean ratio, the "Golden Section."[3]

The relation between illusion and formalism in Plato's day was scarcely simple—as may be instanced even in the "fantastic" art mentioned by Plato in the *Sophist* (235e). Painters and sculptors, he points out, strive for the proportion that will *appear* beautiful. Those who carve colossal figures, for instance, make the upper parts larger so that from the ground they will be seen in usual proportions. A Byzantine Greek chronicler has preserved the story that when Phidias produced his statue of Athena in competition with that of a rival, the people were ready to stone Phidias when the statue was seen lying on the ground.[4] Such proportioned illusion as this Plato classes with the work of the sophist. Yet even the architectural formalism of Plato's day depended on the same adjustments—as in the well-known entasis or swell of the temple columns, in virtue of which they look straight as one sees them from below.

Let us move toward a close of this discussion by placing side by side two more Platonic passages, the first from an early dialogue about verbal images or names, the *Cratylus*.

[2] Pliny, *Natural History*, XXXV, 36, 60: ". . . *uvas pictas tanto successu ut in scaenam aves advolassent.*" See Pierre-Maxime Schuhl, *Platon et L'Art de Son Temps* (Paris, 1933).

[3] Among a number of works on this subject by Jay Hambidge, see especially *Dynamic Symmetry, The Greek Vase* (New Haven, 1920), *The Parthenon and Other Greek Temples, Their Dynamic Symmetry* (New Haven, 1924), *Practical Applications of Dynamic Symmetry* (New Haven, 1932).

[4] Tzetzes, *Historiarum Variarum Chiliades*, VIII, 353–69, ed. T. Kiessling (Lipsiae, 1826), pp. 295–6.

> I should say . . . that the image, if expressing in every point the entire reality, would no longer be an image. Let us suppose the existence of two objects: one of them shall be Cratylus, and the other the image of Cratylus; and we will suppose, further, that some God makes not only a representation such as a painter would make of your outward form and colour, but also creates an inward organization like yours, having the same warmth and softness; and into this infuses motion, and soul, and mind, such as you have, and in a word copies all your qualities, and places them by you in another form; would you say that this was Cratylus and the image of Cratylus, or that there were two Cratyluses?—432

The second, from the attack on poetry in Book X of the *Republic*.

> Then the imitator . . . is a long way off the truth, and can do all things because he lightly touches on a small part of them, and that part an image. For example: A painter will paint a cobbler, carpenter, or any other artist, though he knows nothing of their arts; and, if he is a good artist, he may deceive children or simple persons, when he shows them his picture of a carpenter from a distance, and they will fancy that they are looking at a real carpenter.—598

The minimal conclusion to be drawn from all the evidence would seem to be that Plato has confronted the very difficult problem of the relation between formalism and illusionism in art and, in line with the austerity and subtlety of his basic mathematical view of reality, has expressed his mistrust of the realistic trends of his day and has cast a perennially influential vote in favor of some kind of visual formalism.[5] If this part of his theorizing does not go far in telling us about the nature of poetry, at least it offers a prototype for theories of "stylization" or "detachment" which have never since in the history of poetics been altogether submerged. In what is no doubt its excess of detachment Plato's theory offers an approach by contrast to—as indeed it was historically the point of departure for—the more empirically weighted and warmer theory which we shall encounter in the next chapter.

[5] Plato's formalism seems not to extend to auditory art. See his rules for moral fitness in modes of music, *Republic* III, 398–400, and his censure of "the bare sound of harp and flute," *Laws* II, 669.

CHAPTER 2

ARISTOTLE'S ANSWER: POETRY AS STRUCTURE

§ *Aristotle's* Poetics *in relation to his major works, relation between Plato and Aristotle on universals, the mathematical, the biological,* entelechy, *the Socratic problem of classes—II. theoretical and practical sciences, the* Ethics *and* Politics, *poetry and information, the artistic norm—III. the universal, the probable,* mimēsis, homoiōma, *internal action, music, figures and colors,* opsis, *the ideal (to beltion, hoia einai dei)—IV. growth of tragedy, norms of size and order,* peripeteia, anagnorisis, desis, lusis, *wholeness, beginning, middle, end—V. cohesion of causes,* Posterior Analytics, *the logic of the syllogism, dramatic logic,* Oedipus, *organic unity, Aristotle's six elements of tragedy, reality of the poetic object* §

PLATO'S PUPIL ARISTOTLE CAME TO THE ACADEMY IN THE YEAR 367 OR eighteen years before Plato's death at the age of 80 in 349. Fourteen years later, in 335, Aristotle founded his own school the Lyceum. It was apparently towards the end of his career that he produced his treatise in three books on *Rhetoric* and in some way was responsible for an essay or compilation of notes, in twenty-six chapters, the celebrated *Poetics*. Even if it were to happen that at this late date classical scholars changed their opinion about the authorship of the *Poetics*, one would still turn, for the explication of these condensed and partly chaotic hints, to the system of Greek philosophy which most readily connects with them, the major works of Aristotle, especially his *Metaphysics, Ethics,* and *Politics*. The *Poetics* is a work of the type which Aristotelians have called "acroamatic"—to be interpreted only with the help of other and larger works. The difference between Aristotle and Plato on poetry is a fulfilment of their difference on ideas or universals, and the *Rhetoric* and *Poetics* are parts of a larger answer to Plato. Plato is a teacher and opponent who often appears, or is often just out of sight, in the arguments of Aristotle, and especially in historical parts of the *Metaphysics*.

> . . . having in his youth first become familiar with . . . the Heraclitean doctrines (that all objects of sense are ever in a state of flux and there is no knowledge about them), Plato held these views even in later years. Socrates, however, was busying himself about ethical matters and neglecting the world of nature . . . he fixed thought for the first time on definitions. Plato accepted his teaching but held that the problem applied not to objects of sense but to entities of another kind—for this reason, that common definitions could not be definitions of any objects of sense, as these are always changing. The "entities of another kind," then, he called Ideas, and objects of sense, he said, were all named after Ideas and in virtue of a relation to these; for the many objects of sense exist by participation in the Ideas that have the same name as they.—*Metaphysics* I (A), 6 [1]

> . . . if the Forms exist and "animal" is present in "man" and "horse," it is either one and the same in number, or different. (In formula it is clearly one, for he who states the formula will go through the same formula in either case.) If then there is a "man-in-himself" who is a "this" and exists apart, the parts also of which he consists, e.g. "animal" and "two-footed," must indicate "thises," and be capable of separate existence and substances.—*Metaphysics* VII (Z), 13

> Again, if the Forms are numbers, how can they be causes? Is it because existing things are other numbers, e.g. one number is man, another is Socrates, another Callias?
>
> —*Metaphysics* I (A), 9

It is perhaps best for our purpose to attempt to express the difference between Plato and Aristotle in their view of universals as broadly and as simply as possible. It derives from the fact that whereas Plato, as we have seen, was mathematical, transcendental, and rigorously abstract, Aristotle (whose father, Nicomachus—if a biographical note be relevant—was court physician to Amyntas II of Macedonia—and who was himself

---

[1] Works of Aristotle, other than the *Poetics* and *Rhetoric*, are quoted in this and the following chapter mainly from the Oxford translation, completed in 1931, and largely reprinted in *The Basic Works of Aristotle*, ed. Richard McKeon (New York, Random House, 1941). In the passage from *Metaphysics* I (A), 6 above, the term "sensibles" in the Oxford translation is altered by the present writers to "objects of sense." Some shorter quotations from various Aristotelian works are borrowed from the commentary of S. H. Butcher on the *Poetics*. (Cf. *post*, p. 25, n. 2.)

The Oxford Translation of Aristotle is quoted by permission of the Delegates of The Clarendon Press.

a naturalist and collector of specimens for King Hermias of Atarneus and Assos in Syria) was biological, natural, empirical, and concrete. We shall not go far wrong if we form the habit of imagining behind the universal of Aristotle, rather than a geometric figure like a triangle, some living animal, say a horse. If there was change here, from colthood to death and decay, it was yet possible to say that *something* had changed. (Even if something which is cold becomes hot, a potency has been realized, and potency resides in something.[2]) There is also, especially in a biological object, direction in change, a purpose or *entelechy*, the full self of the object as realized in the object—the horse rather than the colt. "What each thing is when fully developed, we call its nature."[3] Or: ". . . a thing is more properly said to be what it is when it has attained to fulfilment than when it exists potentially."[4] Recurrence in generation also has something to do with it. When a tree is made into a bed, and if the bed then happens to be planted—if anything comes up at all, it will not be a bed but a tree.[5] "Man is born from man, but not bed from bed." The *ousia* or essence, the *eidos* or form, which, as we have seen, was the object of knowledge at the top of Plato's line—but which was apparently transcendental and separate from the horses and beds which are crudely and trustfully known at a lower level by *pistis* (a kind of "animal faith")—is brought down by Aristotle into the things themselves as the dynamic principle of their being which continues through change in a certain direction. The *form* must be in the thing as one of its causes.

> When we are dealing with definite and ordered products of Nature, we must not say that each *is* of a certain quality because it *becomes* so, but rather that they *become* so because they *are* so and so, for the process of becoming attends upon being and is for the sake of being, not *vice versa*.[6]

The Platonic term *ousia* as it appears in Aristotle attracts both "substance" and "essence" for its English translations. The *to ti ēn einai*—the "being what a thing was"—is a relative of *ousia* so close as to be nearly indistinguishable from it. "When we say *what* a thing is, we do not say 'white' or 'hot' or 'three cubits long,' but a 'man' or 'a god.' "[7] Aristotle carries on the Socratic or logical, rather than the Pythagorean or mathematical, strain in Plato's thinking; but he re-enforces this strain ontologically by grounding it more deeply in things themselves, as their vital principle of unity in change. In the *Parmenides* of Plato the younger Socrates, as he is dramatically presented, suffers some embarrassment at

[2] *Metaphysics* IX (Θ); *Physics* I.
[3] *Politics* I, 1.
[4] *Physics* II, 1.
[5] *Physics* II, 1.
[6] *On the Generation of Animals* V, 1.
[7] *Metaphysics* VII (Z), 1.

the questions of the Eleatic Parmenides about the number of things which have *forms*—that is, about the kinds of forms themselves and their number. About some kinds Socrates is sure: there are forms of universal categories such as likeness and difference, of ethical qualities such as justice and goodness, of mathematicals, of elements (fire, air, water, earth), and of natural species, such as man and horse. But about such transitory or inferior classes as, say, mud or hair, the argument is less decided. It is not clear that Aristotle has completely or triumphantly solved this problem. But at least his biological and hence structural emphasis tends to center the concept of form on more complex and stable living things —organic substances. His emphasis falls upon the qualifications which a thing must have in order to be a thing at all, a *this* or a one.[8]

II

THE transition from the more metaphysical areas of Aristotle's thought to his *Poetics* and *Rhetoric* is stepped down or cushioned for us by a distinction again characteristic of the empiricism of Aristotle in reaction against the rational severity of Plato. This is the general distinction which Aristotle makes between theoretical science and a varied range of "practical" philosophies and "productive" arts—or, more briefly, between the demonstrably certain and the arguably probable. The distinction was not pejorative and exclusive, as it tended to be for Plato, but tolerant and inclusive—extending to each kind of discipline a charter to work with the kind of evidence and within the degree of precision which could as a matter of fact be exacted of its peculiar materials. As the ontological and epistemological dialogues of Plato have their themes reflected in the vast museum of his political masterpiece the *Republic*, so the metaphysical, logical and scientific works of Aristotle shade off into his *Ethics*, or philosophy of rational activity along the path of the "mean," and his *Politics*, a more historical inquiry into that activity as it derives from man's role as a member of society. "Man is naturally a social animal" (*Anthrōpos phusei politikon zōon*).[9] Book VIII of the *Politics* deals with education, and more specifically, Chapters 5 and 7 of this Book, with the value of visual, musical, and verbal arts. With the value of poetry, says Aristotle, I have dealt more fully in my *Poetics*. We may think of both his *Poetics* and his *Rhetoric* as expansions of this area of the *Politics* and may safely work on the hypothesis that for Aristotle, as for Plato, poetry is an art to be understood, and praised or blamed, only in its relation to the whole human being of whom it is both the instrument and the reflection.

[8] Cf. *post* Chapter 7, the neo-Platonic development of this conception.
[9] *Politics* I, 1.

Such a basic assumption, however, does not prevent Aristotle from looking at poetry in its own perspective as a thing having its own peculiar character. One of the most interesting passages in the *Poetics*—though it is but an incidental excursion—occurs in Chapter XXV when Aristotle in the course of rejecting several pedantries of criticism apparently prevalent in his day (the reliances, no doubt, of the caviller Zoilus [1] and his friends) alludes to a kind of hyper-literalism, a scientific and informational criterion, such as might easily be imputed to the Socrates of Plato's *Ion*. One may distinguish, says Aristotle, between faults which affect a poem as such and those which do not.

> . . . if the failure is due to a wrong choice—if he has repre-
> sented a horse as throwing out both of his off legs at once, or
> introduced technical inaccuracies in medicine, for example, or
> in any other art—the error is not essential to the poetry.[2]

Or, to shift the example to the sister mimetic art of painting: "Not to know that a hind has no horns is a less serious matter than to paint it inartistically." With the word *inartistically* Aristotle may be thought to have begged the question, and in a sense no doubt he has. In somewhat the same sense all the other poetic theory which we are to consider in this book will do the same—in the sense, that is, that a certain nuclear area of the indefinable will never be reduced by the theory; a scientific or completely analytic definition of poetry has never been achieved. What is *artistically?* What is art? What does an art of words tell us?

III

AMONG the parts of the *Poetics* which have been most often quoted by later theorists are the dicta that poetry is a more philosophic and more serious thing (*philosophōteron kai spoudaioteron*) than "history," that it deals with the universal (here is the direct retort to Plato) while history deals with particulars, that it cares not for what *has* happened but for

---

[1] Zoilus, a critic who flourished about 350 B.C., was the author of a work in nine books probably entitled *Homeromastix* (*A Whip for Homer*).

[2] The *Poetics* of Aristotle is quoted in this and the following chapters from the text and for the most part from the translation of S. H. Butcher, *Aristotle's Theory of Poetry and Fine Art*, 4th Edition, London, 1907. Cf. *ante* p. 22, n. 1. Other editions and English translations which may be very profitably consulted are: *Aristotle on the Art of Poetry*, trans. Ingram Bywater (Oxford, 1909); Allan H. Gilbert's translation of the text according to Gudeman's edition, 1934, in Gilbert's *Literary Criticism, Plato to Dryden* (New York, 1940); Seymour M. Pitcher, "Aristotle on Poetic Art," *The Journal of General Education*, VII (October, 1952), 56–76; L. J. Potts, *Aristotle on the Art of Fiction* (Cambridge, 1953). The last is a highly accomplished translation which confers perhaps more continuity and readability on Aristotle's notes than any other attempt in English. Butcher's translation is quoted by permission of Macmillan & Company Ltd and St. Martin's Press.

what may happen (ch. IX), and that it prefers impossible probabilities (*adunata eikota*) to improbable possibilities (*dunata apithana*).[3] But how can what is impossible be probable? Probable, plausible, or harmonious, by certain approximate laws of spirit, value and desire, we might say, rather than by rules of physical science and measurement. Or, by certain internal laws set up by a work of art for itself, rather than by laws of scientific external reference.

The main effort of the Aristotelian tradition in criticism has been to reconcile such statements with the fact that one of the central terms in Aristotle's system—as might be expected from his proximity to Plato and his purpose of rebuttal—is the term *imitation* (*mimēsis*). A term which meant for Plato removal from reality and distortion (at least when he applied the term to art) is manipulated by Aristotle to mean something apparently better than reality—though we may have difficulty in understanding this. In more scientific contexts Aristotle seems to conceive the mimetic relation between practical art and nature as one of assistance in a teleological process. "Art imitates nature" (*hē technē mimeitai tēn phusin*). This statement occurs not in the *Poetics* but in the *Meteorology* (IV, 3) and refers to the help given to digestion by cookery.[4] Art gives nature a boost in her seeking of the goal. Again: "Every art and educational discipline aims at filling out what nature leaves undone" (*pasa gar technē kai paideia to prosleipon bouletai tēs phuseōs anaplēroun—Politics* IV [VII], 17). Or again: "Art finishes the job when nature fails, or imitates the missing parts" (*hē technē ta men epitelei ha hē phusis adunatei apergasasthai, ta de mimeitai—Physics* II, 8). To go a little further, art in having aims and working by a plan or idea, parallels the work of nature. Nature makes a horse; an artist makes a bed.[5]

It is not precisely these meanings, however, which explain what is meant by the preliminary statements in the *Poetics* that the several arts such as music, dancing, painting, and poetry are all *imitative*. In the end one may decide to try for a synthesis of meanings, but primarily the term *mimēsis* in the *Poetics* must be taken as referring not to some kind of aid or parallel to nature but to the making of a likeness or image of nature. An equivalent term is *homoiōma*, one used instead of *mimēsis* in an important passage of the *Politics* (VIII, 5) which speaks of rhythm and melody as an imitation of passions. From certain allusions to portraiture and to other painting in the *Poetics* one might for a moment suppose that the Aristotelian concept of *mimēsis* was of a very literal and external sort, something like the *technē eikastikē* of Plato in the *Sophist*. On the

---

[3] Ch. XXIV. Cf. XXV: *pros te gar tēn poiēsin hairetōteron pithanon adunaton ē apithanon kai dunaton.*

[4] In the Socratic argument against verbal art (as we shall see, *post* Chapter 4 p. 63), cookery is not an art at all, but a sophistical knack, the false counterpart of medicine.

[5] Cf. *Metaphysics* VII, 9.

other hand music and dancing too are counted in the *Poetics* (as in the *Politics*) as forms of imitation, and the peculiar object of poetic imitation is said in the *Poetics* to be "men in action," their characters, passions, and deeds or experiences (*ēthē, pathē, praxeis*).[6] Aristotle, in short, means that poetic imitation is an imitation of inner human action. The word *homoiōma* in the *Politics* seems to mean a very full imitation, an embodiment, or a "symbol," as it might be called today, of "anger and gentleness . . . courage and temperance, and all the qualities contrary to these." And it is noteworthy that the objects of no other senses, not even the objects of sight, are thought to share this directly emotive and moral quality. "Figures and colors are not imitations, but signs (*sēmeia*), of moral habits, indications which the body gives of states of feeling." As, for example, when a person blushes or grows pale or grimaces. These remarks in the *Politics* may help to explain why at a few places in the *Poetics* Aristotle alludes to the dramatic element of *opsis* or spectacle in a slighting way,[7] as a matter of machinery and costuming rather than poetry, hardly a matter for criticism. Aristotle's emphasis in the *Poetics* falls very clearly on the imitation *in words* of a sort of objects peculiarly suitable for that sort of imitation—namely, human action, passion, and character.

Again, the possible objects of poetic imitation are said in the *Poetics* to be not only men as they are in real life, but men either better (*beltionas*) or worse than they are (ch. II)—and not only things as they were or are, but things as they ought to be (*hoia einai dei*), or as they are said or thought to be (XXV).

> . . . if it be objected that the description is not true to fact, the poet may perhaps reply,—'But the objects are as they ought to be': just as Sophocles said that he drew men as they ought to be; Euripides, as they are.—XXV

> Again, it may be impossible that there should be men such as Zeuxis painted. 'Yes,' we say, 'but the impossible is the higher thing (*beltion*); for the ideal type must surpass the reality.'
> —XXV

The term *beltion* ("better thing" or "higher reality") is a part of Aristotle's general metaphysics of form, growth, direction, or ideal. "Nature," he says in the treatise *On the Parts of Animals* (IV, 10), "makes the best (*to beltiston*) of the materials at her disposal." And in that *On the Generation of Animals* (I, 4): "Nature works either through mechanical necessity (*to anagkaion*) or through a drive toward the ideal (*to beltion*)." But what ideal, we might ask, is presented in the *mimēsis*

---

[6] *Poetics* I–II. Cf. *Problems* XIX, 27: "Though it has no words, music nevertheless has ethical character."

[7] *Poetics* VI, VII, and XIV.

of poetry? Shall we be able through the conception of the ideal to show how poetry as an image is also an imitation in the sense, earlier defined, of a process auxiliary to nature? Shall we say that poetry (taken in the educational sense of the *Politics*) assists or parallels the forces of man's moral nature by offering images of the ideal? If we do say this, we shall come very close to putting a didactic clause in our definition of poetry —closer than Aristotle himself seems to wish. But to say otherwise may terminate in another embarrassment, that of the circular definition. The expression *hoia einai dei* ("things as they ought to be"), says Butcher in his admirable commentary (p. 151), must be taken not in a moral but simply in an aesthetic sense. And with this he confirms the apparently tautological statement of Aristotle that the only *artistic fault* is to paint the animal *inartistically*.

I V

In a characteristic biological analogy Aristotle sums up the history of tragedy as a genre.

> Tragedy, having passed through many phases, reached its natural form, and there it stopped.[8]

The stages of growth in a single organism, from colt to horse, are paralleled in the history of Greek drama from Dionysiac ritual dithyrambics to the tragedies of Sophocles—after which progress ceases. It is possible for the thinker of historical bent to make too much of the fact that Aristotle was an inductive observer and hence to be too confident in assuming that Aristotle's description *a posteriori* of what had been accomplished in the Greek drama of the fifth century was without any implication of value.

Among the simplest norms one might propose for a play is that it should be of a certain size—not too long, so that the mind cannot entertain it (an animal a mile long could not be seen and so would scarcely be called beautiful), but on the other hand, not too short, so as to preclude certain internal relations. The play must in fact be of a certain *magnitude* (*ti megethos*)—because it must be of a certain structure and proportions. "Beauty depends on magnitude and order" (*to gar kalon en megethei kai taxei estin—Poetics* VII).[9] In a simpler and restrictive sense

[8] *Poetics* IV: *pollas metabolas metabalousa hē tragōdia epausato epei esche tēn autēs phusin.*

[9] Cf. *Politics* VII, 4: "Beauty is realized in number and magnitude. . . . To the size of states there is a limit, as there is to other things, plants, animals, implements. . . . For example a ship which is only a span long will not be a ship at all, nor a ship a quarter of a mile long. . . . In like manner a state when composed of too few is not. . . . self-sufficing; when of too many . . . it is not a state, being almost

the action of a tragedy is not longer than one day (*hupo mian periodon hēliou*).[1] In the positive sense, of structure and magnitude, the action must be large enough to admit a change from evil to good or from good to evil (VII)—and, one might add, large enough to display both good and evil adequately. A "complex" action is better than a simple—"complex" being that which includes a *peripeteia* or sudden turn and, as the mechanism of this turn, an *anagnōrisis* or recognition. It is characteristic of Aristotle's thought that these terms, formal in one respect and linking closely with other more formal terms, are in another respect full of implications about the ideal content of tragedy, and in that connection we shall return to them in our next chapter.

The terms *peripeteia* and *anagnōrisis* and also the terms *desis* (complication), *metabasis* (change of fortune—standing in a generic relation to *peripeteia*), and *lusis* (unravelling or denouement)[2] may be looked on as variously intermediate between the sheerly formal and the contentual. The most purified formal terms which Aristotle uses are perhaps *holos* and *teleios;* the action, he says, must be not only of a certain size but whole and complete.[3] The echo from the *Physics* is quite close.

> For thus we define the whole—that from which nothing is wanting, as a whole man or a whole box. . . . "whole" and "complete" are either quite identical or closely akin. Nothing is complete (*teleion*) which has no end (*telos*); and the end is a limit.
> —*Physics* III, 6

The discussion of the whole in the *Poetics* postulates the further formal conceptions of an end (*teleutē*), a beginning (*archē*), and a middle (*meson*). The interdependence of these three formal concepts and that of the *whole* is nicely stated in the *Metaphysics:*

> Of quanta that have a beginning and a middle and an end, those to which the position does not make a difference are called totals, and those to which it does, wholes. V, 26.

---

incapable of constitutional government. For who can be the general of such a vast multitude, or who the herald, unless he have the voice of a Stentor." In *Metaphysics* XIII, 3, beauty consists in symmetry, order, and proportion, and is illustrated by the mathematical sciences in a special degree.

[1] *Poetics* V. The phrase in the context refers clearly to internal length (plot) rather than to external length (duration), although a careless variation in meaning of *mēkos* (size) in V, 4, and VII, 6 and a synonymous use of *chronos* (time) for one of the meanings have raised some doubt among the commentators. For the unities of time and place, see also Chapter II, 3.

[2] *Poetics* XVIII. In Chapter XII occurs the more superficial distinction of the quantitative parts of a play: "Prologue, Episode, Exodos, Choric song; the last being divided into Parodos and Stasimon." This is thought by some to be a non-Aristotelian interpolation.

[3] *Poetics* VII.

A beginning, says the *Poetics*, is that which requires nothing to have come before it; a middle is that which naturally follows something and precedes something else; an end is that something else. Abstract as the terms are, almost truistic as they may appear to us, the heirs of the whole Aristotelian tradition, they yet involve a certain richness of meaning, and they even raise a few problems. That which requires nothing to have come before it will of course not be found very patly in a drama. The beginning of any story is likely to concern a man or a family and hence to imply at least such antecedents as ancestors (who may or may not be mentioned in a prologue or retrospective narration).[4] The acceptable sense of the statement that a story must have a beginning would seem to be that the story must start more or less where its antecedents may be taken for granted, that is, where they are generic rather than specifically relevant. And this has a very special meaning with reference to the stock materials of Greek tragedy, the favorite stories of Thebes or the house of Atreus. These indeed, says Aristotle, are usually the best, because they have the advantage of having really happened and so must be at least probable. One may add—for it is an idea which readily follows —that these stories have the advantage of getting off to a fast start. A comic poet of Aristotle's time complained:

> Your tragedian is altogether the most fortunate of poets. First his plot is familiar to the audience before a line is uttered—he need only give a reminder. If I just say "Oedipus," they know all the rest: his father was Laius, his mother, Jocasta, the names of his sons and daughters, what he has done and what will happen to him. . . . We comic playwrights have no such resources.[5]

It was in virtue of such a well-stocked tradition of fabulous fact that Horace could later give his classic advice about beginning with the siege of Troy, not with the birth of Helen and her sister and brothers (*nec gemini ab ovo, in medias res*). Yet the Horatian *in medias res* stands in a curiously oblique relation to Aristotle's *meson*—which is an actual middle of a plot, not a beginning. And the paradox cannot be resolved if the Aristotelian terms are taken with chronologically complete and measured reference to the external world.

V

The terms *beginning*, *middle*, and *end* emphasize a specially close cohesion of causes. Not everything that happens in the life of one man,

---

[4] Antecedent events introduced in this way are called by Aristotle *ta exōthen* (externals) and are considered as part of the *desis* (XVIII).

[5] Antiphanes, *Poiēsis*, fr. 191, quoted in Gilbert Norwood, *Greek Comedy* (London, 1931), p. 49.

says Aristotle, can be included in one story. Without attempting to force what is mainly a verbal resemblance to the *major, minor,* and *middle* terms of the Aristotelian syllogism, one may yet turn to Aristotle's *Posterior Analytics* for an instance of how the logic of deduction or the syllogism relates to inductive, or as one might say, dramatic reasoning.

> Quick wit is a faculty of hitting upon the middle term instantaneously. It would be exemplified by a man who saw that the moon has her bright side always turned towards the sun, and quickly grasped the cause of this, namely that she borrows her light from *him*; or observed somebody in conversation with a man of wealth and divined that he was borrowing money, or that the friendship of these people sprang from a common enmity. In all these instances he has seen the major and minor terms and then grasped the causes, the middle terms.
>
> —*Posterior Analytics* I, 34

Aristotle proceeds to reduce the reasoning about the sun to syllogistic form somewhat as follows:

> The moon is lighted from the sun. (minor premise)
> That which is lighted from the sun has its bright side
>   sunward. (major premise)
> Therefore: The moon has its bright side sunward.

The syllogistic reduction we observe is a reversal of the actual experience and act of learning. It is a reformation of a certain order derived from raw experience. One may draw a parallel: a man looks up at the moon and speculates how it comes to be so and so; a man witnesses the tragedy of Oedipus and speculates on its significance, the reasons why it should be so and so. One difference between the astronomical act of learning and that which takes place in the presence of tragedy will be that in the latter we have what Aristotle considers not the demonstrably certain middle terms of a science but the probable terms of a practical art. From the play we could derive not strictly a "syllogism" but an "enthymeme," a counterpart of the syllogism in the realm of probability.[6] Another difference might be that the more complicated chain of events in a drama would yield not one but several middle terms, so that we should have the kind of chain of suspended syllogisms known as the Aristotelian sorites. Again, as it is characteristic of poetry to refrain from generalizations or from giving away any messages, we might expect not to find the major premise of our syllogism—though on the other hand Greek tragedy might provide an exception in that its choruses and frequent gnomic utterances serve a highly generalizing purpose. At any rate if we find a drama, let us say *Oedipus the King* by Sophocles (a play

[6] Cf. *post* Chapter 4, p. 67, n. 5.

which Aristotle seems to regard as something like his ideal),[7] if we find this a coherent and orderly structure, we shall tend to carry away from it some dominant impression. And this might be reduced or depoetized, with great overemphasis on the element of generalization, somewhat as follows:

> Oedipus commits patricide and incest.
> He who commits patricide and incest is a criminal, brings a
>   curse on his country, and is doomed to punishment.
> Therefore: Oedipus is a criminal, brings a curse on his country,
>   and is doomed to punishment.

The precise interpretation of the play which we embody in our syllogism is not essential to the general theory. The reader may write in his own middle term or terms (corresponding to whatever he infers about the source of illumination in *Oedipus*). The point of emphasis here is the implicitly reasonable or consistent pattern, the inductive and imaginative cohesion of the dramatic parts, beginning, middle, and end, and in turn the smaller parts of these.

The kind of oneness implied not only in Aristotle's general theory of organic form but in his theory of verbal mimesis is the oneness of a thing which has heterogeneous, interacting parts. The concept is illustrated by a striking analogy in the *Politics* (II, 2):

> Is it not obvious that a state may at length attain such a degree of unity as to be no longer a state?—since the nature of a state is to be a plurality, and in tending to greater unity, from being a state, it becomes a family, and from being a family, an individual. . . . Again, the state is not made up only of so many men, but of different kinds of men; for similars do not constitute a state. It is not like a military alliance. The usefulness of the latter depends upon its quantity . . . but the elements out of which a unity is to be formed differ in kind.

"The parts of the action," says the *Poetics* (VIII), "stand together." Aristotle's speculations begin with the observation of life, but they do not end in atomistic analysis. He sees the whole as more than the sum of its parts if only in that it includes the relations among the parts.

To make a final application of these notions to the literary object, let us say that rightly understood Aristotle asks us to distinguish between what is really a verbal object (a unity, a thing, and hence an analogue of substantial being) and what only pretends in certain superficial ways to be so. The unity of the verbal object is one which penetrates to many levels and one which requires the complement of all these

[7] See *Poetics* XI, XIII, XV, XVI, XXIV, XXVI.

levels—as perhaps Aristotle indicates in his list of the six elements of tragedy: *muthos* (plot), *ēthos* (character), *dianoia* (thought)—these, he says, are the "matter"; [8] *lexis* (diction), *melos* (song)—*these* are the "medium";[8] *opsis* (spectacle)—this is the "manner."[8] The integration of these six is not a thing to be lightly supposed, nor, for that matter, is the legitimacy of the triple distinction: matter, medium, manner—on these issues we shall have occasion to say more. For the moment we assume that the integration, which we discuss now mainly with reference to plot, will in the fullness of fact include the other five elements. Let us put our stress for the moment upon the unity and reality of the play, as distinct from, but analogous to, that of objects in other areas of our experience.

> A sentence or phrase may form a unity in two ways—either as signifying one thing, or as consisting of several parts linked together. Thus the Iliad is one by the linking together of parts, the definition of man by the unity of the thing signified.
>
> —*Poetics* XX

A passage in the *Metaphysics* (VII, 4) makes it clear, indeed, that the oneness of a thing signified, man, for instance, was for Aristotle a oneness of greater metaphysical dignity than the oneness of verbal composition.

> . . . we have a definition not where we have a word and a formula identical in meaning (for in that case all formulae or sets of words would be definitions; for there will be some name for any set of words whatever, so that even the *Iliad* will be a definition), but where there is a formula of something primary. . . .

Nevertheless, the unity of the verbal composition, "by the linking together of parts," has a worth of its own—quite different from that of the other kind of verbal unity, the more abstract unity of definition or statement. *Oedipus the King* is more than its title, and it is more than a certain number of scenes placed together under one title—just as an actual man is more than his name or his definition, and, within the world of physical substances, is more of a thing than a number of cardboard boxes wrapped together and identified with a label. The *Oedipus* has a far more cohesive actuality and substantiality than, for instance, the entries for a year in the *Anglo-Saxon Chronicle* or a chapter of Xenophon's *Anabasis*. It has a great deal more than certain other Greek plays, notably than some by Euripides, a dramatist to whom Aristotle refers

[8] For the relation of these terms to the term "form" as that appears throughout this history, see *post* Chapter 32, Epilogue, pp. 747–8.

with markedly less approval. The *Andromache* of Euripides, for example, falls in half (if not into smaller parts) and might easily be viewed as fragments of at least two unfinished plays stuck together by means of the title and certain other abstract indexes. Its unity is somewhat illusory. *Oedipus*, on the contrary, not only presents a certain unified and significant image of reality, but is itself a form of reality.

CHAPTER 3

ARISTOTLE: TRAGEDY AND COMEDY

§ *The tragic focus, definition of tragedy, catharsis—II. plot and character, spectacle, the ideal tragic hero—III. hamartia (three interpretations), Aristotelian vs. Socratic ethics, good and bad luck, theological blunders,* Oedipus— *IV.* peripeteia *and* anagnōrisis *as dramatic content—V. definition of comedy, comic catharsis, Old Comedy and New, lampooning vs. general significance, label names, comic types in Aristotle's* Ethics, *Theophrastan Characters, the comic universal, tragic and comic* hamartia—*VI. tragic and comic antinomies, importance of Aristotle's answer to Plato, a double concern for the universal, escape from both Thracian and Boeotian theory, Abbé Bremond, mystery vs. criticism* §

WE HAVE BEEN USING THE TERM "TRAGEDY" ALMOST AS IF IT WERE synonymous with "poetry." Aristotle does the same, or at least he devotes a large part of his *Poetics*, Chapters VI–XIX, to talking about tragedy. Not only had tragedy evolved, as we have seen, through several phases to its entelechy or full form, but this same evolution was in a broader sense the evolution of poetry to *its* full form, which was no other than that of tragedy. Epic, which Aristotle treats in the last four chapters of the *Poetics*, had been a phase in the genesis of tragedy, it might be discussed in much the same terms, and—though this seems to have run contrary to the prevailing opinion—it was inferior to tragedy because less concentrated, less ideal. Dithyramb was a more recent ritual approach to tragedy, surviving in lyric and choral parts, which ought to be closely integrated with the action. The philosophy of lyric as such does not appear in the *Poetics*. The didactic is clearly not countenanced —the physics of Empedocles being adduced as an instance of what is verse but not poetry. The literary genres as such make a post-Aristotelian chapter of critical history. But it may be observed here that the dominance of one genre or another at different periods of critical history may strongly affect whole systems of criticism and may afford the insights through which they make their most permanent statements. The Aristotelian poetics is the poetics of the drama and especially of tragedy. We now quote the celebrated definition of tragedy from Chapter VI. Tragedy is:

> an imitation of an action that is serious, complete, and of a certain magnitude; in language embellished with each kind of artistic ornament, the several kinds being found in separate parts of the play; in the form of action, not of narrative; through pity and fear (*di' eleou kai phobou*) effecting the proper purgation (*katharsis*) of these emotions.

One of the most debated clauses of this definition is the last, concerning catharsis. It will be noted that just as Aristotle is in the main intent on answering Plato in metaphysical terms—putting his poetic "universal" against Plato's imitation of an imitation—so here he has thrown out a brief answer in emotive terms to Plato's argument that poetry inflames the passions and weakens moral fiber. Perhaps Aristotle said more about catharsis in a lost second part of his *Poetics*. In the section of the *Politics* on education there is a parallel statement about the benefit of music in working off emotions of religious frenzy. "When hereafter we treat of poetry," he says, "we will treat the subject with more precision" (*Politics* V [VIII], 7). The exegetes of Aristotelian catharsis have chiefly devoted their efforts to arguing the question whether the term "catharsis" is a medical, Hippocratic metaphor implying the purgation or expulsion of something harmful, the emotions themselves—or is a religious or moral metaphor, implying the purification or aesthetic depersonalization of our usually selfish emotions of pity and fear. (Various intermediate theories, of tempering or moderation, appeared in the late Renaissance, and will claim our attention in a later chapter.) The first or hygienic view, though cruder, appears to be what Aristotle meant—if we may judge from what he says of music in the *Politics* and from the usual syntax of the noun *katharsis* with an objective genitive of the harmful thing purged away (rather than of the other thing purified and retained), as in the phrase of Plato's *Phaedo*, *katharsis tis tōn toioutōn pantōn* (i.e. *hēdonōn kai phobōn*),[1] which may be Aristotle's model.[2] The second or

---

[1] *Phaedo* 69: "Truth is in fact a kind of purgation of all such [pleasures and fears]."

[2] A third argument may be found in the fact that Aristotle's *Rhetoric* (II, 5, 8) speaks of pity and fear as naturally related. This seems to tell against the view (Butcher, p. 265) that these emotions are specially brought together in tragedy so that they may purify each other of sentiment and selfishness.

lustratory view is that adopted by Butcher in his influential essay. It connects more readily with normal modern views about the dignity of the tragic experience and its enlargement of our souls; it is doubtless nearer not only to what most of us would like to say but to the truth. It has at least the advantage of making the enjoyment of tragedy occur while we are witnessing it, rather than in a sounder sleep when we get home, a relief after emotional orgy. But both views concern after all not what tragedy says or what tragedy is so much as what tragedy may do to us; they lie rather in the realm of experimental psychology than in that of literary criticism. They treat "pity and fear" as a reference to something in the audience rather than to something (scenes or elements) in the play, "scenes of pity and fear," as the phrase may justly be rendered.

II

ANOTHER question vigorously debated by the exegetes has concerned the statement (*Poetics* VI) that the plot (*muthos*) is the soul and first principle (*archē kai psuchē*) of tragedy. A shift of interest to character as a thing somehow appearing apart from or prior to plot is associated historically with the rise of romantic criticism and the drama of soul-analysis through reverie and soliloquy. Today a rigorously minded classical critic may write an essay [3] rebuking Shakespearian studies for overlooking a central Aristotelian principle and indulging too much in thoughts about Shakespeare's characters. But in an earlier chapter of the *Poetics* Aristotle says that poetry imitates men not only in their actions but in their characters and feelings. And he says too that *ēthos* as well as *muthos* is one of the six elements of tragedy. One might be content to say that—whatever the possibly successful imbalances of character or of action in drama, and they are doubtless many—there can be no basic consideration of character and action separately. Or, one might say, plot without character is a puzzle, as in a detective story; character without plot is a series of conversations or soliloquies, as in some romantic closet dramas. "What is character but the determination of incident?" asks Henry James. "What is incident but the illustration of character?" "If a woman stands with her hand on a table and looks at me a certain way it is an incident."[4]

Perhaps not enough has ever been said about Aristotle's slight regard for the sixth element of tragedy in his list, *opsis*, the optical part or spectacle. Mere scene-shifting, he considers it, and scarcely a concern of

[3] E. E. Stoll, "Poetry and the Passions: An Aftermath," *PMLA*, LV (December, 1940), 979–92.

[4] Henry James, *The Art of Fiction*, ed. L. N. Richardson (New York, 1941), p. 86.

criticism.[5] He seems to concur in Plato's disapproval of animal mimicry and artificial thunder claps (*Republic* III, 396) and is thus the second critic of antiquity to take up the long fight by men of good sense against the usurpation of the stage by vaudeville, operatic diversions, and slapstick—"Cato's long wig" and "Flowered gown," Pinkie and the chicken swallowed whole. It is better,—says Aristotle, "to depend on an artistic handling of the story." We ought to get the effect from simply hearing (or reading). This may be an armchair view and rather extreme—but it has the advantage of stressing the verbal and poetic element of drama, that which is most stable and permanently eligible for criticism.

In our last chapter we have considered *to beltion,* or the ideal aim of nature's working in the Aristotelian scheme of universals, as that aim is reflected or paralleled in the human work, the poem, taken as itself a structural entity. It is more difficult—though equally important—to consider how the Aristotelian ideal may relate to nature as an object which the poem represents or imitates. Perhaps Aristotle meant, in an affective sense, that poetry helps our nature towards its norm (catharsis aids nature's ethical purposes as cooking aids digestion). And he does seem to say that nature as imitated in poems is chosen with some kind of reference to ethical values. But this reference, whatever it may be, scarcely seems to be the same thing as measurement by an ethical norm.

Tragic poetry, says Aristotle, may represent men as better than they are, or as they are. Sophocles represented them as better; Euripides, as they are. Poetry, he says again, defending tales of the marvellous against literalistic criticism, may even plead that it is giving us things as they are said to be or as they are thought to be. So far as rewards and punishments are concerned—and they are a great concern in tragedy—distributive justice, to each according to his desert, is a weak dramatic form, a concession to the audience. It appears in comedy. Another weak form is that which only shows the villain suffering an appropriate downfall. It is difficult to entertain any very intense feelings about such an outcome.

The moral bent of the theory comes out more distinctly in the exclusion of two other cases, that where the virtuous man suffers adversity (this produces only shock—*to miaron*), or that where the villain prospers (this is against our moral sense or human feeling—*to philanthrōpon*). Tragedy appears in the nicely balanced and complicated instance where a man of strong character—and of eminent worldly position, like

[5] *Poetics* VI. We have already noticed (*ante* Chapter 2, p. 27) the opinion expressed in the *Politics* that the objects of vision, color, and figure, have a much weaker claim than music to serve as symbols of ethical experience. In a passage near the beginning of the *Poetics* (Ch. IV) concerning the pleasure we experience in recognizing the picture of a person we know, the emphasis seems to be on the universality of the mimetic pleasure: it occurs even in such a simple instance as that of portraiture.

Oedipus or Thyestes—suffers downfall as a result of some error (*di' hamartian tina, di' hamartian megalēn*). And yet he is undeserving (*anaxios*) of so great a downfall (so we may pity him); and he is a man much like ourselves (*homoios*), so we may experience fear at the spectacle of his downfall.[6]

III

A LARGE difference of opinion about Greek tragedy may be epitomized in a difference about the term *hamartia*. Etymologically, this means the missing of a mark with bow and arrow, an unskillful but not morally culpable act. And according to one school of thought *hamartia* in Greek drama is mainly an accent upon a larger tragedy of fate, man's larger suffering, unpredictably and without measure, at the hands of the gods, and man's stoic endurance.[7]

> As flies to wanton boys, are we to the gods;
> They kill us for their sport.

But the term may also be thought to have implications of moral responsibility (it means *sin* in the Greek of the New Testament). And according to another school, *hamartia* is the crux of a deeply moral (and even Christian) kind of tragedy, the story of man's culpable weakness and his due punishment. Classic Greek literature, from Homer to the tragedians, is full of human character and will engaged in responsible action. Even Antigone, when she hangs herself in the sealed cave, does not elude the criterion. Imagine in the same predicament the much-enduring Odysseus—or remember his courageous and ingenious tactics when a prisoner in the cave of the Cyclops.[8]

But again another, though a somewhat more difficult, notion is possible—one which may do more justice to the uneasy tension between willing and knowing observable in some Greek plays, notably in *Oedipus the King*, and may at the same time be more consonant with the hints of Aristotle when the latter are taken in relation to the main tenor of his thought. Error arises only through ignorance, Socrates had argued again and again, and most eloquently in the *Protagoras* (352). It is not

---

[6] In another chapter of the *Poetics*, XV, the tragic character must be good (*chrēston*), appropriate (*harmotton*), true to life (*homoion*), and consistent (*homalon*). The second, third, and fourth, if they may be distinguished, make the classical doctrine of character decorum. Cf. *post* Chapter 5.

[7] Seymour M. Pitcher, "Aristotle's Good and Just Heroes," *PQ*, XXIV (January, 1945), 1–11; (April, 1945), 190–1; C. M. Bowra, *Sophoclean Tragedy* (Oxford, 1944), Ch. V.

[8] Lane Cooper, *Aristotelian Papers* (Ithaca, 1939), "The Villain as Hero"; and "'Αμαρτία Again—AND AGAIN," *The Classical Journal*, XLIII (October, 1947), 39–40.

really possible to know what is correct and to do otherwise. But the psychology of Aristotle's *Ethics* is more complicated. Concerned, as so often, to rebut or to qualify the view of Plato or Socrates, he argues in Book VII of the *Nicomachean Ethics:*

> Now we may ask . . . how a man who judges rightly can behave incontinently. That he should behave so when he has knowledge, some say is impossible; for it would be strange—so Socrates thought—if when knowledge was in a man something else could master it and drag it about like a slave. For Socrates was entirely opposed to the view in question, holding that there is no such thing as incontinence; no one, he said, when he judges acts against what he judges best—people act so only by reason of ignorance. Now this view plainly contradicts the observed facts, and we must inquire about what happens to such a man. . . .
>
> . . . . since there are two kinds of premises, there is nothing to prevent a man's having both premises and acting against his knowledge, provided that he is using only the universal premise and not the particular; for it is particular acts that have to be done. . . .
>
> But now this is just the condition of men under the influence of passion; for outbursts of anger and sexual appetites and some other such passions, it is evident, actually alter our bodily condition, and in some men even produce fits of madness. It is plain, then, that incontinent people must be said to be in a similar condition to men asleep, mad, or drunk.—VII, 2–3

Somehow or other, experience teaches us, it is possible to know the better and do the worse. (*Video meliora, proboque. Deteriora sequor.*)[9] But the degrees of responsibility may be very elusive of definition.

> Now when (1) the injury takes place contrary to reasonable expectation, it is a *misadventure* (*atuchēma*). When (2) it is not contrary to reasonable expectation, but does not imply vice, it is a *mistake* (*hamartēma*) (for a man makes a mistake (*hamartanei*) when the fault originates in him, but is the victim of accident when the origin lies outside him). When (3) he acts with knowledge but not after deliberation, it is an *act of injustice* (*adikēma*)—e.g. the acts due to anger or to other passions necessary or natural to man; for when men do such harmful and mistaken acts (*blaptontes kai hamartanontes*) they act unjustly, and the acts are acts of injustice, but this does not imply that the doers are unjust or wicked; for the injury is not due to

[9] Ovid, *Metamorphoses* VII, 20.

vice (*mochthēria*). But when (4) a man acts from choice, he is
an *unjust man* and a vicious man.—*Ethics* V, 8

A close affinity between (3) in this list, the act of passion, and (2), the
act of culpable negligence, is further suggested in the continuation of
the passage quoted just above from Book VII.

> . . . incontinence . . . is blamed not only as a fault (*hamartia*)
> but as a kind of vice (*kakia*).[1] VII, 4

In yet another passage (*Ethics* III, 1) even rooted and wicked ignorance,
(4) in the list above, is alluded to as *hamartia*. *Hamartia* (error) and its
concrete equivalent *hamartēma* (an erroneous act) and the cognate verb
hamartanein seem to connote an area of senses shading in from a peri-
phery of vice and passion to a center of rash and culpable negligence.[2]
Both V, 8 and III, 1 of the *Ethics* include very helpful descriptions of
the latter.

> . . . those done in ignorance are *mistakes* (*hamartēmata*) when
> the person acted on, the act, the instrument, or the end that will
> be attained is other than the agent supposed; the agent thought
> either that he was not hitting anyone or that he was not hitting
> with this missile or not hitting this person or to this end, but a
> result followed other than that which he thought likely (e.g.,
> he threw not with intent to wound but only to prick), or the
> person hit or the missile was other than he supposed.—V, 8

> A man may be ignorant, then, of who he is, what he is doing,
> what or whom he is acting on . . . and to what end (e.g. he
> may think his act will conduce to someone's safety). . . . of
> what a man is doing he might be ignorant, as for instance peo-
> ple say, "it slipped out of their mouths as they were speaking,"
> or "they did not know it was a secret," as Aeschylus said of the
> mysteries, or a man might say he "let it go off when he merely
> wanted to show its working," as the man did with the catapult.
> Again, one might think one's son was an enemy, as Merope did,
> or that a pointed spear had a button on it, or that a stone was
> pumice-stone; or one might give a man a draught to save, and
> really kill him; or one might want to touch a man, as people do
> in sparring, and really wound him.—III, 1

Or—if we may take a very slight liberty of interpolation—one might meet
an old man and his retinue at a cross-roads, fall into an altercation, and

---

[1] *Kakia* seems to be approximately equivalent to the *mochthēria* (vice) mentioned in *Ethics* V, 8 and distinguished from *hamartia* in *Poetics* XIII.

[2] Butcher, pp. 320–1, points out a passage in *Oedipus at Colonus*, ll. 966 ff., where
hamartia and *hamartanein* shift in successive lines from the connotation of the volun-
tary to that of the involuntary.

end by killing them all—and one might be ignorant that the old man was one's father. Or one might serve the people of a foreign state by solving a riddle and one might be rewarded with the hand of their queen—and one might be ignorant that the queen was one's mother. "The doing of an act that is called involuntary in virtue of ignorance of this sort," says the *Ethics* (III, 1), "must be painful and involve repentance." It is upon "ignorance of particulars" that "pity and pardon depend." [3]

The matter in question may be even further illustrated by another Aristotelian distinction, that made in the *Physics* between what he called the *spontaneous* (the mechanically determined natural event) and *chance* (the stroke of good or evil fortune).

> Chance (*tuchē*) and what results from chance are appropriate to agents that are capable of good fortune and of moral action generally. Therefore necessarily chance is in the sphere of moral actions. This is indicated by the fact that good fortune (*eutuchia*) is thought to be the same, or nearly the same, as happiness, and happiness to be a kind of moral action, since it is well-doing.
>
> . . . spontaneous events (*hosa apo tou automatou*) are said to be "from chance" if they have the further characteristics of being the objects of deliberate intention and due to agents capable of that mode of action.—*Physics* II, 6

The moral application is developed in passages of the *Rhetoric* concerning the psychology of praise and blame.

> Since praise is founded on actions, and acting according to moral purpose is characteristic of the worthy man, we must endeavour to show that a man is acting in that manner, and it is useful that it should appear that he has done so on several occasions. For this reason also one must assume that accidents and strokes of good fortune are due to moral purpose; for if a number of similar examples can be adduced, they will be thought to be signs of virtue and moral purpose.—I, 9 [4]

[3] Another class of actions treated in Aristotle's *Ethics* (III, 1) as perhaps involuntary are those "done from fear of greater evils or for some noble object." One might perform such an action, for example, "if a tyrant were to order one to do something base, having one's parents and children in his power, and if one did the action they were to be saved, but otherwise would be put to death." The concept of the involuntary defined here, though it does not seem to be central to the *hamartia* discussed in the *Poetics* and *Ethics,* would be clearly available in discussing such a tragic fault as Agamemnon's sacrifice of Iphigenia to gain a favoring wind for the expedition against Troy.

[4] Passages of Aristotle's *Rhetoric* quoted in this chapter and the following are reprinted by permission of the publishers from *Aristotle . . . The "Art" of Rhetoric,* translated by John Henry Freese, The Loeb Classical Library, Cambridge, Mass.: Harvard University Press, 1939.

Or, as the poet Simonides had already put it:

> . . . a man . . . cannot but be evil if he be overtaken by hope-
> less calamity; for any man is good in good fortune and bad in
> bad, and take it all in all, they are best who are loved by the
> gods.[5]

Fortes fortuna juvat. God helps him that helps himself. The darker side
of this wisdom has perhaps always been the one more likely to receive
literary treatment, even though the treatment may be comic. Chekhov's
Cherry Orchard, for instance, provides a diminished figure from Greek
tragedy in the melancholy, unlovable, and unlucky philosopher servant
Epihodof, whose "Twenty Misfortunes a Day" (if he opens a door, the
knob comes off in his hand; if he plays billiards, he rips the cloth) are
clearly a part of his miserable character. In Greek thought what we encounter is no doubt a primitive notion of Providence: If the gods superintend all things, then both good and bad luck must somehow be their
doing, and for sufficient reason. A modern version will be psychological
—a Freudian theory of unconsciously deliberate slips, cultivated bad
luck, accident-prone persons.[6]

To be responsible for mistakes which are partly unavoidable is bad
enough in any area of human activity—it must be worst, and overwhelming, when the area is that of man's relation to the supernatural.
An Ancient Mariner shoots a friendly albatross with his crossbow
(*hamartia* by hitting the mark) and brings down an appalling punishment on himself and on all his shipmates. When an elderly female novelist complained to Coleridge that the poem did not have any moral, he
answered that in his opinion it had "too much." And he went on to say
that it should have been altogether without moral like the Arabian Nights
story of the merchant who threw date shells down a well putting out, by
ill luck, the eye of a genie's son. The genie rose from the well and claimed
in retaliation the merchant's life.

It is in this department of man's blundering, that which is committed against the supernatural and is hence boundless in its import and
consequences—that we shall have to place the *hamartia* of Aristotle's
ideal Greek tragedy, *Oedipus the King.* In the partly analogous Hebrew
tragedy of *Job,* the meaning announced at the end by the Voice from
the Whirlwind is that Job's sufferings have not been strictly determined
by the extent of his own sins. The same meaning is implicit in the *Oedipus,* but the tilt of the emphasis is toward a responsibility, which though
it could never have been satisfactorily discharged, Oedipus was yet not

---

[5] "Eulogy to Scopas," in *Lyra Graeca,* trans. J. M. Edmonds (London: Loeb
Classical Library, 1924), vol. II, fr. 19. The fragment is preserved in the *Protagoras*
of Plato, 339, 347.

[6] See Freud, *The Psychopathology of Everyday Life,* trans. A. A. Brill (New
York, 1914).

free to evade. If on the one hand Oedipus is predestined to destruction, on the other hand, the particular time, features, and fullness of his suffering are determined ironically by the kind of militant scepticism which he shares with his mother, and by his own violent efforts to get free. The rashness which may be traced in his early actions—the flight from Corinth and the murder of Laius—only prefigures the hasty, ill-tempered, and irreverent steps of his inquisition on the day of downfall.[7]

I V

WE HAVE talked in our last chapter about Aristotle's theory of poetry as a theory of poetic form. But it is a theory of form only in the sense by which *form* has plenary implications for what may be thought of, from another point of view, as poetic content. Two precise and technical Aristotelian concepts, already mentioned briefly in our last chapter, serve very well to show the interdependence of the two sides of the theory. *Peripeteia* (sudden reversal) and *anagnōrisis* (recognition) are the pivots of the complex action (*peplegmenē praxis*) preferred by Aristotle; they are a formal necessity in the well-developed whole of a certain size, the action with beginning, middle, and end, where good and evil are adequately set against each other. At the same time, *peripeteia* and *anagnōrisis* are key incidents in the serious story (*muthos*) of the upright protagonist, his *hamartia*, and his suffering. *Peripeteia* is an acute form of *metabasis* or change from good to bad. In the light of Aristotle's examples (the messenger from Corinth comes to cheer Oedipus but clinches the revelation of horror; Danaus leads off Lynceus for the purpose of executing him but is himself executed—) it would seem that *peripeteia* means something very much like a reversal of expectation or frustration of purpose, an "unexpected catastrophe resulting from a deed unwittingly done."[8] *Peripeteia*, says one classical scholar, is a kind of irony of action. Irony of words, so frequent also in Greek tragedy and so telling, occurs "when words, are caught up by circumstances and charged with a fuller meaning than the speaker meant." Irony of action occurs when "deeds are caught up out of an agent's grasp and charged with a meaning the very opposite" of what was meant.[9] *Anagnōrisis*, when used, as it may be, in close junction with *peripeteia*, is the hero's realization of the truth, the full meaning of the deed done in error. There

---

[7] For a detailed exposition of the play as a "critique of rationalism," see Cleanth Brooks and Robert B. Heilman, *Understanding Drama* (New York, 1948), pp. 573 ff.

[8] Atkins, I, 91; F. L. Lucas, "The Reverse of Aristotle," *Classical Review*, XXXVII (1923), 98–104; and his *Tragedy in Relation to Aristotle's "Poetics"* (London, 1928), pp. 91 ff.

[9] Atkins, I, 92; W. Lock, "The Use of περιπέτεια in Aristotle's Poetics," *Classical Review*, IX (1895), 251–3.

are six kinds, says Aristotle, of which the most effective is not that of
the scar discovered in the bath (as on the return of Odysseus to Ithaca)
or that deliberately contrived by one of the characters (as when Orestes
makes himself known to Iphigenia) but that which grows naturally from
the very workings of the plot—and the example is that of the messenger
in *Oedipus*. *Peripeteia* and *anagnōrisis*, we suggest, are but the due developments and complements of *hamartia;* they are the surprising, but
natural, aftermath of the partly responsible act of error. The reversal,
says Aristotle, should follow its antecedents in a way that is probable or
necessary—but it is much better if the way is also surprising. If there
were no surprise—that is, if the downfall were clearly predictable or acceptable from the start as the only plausible outcome of the protagonist's fault—we should have not *hamartia* as it may be accurately conceived, but the fully vicious act of the villain. *Peripeteia* and *anagnōrisis*
are requirements for the action of a certain magnitude—an action large
enough to exhibit the development of a character through confidence,
error, recognition and suffering. These two technicalities are specifications for the kind of moral consequence, crossed by surprise, which
makes the cohesive beginning, middle, and end, the whole and unity of
Aristotle's formal theory. "It may perhaps be," said a later Greek writer
in the Aristotelian vein, "that nature has a liking for contraries and
evolves harmony out of them and not out of similarities. . . . The arts
. . . apparently imitate nature in this respect."[1]

V

WHAT of comedy? Opposite and complement of tragedy, the other
half of Greek drama, it is so different a half, and may seem in its marked
physical response of laughter so different from all the rest of poetry
as to resist being assimilated into any general poetics either of form or
of content. Like catharsis, comedy is a topic upon which Aristotle may
have said more in a second part of his *Poetics*.[2] It is a topic to which he
refers several times in the extant part of the *Poetics*, but rather casually,
as if comedy were a minor genre, a reverse or grotesque of serious poetry. This was the kind of poetry that would deal with men as worse
than they are (II) or at least as uglier than they are. Plato in the *Philebus*
(48–50) had thought the comic response a kind of malicious joy or emotion of self-enhancement at the spectacle of obnoxious characters (those
who in real life could hurt us) made innocuous on the stage. Aristotle,
with a more kindly insight, is concerned about the pain which those who

---

[1] *De Mundo,* Chapter 5 (trans. E. S. Forster [Oxford, 1914], 396[b]).
[2] Cf. *Rhetoric* III, 18; I, 11; *Poetics* VI.

exhibit deformities may themselves be imagined to suffer or not to suffer. The well-known definition runs as follows:

> Comedy is, as we have said, an imitation of characters of a lower type,—not, however, in the full sense of the word bad, the ludicrous (*to geloion*) being merely a subdivision of the ugly (*to aischron*). It consists of some defect (*hamartēma*) or ugliness which is not painful (*anōdunon*) and not destructive [3] (*ou phthartikon*). To take an obvious example, the comic mask (*to geloion prosōpon*) is ugly and distorted, but does not imply pain.—V

A recently too much celebrated document, the *Tractatus Coislinianus*,[4] a late peripatetic deductive parallel to the chapters of the *Poetics* on tragedy, adds to our definition a cathartic clause.

> Comedy is an imitation of an action that is ludicrous and imperfect . . . through pleasure and laughter effecting the purgation of the like emotions.

This seems a plausible guess. It is supported by our finding in Aristotle's *Ethics* (X, 6) the thesis that happiness consists not in amusement but in rational activity, and by the fact that both Plato and Aristotle include laughter among the politically dangerous emotions. Plato in both the *Republic* (III, 388–395) and *Laws* (VII, 816–17; XI, 934–6) looks on the act of comic mimesis as a dangerous contagion; he would man the comic stage with slaves and hired strangers. Aristotle remarks in his *Politics* (VII, 7) that "the legislator should not allow youth to be spectators of iambi or of comedy until they are of an age to sit at the public tables or to drink strong wine." [5] This kind of catharsis for comedy would be homeopathic (the purging of laughter by working it off) and would be neatly symmetrical with Aristotle's answer to Plato concerning the tragic catharsis. At the same time, it is at least possible to construct another theory of comic catharsis along lines suggested in Plato's *Philebus*, where, as we have noted, laughter is release from the mental pain of envy, and in a passage of Aristotle's *Rhetoric* (II, 3) asserting that "We

---

[3] The example of the comic mask which follows seems to refute those who would translate this "destructive to others."

[4] Called so from the De Coislin Collection in the Bibliothèque Nationale at Paris, from which it was printed by J. A. Cramer in his *Anecdota Graeca* in 1839. The manuscript is of the tenth century A.D.; the contents date apparently from about the first century B.C. See Lane Cooper, *An Aristotelian Theory of Comedy* (New York, 1922), p. 10.

[5] Among the "Characters" of Aristotle's successor Theophrastus is the Ruffian or Reckless Man who "is not ashamed, even while sober, to exhibit himself in the lascivious dance, or to play a part in comedy unmasked." For a recent exposition of this view of comic catharsis, see J. C. Ransom, *The World's Body* (New York, 1938), "The Cathartic Principle," pp. 188–9.

are placable when we are in a condition opposed to angry feeling, for example, at a time of sport or laughter or festivity." [6] But this would be allopathic catharsis and not symmetrical with the tragic. The present writers are content to leave this problem where it stands.

A more specifically critical problem is posed in the *Poetics* by a series of statements in which Aristotle draws a comparison between the "Old," lampooning, or Aristophanic comedy (for the sake of convenience it may be said to have ended with the Athenian downfall of 404) and the "New" or Menandrian comedy (dating after the conquest by the Macedonians in 338). Tragedy had originated in Dionysiac ritual dithyrambics; comedy had originated with the leaders of phallic songs in the *kōmoi* or village Dionysiac revels (IV). Back of each at another remove stood Homer.

> Homer . . . first laid down the main lines of Comedy, by dramatizing the ludicrous instead of writing personal satire. His Margites bears the same relation to Comedy that the Iliad and Odyssey do to Tragedy. . . . lampooners became writers of Comedy, and the Epic poets were succeeded by Tragedians.
> —IV

Lampoon, however, seems to have been a deviation from Homer in the wrong direction toward personality; lampoon was not all it should be.

> As for the plot, it came originally from Sicily; but of Athenian writers Crates was the first who, abandoning the "iambic" or lampooning form, generalized his themes and plots.—V

> In comedy . . . the poet first constructs the plot on the lines of probability, and then inserts characteristic names;—unlike the lampooners who write about particular individuals.—IX

Aristotle's conception of comedy seems even better satisfied by later Hellenistic new comedy and the Roman translations of Terence and Plautus than by the sentimental intrigues found actually in the Middle Comedy and the New Comedy of his own day. It may seem rash to say [7] that he did not appreciate the hilarity of the older lampooning comedy. But at least he must have thought comedy had been moving in the right direction. His remarks about comedy are better illustrated by almost any play of Plautus than by the masterpieces of Aristophanes.

In tragedy, he says, the poet took the already legendary name and rewrote the already known story around it. In comedy he took "characteristic" names (*ou ta tuchonta onomata*). The phrase is an emendation by Butcher, but seems eminently plausible. The plays of Plautus and Terence and the fragments and titles of Greek New Comedy and Mid-

---

[6] Lane Cooper, *op. cit.*, pp. 66–70.
[7] With Butcher, p. 380.

dle Comedy yield a large and various collection of label names [8]—racial names of slaves, like *Cario* or *Syrus*, type names like *Monotropos* (Hermit) or *Polypragmon* (Busybody), compound suggestions like *Philocomasium* (Village Revel Girl), *Artotrogus* (Breadnibbler), *Pamphile* (All-dear), or the monstrosity *Pyrgopolynices* (Conqueror of Towered Cities). Such names illustrate in a nicely definable and tabloid form a difficult poetic choice, that between naturalism (truth to life) and significance. Shall a playwright sacrifice reality for the easy symbolism of the label name, or shall he sacrifice significance for the convincing realism of a name which is as pointless as most of those in real life? Or shall he escape the dilemma by using a common noun, a "citizen," a "tapster," a "slave," a "messenger," or a "soldier," a "1st man in blue serge," a "2nd man in blue serge" (the names of minor dramatic characters from Aeschylus to our own day)?

Both Greek comedy and Greek tragedy decided mainly for the significant name, that of the type or that of the known historic person, the difference between the two being a part of the difference between the meaning of the comic character and that of the tragic. In the *Ethics* of Aristotle virtue is reasonable activity along a line of moderation, on both sides of which are the vices of extremity. A slant toward comic theory is quite pronounced in the description (IV, 8; II, 7) of the tasteful or ready-witted gentleman joker (*eutrapelos*) [9] and the extremes between which he stands, the uncultivated boor, an enemy of jokes (*agroikos*), and the buffoon (*bōmolochos*), who tries to be funny at all costs. One may see the difference between good and bad taste in wit, says Aristotle, "in the old and the new [1] comedies; to the authors of the former indecency (*aischrologia*) of language was amusing; to those of the latter innuendo (*huponoia*) [2] is more so." Again, we encounter (IV, 7) the admirably mock-modest or Socratic man (*eirōn*) and his antitypes the humbug, he who assumes modesty about trifles, and the boaster (*alazōn*), obvious precursor of the Hellenistic *Alazōn* and the Plautine Miles Gloriosus.[3] But if comedy deals with inferior examples of humanity, how, one may wonder, is the ironist, a near neighbor of the

[8] The term "charactonym" has been recently suggested to fill a kind of gap in English critical vocabulary (Thomas E. Berry, in *Word Study*, XXV, December, 1949, 1).
The plays of Plautus contain more of these significant names than of the opposite kind.

[9] Cf. *Rhetoric* II, 12, wit (*eutrapelia*) as "cultured insolence."

[1] I.e., Middle.

[2] The *Tractatus Coislinianus* uses the terms *loidoria* and *emphasis* for the same contrast.

[3] The buffoon, the ironist, and the boaster are named as specific comic types in the *Tractatus Coislinianus*. A near equivalence between *eirōneia* and *huponoia* is indicated in a passage of the *Rhetoric* (III, 18), where the gentleman, or ironist, who jokes to amuse himself, is set against the buffoon (*bōmolochos* again), who tries too hard to amuse others.

truthful mean, to be taken as a comic type? How is *huponoia*, the conversational style of the gentleman, to be associated with "New Comedy" or with any form of comedy at all? The answer is perhaps not explicit in ancient documents but may be suggested in the speculation that comedy has always required in addition to its gulls and butts such critical agents as the clever slave and planner, the gentleman commentator and wit. It might almost be a definition of a certain more sophisticated kind of comedy to say that it arises from the opposition of mixed characters or sets of mixed characters, composites who serve reciprocally as butts and critics.

Aristotle treats virtues no less than vices as clearly conceptualized types, but he has a tendency to see the vices more vividly. The tendency is continued and accentuated by his pupil and successor Theophrastus, in whose *Characters* [4] we find such contrasting pairs as the obsequious man (*areskos*) and the surly (*authadēs*), the boaster (*alazōn*) and the mock-modest (*eirōn*), and with these such companions in unattractiveness as the loquacious and the garrulous, the flatterer and the complaisant, the penurious, the avaricious, and the mean. Theophrastus gives us a nosology, a gallery of nasty persons. Greek ethical theory and comic theory are strongly alike in finding vice, much more than virtue, susceptible of fixed portraiture. The names of six out of the thirty Theophrastan Characters are the same as titles of lost plays by Menander. [5] And Menander is said to have been the pupil of Theophrastus.

These correlations between vice and comedy may be taken as the reverse of the truth that virtue is not only a mean but a course of conduct which requires such positive qualities as strength of purpose and courage, and which is best seen in a dynamic form, in motion toward an object. The comically evil character stands still, despite warnings and punishments, and his "sufficient destiny" is simply to go on revealing himself. [6] "Greek tragedy . . ." says Butcher, "combines in one harmonious representation the individual and the universal. Whereas comedy tends to merge the individual in the type, tragedy manifests the type through the individual" (p. 388). This may not be so easy a distinction as it sounds. But at least we can say that in tragedy we start with a known individual, Oedipus or Agamemnon, and see what he comes to—at what being and meaning he arrives through a certain development. In comedy (or at least in Greek New Comedy) we start, on the other hand, with the defined meaning, and it remains defined or fixed. We only more or less fill it out with examples. (It is a mechanism which we employ to-

---

[4] *Ēthikoi charaktēres*, they were called by Diogenes Laertius, the earliest extant writer of antiquity to refer to them. See *The Characters of Theophrastus*, trans. R. C. Jebb (London, 1870).

[5] *Menander*, ed. F. G. Allinson (London: Loeb Classical Library, 1921), p. xiii. Cf. Butcher, pp. 377–9.

[6] Cf. Maynard Mack, ed. *Joseph Andrews* (New York, 1948), pp. xiii–xiv.

ward some more complex overall end.) And this is partly because, just as Aristotle says, comedy deals with the inferior—and hence with a kind of human character which may at least be supposed to occur very readily in everyday life. The Aristotelian notion of the tragic protagonist as king or at least as man of eminence was complemented more explicitly, with an opposite notion for comedy, perhaps by Aristotle himself in a lost dialogue *On Poets*, perhaps by his pupil Theophrastus,[7] certainly by later theorists. "Imitatio vitae," Cicero was to call comedy, "speculum consuetudinis, imago veritatis." [8]

Tragedy and comedy show different, though understandably different, relations to the Aristotelian universal. One hinge of this unity and difference is *hamartia*. (The nearly synonymous *hamartēma* is the name of the comic flaw in Aristotle's definition of comedy.) Tragedy takes *hamartia* literally but magnifies its punishment—and is thus fearful and pitiful. Comedy distorts *hamartia* by caricature, reduces punishment to discomfiture and mortification, and is thus ridiculous. The victorious general Agamemnon returns to Argos with the captive princess Cassandra; Pyrgopolynices, the braggart captain, arrives at Ephesus with the captured slave girl Philocomasium. In the second half of the *Miles Gloriosus*, when Pyrgopolynices is tricked into attempting a marriage with a harlot supposed to be his next-door neighbor's wife, we are at least in the general region of the Oedipus transgression. But where the tragic heroes suffered death and self-inflicted blindness, the braggart soldier meets the catastrophe of an ignominious beating and responds by bellowing out a confession of his several errors.[9] In the fragmentary *Perikeiromenē* (*She Who Got Sheared*) of Menander, the girl describes the rape of her locks by the sailor lover with the verb *hubrizein*,[1] cognate with the tragic name (*hubris*) for man's eruption out of his proper sphere. These parallels are consistent with what has been observed as a broader degeneration during the fifth and fourth centuries in Greek concepts of character, from the *authadeia* which with Aeschylus was Promethean self-will to the mere "surliness" which adequately renders the term in the *Character* by Theophrastus,[2] from *eirōneia* as a philosophic stratagem in the Platonic dia-

---

[7] Atkins I, 159; A. P. McMahon, "On the Second Book of Aristotle's *Poetics* and the Source of Theophrastus' Definition of Tragedy" and "Seven Questions on Aristotelian Definitions of Tragedy and Comedy," *Harvard Studies in Classical Philology*, XXVIII (1917), 1–46; XL (1929), esp. 100–3. The argument rests on statements made by the fourth-century grammarians Diomedes and Donatus.

[8] Cicero, *De Re Publica* IV, 13, quoted by Donatus, *Excerpta de Comoedia* (Atkins II, 38).

[9] Pyrgopolynices might also be profitably compared with the romantically successful bully fellow Hercules in the *Alcestis* of Euripides, or the mock Hercules Dionysus in the *Frogs* of Aristophanes.

[1] Act IV, l. 600 (Loeb *Menander*, p. 256): Glycera: [*eis allas koras*] *hubrizetō to loipon*.

[2] Cf. G. Gordon, "Theophrastus and His Imitators" in *English Literature and the Classics* (Oxford, 1912), p. 53.

logues and a gentlemanly form of modesty in Aristotle's *Ethics* to the chicanery of the Theophrastan Dissembler: "A man of this sort (*ho de eirōn*) approaches his enemy with professions of friendship; he flatters those against whom he is plotting mischief; and he condoles with them in the way of their calamity."

VI

THE division of Greek drama into comic and tragic and Aristotle's corresponding theory would seem to represent a tension of principles that extends into literature and life perhaps not so deeply as some recent speculators have maintained, but deeply enough. We reduce the following table of mutually dependent "antinomic symbols" from Mr. Albert Cook's *The Dark Voyage and the Golden Mean, A Philosophy of Comedy.*[3] Under one or the other of these two opposed but interdependent headings we have nearly all that may be conceived in the realm of human interests.

TRAGEDY	COMEDY
The Wonderful	*The Probable*
Imagination	*Reason*
Ethics	*Manners*
The Individual	*Society*
The Extreme (Christianity)	*The Mean (Aristotle)*
Symbol	*Concept*
Death	*Politics, Sex*
Good and Evil	*Conformity or Expulsion*
The Handsome Actor	*The Ugly Actor*
The Pariah Artist	*The Diplomatic Artist*
Failure	*Success*
Soliloquy	*Aside*
The Superhuman	*The Subhuman (beast, machine)*
Aristocrat	*Bourgeois*
Paradox	*Contrast*

We venture to add this tentative thought: that the two sides of this interesting dichotomy may be more closely interdependent in literature than in life—that a certain union of the two may well be near to the center of whatever is universal in poetry.

Aristotle, by his formal analysis of the two dominant genres of Greek literature, made a respectable effort to rebut Plato's arguments against poetry and to answer the business-like and Rotarian questions of Socrates in the *Ion*. The answer is perhaps not ironclad, but it has at least one important virtue, namely, that it tends to shift the emphasis of inquiry

[3] Cambridge, Mass., 1949. Our table is selected and adapted from pp. 28 and 50–1.

away from what poetry may *say*, or tell us, in a practical or even in a philosophic sense, toward what poetry may embody or in itself *be*. And this the answer accomplishes through its *double* concern for the universal—that is, its concern both for what is imitated or reflected in the poem and for the poem itself as a form or kind of being in which the imitation is realized. As Aristotle's theory is a theory of imitation, it is a theory of reference (what the poem *is* never really escapes entanglement with what the poem *says*); it is a theory of a universal and an ideal in the field of reference, and this ideal tends to be the ethical man. Still this ideal is never quite that. The theory never quite says that the poetic worth of the imitation is to be decided directly in terms of the practical ideal. Whether poetry is something which charms (as Homer and the Thracians had said) or something which teaches (as Hesiod and the Boeotians said) [4] was an inherited issue which Aristotle met not head on but by the oblique device of saying that poetry is something which pleases us by being an image and by being at the same time very serious and very philosophic (*philosophōteron kai spoudaioteron*).

We conclude our account of Aristotle's debate with Plato by alluding to the spirited judgment of a modern French critic, the Abbé Henri Bremond in his *Prière et Poésie*. His first chapter, "*Platon et la Poésie Exilée*," speaks well enough for present purposes in its title. From the second chapter, "*Aristote et la Poésie Dépoétisée*," we attempt the following translation of an apologia put in the mouth of Aristotle.

As for the meaning which is captured in a poem, though it may have been as it were divinely discovered through that *theia dunamis* of which professor Socrates tells us, it remains nevertheless intelligible and as a result definable. If a doctor is able to enumerate the parts of a human skeleton, it hardly follows that he is open to censure for not being interested in life. He follows his anatomical bent; I follow mine as logician. You profess to deplore the fact that I have put poetry under "the absolute yoke of reason." But it is not quite clear to me where you get that idea. That fantastic line about "sole reason," the first principle of all poetic beauty, is not to be found in my own writings so far as I know. . . . It is not as if I had overlooked, as you seem to suppose, that specific and ineffable quality which constitutes the poetic experience. It is simply that I am not concerned with it—unless in that famous statement of mine about catharsis [5]—a somewhat obscure expression, I admit, but one

---

[4] Atkins I, 80–1; W. C. Greene, "The Greek Criticism of Poetry" in *Perspectives of Criticism*, ed. Harry Levin (Cambridge, Mass., 1950), p. 21.

[5] As a matter of fact Aristotle makes some casual acknowledgements of poetic inspiration. In the *Poetics* (XVII) he speaks of the poet as *euphuēs* rather than *manikos;* in the *Rhetoric* (III, 7) poetry is an inspired thing (*entheon hē poiēsis*).

from which they will someday derive a thoroughgoing mystical poetics.

And the Abbé's comment on this:

> He tells the truth. There is no metaphysic, either right or wrong, in his *Poetics*. There is no other heresy than that of silence—the most dangerous of all—Aristotle's sin of omission, his disappearing trick. He has not written a single sentence from which one might convict him of setting aside the traditional view of the poet's inspiration and identifying poetic knowledge with rational. But then he has not written a sentence either—except to be sure that about catharsis—from which one might even suspect the contrary. To remain silent is to consent. Aristotle has kept his silence—silence forever to be deplored—silence pregnant with catastrophe, pregnant, if I may so express myself, with Boileau.[6]

This seems the place for a candid assertion that our own view as theorists of poetry is something like that which Aristotle is made to confess. We argue that criticism, if it is to occur at all, must be like that. It must be rational and aim at definitions, whether it can or cannot quite achieve them. But what is left over and above definition, we argue furthermore, is still an objective quality of poems, knowable if indefinable, and distinguishable from that other realm, the dark well of mystery and inspiration [7]—which is the poet's alone. If these two areas, the knowable yet indefinable individuality of the poem, and the unknowable or incommunicable mystery of the poet's inspiration, are alleged to show limits to the critic's activity, we concede the point. The first area, the individuality of the poetic utterance, may tease the critic's ambition. He would conquer it if he could though this is not required of him. With the second, the inspiration, he is scarcely concerned.

[6] Henri Bremond, *Prière et Poésie* (Paris, 1926), Chapter II, translated by permission of Burns Oates & Washbourne Ltd., London.

[7] A more recent, and to the present time perhaps the largest and most brilliant celebration of this "translucid spiritual night" is Jacques Maritain's *Creative Intuition in Art and Poetry* (New York: Pantheon Books, 1953). Mr. Maritain, so far as he would grant any significance at all to the concerns of the present narrative, would say that they are the concerns of "art," not of "poetry." There is a partial sense in which he would be perfectly right.

SUPPLEMENT

I connect the essential distinction between tragedy and comedy with two opposing impulses deeply rooted in human nature. Until we can find a way of reconciling the antinomy in our nature we are all torn between the desire to *find* ourselves and the desire to *lose* ourselves. It is on some such antithesis as this that Coleridge based his whole philosophy and in particular his theory of imagination.

We are impelled to preserve and accentuate and glory in our separate lives; we believe that every member of our species has his particular and distinct destiny; there are even atheists who cannot bring themselves to believe in the possibility of their own extinction. This natural pride of man and in man I believe to be the psychological foundation of tragedy. . . .

But if there is a proper human pride, there is also a proper human modesty; and the two are never, I think, far from each other. We cherish our separateness jealously; but we need also to merge it in the life of the world into which we were born, to mix with other people, to adjust our own wills and even our characters to the *milieu* in which by choice or necessity we live and to the general laws of nature. This second impulse is surely as healthy and strong as the other, and it is found in men of the most vigorous and robust character; Blake, for instance, cries in one of his most moving lines

"O why was I born with a different face?"

We cannot be satisfied with the mere assertion of our individuality; we must recognize a destiny other than our individual destinies: the *destiny of our race.* From one point of view every sparrow is infinitely important; from another the greatest man is completely unimportant. These two truths are complementary, and perhaps neither has much meaning without the other. This is one of the great paradoxes of the Christian religion; but one does not need to be a Christian to recognize its truth.

—L. J. Potts, *Comedy* (London, 1949), pp. 16–18, by permission of Hutchinson & Co. (Publishers) Limited, London

It may be said that whereas tragedy deals with the unusual but normal, comedy deals with the abnormal but not unusual. The abnormality of comic characters is not absolute; we should feel that they are capable of behaving normally if they would. But it is the main concern of the comic writer to discriminate between what is normal and abnormal in human behaviour; he is detached from his subject-matter in a sense in which other artists are not. He needs not merely a strong feeling for normality, but also a clear notion of it. It is therefore necessary for him to be in some measure a moral philosopher; for the norm is a philosophical concept. The usual, or average, is not; it can be calculated statistically from observed facts. But normality, like the cognate concepts of health and sanity, is not a fact, nor a complex of facts, nor even a simplification of facts; it is an idea, and exists only in the mind that has brought itself to bear on all the relevant facts. There is not one norm of human behaviour, but many: some of them widely divergent and even contradictory. Jane Austen's norm differs drastically in some respects from Chaucer's or Fielding's. But all comic writers must have a norm in view. To detect eccentricity you must have a centre: that is to say a consistent, if not consciously worked out, standard of character and conduct.

—L. J. Potts, *Comedy*, pp. 46–7

Greek tragedy is the tragedy of necessity: i.e., the feeling aroused in the spectator is "What a pity it had to be this way"; Christian tragedy is the tragedy of possibility, "What a pity it was this way when it might have been otherwise." . . . the hubris which is the flaw in the Greek hero's character is the illusion of a man who knows himself strong and believes that nothing can shake that strength, while the corresponding Christian sin of Pride is the illusion of a man who knows himself weak but believes he can by his own efforts transcend that weakness and become strong. . . .

A modern reader, accustomed to the tragedy of possibility, instinctively asks, "Where and when did he make the wrong choice?" and as instinctively answers, "He should not have listened to the prophecy in the first place, or, having done so, then he should never have struck the old man or anyone else, and should never have married Jocasta or anyone else." But such thoughts would never have occurred to Sophocles or his audience. Macbeth and Captain Ahab are wrong to listen to the prophecies about them, because they are equivocal, and each reads into his a possibility he is wrong to desire; the prophecy Oedipus hears is not only not unequivocal but something he is right to wish to avoid. When he kills the old man he feels no guilt, neither is he expected to feel any, and when he marries Jocasta there is nothing the matter with the relation as such. It is only when it turns out that, as a matter of fact, the former was his father and the latter is his mother that the guilt begins. . . .

Other Greek heroes are faced with the tragic choice between two evils: Agamemnon must either sacrifice his daughter or fail in his duty to the Greek Army; Antigone must be false either to her loyalty to her brother or to her loyalty to her city.

The tragic situation, of learning that one is a criminal or of being forced to become one, is not created by the flaw in the hero's character, but is sent him by the gods as a punishment for having such a flaw.

The pessimistic conclusion that underlies Greek tragedy seems to be this: that if one is a hero, i.e., an exceptional individual, one must be guilty of hubris and be punished by a tragic fate; the only alternative and not one a person can choose for himself is to be a member of the chorus, i.e., one of the average mass; to be both exceptional and good is impossible.

How does "Moby Dick" compare with this?

The hero, Captain Ahab, far from being exceptionally fortunate, is at the beginning, what in a Greek tragedy he could only be at the end, exceptionally unfortunate. He is already the victim of what the modern newspaper, which is Greek in this respect, would call a tragedy; a whale has bitten off his leg. What to the Greeks could only have been a punishment for sin is here a temptation to sin, an opportunity to choose; by making the wrong choice and continuing to make it, Ahab punishes himself.

—W. H. Auden, "The Christian Tragic Hero," *The New York Times Book Review*, December 16, 1945, p. 1, by permission of the author and *The New York Times*

It is . . . a strange and a rather embarrassing phenomenon that precisely the centuries which were thoroughly unconversant with such an enthusiastic and flying humanism produced great tragedy; while precisely those periods that had dedicated themselves entirely and without reserve to the possibility of progress and social surge failed again and again to hit off the true tragic note. Indeed, as one courses through these readings and commentaries of a half-generation ago on modern tragedy, one cannot quite get rid of the constant suspicion that *all* the evidence had been tampered with, subtly, better still, unconsciously. The facts had been rather badly twisted, so badly that as a consequence we are now in rapid danger of having our sense of the tragic completely perverted. The truth of the matter comes down to this: that it was our modern tragic literature and theory that alone inserted these strange concepts of exaltation and triumph (and did not write tragedy); while in other periods these notions have been remarkable for their absence, indeed for their rejection (yet tragedy was written). And though this writer hesitates to broach so scandalous a thesis, yet he cannot contain the suspicion that it was exactly this heresy of exaltation, and all the splendid adjectives out of which it was compounded, that was partly responsible in our times for our very great failure in the theater. . . .

We have but to try anything mightily and see what happens. In the end we come back to the decision of everyone of the great tragedies that, left to itself, the human will at the very height of its straining stands broken and defeated. . . . If, for example, we should picture the fact of defeat in terms of the metrical pattern of a production of the *Oedipus*, it should be in terms of the confident forward iambics of a machine of perfect dignity that bit by bit begins to disintegrate, in the end loses all sense of an ictus in the pattering, stuttering rows of consecutive short-syllabled feet of a blinded man, and in the very end does not even have the energy to complete the final iamb. It hangs in the air and there is nothing left. There is neither room nor energy for those artificial endings of defiance and mystical victory that we love to tack on to our tragedies. These things are lies, at least in the sense that there is no evidence for their possibility or validity. They are completely outside the *human* story and neither history nor theology can give any ground for them.

—William F. Lynch, "Confusion in Our Theater," *Thought, Fordham University Quarterly*, XXVI (Autumn, 1951), 346, 349, by permission of the editors of *Thought*

CHAPTER 4

THE VERBAL MEDIUM: PLATO AND ARISTOTLE

§ *The verbal medium, "rhetoric" as verbal artifice, Sicilian rhetoricians—II. Plato's* Phaedrus: *love, beauty, rhetoric, the speech of Lysias (a bad speech badly written), the mock speech of Socrates (style without truth), second speech of Socrates (eloquent truth)—III. theoretical discussion by Socrates: dialectic,* psuchagogia, *Socratic ethic, rhetoric as an ignorant "knack," rhetorical technicalities, written vs. spoken words—IV. Isocrates, epideictic rhetoric, a florid* paideia—*V. Aristotle's* Rhetoric: *a practical defence, rhetoric, dialectic, and the probable, ethical and emotive arguments, verbal style, something superficial yet significant, clarity, propriety, and the ornate, metaphor, related figures—VI. Isocrates again, the power of words, the Logos, grammar, dialecticians vs. rhetoricians, Ciceronian retrospect* §

W E HAVE BEEN TALKING ABOUT POETIC IMITATION AS IF IT WERE a straight copy of its objects, or a vision of them through plate glass; and in so doing we have minimized the possibility of talking about the poem rather than about its objects, about what it may *be* rather than about what it may *say*. In our first three chapters we have heard a debate conducted upon grounds of maximum advantage to the Platonic moral cause. Let us return now to the fact that Aristotle treated plot, character, and thought—the *content* of drama—as only some of its elements. Let us recall that he treated also, by a method of separation which may have seemed to us at first glance rather crude, two elements which he called the *medium*—language and music—and that there was even another element which he called the *manner*—the stage spectacle. Among these three elements, language stands out as a thing basic to all literature. Language is an inevitable concern of literary criticism. And this fact invites us to canvass a part of ancient critical history which for want of a better name we shall call *Rhetoric*.

It is a commonplace of recent critical history to observe that ancient rhetoric, from its formal beginning near the end of the fifth century B.C. to its second sophistication in the early Christian centuries, was basically a practical art, concerned, that is, with the business of persuading judges in law courts, senators in assemblies, and congregations in churches. The counter facts which we insist on here are that this legal or political art came in Roman times to be practically equivalent to higher education, and that from first to last it dwelt characteristically upon verbal artifice. It was in this art rather than in that of poetics that words were most often deliberately studied, and its examples were drawn indiscriminately from poetry and prose. "The art of contention in speech," says Socrates in the *Phaedrus*,

> is not confined to courts and political gatherings, but apparently, if it is an art at all, it would be one and the same in all kinds of speaking, the art by which a man will be able to produce a resemblance between all things between which it can be produced.—261 [1]

The term *rhetoric* has, and has had from early times, the highly useful secondary sense: *a study of how words work*. It is primarily in this sense that we shall use the term throughout this book.

Corax and Tisias were Sicilian sophists who flourished about fifty years before the birth of Aristotle. They taught legal rhetoric in Syracuse and wrote the earliest recorded treatises on the art, but these have perished. One of their successors was Gorgias of Leontini, who came to Athens on an embassy in 427 and remained to instruct and fascinate the generation of young intellectuals and aesthetes portrayed in the *Clouds* of Aristophanes. A later Sicilian Greek historian has left this account of the matter:

> On arriving at Athens and being allowed to address the people, he [Gorgias] spoke on the theme of federation in a style of such exotic artifice that he cast a spell over his audience, euphuistically inclined as they were and devoted to the ideal of eloquence. He was the first to use the strikingly artificial figures of antithesis, isocolon, parison, homoeoteleuton, and sundry other embellishments of this kind, which came at that time as admired

---

[1] With one exception, indicated in a note, quotations from Plato's *Phaedrus* in this chapter are reprinted by permission of the publishers from the translation of H. N. Fowler, *Plato . . . Euthyphro, Apology, Crito, Phaedo, Phaedrus*, 1938, Loeb Classical Library, Cambridge, Mass.: Harvard University Press.

novelties, though now they seem rather ridiculously affected and precious.[2]

Gorgias and a fellow rhetorician Polus are the antagonists of Socrates in an early and lengthy Platonic attack on rhetoric, the dialogue entitled *Gorgias;* and the same rhetorical school is the subject of criticism in the mature, highly sophisticated and dramatic *Phaedrus,* a document which is not only the earliest substantial counter-rhetoric now surviving but is still one of the most formidable in all rhetorical history.

II

THE *Phaedrus* contains some of the best-known Platonic passages on love and beauty—ones which we have alluded to in an earlier chapter —most notably the illustrative oration by Socrates built on the elaborate allegory of the soul or intellective principle as charioteer, with difficulty driving his two horses, a noble steed of the higher desires and a balky beast of the lower passions, toward the empyreal sphere of divine forms. Classical scholars have disagreed as to whether this main motif of the dialogue shows sufficient relevance to an equally conspicuous second motif—an examination of the art of rhetoric. The relevance between the two motifs (and hence the unity of the whole dialogue) actually seems very close. It is the relevance of ideal illustration to a theory of an art ideally conceived. A main assumption of the whole dialogue is the Socratic principle that virtue is knowledge, and, springing from this, the main argument is that a worthy rhetoric—one aimed at the highest good—will be, not a way of fooling people in law courts, but an approach to knowledge, or an embodiment of it—a kind of inspired philosophy. The theme of love and beauty, which Plato believed to be the only adequate theme of philosophy, was the only one which he could have employed for the full illustration of the thesis.

The argument begins adroitly with an enthusiastic reading by Phaedrus, and a cool analysis by Socrates, of a shoddy speech—either an actual speech of the orator Lysias or a parody—an academic invective against ardent lovers.[3] The objections of Socrates are two: that the speech is wrongheaded (though he ironically professes not to urge this) and that its style is confused. Some sort of connection between these two facts is perhaps a main innuendo.

SOCRATES: How now? Are you and I to praise the speech because the author has said what was called for, or is the sole

---

[2] Diodorus Siculus, *Historical Library* XII, 53.

[3] The homosexual meaning alluded to in our first chapter is to be assumed throughout this discussion.

point whether the expressions, taken singly, are clear, compact, and finely turned? If we must judge it by the substance, I readily give way to your opinion; the substance because of my ineptitude, escaped me. I paid attention to the rhetoric of it only, and this I doubted whether Lysias himself would consider adequate. If you will let me say so, Phaedrus, it seemed to me he said the same things over twice or thrice, perhaps because he wasn't very well supplied with things to say on a given subject, or perhaps he didn't bother about a point like that. And then it seemed to me that he was showing off in youthful fashion how well he could say the same thing over in two different ways.

PHAEDRUS: Nonsense, Socrates! What you call repetition is the peculiar merit of the speech. . . .[4]

The speech of Lysias is in fact a tediously overlapping enumeration of reasons against the eager lover and in favor of the person who is more calculating in his approach, or, as he is called, the "non-lover." At a later point in the argument (264) Socrates likens it to an inscription that was said to appear on the tomb of Midas the Phrygian. Any line of it could be put first or last.

> A bronze maiden am I; and I am placed upon the tomb of
>   Midas.
> So long as water runs and tall trees put forth leaves,
> Remaining in this very spot upon a much lamented tomb,
> I shall declare to passers by that Midas is buried here.

Some of the distortions of style which the basically careless structure of thought has forced upon the writer—the "two different ways" of saying the same thing to which Socrates alluded—may be more apparent in the Greek than in English translations where efforts of translators to tidy up have missed the point.

> For lovers repent (*ekeinois . . . metamelei*) of the kindnesses
> they have done when their passion ceases; but there is no time
> when non-lovers naturally repent (*metagnōnai prosēkei*).—231

Here the translator's logical repetition of *repent* covers up the pointless "elegant variation" of the Greek. The following example is more faithful to the Greek text.

> And besides, lovers consider the *injury they have done to their
> own concerns* on account of their love, and the benefits they
> have conferred, and they add *the trouble they have had*, . . . ;

[4] *Phaedrus* 234-5. We quote the translation by Professor Lane Cooper, *Phaedrus, Ion, Gorgias* (London, 1938), p. 15, by permission of the Oxford University Press, Inc., New York.

but non-lovers cannot aver *neglect of their own affairs* because
of their condition, nor can they take account of the *pains they
have been at in the past.*—231

The italicized phrases tease a very simple meaning into coy but drab
variations. The gist of the matter is that this is a bad speech, and that
it is badly written. And both these things are true, implies Socrates,
because the author does not know what he is talking about.

The next step in the dramatically conceived argument is accomplished by a second speech on the same theme—one delivered by Socrates, *ex tempore*, with his head wrapped up for shame, in the character
of a crafty lover who tries to gain favors by pretending to be a non-
lover. It is a better speech than the first, because it begins with a definition of love (as desire) and proceeds, in a style which is at least orderly, to expound the evil of being ruled by that force. Socrates even
makes a pretense of being in a kind of dithyrambic frenzy and winds
up his speech with a hexameter.[5] But the whole argument is negative,
at the expense of the lover, and stops without saying a word in actual
favor of the non-lover—because, of course, nothing can be said in his
favor. Whereas the first speech and the critique of it has suggested the
union or even identity of bad, ignorant thinking and bad style, the second
speech exhibits the severe handicap imposed upon himself by the person
who in a sense knows the truth but who pretends not to know it—
and leads "his hearers on with sportive words" (262).

Almost immediately Socrates is stricken with remorse at having
participated in a blasphemy and, in the manner of a man who not only
knows the truth but is inspired to speak in its defence, launches into
his palinode, the prolonged and eloquent allegorical discourse upon
love, beauty, and immortality to which we have already alluded. Despite
its enthusiasm and lavish invention, the speech is well ordered, beginning with a fourfold celebration of *mania* (244–245) or inspired madness and pursuing the theme of the soul's immortality in the figure
of the charioteer and his two horses. This figure itself might be taken
as a symbol of orderly composition and division.

The rhetorical significance of the three speeches on love becomes
unmistakable in the comparison of their merits and the theoretical discussion which follows.

But I do think you will agree to this, that every discourse must
be organised, like a living being, with a body of its own, as it
were, so as not to be headless or footless, but to have a middle
and members, composed in fitting relation to each other and to
the whole.—264

[5] *Phaedrus* 238, 241. Aristotle is apparently thinking of these passages when in
his *Rhetoric* (III, 7) he alludes to the ironic use of emotive language in the *Phaedrus*.

The second speech of Socrates is described apologetically as figurative, plausible, perhaps expressive of some truth—a "sportive jest."

> . . . but in these chance utterances were involved two principles, the essence of which it would be gratifying to learn, if art could teach it.
>
> PHAEDRUS: What principles?
>
> SOCRATES: That of perceiving and bringing together in one idea the scattered particulars, that one may make clear by definition the particular thing which he wishes to explain; just as now, in speaking of love, we said what he is and defined it whether well or ill. Certainly by this means the discourse acquired clearness and consistency.
>
> PHAEDRUS: And what is the other principle, Socrates?
>
> SOCRATES: That of dividing things by classes; where the natural joints are, and not trying to break any part, after the manner of a bad carver.—265.
>
> Now I myself, Phaedrus, am a lover of these processes of division and bringing together, as aids to speech and thought; and if I think any other man is able to see things that can naturally be collected into one and divided into many, him I follow after and "walk in his footsteps as if he were a god." And whether the name I give to those who can do this is right or wrong, God knows, but I have called them hitherto dialecticians.—266

In short, rhetoric, so far as it is anything at all but a sham, is philosophy. To be able to define and divide, the rhetorician has to be able to think; he has to know the truth. There would seem to be some hedging on the part of Plato in this dialogue—as to whether the truth to be known is the cognitive content, the doctrine, about which the rhetorician would persuade his hearers, or another kind of truth, the psychological truth about their individual temperaments, which he must know if his discourse is to be a successfully administered persuasion (*psuchagōgia*).—271.

> He must understand the nature of the soul, must find out the the class of speech adapted to each nature, and must arrange and adorn his discourse accordingly, offering to the complex soul elaborate and harmonious discourses, and simple tales to the simple soul.—277.

But the emphasis of the dialogue is very largely upon the question *what* is to be said, not upon the question *to whom*, and the chief distinction is between the politico-legal rhetorician, who prefers "what seems to be true," or what is probable, to actual truth, and the philosophic rhetorician, who labors "not for the sake of speaking and acting before men, but that he may be able to speak and to do everything, so far as possible, in a manner pleasing to the gods." (273) In short, the main distinction is between professional rhetoricians as they are actually found to be, and the ideal rhetorician as he may be conceived to be. And here the Socratic identification of virtue with knowledge works relentlessly. If he who knows what is right will always do it, then he who does wrong (a sophistical rhetorician who uses his "art" to work evil) cannot know the right—or at least the so-called "art" by which he works evil cannot be a way of knowing it. As in the *Ion* the retreat was ironically from poetry as an art or form of knowledge to poetry as divine insanity (and indeed the same retreat occurs in the *Phaedrus* on several planes of irony and seriousness), so the specific resort imputed to rhetoric (a close relative of poetry) is from artful knowledge to the cheapness of a knack or trick (*tribē*). That is the only way to explain its undoubtedly effective, but subversive, performance.

> I seem, as it were, to hear some arguments approaching and protesting that . . . ["the art of speaking"] is lying and is not an art, but a craft devoid of art (*hoti pseudetai kai ouk esti technē all' atechnos tribē*). A real art of speaking . . . which does not seize hold of truth, does not exist and never will.—260

This explanation had been given a fancier (and no doubt to the rhetoricians an even more exasperating) shape in the earlier *Gorgias*, where the same key concept, *tribē* or knack, is applied in a four-point analogy. As the cheap knack of *cosmetic* is to the art of *gymnastic* in building health, and as *cookery* is to *medicine* in repairing health, so in the field of politics, *sophistic* is the meretricious rival of *legislation*, and *rhetoric* is that of *jurisprudence*.

At one place in the *Phaedrus* (267), Socrates makes a scornful review of contemporary rhetoricians and the niceties of their art (*ta kompsa tēs technēs*): Theodorus of Byzantium, with his introduction, narrative, testimony, proofs, probability, confirmation and further confirmation, refutation and further refutation; the "illustrious Parian" Evenus, with his covert allusion, indirect praises (*parepainoi*), and indirect censures (*parapsogoi*); Gorgias and Tisias, who make small things seem great and great things small, and new things old and old things new, and who invented conciseness (*suntomia logōn*) and measureless length on all subjects (*apeira mēkē peri pantōn*); Prodicus and Hippias of Elis; Polus, with his duplication (*diplasiologia*), sententiousness (*gnōmologia*), and figurativeness (*eikonologia*); Licymnius, with his beautiful diction (*euepeia*); Protagoras, with his correctness of diction (*orthoepeia*); the "mighty Chalcedonian" Thrasymachus, with his genius for rousing audiences to wrath and for soothing them again, for devising or for refuting calumnies on any grounds whatsoever. On one piece of technique, that of summarizing a speech at the end, all seem to be agreed, though some call it recapitulation (*epanodos*), others something else. This is a section of the *Phaedrus* which might be transplanted almost verbatim into Benedetto Croce's expressionistic history of *Aesthetic*.

The ground of Plato's objection to rhetoric may be perhaps most deeply understood, near the end of the *Phaedrus*, in a distinction between written and spoken words, a distinction which is the more relevant to the argument because of the fact that Attic oratory made no pretense of being *ex tempore*. The written word, urges Socrates, is a static thing useful only to tell people what they already know, an amusement, a reminder for the forgetfulness of old age. But the spoken word is the true, vital, and dialectic word—it is written in the mind of the hearer and is able to defend itself in the process of question and answer.

> But the man who thinks that in the written word there is necessarily much that is playful, and that no written discourse, whether in metre or in prose, deserves to be treated very seriously (and this applies also to the recitations of the rhapsodes, delivered to sway people's minds, without opportunity for questioning and teaching), but that the best of them really serve only to remind us of what we know; and who thinks that only in words about justice and beauty and goodness spoken by teachers for the sake of instruction and really written in a soul is clearness and perfection and serious value, that such words should be considered the speaker's own legitimate offspring, first the word within himself, if it be found there, and secondly its descendants or brothers which may have sprung up in worthy manner in the souls of others, and who pays no attention to the other words,—that man, Phaedrus, is likely to be such as you and I might pray that we ourselves may become.
> —277–8 [6]

In this clear confirmation of the anti-mimetic doctrine of the *Republic*, we may see that in theory at least (or at least in this dialogue) Plato prefers the object imitated in his dialogues, the actual conversations as they may be supposed to have taken place, to his own highly artful or poetic embodiment of them in fixed words. And this may remind us that poetic quality does indeed reside in fixity, or determinacy, of words. Not only meter and rhyme and all the minute effects of a lyric but the

---

[6] Cf. Atkins, I, 148 on the niceties possible in written style and on the "deliberative" oratorical style as shadow-painting (*skiagraphia*).

dialogue and succession of scenes in a tragedy, the whole economy and precision of poetic power in words, depend on choice, limitation, and fixation, and hence are opposed to the fluid character of dialectic or of the bull session—though the latter, in virtue of its capacity to shift words, correct, repeat, rephrase, paraphrase, and in general adjust itself to the exigencies of debate, may in a sense fit closer to the truth of the matter which is discussed.

IV

IT WAS no less against literary than against oratorical interests that Plato was fighting. The close alliance of rhetoric and poetry as his enemies, seen more than once in the *Phaedrus*,[7] is suggested a final time in a closing allusion to the rhetorician Isocrates.

> I think he has a nature above the speeches of Lysias and possesses a nobler character; so that I should not be surprised if, as he grows older, he should so excel in his present studies that all who have ever treated of rhetoric shall seem less than children; and I suspect that these studies will not satisfy him, but a more divine impulse will lead him to greater things; for my friend, something of philosophy is inborn in his mind.—279

The fictional date of the dialogue is about 410 B.C., when Isocrates, the pupil of Gorgias, was making his first appearance on the scene. But the dialogue was written perhaps as late as 370,[8] at a time when Isocrates was the most eminent and affluent teacher of rhetoric at Athens and hence the chief rhetorical antagonist of the Platonic school. The *Art of Rhetoric* which Isocrates wrote survives only in a few fragments. But from several of his discourses, especially that *Against the Sophists* and the *Antidosis*, which deal with education—and from the style itself of his writing—we get an idea of the kind of campaign which he waged against law-court and assembly rhetoric and the debased form of ethical dialectic which he calls "eristic." Although he discountenanced the academic exercise on mythological topics or on paradoxical themes such as those affected by Gorgias and Protagoras—"that we cannot lie," or "that nothing exists"—or on such anticipations of Swift's broomstick as "humble bees" or "salt," the theory of Isocrates was literary rather than practically oratorical. The form of speech which he chiefly sponsored was the epideictic (the encomiastic or the invective declamation), and this was an oratory that had moved as far as possible away from the give and take of dialectic toward the fixity of a set piece or essay—

---

[7] See for instance, 258, 261.
[8] R. Hackforth, *Plato's Phaedrus* (Cambridge, 1952), pp. 3–8.

albeit an essay that would seem by our standards a rather florid one. The epideictic style, Aristotle would say in his *Rhetoric* (III, 12), is especially suited to written compositions; it aims at being read. Isocrates hoped that his *Antidosis* would prove a "monument more noble than statues of bronze." The rhetoric of Isocrates was a scheme of general education (*paideia*) which aimed at a liberal union of philosophy and persuasion, an understanding of elevated and large political topics, and withal an artistic verbal style, imaginative (*poiētikos*) and diverse. The "thoughts" of the graduate rhetorician were to be not only "dignified and original" but "adorned with a number of striking figures." What was desired was a kind of poetic prose oratory, or literary prose, something which would serve not only for statesmen but for critics of poetry, for historians, for writers of panegyric. Isocrates entertained a highly integrated view of life and letters; he conceived the former as greatly in need of the latter. The sum of his teaching was a genial, flowery, belletristic kind of humanism.[9]

V

THIS was one kind of answer both to the Sophists and to Plato. A rhetorician of later antiquity [1] reports that Aristotle's systematic treatise on the question, his *Rhetoric* in three books, was the outcome of a feud with Isocrates. The story says that during his first residence in Athens (367–347 B.C.) Aristotle sneered at the ideas of Isocrates and the method of their dissemination in bundles of speeches hawked by the booksellers. Yet the difference between the two as theorists of rhetoric is not so profound. Aristotle takes more examples from the orations of Isocrates than from the works of any other author. The difference between them might be summed up, without great distortion, in the statement that Aristotle, looking on rhetoric in a far more utilitarian way than Isocrates, is somewhat closer to being sophistical; as a philosopher, however, as a teacher of rhetoric in Plato's Academy, he is at the same time more systematic than Isocrates. The latter virtue is the one by which Aristotle gains the advantage of having his ideas preserved not in speeches but in a treatise.[2]

"Do you think we have reproached the art of speaking too harshly?" asks Socrates in the *Phaedrus*. "Perhaps she might say:

> 'Why do you talk such nonsense, you strange men? I do not compel anyone to learn to speak without knowing the truth,

---

[9] See Atkins, I, 124–8, 148, 154–5.
[1] Dionysius of Halicarnassus, *On Isocrates* 18; Atkins, I, 133.
[2] Aristotle's *Theodectia*, on style, and other works on rhetoric are lost. Atkins, I, 133, 135, 136.

but if my advice is of any value, he learns that first and then acquires me. So what I claim is this, that without my help the knowledge of the truth does not give the art of persuasion.'—260

It would not be unfair to say that Plato has here anticipated the gist of Aristotle's doctrine. "What makes the sophist," says Aristotle, "is not skill in argument, but [defect of] moral purpose." [3]

Aristotle's *Rhetoric* opens with the statement: "Rhetoric is a counterpart of dialectic." But the term *dialectic* has for Aristotle a softer meaning than for Plato—the meaning of a conversationally plausible inquiry rather than of a metaphysically compelling demonstration. Dialectic is a comfortable neighbor to rhetoric, on the higher side. Both dialectic and its practical counterpart, rhetoric, enjoy a kind of cushioning from the severity of theoretical science (mathematics, physics, metaphysics). Dialectic is the argumentative technique of the social, practical, deliberative and "alternative" sciences (ethics and politics). "It is the mark of an educated man" says Aristotle in his *Ethics*, "to look for precision in each class of things just so far as the nature of the subject admits; it is . . . equally foolish to accept probable reasoning from a mathematician and to demand from a rhetorician scientific proofs." [4]

Even that much would have been enough to protect rhetoric from the full brunt of the Platonic inquisition. But Aristotle does more. There is a moment in the first chapter of Book I when he seems bent on treating rhetoric rather rigorously within the limits of its probable arguments (its "examples" and "enthymemes"). [5] "Proofs," he says, "are the only things in . . . [rhetoric] that come within the province of art." And he is severe upon the previous compilers of handbooks who have devoted their attention chiefly to methods of arousing prejudice. Nevertheless, the argument begins to change even in the same chapter; there is a disposition to talk more about persuasion than about proof. The truth may be the truth, but it may need help before it is accepted. Not all persons are easy to persuade by reason. The orator should be able to prove opposites—like a logician—not for the sake of doing this,

---

[3] *Ho gar sophistikos ouk en tē dunamei all' en tē proairesei* (*Rhetoric*, I, 1).

[4] *Nicomachean Ethics* I, 3.

[5] The term "enthymeme" was used by Aristotle's successors, as it is by modern logicians, to refer to the elliptical syllogism. But for Aristotle, in his *Rhetoric* and in his logical writings, "enthymeme" is the name of the rhetorical syllogism, which is a *probable* argument for a *particular* conclusion. The enthymeme is thus distinguishable from two other kinds of syllogism, the dialectic syllogism, which is a probable argument for a general conclusion, and the apodeictic or scientific syllogism, which is a certain argument for a universal conclusion. See J. H. Freese, *Aristotle . . . the "Art" of Rhetoric* (London: Loeb Classical Library, 1939), p. 474, Glossary, s.v. *Dialektikē;* James H. McBurney, "Some Recent Interpretations of the Aristotelian Enthymeme," *Papers of the Michigan Academy of Science, Arts and Letters,* XXI (Ann Arbor, 1936), 489–500.

but just for understanding. All good things except virtue itself may be abused. The function of rhetoric is not so much to persuade as to find out the existing means of persuasion. Thus runs what would seem to be almost the dialogue of Aristotle with his own conscience, as he moves toward the empirical and anti-Platonic procedure of justifying rhetoric as it is found in fact to be. The second chapter begins by "defining rhetoric anew." "Rhetoric then may be defined as the faculty of discovering the possible means of persuasion in reference to any subject whatever." And we learn in this chapter that there are no fewer than four kinds of "artificial proof" [6] or means of persuasion: (1) the ethical or those depending on the moral character of the orator himself —by which he elicits confidence in himself; (2) the affective or those which appeal to the emotions of the audience (It was only the *exclusive* use of such proofs to which I alluded disparagingly in my first chapter, he explains); (3) valid arguments, which tend to establish the truth of whatever we are maintaining; and (4) apparent arguments, which only seem to establish it. The first two books of Aristotle's *Rhetoric* do in fact proceed in that pattern, the first Book telling about materials, or areas of argumentative probability, the second Book giving us mainly the psychology of good relations between speaker and audience. Aristotle has put a four-layered mattress between rhetoric and the inexorable or scientific truth—two of the layers being psychological, that is, relating to the character and feelings of the speaker and audience, one, the layer of probable cognitive arguments being at least nonscientific, and the fourth, the layer of apparent arguments, being feathered with actual deception. Aristotle thus defends rhetoric on approximately the same grounds as those on which Plato condemns it.

These Aristotelian graduations away from the strictness of scientific demonstration are not the immediate stuff for a rhetoric of verbal surface. But they do provide the underlying contour of such a rhetoric. They enable or make plausible a fifth and a sixth graduation—verbal style (*lexis*) and structure or architecture (*taxis*), the subjects of Aristotle's third book. About Aristotle's conception of *taxis* Plato could not have complained, though he might have related this (the organic order, beginning, middle, and end named in the *Phaedrus*) more intimately to "dialectic." But *lexis* is the apex and epitome of the difference between Plato and Aristotle as rhetoricians, and not so much the details of what Aristotle said about *lexis* as the very fact that he thought it reasonable to devote twelve chapters to the topic.

"We have therefore next to speak of style; for it is not sufficient to know what one ought to say,—but one must also know how to say it, and this largely contributes to making the speech appear of a certain

---

[6] I.e., artful, as distinguished from the inartificial or ready-made, such as witnesses, tortures, contracts.

character" (III, 1). It is almost as if this matter of style should be grouped with the newly acknowledged and even more external art of delivery (a kind of acting, *hupokrisis*), a thing that has to be conceded, not as right but as necessary, owing to the corruption of politicians and judges. Just a little more can be said for style:

> . . . it does make a difference, for the purpose of making a thing clear, to speak in this or that manner; still, the difference is not so very great, . . . all these things are mere outward show for pleasing the hearer; wherefore no one teaches geometry in this way.[7] III, 1

It is a cautiously divided account of style, giving due recognition to clarity and purity (*esti d' archē tēs lexeōs to hellēnizein*—the first principle of style is to use good Greek [8]) and in general to propriety, but at the same time showing considerable respect for the elevated and ornate, for a certain strangeness or departure from the ordinary which (like a foreigner among our fellow citizens) appears more distinguished (III, 2 and 5).

One of the most interesting technical features [9] of the discussion is a marked concern for metaphor. The section of his *Poetics* (Chs. XXI–XXIV) devoted to the element of tragedy which Aristotle calls diction or style, *lexis*, is mentioned four times in the first two chapters of Book III of the *Rhetoric*. If we turn back to the *Poetics*, we find the often-quoted statement that to be a master of metaphor is the greatest poetic gift, because metaphor shows an eye for resemblances, and metaphor cannot be learnt from anyone else.[1] We find also the definition: "Metaphor consists in assigning to a thing the name of something else," and the four classes of metaphoric reference: from genus to species, from species to genus, from species to species, and by propor-

---

[7] He continues: ". . . . written speeches owe their effect not so much to the sense as to the style. The poets, as was natural, were the first to give an impulse to style; for words are imitations, and the voice also, which of all our parts is best adapted for imitation, was ready to hand; thus the arts of the rhapsodists, actors, and others, were fashioned. And as the poets, although their utterances were devoid of sense, appeared to have gained their reputation through their style, it was a poetical style that first came into being, as that of Gorgias." In the *Poetics* (XXIV) appears the rather frigid statement: "The diction should be elaborated in the pauses of the action, where there is no expression of character and thought. For . . . character and thought are merely obscured by a diction that is over brilliant."

[8] Under this head comes a censure of ambiguity (*amphiboloi*), III, 5.

[9] The statements in III, 8 that prose should have rhythm but not meter (*rhythmon dei echein tōn logōn, metron de mē*) and that the best rhythm for prose is the paeonic, are Aristotle's attempt to reconcile the Pythagorean and Platonic doctrine that number confers order and limit (see the literary application in *Philebus* 23) with the fact that the "rhythm" or movement of good prose is not really a matter of number or measure.

[1] A thought repeated in *Rhetoric* III, 2.

tion.[2] Somewhat more specific, if miscellaneous, remarks on the same subject appear in the *Rhetoric*. "It is metaphor above all that gives perspicuity, pleasure, and a foreign air" (III, 2). "It must be appropriate and not far-fetched," but not too obvious either (III, 11). It can make things look either better or worse—as when a pirate calls himself a "purveyor" or an actor calls himself an artist, or someone else calls the actor a flatterer of Dionysus. A metaphor is like a riddle. Metaphors should mostly be "derived from things that are beautiful." "It does make a difference, for instance, whether one says 'rosy-fingered morn,' rather than 'purple-fingered,' or, what is still worse, 'red-fingered'" (III, 2). A climax to these obiter dicta and to the whole treatment of *lexis* occurs in Chapters 10 and 11, where metaphor is joined with figures of parallel sound and sense and with various verbal deceptions or jokes shading into paronomasia or pun.

> "And he strode on, under his feet—chilblains," whereas the hearer thought he was going to say "sandals."

> The more special qualities the expression possesses, the smarter it appears; for instance, if the words contain a metaphor, and a metaphor of a special kind, antithesis, and equality of clauses, and actuality.

"Actuality" or vividness (*energeia*)[3] is perhaps better taken as a term for summing up the effect of rhetorical figures than as a name for another figure on the same footing. But we may say that Aristotle has here very shrewdly observed a close relation among rhetorical features which are not always or easily seen as so closely related—the logic of parallel and distinction, the apparently alien pun or trick with sounds, and mediating these extremes the imaginative force of metaphor. He has thus come not far from supplying an accurate formula for a long tradition of poetical wit.

> Here Britain's statesmen oft the fall foredoom
> Of foreign Tyrants and of Nymphs at home;
> Here thou, great ANNA! whom three realms obey,
> Dost sometimes counsel take—and sometimes Tea.

---

[2] Proportion is defined in *Ethics* V, 3 as "an equality of ratios, implying four terms at least." See *Rhetoric* III, 4: "If the goblet is the shield of Dionysus, then the shield may properly be called the goblet of Ares."

[3] Roman rhetoricians (Dionysius of Halicarnassus, *De Lysia*, VII; Longinus, *Peri Hupsous*, XV; Quintilian, *Institutio Oratoria* VIII, 3, 62) use the term *enargeia* in approximately the same sense. Cf. W. Rhys Roberts, *Longinus on the Sublime* (Cambridge, 1935), pp. 197-8.

VI

THE important thing about both Aristotle and Isocrates as rhetoricians is, in brief, that they affirm the power of the word—Aristotle the more systematically and analytically, Isocrates the more eloquently. This is the point at which to make a brief return to Isocrates for the sake of introducing some of his enthusiastic conceptions. According to Isocrates eloquence is creative process (*poiētikon pragma*), the source of civilization, of laws and arts, and of most other human blessings, the mark which distinguishes men from the brutes, the instrument and test of wisdom. It is the adorner and transformer of experience, making old things new and new things old, the big little and the little big. It is an expression of intelligence, a reflection of character, an outward image of a true and virtuous soul (*psuchēs agathēs kai pistēs eidōlon*).[4] The rhetorical doctrine made current by Isocrates had been heard before from sophists and much earlier had had a more lyric orientation, as in the myth of Orpheus taming savage men and beasts by his music, and that of Amphion charming stones with his poetry and building the Theban walls.[5] It had been aligned with such verbal and poetic interests as the allegorical interpretation of Homer rejected by Plato in Book III of the *Republic* or the semi-facetious etymological reasoning about the right sense of words, the natural relation between words and things, in Plato's *Cratylus*. The Stoic Zeno's *Homeric Problems* would later establish the school of allegorical criticism for the post-Aristotelian or Hellenistic age;[6] the natural expressiveness of language would be defended by the school of Analogists among the Alexandrian grammarians and critics.[7] A commonplace of antiquity, especially among the Stoic philosophers,[8] was a doctrine which we may call simply that of the *Logos*—the word as the expression and hence the mold and determination of reason and intelligence: in a mathematical sense, as in the logos of Euclid, in grammatical, etymological, symbolic, exegetic, rhetorical, and moral senses—in the grand and synthesizing sense that eloquence and wisdom are inseparable. The relation of this doctrine to literary criticism may be hinted by allusion to the earliest extant Greek *Grammar*, the sixteen pages of the second-century Dionysius Thrax, a standard for centuries, in which we ascend through six stages, from accurate reading aloud and interpretation of figures of speech, to the crown of

---

[4] *Against the Sophists* 12; *Nicocles* 5–9; *Antidosis* 254; *Panegyricus* 8; all cited in Atkins, I, 125–6.
[5] Atkins, I, 13, 29, 127.
[6] Atkins, I, 187.
[7] Atkins, I, 184; II, 17.
[8] E. Vernon Arnold, *Roman Stoicism* (Cambridge, 1911), esp. pp. 128–49.

all, the criticism of poetry. The *Grammaticus* of this age was scarcely the figure for a mid-19th-century *Grammarian's Funeral*. He was the professionally qualified *poetarum interpres*.[9] Finally, the doctrine of the *Logos* with all that it implied was a doctrine less dear even to poets and grammarians than to statesmen. It was one of the main theoretical supports of a life devoted to public leadership. "I am grateful to the Stoics," said Cicero, "for this reason: that they alone of all the philosophers have declared eloquence to be virtue and wisdom."[1] The debate about rhetoric which we have been considering is but an early chapter, though an important one, of a controversial history which continues through later antiquity, the Middle Ages, and the Renaissance. The ancient quarrel between the philosophers and the poets to which Plato alludes in the *Republic* was the same in principle as a later and much longer quarrel between dialecticians (in the Platonic sense, philosophers tending toward science) and rhetoricians.[2] On the side of the dialecticians one might align in one consistent team: Plato, Abelard, Occam, Ramus, Descartes. On the side of the rhetoricians, poets and grammarians: Aristotle, Cicero, Quintilian, Augustine,[3] John of Salisbury, Bonaventure, and Richard Hooker.[4] The following retrospective passages in the *De Oratore* of Cicero define the role of Socrates in the long debate and the importance of the whole incident in which Plato, Isocrates, and Aristotle were the other chief participants.

> It was Socrates who . . . separated the ability to think wisely from the ability to speak gracefully, though these are naturally united—Socrates! the philosopher whose genius and varied con-

[9] Atkins I, 182–3; J. E. Sandys, *A History of Classical Scholarship* (Cambridge, 1921), I, 6–11; Richard McKeon, "The Philosophic Bases of Criticism," in R. S. Crane, *Critics and Criticism*, p. 507.

[1] "*Stoicis hanc habeo gratiam, quod soli ex omnibus eloquentiam virtutem ac sapientiam esse dixerunt*" (quoted in Arnold, *Roman Stoicism*, p. 149). Cf. J. S. Watson, *Cicero on Oratory and Orators*, 1890, p. 210; *De Oratore* III, 18.

[2] The Stoic philosopher Zeno made a comparison (recorded in Cicero's *Orator* XXXII, 113) between the concise form of dialectic utterance, a "closed fist," and the expanded expression of rhetoric, an "open palm." The fact that Stoic philosophers promoted the doctrine of the Logos (or verbal power) but at the same time favored a concise and severe dialectic style must be looked on as an anomaly arising characteristically enough out of the complex issue concerning verbal style and content. Cf. *post* Chapter 12, our account of Ramism and 17th-century rhetoric.

[3] The theological aspect is well illustrated in this passage from the *Adversus Praxean* of Tertullian (about A.D. 213): "This reason is His own thought; this is what the Greeks call 'Logos,' which word we translate also by 'speech.'. . . . To understand it more easily, take knowledge from yourself, I pray you, as from 'the image and likeness' of God. . . . See, when you silently meet with yourself in the process of thinking, that this very process goes on within you by reason meeting you along with word at every movement of your thought, at every beat of your understanding. Whatsoever you think is word; whatsoever you understand is speech" (*Tertullian Against Praxeas*, trans. A. Souter, London, 1920, pp. 36–7, Par. 5).

[4] See H. M. McLuhan, "Edgar Poe's Tradition," *Sewanee Review*, LII (January–March, 1944), 24–33.

versation Plato's dialogues have committed to immortality, but who himself has left us nothing in writing. Hence arose that divorce of the tongue from the heart (*discidium illud . . . quasi linguae atque cordis*), that absurd, needless, and deplorable conception, that one set of persons should teach us to think, and another should teach us to speak.—*De Oratore* III, 16

The ancients, till the time of Socrates, used to combine the whole of their study and science pertaining to morality, to the duties of life, to virtue, and to civil government, with the art of speaking; but afterward, the eloquent being separated by Socrates from the philosophic, and the distinction being continued by all the followers of Socrates, the philosophers despised eloquence, and the orators philosophy. . . . the followers of Socrates excluded the pleaders of causes from their own ranks, and from the common title of philosophers—though the ancients had been of the opinion that the faculty of speaking and that of understanding were allied in a marvellous harmony.—*De Oratore* III, 19 [5]

Aristotle . . . said it was disgraceful that he should remain silent and let Isocrates do all the speaking. He therefore undertook to equip that philosophy of his with due illustrations and ornament and to connect the knowledge of things with skill in speaking. This of course came to the notice of that sagacious monarch Philip, who summoned Aristotle as a tutor for his son Alexander. Let the boy get from the same teacher instructions in behavior and in language.

Now, if anybody desires to call that philosopher who instructs us fully in things and words an orator, he may do so without opposition from me; or if he prefers to call that orator whom I describe as having wisdom united with eloquence a philosopher, I shall make no objection. . . . If I had to choose one of the two, I should prefer uneloquent good sense to loquacious folly. But if it be inquired which is the more eminent excellence, I give the palm to the learned orator, and if you will admit that this person is also a philosopher, there is an end of controversy; but if you insist on distinguishing the orator from the philosopher, the philosopher will be inferior—for the equipment of a complete orator includes the knowledge of philosopher, but the knowledge of the philosopher does not necessarily include the eloquence of the orator.—*De Oratore* III, 35 [6]

[5] Adapted from J. S. Watson, *Cicero on Oratory and Orators* (New York, 1890), pp. 209, 212.
[6] Adapted from J. S. Watson, p. 233.

SUPPLEMENT

This tradition [the oratorical] has been a continuous force in European law, letters, and politics from the time of the Greek sophists. It is most conveniently referred to as the Ciceronian ideal, since Cicero gave it to St. Augustine and St. Jerome, who in turn saw to it that it has never ceased to influence Western society. The Ciceronian ideal as expressed in the *De Oratore* or in St. Augustine's *De Doctrina Christiana* is the ideal of rational man reaching his noblest attainment in the expression of an eloquent wisdom. Necessary steps in the attainment of this ideal are careful drill in the poets followed by a program of encyclopedic scope directed to the forensic end of political power. Thus, the *doctus orator* is, explicitly, Cicero's sophistic version of Plato's philosopher-king. This ideal became the basis for hundreds of manuals written by eloquent scholars for the education of monarchs from the fifth century, through John of Salisbury and Vincent of Beauvais, to the famous treatises of Erasmus and Castiglione.

So far as America is concerned, this was a fact of decisive importance, since Virginia, and the South in general, was to receive the permanent stamp of this Ciceronian ideal. . . . It is thus no accident that the creative political figures of American life have been moulded in the South. Whether one considers Jefferson or Lincoln, one is confronted with a mind aristocratic, legalistic, encyclopedic, forensic, habitually expressing itself in the mode of an eloquent wisdom.

New England is in the scholastic tradition, and profoundly opposed to "humanism." Briefly, the theocratic founders of Harvard and rulers of New England were Calvinist divines, fully trained in the speculative theology which had arisen for the first time in the twelfth century—the product of that dialectical method in theology which is rightly associated with Peter Abelard. Unlike Luther and many English Protestants, Calvin and his followers were schoolmen, opposed to the old theology of the Fathers which Erasmus and the humanist-Ciceronians had brought back to general attention after the continuous predominance of scholastic theology since the twelfth century. To the humanists nobody could be a true interpreter of Scripture, a true exponent of the *philosophi Christi*, who had not had a full classical training. So Catholic and Protestant schoolmen alike, were, for these men, the "barbarians," the "Goths of the Sorbonne," corrupting with "modernistic" trash (the schoolmen were called the *moderni* from the first) the eloquent piety and wisdom of the Fathers. (The Fathers were called the "ancients" or *antiqui theologi*.)

Harvard . . . originated as a little Sorbonne, where in 1650 the scholastic methods of Ockham and Calvin, as streamlined by Petrus Ramus, were the staple of education. Logic and dialectics were the basis of theological method, as of everything else at Harvard. Here rhetoric was taught, not for eloquence, but in order to teach the young seminarian how to rub off the cosmetic tropes of Scripture before going to work on the doctrine with dialectical dichotomies. Ramus taught a utilitarian logic for which he made the same claims as pragmatists do for "scientific method." In fact, Peirce, James, and Dewey could never have been heard of had they not been nurtured in the Speculative tradition of the scholastic theologians Calvin and Ramus.

—H. M. McLuhan, "Edgar Poe's Tradition," *The Sewanee Review*, LII (January–March, 1944), 25–8, selected passages, by permission of the author and *The Sewanee Review*

Until Gutenberg, poetic publication meant the reading or singing of one's poems to a small audience. When poetry began to exist primarily on the printed page, in the seventeenth century, there occurred that strange mixture of sight and sound later known as "metaphysical poetry" which has so much in common with modern poetry.

The printed page was itself a highly specialized (and spatialized) form of communication. In 1500 A.D. it was revolutionary. And Erasmus was perhaps the first to grasp the fact that the revolution was going to occur above all in the classroom. He devoted himself to the production of text-books and to the setting up of grammar schools. The printed book soon liquidated two thousand years of manuscript culture. It created the solitary student. It set up the rule of private interpretation against public disputation. It established the divorce between "literature and life."

We have long been accustomed to the notion that a person's beliefs shape and color his existence. They provide the windows which frame, and through which he views, all events. We are less accustomed to the notion that the shapes of a technological environment are also idea-windows. Every shape (gimmick or metropolis), every situation planned and realized by man's factive intelligence, is a window which reveals or distorts reality. Today when power technology has taken over the entire global environment to be manipulated as the material of art, nature has disappeared with nature-poetry.

From the point of view of its format, the press as a daily cross-section of the globe is a mirror of the technological instruments of communication. It is the popular daily book, the great collective poem, the universal entertainment of our age. As such it has modified poetic techniques and in turn has already been modified by the newer media of movie, radio, and television. These represent revolutions in communication as radical as printing itself.

James Joyce was the first to seize upon newspaper, radio, movie, and television to set up his "verbivocovisual" drama in *Finnegan's Wake*. Pound and Eliot are, in comparison with Joyce, timid devotees of the book as art form.

In cognition we have to interiorize the exterior world. We have to recreate in the medium of our senses and inner faculties the drama of existence. This is the work of the *logos poietikos*, the agent intellect. In speech we utter that drama which we have analogously re-created within us. In speech we make or *poet* the world even as we may say that the movie parrots the world. Languages themselves are thus the greatest of all works of art. They are the collective hymns to existence. For in cognition itself is the whole of the poetic process. But the artist differs from most men in his power to arrest and then reverse the stages of human apprehension. He learns how to embody the stages of cognition (Aristotle's "plot") in an exterior work which can be held up for contemplation.

It is only common sense to recognize that the general situation created by a communicative channel and its audience is a large part of that in which and by which the individuals commune. The encoded message cannot be regarded as a mere capsule or pellet introduced at one point and consumed at another. Communication is communication all along the line. One might illustrate from sports. The best brand of football played before fifty people would lack something of the power to communicate.

What we have to defend today is not the values developed in any particular culture or by any one mode of communication. Modern technology presumes to attempt a total transformation of man and his environment. This calls in turn for an inspection and defense of all human values. And so far as merely human aid goes, the citadel of this defense must be located in analytical awareness of the nature of the creative process involved in human cognition. For it is in this citadel that science and technology have already established themselves in their manipulation of the new media.

—H. M. McLuhan, "Sight, Sound and the Fury," *The Commonweal*, LX (April 9, 1954), 7–11, selected passages, by permission of the author and *The Commonweal*

CHAPTER 5

ROMAN CLASSICISM: HORACE

§ *Hellenistic criticism—II. the context of the* Ars Poetica
*—III. its meaning: literary genres, Platonic forms, Aris-
totelian decorum, formulas and examples, imitation of
models—IV. nature and convention, the audience—V. theory and practice in Horace, a modern problem: imperfection vs. objectivity—VI. (literary ideas in the* Satires *and
other* Epistles*) satire and comedy as poetry, the language
of poetry, usage, the* callida junctura*—VII. mediocrity
in poems—VIII. the structure of the* Ars Poetica, *Peripatetic topics: matter and form, hedonism and didacticism,
poet and poem, divine inspiration, genius and technique—
IX. Augustan studio advice* §

MORE THAN TWO CENTURIES OF HELLENISTIC CIVILIZATION LIE
between Aristotle and the literary theorist who is next to
claim our attention, the Roman poet Horace. This period,
during which we hear of literary studies no longer in Athens, but in
the capital of the Attalids at Pergamum and in that of the Ptolemies
at Alexandria, is not celebrated for important literary theory. The reason
is, in one sense, simply that the writings have disappeared. The history
has to be pieced out inferentially from titles of lost works, from later
writers like the geographer Strabo, the biographer Plutarch, or the encyclopedist Diogenes Laertius, and from certain very recently recovered papyrus fragments. Yet the reason for the paucity of documents
in turn would seem to be that the Hellenistic period produced no literary
theory which could compare in seriousness with that of the fourth century in Athens and no literary art which could compare with that of
the Periclean or that of the Homeric age. It is a period known for historically rigorous studies, formalism, and technicalities, and at the same

77

time for extreme aestheticism, literary novelties, and *préciosité*. It is known for genre naturalism and at the same time for romantic fantasy. It was the heyday not only of the grammarian, the scholiast, the philologist, but also of the epigrammatist, the idyllist, the "Asiatic" rhetorician.[1] The communal interest in religious and patriotic issues which during more ancient times had produced the great genres of drama and epic dwindled during the Hellenistic age to an esoteric and merely literary cultivation of smaller forms—epigram, elegy, idyll, pastoral, didactic, epyllion. Scholar poets developed the utmost nicety in exploring the byways of myth. When Apollonius of Rhodes published about the middle of the third century the four books of his romance epic *Argonautica*, his former instructor Callimachus, the epigrammatist and scholar, led the critics of the day in censure of its long-windedness. "I hate the cyclic poem," said Callimachus, "the common road which everyone uses." And he said also: "a big book is a big nuisance" (*mega biblion mega kakon*).[2] The portrait of the age on the historico-critical side can be suggested in the production by Callimachus of the massive bio-bibliographical catalogue of the Alexandrian Library, *Lists of Illustrious Writers and Their Works*, in 120 volumes.[3] The century is celebrated for the editing and textual criticism of Homer and of the dramatists and lyric poets, the most learned laborers in this field having been Zenodotus (325–234 B.C.), the first librarian of the Alexandrian Museum, and his later contemporaries Eratosthenes, Aristophanes of Byzantium, and Aristarchus. Aristarchus, who centuries later was to be known as the first "critic" in antiquity (the antitype of Aristotle's equally eponymous contemporary the snarling critic Zoilus), earned his fame by a program of studying Homer in the light of the Homeric age, dialect, and idiom. In place of the allegorical or symbolic defence (still employed by the Stoics in the tradition of Zeno), he introduced the concepts of racial childhood, the naively heroic, and the poet as their faithful reporter.[4] Another way of summing up the Alexandrian period in polite letters is to say that it was one of tension between history and criticism, a prolonged Quarrel of Ancients and Moderns, which, even dimly known as it is, forecasts some of the main issues of much later critical history.

---

[1] Hegesias of Magnesia, who flourished about the middle of the third century, was the champion of the oratorical school known to modern scholars as the First Sophistic.

[2] Atkins, I, 177–9.

[3] Of the same order were a treatise *On Comedy* in eleven books by Lycophron and *The Old Attic Comedy* in twelve volumes by Eratosthenes. The forty-volume *History* of the Graeco-Roman world by Polybius (c. 210–125 B.C.) was a pioneer effort to trace philosophic, political, and social causes.

[4] During the same century Euhemerus of Messina maintained that the Homeric gods were apotheosized primitive benefactors of mankind—and thus gave his name to the "euhemeristic" tradition of mythic interpretation.

II

AT THE death of Theophrastus in 287 B.C., the texts of Aristotle's works
are said to have passed to a disciple who hid them from the bibliomania
of the Attalid kings in a cave at Scepsis in the Troad. There they lay
unknown until about 100 B.C., when they were taken back to Athens.
From Athens they were taken by the Roman general Marius to Rome
in 86 B.C.[5] The Peripatetics meanwhile carried on in their own fashion,
formalizing and fixing the system which Aristotle had sketched. One
of these was Neoptolemus, a grammarian-poet of Parium in Bithynia,
whose name is connected with that of Horace by the scholiast Porphyrio
in the third century A.D. Horace, says Porphyrio in his introductory
note to the classic *Ars Poetica*, "epitomized the precepts (*congessit
praecepta*) of Neoptolemus of Parium—or at least the most important
of them." The assertion has been verified in modern times by the re-
covery at Herculaneum of some charred papyrus scraps containing a
partial digest of Neoptolemus in passages from a work *On Poems* (*Peri
Poiēmatōn*) by a first-century Epicurean philosopher Philodemus of Gadara.[6] The connection with Horace is made biographically plausible by
the fact that the papyri were recovered from the villa of Lucius Piso
Caesonius, Roman consul in 58 B.C. and father of Lucius Calpurnius
Piso, who in turn was consul in 15 B.C. and father of the two young
men to whom Horace addressed his epistle on the art of writing. It has
been easy for historians to imagine the youthful Horace as member of
a literary coterie attending the "garden school" at Naples, where Philodemus was a professor, or gathering at the Herculanean villa of the consul Caesonius to discuss with Philodemus the opposed philosophies of
Peripatetic utilitarianism and Epicureanism.

The *Epistola ad Pisones* (in the next century dubbed *Ars Poetica*
by Quintilian, VIII, 3) is a slick piece of writing, produced by Horace
apparently toward the end of his life (65–8 B.C.) after he was the established author of the four books of *Odes*, one of *Epodes*, two of
Satires, and two of *Epistles*. The whole poetic career of Horace is part
of an Augustan and patriotic reaction against Alexandrian belletristic
trends and at the same time against Patrician antiquarianism. But there
is a great difference in ethical and metaphysical resonance between the
Ars of Horace and the *Poetics* of Aristotle or the *Phaedrus* of Plato.

[5] Atkins, I, 167. The authorities are Strabo, *Geography* XIII, 1; Plutarch, *Life of
Sulla*; Diogenes Laertius, *Lives of the Philosophers*, chapters on Aristotle and Theophrastus.
[6] Atkins, I, 170; II, 54; and L. P. Wilkinson, *Horace and His Lyric Poetry*
(Cambridge, 1945), pp. 87 ff. The work of Philodemus *On Poems* appears in the edition of C. Jensen, *Philodemos über die Gedichte (fünftes Buch)*, Berlin, 1923.

In the rugged days of the Republic, when high political aims governed taste in literature, Cicero had said: "If I had twice as long to live, I should have no time to read lyric poetry." [7] And the soldier dictator Caesar had said: "Avoid a curious word as you would a rock." [8] But Horace practised his art in the day of aristocratic and imperial patronage and polish, when there was need not so much for powerful speeches to decide political issues as for elegant poems to celebrate ancestral grandeur, military triumph, peaceful and benevolent sway. The poetry and criticism of Horace was part of an Augustan classical movement—back toward the high seriousness, if not the moral intensity, of Greek classical art. At the same time Horace had become a refined poet under the Epicurean influence of the school at Naples and along with the neoteric and Hellenizing coteries of the mid-century. He emerged from an Alexandrian atmosphere which may be symbolized equally by Catullus' lament of Lesbia for her sparrow and the sojourn of Cleopatra at Rome for the two years preceding the assassination of Caesar. Whatever earnest pleading Horace does is that of a poet for the poet's cause, as in the two long epistles of his Second Book, to Augustus and to Florus. His opponents are not politicians, sophists, or philosophers, but his fellow poets and various kinds of literary pretenders—the poetasters, criticasters, buffoons, libellers, aesthetes, and fops. "The Socratic dialogues (*Socraticae chartae*)," says Horace, "will provide you with ideas." His specialty is not the deep question or the tenacious train of reasoning, but the tacit assumption and upon this the neatly erected formula. Yet he is, in a way that is curiously his own, eminently worth while.

III

THE main thing assumed in the criticism of Horace is the normative value of the literary "species," [9] the genre, kind, or type, and of the companion principle designated by the term "propriety"—*to prepon* in Aristotelian criticism, *decorum* in Latin.[1] The ultimate reference for both genre and decorum was the Greek doctrine of ideas or forms, either in the Platonic or in the Aristotelian version. The Platonic, or supposedly Platonic, perfect idea of a thing had by the time of Horace developed a literary application which may be conveniently illustrated in these passages from Cicero's *Orator*.

> When that great artist [Phidias] was working on a statue of Jupiter or Minerva, he was not trying to copy an actually existing model but was intent on some vision of perfect beauty

[7] Seneca, *Epistles* XLIX, 5; Atkins, II, 44.
[8] Aulus Gellius, *Noctes Atticae* I, 10; Atkins, II, 53.
[9] As it was accurately called in English criticism of the 18th century.
[1] Cicero, *Orator* XXI.

(*species pulchritudinis eximia quaedam*). By that he directed
his hand and chisel. And just as visible forms and figures each
participate in a certain perfection or excellence, an intelligible
ideal by reference to which the artist transcends mere ocular
experience, so eloquence has its ideal, which we conceive in
our minds and attempt to copy in audible words. These forms
of things were called *ideas* by that eminent philosopher, that
master of thought and speech, Plato. He said that they were an
innate part of our minds and did not, like all other things,
suffer beginning and end, flux and lapse, continual passage from
one state to another. It follows that whatever topic a person
undertakes to discuss rationally and methodically, he ought to
reduce it to its ultimate and proper character and form.

I confess that I myself have learned whatever I may know
about the art of oratory not from the workshops of the rhetoricians but from the spacious walks of the Academy.—*Orator*
II–III, 9–10, 12

A fairly specific encouragement for such a literary doctrine had actually been given by Aristotle in those passages of his *Poetics* where
he said that tragedy having passed through many stages of growth
(*pollas metabolas metabalousa*) had reached its final and perfect stage,
and where he said that characters should be true to life and internally
consistent—or in those passages of the *Rhetoric* where he insisted that
style should be appropriate to theme, or where he spoke of the differences between poetic and prose style and of the three main oratorical
styles (matching the three main types of oratorical purpose), forensic,
deliberative, epideictic. By the time of Horace, such notions had under-
gone a marked development in the subdivision and multiplication of
fixed literary types and had acquired a nearly legislative prestige. Instead of the three literary genres, epic, tragedy and comedy, which are
mainly treated by Aristotle, we have in the time of Horace a spectrum
of genres including epic, tragedy, comedy, lyric, pastoral, satire, elegy,
and epigram.[2] The aim of criticism was to expound for each of these
types an *operis lex*[3] and its corollaries.

Horace begins his *Ars Poetica* with the negatively Aristotelian example of a mixed species, a beautiful woman sporting a fishtail, and
after laughing at this, adds his sufficiently generalized but nonetheless

[2] Cf. Horace, *Satires* I, 10; *Epistles* II, 2; *Ars Poetica* 73; J. F. D'Alton, *Roman
Literary Theory and Criticism* (London, 1931), Ch. VI.

[3] *Ars Poetica* 135. The edition of Horace mainly consulted here is that of
the Loeb Classical Library: *Satires, Epistles and Ars Poetica*, ed. H. Rushton Fairclough, Cambridge, Mass., 1936; *The Odes and Epodes*, ed. C. E. Bennett, Cambridge,
Mass., 1934. For a few longer passages, the "imitations" of Alexander Pope appear in
lieu of translations. The prose paraphrases of shorter passages are the work of the
present authors.

memorable advice about purple patches and unity. "Make it anything at all, so long as it hangs together" (*Sit quod vis, simplex dumtaxat et unum*). A long middle section of the poem, devoted in a rambling fashion to the history and rules of literary genres, manages to formulate a good many very explicit instructions:

> Five acts, no more, no less.
> *Neve minor neu sit quinto productior actu*
> *fabula.* 189

> Only three speakers at a time.
> *. . . nec quarta loqui persona laboret.* 192

> Scenes of butchery offstage.
> *ne pueros coram populo Medea trucidet.* 185

> Plunge right in.
> *Semper ad eventum festinat et in medias res.* 148

> Hexameter verse for war poems.
> *Res gestae regumque ducumque et tristia bella*
> *quo scribi possent numero, monstravit Homerus.* 73–4

Along with such rules come the more interesting gallery of capsule character types, from carefree boy to crotchety old man, " full of difficulties and complaints, the encomiast of days gone by" (*difficilis, querulus, laudator temporis acti,* 173)—and the formulas for historical figures, like the well-known thumbnail sketch of Achilles: "restless, wrathful, ruthless, fierce" (*impiger, iracundus, inexorabilis, acer,* 121). A very reasonable corollary of the doctrines of decorum and genre had been a shift from the Aristotelian *mimēsis* of nature to the fully classical and traditional kind of imitation,[4] that of models, a matter nicely epitomized by Horace:

> Be Homer's works your study and delight,
> Read them by day, and meditate by night.

> *vos exemplaria Graeca*
> *nocturna versate manu, versate diurna.*—268–9

IV

WE HAVE already suggested that it is one thing to make neatly turned pronouncements of this sort—perhaps even with semi-playful amusement

---

[4] George Converse Fiske, *Lucilius and Horace* (Madison, 1920), Chapter I; Richard McKeon, in *MP*, XXXIV (August 1936), 1–35. The imitation of models was consistent with the notion, occasionally expressed in classical antiquity and in the later age of neo-classicism, that primary topics of literary imitation had already all been imitated. Thus: *nullumst iam dictum quod non dictum sit prius* (Terence, *Eunuchus*, l. 41); *omnis ad accessus Heliconis semita trita est* (Manilius, *Astronomica* III, Prol.). Cf. *post* Ch. 10, pp. 178–81; Ch. 12, pp. 234–5; Ch. 15, pp. 326–7.

in the so tidy control of a situation—another to entertain a profound rationale in support of them or to be able to expound this. One question which modern scholars have asked about the critical assumptions of Horace is whether the notion of *decorum* entertained by him refers to something intrinsic to the nature of things or to something established by human convention.[5] This question can hardly be answered without one's taking some notice of a more general and more important question—that of how conventions in general are related to nature. Does the convention of a man's opening a door for a lady, or the salutation *dear* at the beginning of a letter, have any rightness in nature? Are these any better than others that might be imagined? There is little direct evidence of what Horace thought about this difficult question. His criticism does, however, offer a good example of the thorough interpenetration of nature and convention in the classical literary tradition. One recent way of stating the matter has been to say that the decorum of Horace is something affectively and socially oriented—toward the taste and standards of the aristocratic theater audience of his day rather than toward an Aristotelian or natural objectivity.[6] Does not the *Ars Poetica* allude to this audience repeatedly?

> Both highbrow and lowbrow will raise the loud guffaw.
> *Romani tollent equites peditesque cachinnum.*   113

> Take my advice—I know what your public wants.
> *Tu quid ego et populus mecum desideret audi.*   153

> The orchestra will be harder to please than the peanut gallery.
> *offenduntur enim, quibus est equus et pater et res,*
> *nec, si quid fricti ciceris probat et nucis emptor,*
> *aequis accipiunt animis donantve corona.*   248–50

But such an argument, we venture to suggest, lays too much theoretical stress on what can more plausibly be taken as only the most convenient and dramatic way of impressing young literary aspirants with the ideas of success and failure. The peanut gallery may cheer. The literati will laugh. Such are always among the possible rewards of trying to write poetry. But rewards do not constitute definitions. Horace himself has implied as much, in his *Epistle to Augustus*, where he despises the playwright's dependence on a public, and in his tenth *Satire*, where he asserts the sophistication of his satirical standard.

> Never mind what the mob thinks—"fit audience find, though few."

[5] Craig LaDrière, review of Wolf Steidle, *Studien zur Ars Poetica des Horaz,* 1939, in *American Journal of Philology*, LXIII (April, 1942), 241–3.

[6] R. S. Crane, review of Paul F. Saintonge *et al., Horace: Three Phases of His Influence*, Chicago, 1936, in *Philological Quarterly* XVI (April, 1937), 162–3.

. . . neque te ut miretur turba labores,
contentus paucis lectoribus. 73–4

"Let but Plotius and Varius approve of these verses. . . ." Horace appeals to an audience selected not by social or political standards but just by literary standards—to his fellow poets and his literary friends, to Maecenas and the other patrons and arbiters of the day. This procedure may be close to the fallacy which in our day C. S. Lewis has amusingly imputed to T. S. Eliot,[7] of crowning and mitring himself king and pope of pointland. (On Eliot's view that only a poet can judge of poetry, it must be only as a poet that he knows that his judges are poets and hence competent judges of his own poetry.) But it is a procedure which is the opposite of sociological. It is the opposite of an appeal to any decorum, or convention, established merely by the taste of the Roman gentlemen.

V

ANOTHER difficulty in interpreting Horace (rather a biographical than a strictly critical difficulty) may arise if we observe that some of his neatly turned dicta are not very readily squared with his own practice as a poet. His *Odes* and *Epodes*, for instance, are far too varied and original in their union of meter and matter to be accountable to such rules of the *Ars Poetica* as those which say that anger should be expressed in iambs, that only gods, sporting events, young love and the banquet should be treated in lyric meters. There is no place in the *Ars Poetica* for a facetious lyric like the Horatian *Integer vitae*, beginning with its over-confident claims for the man of sterling character ("he needs no barbaric armory"—*non eget Mauris jaculis*) and ending with the poet's lighthearted determination to keep thinking fondly of his Dulcinea no matter what happens (*dulce ridentem Lalagen amabo, dulce loquentem*). A scholar writing early in this century, and perhaps in a mood of over-responsiveness to the triumphant aesthetic of Benedetto Croce, has defended the practice of Horace against the theory of Horace in the following manner:

> It was the settled practice of the Renaissance that classical poetry should be regarded as the achievement of objective perfection; a practice which has had the most disastrous consequences. The very name of the "humanities" forbids that they be tried by the criterion of impeccability. . . . a genuine poem is not a machine, and is always subjective.
>
> • • •

[7] *A Preface to "Paradise Lost"* (Oxford, 1942), pp. 9–11.

Integer vitae has long been felt to present difficulties. It begins
like a hymn with the more or less solemn proclamation of the
poet's inviolability, and ends with . . . gaiety.[8]

The alignment of ideas implicit, or even largely explicit, in this passage
makes a curious antithesis. *Objectivity, perfection* or *impeccability*, and
the machine go together as unpoetic and apparently almost equivalent,
and in the opposite or poetic scale, *subjectivity* (and implicitly *imperfection*) and *spontaneity*. By such a division the only term which gains
anything is *imperfection*, and this is a gain which poetry may not be
grateful to find transferred to itself. The charm of the lyric *Integer
vitae* for this critic lies in the supposed fact that its ending is an afterthought, "purely decorative," connected to the beginning by very slight
ties (though he says that this ending is "appropriate to the theme").
The difficulty might not have occurred had the critic noticed that *Integer vitae* does not in fact begin with the solemnity of a hymn (though
it has been mistakenly set to hymn music) but with a playful exaggeration which is perfectly in keeping with its conclusion—and with its
even more preposterous middle stanza, about a wolf that fled from the
poet in the Apulian woods. It is perhaps stretching the evidence to say
with another modern interpreter that the theory of decorum expounded
by Horace is flexible enough to account entirely for his own practice.

> An organic, a vital, coherency, a beauty neither less nor more
> dependent on the adaptation (not ruthless subjugation) of
> means to ends than is the beauty of the creations of Nature
> herself, is the ideal pointed to by the school of criticism prop-
> erly called Classic.[9]

Such a view does, however, have the advantage that it avoids the critical
nonsense of applauding Horace for imperfections.

> I am annoyed when I come across mistakes in a classic like
> Homer. *indignor quandoque bonus dormitat Homerus.—Ars
> Poetica* 359

And such a view finds added support when we survey not only certain
passages in the *Ars Poetica* which tell against taking the rules too
seriously but other more casually critical passages in the *Satires* and
Epistles.

VI

THERE are places, we might say, where the conservative critical theory
of Horace frays out or blurs into his actual practice, places where he is

[8] Roy Kenneth Hack, "The Doctrine of Literary Forms," *Harvard Studies in
Classical Philology*, XXVII (1916), 35–6.
[9] A. Y. Campbell, *Horace, A New Interpretation* (London, 1924), p. 256.

less on guard as a theorist and mainly on the alert to catch every shade
of advantage in writing the poet's apologia. Thus in the *Epistle to Augustus* he defends the innovating poets of his own circle against the
archaizing snobbery and faddism of the patrician audience. And this in-
volves him in the view that the classics were in their own day innovations.

> Had ancient times conspired to disallow
> What then was new, what had been ancient now?
> *Quod si tam Graecis novitas invisa fuisset*
> *quam nobis, quid nunc esset vetus?*   90–1

And we have the curious side look at Horace's theory of decorum which
is provided through *Satires* I, 4 and 10, where he appears as if struggling,
though scarcely in any theoretical anguish, with the opposed facts that
satire had been a parvenu, a latter-day genre and a low one, but that to
have invented it, as Lucilius did in the second century, was a great thing.
Horace considers himself to be less than the inventor (*inventore minor*), though at the same time he can be scornful of Lucilius for his
lack of polish and proud of himself for having added this quality. As
Aristotle distinguished the abusive fun of Old Comedy from the witty
innuendo of the New, Horace prefers the liberal polite jest and the
shaded style, by turns grave and gay (*modo tristi, saepe jocoso*), to the
harsher and coarser, the careless, satire of Lucilius written two hundred
lines at a breath, "standing on one foot." (*In hora saepe ducentos, ut
magnum, versus dictabat stans pede in uno.* I, 4, l.10.) A fairly strict theory of decorum begins to operate no doubt where Horace gives up the
defence of both himself and Lucilius as poets, saying that satire is after
all not poetry at all—not noble enough—just words put together in verse
though they might as well be in prose (*sermoni propiora*, I, 4, l.42).[1] The
name for his satires is in fact "Talks," "Causeries"—*Sermones*.[2] To support this humility, Horace is even willing to countenance the question,
raised by some others, whether comedy is or is not poetry—for it lacks
fire and force both in words and matter (*quod acer spiritus ac vis nec
verbis nec rebus inest.* I, 4, ll. 45–6). There is evidence in the *Epistle to
Augustus*, however, and in the *Ars Poetica*, that Horace actually considered comedy when it was polished, like that of Menander and Terence
(scarcely that of Plautus), to be real poetry. Satire too, if we allow ourselves the indulgence of speculating about what Horace most sincerely
thought, probably stood a little higher in his estimation than the tactical

---

[1] Cf. H. R. Fairclough, "Horace's View of the Relations between Satire and
Comedy," *American Journal of Philology*, XXXIV (1913), 186, 190; G. L. Hen-
drickson, "Horace, Serm. I, 4: A Protest and a Programme," *American Journal of
Philology*, XXI (1900), 121–42.

[2] Lucilius had used the term *sermones* of his own satires (Fairclough, *loc. cit.*,
pp. 187, 191). In *Satire* II, 6, l. 17 Horace is content to be inspired by a *musa pedestris*.

modesty of his apologia would indicate. He concludes his confession
with an evasion. "Some other time we'll see whether this kind of writing
is true poetry or not" (*alias justum sit necne poema . . . genus hoc
scribendi.* I, 4, ll. 63–5).

The least rigid of all Horatian doctrines is that concerning the low
and the lofty in language. Here we see the idea of decorum placed in
the most softening and concessive light. Horace pays his notable respects
to dignity and splendor of diction in a passage of his *Epistle to Florus*
often quoted in neo-classic times—for instance, as the motto of Samuel
Johnson's *Dictionary:*

> at qui legitimum cupiet fecisse poema,
> cum tabulis animum censoris sumet honesti;
> audebit, quaecunque parum splendoris habebunt
> et sine pondere erunt et honore indigna ferentur,
> verba movere loco, quamvis invita recedant
> et versentur adhuc intra penetralia Vestae;
> obscurata diu populo bonus eruet atque
> proferet in lucem speciosa vocabula rerum,
> quae priscis memorata Catonibus atque Cethegis
> nunc situs informis premit et deserta vetustas;
> adsciscet nova, quae genitor produxerit usus.
> —*Epistle* II, 2, ll. 109ff.

In the adaptation of Pope:

> But how severely with themselves proceed
> The men who write such Verse as we can read?
> Their own strict Judges, not a word they spare
> That wants or force, or light, or weight, or care,
> Howe'er unwillingly it quits its place,
> Nay tho' at Court (perhaps) it may find grace:
> Such they'll degrade; and sometimes, in its stead,
> In downright Charity revive the dead;
> Mark where a bold expressive phrase appears,
> Bright thro' the rubbish of some hundred years;
> Command old words that long have slept, to wake,
> Words, that wise Bacon, or brave Raleigh spake;
> Or bid the new be English, ages hence,
> (For Use will father what's begot by Sense).

It is a plea for coinages and revivals almost the opposite in emphasis from
those cautious words of Pope in his own *Essay on Criticism* recommend-
ing the mean between the old-fashioned and the new-fangled.

> In words, as fashions, the same rule will hold;
> Alike fantastic, if too new, or old:

> Be not the first by whom the new are tried,
> Nor yet the last to lay the old aside. II, 333 ff.

In *Satire* I, 10 Horace has his fun at the expense of the affected neoterics who salted their Latin with Greek (*At magnum fecit, quod verbis Graeca Latinis miscuit,* 20), but in the *Ars Poetica* he recognizes the principle (later rampant in vernacular poetics of the Renaissance) that a language may be enriched by adaptations from one older and more impressive:

> Newly coined words will get by if they are taken from the Greek, a few at a time.

> *et nova fictaque nuper habebunt verba fidem, si*
> *Graeco fonte cadent parce detorta.* 52–3

Yet Alexander Pope probably considered the passage quoted above from his *Essay on Criticism* Horatian enough in spirit—and he was not far wrong. The double principle of decorum and fertility which appears in the last line of Johnson's *Dictionary* motto (*quae genitor produxerit usus*) may not express the emphatic idea of the whole passage, but it still expresses something central to Horace's view of language, an implicit key or point of control. Horace takes the middle way, that of living speech. Both with regard to obsolescence, the passing away of fine old words, and with regard to revivals, the norm is usage.[3] Usage is the final court of appeal.

> Many words that have perished will be reborn, and many will perish that now live respected—if Usage says so. Usage is judge and law and rule of speech.

> *multa renascentur quae jam cecidere, cadentque*
> *quae nunc sunt in honore vocabula* (the hexameter falls with
> a wistful cadence), *si volet usus,*
> *quem penes arbitrium est et jus et norma loquendi. Ars Poetica*
> 70–2

The Horatian doctrine of usage—steering between Attic purism on the one hand and on the other aristocratic archaizing and macaronic Hellenizing—defines the vital speech of a satirist, a social poet of everyday words (*sermoni propiora*). This is the more remarkable when we consider the degree of formal codification at which contemporary rhetoric had arrived. Such a view of the poetic idiom owes something, no doubt, to the kind of humility which is seen also in the Horatian apology, or

---

[3] In the third-century debate between Analogists and Anomalists to which we have referred above (Chapter 4), Horace would have been among the latter, the sceptics about any natural fitness of words for things.

mock apology, for the satiric genre. The view can scarcely be separated either from the realist theory of comedy coming down from Aristotle [4] and expressed for Augustan Rome in the Ciceronian phrases (preserved by Donatus) *comoedia . . . imitatio vitae, speculum consuetudinis, imago veritatis.* [5] In his Epistle to Augustus (168–70) Horace advances in defence of comedy the argument that, although its everyday materials are easy enough to come by, yet the comic writer's task is an especially exacting one because his descriptions of life are so easily held to account (*habet Comoedia tanto plus oneris, quanto veniae minus*). Despite the fact that the *Ars Poetica* says so much about epic and drama, even noting satyr plays and stage music,[6] and despite the modest claim for satire which we have quoted, the satire and epistle and the conversational lyric are the Horatian genres. It is through these that the more general insights of Horace into poetry are focussed—as those of Aristotle were focussed through the theatrical genres of tragedy and comedy. For in a wider sense Horace does define the idiom of all poetry. As a modern poet has put it, in all solemnity:

> The word neither diffident nor ostentatious,
> An easy commerce of the old and the new,
> The common word exact without vulgarity,
> The formal word precise but not pedantic.[7]

Add to this conception of idiom another conception, casually asserted by Horace, that of "order and juncture"—the "cunning juncture" of words (*series juncturaque, callida junctura—Ars Poetica*, 242, 47), and we recognize the precept of the cliché-breaker, the mind persistently on the verge of metaphor.

> I'll give a twist to the familiar that will make anybody think he could do the same—but he will waste his perspiration if he tries.

> *ex noto fictum carmen sequar, ut sibi quivis*
> *speret idem, sudet multum frustraque laboret ausus idem.*   240–2

VII

ONE of the most widely read amateurs of criticism in recent times, G. E. B. Saintsbury, called Horace's *Ars Poetica* a treatise *De Medio-*

---

[4] Cf. *ante* Chapter 3.

[5] Atkins, II, 38; H. R. Fairclough, *American Journal of Philology*, XXXIV, 183. Cf. *ante* Chapter 3, p. 50.

[6] A fact which has been taken to argue the construction of the *Ars Poetica* upon a Hellenistic model (Atkins, II, 71–2).

[7] T. S. Eliot, *Little Gidding*, V.

critate. To inquire into the justice of this disparagement would be to raise again, as with Hack, the question whether perfection (of precisely turned idiomatic speech) is the contrary of poetic force and a check upon it or is not rather its appropriate channel and its only realization. But Saintsbury's *mot*, set against certain conspicuous features of Horace's poem, may remind us of another perennial question for criticism. An academic wit of our own day has observed that pretty good poetry is like pretty good eggs. In the 18th century, when James Boswell once argued, for the sake of argument, that "poetry of a middle sort was entitled to some esteem," Samuel Johnson retorted that since poetry is a luxury and there is no necessity for our having it at all, it can have no value unless exquisite.[8] The perennial inclination of both critic and poet toward a kind of perfectionism, perhaps snobbishness, which sets them apart from producers and critics in other fields, even in some of the other arts, poses, besides social and editorial problems, a difficult critical problem. If there is some sort of absolute difference between the poem which is really a poem and that which is not—if there are no middle grounds, as there are with most human values, no shades of goodness, grace, and nourishment—why is this so? Is it so? We shall see the opposite implication in some of the most metaphysical defences of aesthetic value. The point here is that the tradition of perfectionism has one of its most insistent formulas in the *Ars Poetica* of Horace—not only in the whole drift of the treatise, its plenary range of decorums, but in the celebrated dictum: "Neither gods nor mortals—nor booksellers—have any use for the middling poet."

> *mediocribus esse poetis*
> *non homines, non di, non concessere columnae.* 372–3

If Horace's treatise was *De Mediocritate*, this was surely not according to his own conception. And it is in fact only by the odd equation "Perfection=Mediocrity" that one can make it so. Nevertheless, it is one of the curiosities of critical history, perhaps symptomatic of a deeply founded and irreconcilable paradox, that this equation has often been assumed—and not necessarily in opposition to high ideals but apparently in support of them. We shall see a classical source of the equation in our next chapter.

VIII

IF ONE were looking for an ironic illustration of the doctrine of genres, it could most readily be found in the fact that classical scholars have seriously debated the question whether the *Ars Poetica* is to be taken as

[8] Boswell's *Life*, April 10, 1775.

a theoretical treatise (a formal *poetics*), or as an introductory and practical guide (an *isagoge*), or, its haphazard sequence of topics considered,
as merely an *epistle* to a friend.[9] As a critical question this may be readily
dismissed for its utter vacuity. It may have some historical or genetic
sense—what genre would Horace, if asked, have said that he was writing? The fact is that the poem presents a rather random structure—it
tends itself to be an instance of beautiful woman shading into fish
(. . . *in piscem mulier formosa superne*). It can scarcely be invoked to
illustrate its own dictum:

> a place for everything and everything in its place.
> *ut iam nunc dicat iam nunc debentia dici.*   43

"Horace still charms with graceful negligence and without method talks
us into sense." [1] So far as one can discern an overall order, it is roughly
this: Lines 1–72 present a miscellaneous bundle of topics: *purple patches,
unity, brevity, writing within one's own powers, order of ideas, verbal
usage,*—all of which might be conceived under some such head as *poesis,*
the qualities that go into poems, the common sinews. Lines 73–294 speak
of various genres, their history, decorum, and rules—the form of the
whole poem itself—*poema.* Lines 295–476 tell some jokes about poets
and give some partly jocular good advice about what to do and what not
to do in being a poet; they present a miscellaneous bundle of ideas about
poeta. This threefold division is one of the main resemblances which
Horace is thought to show to the Peripateticism of Neoptolemus rather
than to the more simplified Epicureanism of Philodemus. It is a division
deriving from two distinctions which had been made by theoretical critics with increasing explicitness from early times: that between the matter (or statement) of poetry and its poetic "form," and that between the
poem and the poet. The first of these distinctions we have seen entertained by Aristotle, but with a restraint dictated by his basic view that
the residence of forms is only in concrete things. The threefold arrangement of Neoptolemus, his *poiēsis* (matter), *poiēma* (form), *poiētēs* (poet)
—was more clearly divisive—though of course Neoptolemus, like most
Hellenists, asserted that "matter" and "form" were alike important.[2] As
the emphasis fell on "form" or on "matter", one other thing had usually
been decided in Hellenistic criticism—the question whether the function
of poetry is hedonistic or didactic—whether the correct view is the Io-
nian and Homeric, that the aim of poetry is pleasure through enchantment, or the Boeotian and Hesiodic, that it is teaching. Stoic philosophers
held more or less consistently to the contentual or didactic view. Profes-

---

[9] R. K. Hack, *loc. cit.,* pp. 9–10.
[1] Scaliger was to call the poem "an art written without art." Heinsius transposed
passages to improve it. *Atkins,* II, 69.
[2] Atkins, I, 170–3.

sional scholars and critics, like Heracliodorus and Eratosthenes, dwelt on diversion and the enchantment of beautiful words. But Horace's model Neoptolemus adopted what we may call a Peripatetic compromise, Aristotelian in spirit but more specific than Aristotle,[3] the doctrine that the aim of poetry is twofold, to charm and at the same time to be a useful teacher.[4] It is this adjustment of the issue, the hedonistic-pedagogic compromise, which we find in one of the passages of the *Ars Poetica* most often quoted by posterity. "Either a poet tries to give good advice, or he tries to be amusing—or he tries to do both. . . . A mixture of pleasure and profit appeals to every reader—an equal administration of sermon and tickle."

> *Aut prodesse volunt aut delectare poetae*
> *aut simul et iucunda et idonea dicere vitae.* 333–4
>
> *omne tulit punctum qui miscuit utile dulci,*
> *lectorem delectando pariterque monendo.* 343–4

The second main distinction which enters into the threefold division of the *Ars Poetica*, that between poem and poet, is one with which we have already been concerned in several earlier places—in alluding to the personal invocations of the muse by Homer and Hesiod, in discussing the semi-ironic retreat by Socrates from the analysis of poetry to the *theia moira* (divine dispensation) or magnetic irradiation of the poet himself. The *Odes* of Horace offer enough evidence that the poet's divine inspiration was still a current concept—if perhaps largely a tacit myth or poetical figure. But divine inspiration bears a close resemblance to another mysterious thing, that which is often called "genius" or a natural gift. A different version of the antithesis poet-poem occurs in Pindar's contention that poetry is nature (*phua*, not *technē*), in Aristotle's passing word about the poet's special sensibility (*Poetics* XVII), in the remarks dropped in his *Rhetoric* to the effect that certain things are to be learned either by native insight or by technical training (I, i; III, i), and in the four requirements for good rhetoric named by Isocrates: native ability (*phusis*), practice (*epimeleia*), technical knowledge (*epistēmē*), and imitation of models.[5] An intimate correspondence between the character of the verbal artist and the worth of his utterance was a reiterated doctrine of antiquity which received such neat epitomes as the Stoic definition of an orator, "a morally good verbal technician"

---

[3] Aristotle, despite the cathartic clause in his theory, had indicated that the aim of each kind of fine art is to give the pleasure proper to it (*Poetics* XIV).

[4] Atkins, I, 175–7. Cf. the Lucretian figure of bitter medicine in the honeyed cup (*De Rerum Natura* I, 936–50) and the ancient definition quoted in Strabo's *Geography* I, 2: poetry is "a primitive philosophy guiding our morals, our tastes, and our actions."

[5] Atkins, I, 127–8.

(*vir bonus dicendi peritus*),[6] or the statement of the younger Seneca that a man's oratory could be no better than his life (*talis hominum oratio qualis vita*).[7] It is this branch of the doctrine, rather than that referring to divine inspiration, which appears in the Peripatetic arrangement: *poiēsis, poiēma, poiētēs*. But apparently *poiētēs*, on any terms, lent himself much less readily to formal analysis than did his product. Neoptolemus is able to observe that native gifts (*dunamis hē poiētikē*) as well as technical skill (*technē*) are requisite. He can distinguish between the technically skilful writer and the born poet.[8] And this was about all anybody had been able to say about the poet himself as distinct from his poems. Perhaps even this distinction between genius and technique was no more than a translation of the initial distinction, from which it stemmed, that between poet and poem. A fragment ascribed to Simylus,[9] a didactic poet, probably of the Hellenistic period, reduces the issue to absurdity by asserting that neither genius (*phusis*) nor art (*technē*) is any good alone, nor both together without practice (*meletē*), good luck (*kairos euphuēs*) and a well-disposed critic (*kritēs*).

IX

THE *Ars Poetica* of Horace is a climax to all this history in the neat compression of his statement about a choice that was no choice at all. "People like to ask whether a good poem comes natural or is produced by craft. So far as I can see, neither book-learning without a lot of inspiration nor unimproved genius can get very far. The two things work together and need each other."

> *Natura fieret laudabile carmen an arte,*
> *quaesitum est: ego nec studium sine divite vena*
> *nec rude quid prosit video ingenium; alterius sic*
> *altera poscit opem res et coniurat amice.*   408–11

For Horace neither the distinction between poem and poet nor that between *ars* and *ingenium* was very rigorous, as may be seen indeed in the number of rather mixed statements which he contrived to make about the poet, a few of them even in the first two sections of the *Ars*, sections which are ostensibly concerned with poetry and poems. Shortly after the advice about brevity running the danger of obscurity (*brevis esse laboro, obscurus fio*), comes that about knowing our own limitations

---

[6] Preserved from a lost treatise on rhetoric by the elder Cato (Atkins, II, 16). The same source gives us the memorable advice about content and form: *rem tene, verba sequentur.*

[7] *Letters to Lucilius*, CXIV, 16; Atkins, II, 168, 325. Such ideas were given a reverse twist by Epicurus: the wise man would "live poems" rather than write them.

[8] Atkins, I, 173.

[9] Preserved by Stobaeus (A.D. c. 500) in his *Florilegium*; Atkins, I, 180. The fragment is quoted by Ben Jonson in his *Discoveries*.

(*Sumite materiam vestris, qui scribitis, aequam viribus,* 38–9). After the history of the tragic and comic genres, comes "patience and revision" (*limae labor et mora,* 291).[1] Almost the whole third section of the poem is of course not theory of poetry at all but theory of being a poet (if we may take the liberty of turning some of Horace's satirical descriptions into terms of advice): Don't be a Bohemian; a bath won't wash off your inspiration. Read Socrates and get wisdom. Too bad for your poetic chances if you have been exposed to the standard Roman commercial education. Be careful, but not paralysed with scruples (*non ego paucis offendar maculis*). Aim at the top (*mediocribus esse poetis . . .*) Don't force your inspiration (*Tu nihil invita dices faciesve Minerva*). Don't rush into print (*nonumque prematur in annum*). Remember the glorious history of poetry, its sacred function. Don't take the praise of your friends and retainers too seriously. Get the advice of an honest critic—and follow it. Be steady, the best poet is not the mad one. The concluding paragraph of Horace's eipstle, an almost Rabelaisian portrait of the crazy poet—victim of the itch (*scabies*), of the king's disease (*morbus regius*), of some frantic hallucination (*fanaticus error*), or of lunacy (*iracunda Diana*), or perhaps a man who has defiled ancestral ashes or disturbed a consecrated spot—shows how far the sophisticated Augustan age had moved away from the ancient theory of the poet as a vessel of Dionysiac enthusiasm.[2] The Horatian view of poetic inspiration lies in the field of author-psychology and professional strategy.

The *Ars Poetica* of Horace is a nice mélange of objective and critical rules with snatches of studio wisdom. Keep your pencils sharpened, carry a pocket notebook, drink a pint of beer with lunch, go walking in the country, listen to the muse when she speaks, recollect your emotions in tranquillity, revise carefully, take your time in publishing. It is no derogation from such statements to say that they are not strictly parts of criticism. In the *Ars Poetica* of Horace they are, despite the random structure of the poem, not actually in great danger of being confused with criticism. One of the advantages of the aphoristic style is that its ideas tend to stay detached and clean. The implications of a given *dictum* do not operate very far in any direction.

---

[1] The oft-quoted "*si vis me flere, dolendum est primum ipsi tibi,*" 102–3, is not in its context a genetic rule. It refers to the roles of tragic characters, Telephus or Peleus.

[2] Cf. Persius, Prologue to *Satires;* Lucian, *Discussion with Hesiod.*

SUPPLEMENT

THE SONNET

Sir,— The sonnet has a universally accepted rhythm, beat, rhyme and number of lines. The rules apply not only to English sonnets but to those of all cultivated lands. You do our nation and yourselves, as a critical literary journal, a real disservice when (October 13) you accept the line "My moon is brought down from the sky in kindness" as a sonnet line, without any comment or reproof to the author who perpetrates it. However charming Mr. Warner's poems from which you quote may be as lyrics, the one you quote without comment as a sonnet is simply not a sonnet. In these days of weak and gagged critics, we look to your paper for a cultivated criticism to arrest the decay of English letters by ardent but lazy and conceited young writers who do not take the trouble to learn the elements of their craft.

Marie Carmichael Stopes

—*The Times Literary Supplement*, London, November 3, 1945, p. 523, quoted by permission of *The Times*

Analysis

Last Tuesday morning a young lady employed as a reader by one of the local book publishers turned in a report on the manuscript of a novel she had been reading. She had this to say about one of the leading characters: "I do not think this man should be identified as a bookmaker. He seems too uncouth, even sporty, a character to be wholly convincing as a craftsman."

—*The New Yorker*, December 2, 1944, by permission; © 1944 The New Yorker Magazine, Inc.

The unskilful poet will portray a dolphin living in the woods and a wild boar on the ocean. (*Delphinum silvis adpingit, fluctibus aprum.*)

—Horace, *Ars Poetica*, l. 29

The fishes got stuck in the tops of the elms, where the doves usually sat, and frightened deer were swimming on the flood.

> (*Piscium et summa genus haesit ulmo*
> *Nota quae sedes fuerat columbis*
> *Et superjecto pavidae natarunt*
>   *Aequore dammae.*)

—Horace, *Odes*, I, 2, 9–12

He is to consider himself as a Grotesque painter, whose works would be spoiled by an imitation of nature, or uniformity of design. He is to mingle bits of the most various, or discordant kinds, landscape, history, portraits, animals, and connect them with a great deal of flourishing, by heads or tails, as it shall please his imagination, and contribute to his principal end, which is to glare by strong oppositions of colours, and surprise by contrariety of images.

Serpentes avibus geminentur, tigribus agni. Horace.

His design ought to be like a labyrinth, out of which nobody can get clear but himself. And since the great Art of all Poetry is to mix Truth with Fiction, in order to join the *Credible* with the *Suprising;* our author shall produce the Credible, by painting nature in her lowest simplicity; and the Surprising, by contradicting common opinion. In the very Manners he will affect the *Marvellous;* he will draw Achilles with the patience of Job; a Prince talking like a Jack-Pudding; a Maid of honour selling bargains; a footman speaking like a philosopher; and a fine gentleman like a scholar. Whoever is conversant in modern Plays, may make a most noble collection of this kind, and, at the same time, form a complete body of modern *Ethics and Morality.*

—Alexander Pope and friends, *Peri Bathous: or of the Art of Sinking in Poetry* (1728), Chapter V, "Of the true Genius for the Profund, and by what it is constituted"

CHAPTER 6

ROMAN CLASSICISM: LONGINUS

§ *date and context of* Peri Hupsous—*II. elevation (the sublime),* ekstasis, *the five "sources": great ideas, passion, figures, diction, synthesis, little actually said about the first two—III. political and ethical differences between the Augustan and Imperial eras, interest in the poet's soul, imitation as inspiration, the five sources not co-ordinate, the "diagonal distinction"—IV. development of verbal rhetoric in the Hellenistic and Roman eras—V. Longinian rhetorical technicalities, devices for reconciling them with elevation and passion, correctness vs. grandeur—VI. variety of criteria considered in* Peri Hupsous, *universality, physical grandeur, Petronius, anticipations of heroic drama and Kant—VII. occasional subtleties, synthesis as rhythm or as verbal ordonnance, Sappho's Ode, "synaesthesis," Longinian decorum of transport* §

THE HORATIAN INTEREST IN THE AUTHOR NO DOUBT OWED SOMETHING to the Epicurean and anti-rhetorical teaching of Philodemus of Gadara, the professor to whom Horace may have been exposed in his youth. Viewed in that way the ideas of Horace become part of a critical trend, a "romantic" concern for the poet's inspiration which, if we may generalize somewhat broadly, came to its climax only in the second half of the next century. This climax is recorded for us not in the writing of a school but in the single extraordinary essay entitled *Peri Hupsous,* to which (or to the major part of the essay which survives) the name of an otherwise unknown "Longinus" has become attached. An alignment with the age of Horace is specially suggested by the fact that Longinus refers (Chapter III) with the deference of an old pupil or epigonist to another Gadarine or Epicurean philosopher, Theodorus, and

even more by the fact that the main argument of the essay is directed
against a certain Caecilius of Calacte, a rhetorician and a friend of the
famous rhetorical critic Dionysius of Halicarnassus, who flourished at
Rome during the Augustan period.[1] A certain slant of the essay toward
the *somnia Pythagorea* of neo-Platonism has led one recent commentator[2] to return to the accepted Renaissance view that Longinus was Cassius Longinus, philosopher-rhetorician of the third century, friend of
Plotinus, teacher of Porphyry at Athens, and unfortunate counsellor of
the rebellious Palmyran Queen Zenobia. But the internal evidence, especially the range of quotations and allusions, from Homer to Caecilius
and other Augustan rhetoricians, sufficiently argues for a Greek rhetorician at Rome in the first century.[3] The text of the *Peri Hupsous* is a discovery of the 16th century—in the first edition by Robortello at
Basel in 1554. No reference to the essay from either classical or medieval
times survives.

II

UNDERTAKING to improve on the work of the Augustan Caecilius, Longinus insists that Caecilius has said little about the sources, or components, of what both authors call *hupsos*,[4] a quality of "elevation" in writing, of intensity or eloquence, the "sublime," as it was much later to be
called. It could appear in prose or in poetry, in the oratory of Demosthenes, the dialogues of Plato, the epic narrative of Homer, the Greek
drama, the lyric poetry of Sappho, the opening of the Hebrew Lawgiver's *Genesis:* " 'God said'—what? 'Let there be light, and there was
light; let there be land, and there was land' " (IX). The range of the author's reading and his capacity for enthusiasm are among the most striking characters of the essay. A strong interest in the emotional response
of the poetic audience is indicated by a distinction between rhetoric and
poetry made in the first chapter: "The effect of elevated language upon

[1] Caecilius was a member of the reigning school of Apollodorus, the more
doctrinaire champions of rhetorical rule. See Atkins, II, 214.

[2] R. A. Scott-James, *The Making of Literature* (London, 1936), ch. VIII, "The
First Romantic Critic," pp. 81–3.

[3] W. Rhys Roberts, *Longinus on the Sublime* (Cambridge, 1935), Introduction.
We quote the translation of Roberts throughout this chapter, by permission of the
Cambridge University Press.

[4] Other similar expressions used by the author are *ta huperphua, ta megala, ta
megathē, to megalophuēs, hē hupsēgoria, to thaumasion, to hupertetamenon.* The
term *bathos*, used in Chapter II, is apparently a synonym (though taken waggishly
by Alexander Pope as an antonym and hence given its modern English meaning).
Cf. Atkins, II, 253; Roberts, Appendix B; St. Paul, *Romans* XI, 33–6; *Ephesians*
III, 13–21. The earliest English translations were *Of the Height of Eloquence*, by
John Hall, 1662, and *Of the Loftiness or Elegancy of Speech*, by John Pulteney,
1680. After the translation by Boileau in 1674 the term "sublime" prevailed. Cf.
A. F. B. Clark, *Boileau and the French Classical Critics* (Paris, 1925), pp. 371–5.

an audience is not persuasion but transport." And transport (*ekstasis*) [5] has been one of the ideas principally associated with Longinus by posterity. The chief theoretical challenge of the essay, however, lies in a certain peculiarity to be observed in the basic layout of the whole upon a five-fold division of the "sources" of "elevation." These five, announced and briefly defined in chapter VIII, are: (1) the power of forming great conceptions (*noēseis*), (2) inspired and vehement passion (*sphodron kai enthousiastikon pathos*), (3) formation of figures (*schēmata*), (4) noble diction (*phrasis*), (5) dignified and elevated "composition" (*sunthesis*). It is a regrettable matter that we do not actually hear as much about the first two of these sources, great conceptions and vehement passions, as we should like and as we may be led to expect from the plan announced in chapter VIII. The emotions, we learn in a later chapter (XLIV), were to be treated in another, now unknown, essay. And one of the most distressing lacunae in the Paris manuscript, that of six leaves from the second quaternion (KE), occurs in the very midst of the discussion about great conceptions.[6] "Sublimity is the echo of a great soul" (*hupsos megalophrosunēs apēchēma*). And after a few more lines, *Desunt sex folia.* Nevertheless it is clear enough that "sources" (1) and (2), conceptions and passions, refer to the state of the poet's soul more emphatically than to anything in poems themselves. They are both parts of greatness of soul, both, as Longinus puts it, on the side of nature, whereas "sources" (3), (4), and (5), figures, diction, and composition, are on the side of art.

III

ONE of the differences between Horace and Longinus is the difference between the ethical and patriotic Augustan era (conducive, it seemed, to great poetry) in which Horace wrote and the later corrupt and discouraging times to which Longinus in the closing chapter of his essay attributes a decline in poetic power and eloquence. It was common for philosophers during the reign of Vespasian to look back wistfully (*laudatores temporis acti*) to Republican institutions, to argue that democratic freedom had nurtured genius, and to impute a contemporary decline in oratory to political servitude. Longinus, like other literary men,[7]

    [5] In Chapter XV vivid poetical images (*phantasiai*) aim at enthrallment (*ekplēksis*).

    [6] A fact which might seem remarkable, that in a manuscript of which more than a third is missing, the forty-four chapter numbers remain, is explained by the further fact that the chapter headings are in a later hand than that of the scribe who wrote *Parisinus 2036*, the primary surviving manuscript, of the tenth century. This manuscript lacks actually eight leaves at the place mentioned, but the first and last are supplied from another manuscript. See Roberts, pp. 166, 169.

    [7] "Similar speculations" may be "traced in the writings of the two Senecas, Petronius, Tacitus, and Velleius Paterculus; and to these discussions later contributions were to be made by Quintilian and the younger Pliny" (Atkins, II, 215).

though agreeing with the philosophers about the literary decline, professed to have more confidence in the restorative power of enlightened autocracy. He puts the argument against autocracy in the mouths of the philosophers and for his own part lays the blame for decline on ethical rather than political causes, on the prevailing vices of the day, love of money and pleasure, insolence, and lawlessness—the general atrophy of man's immortal part, the soul. "It is not possible that men with mean and servile ideas . . . should produce anything that is admirable and worthy of immortality." Such an interest in the causes of poetic decline was the legitimate complement of his profound interest in the cultivation of the poet's soul as the way to sublimity. "Homer enters into the sublime action of his heroes." He "shares the full inspiration of the combat" (IX). In the first chapter of the essay a point of complaint against the Augustan critic Caecilius is that he has, "strangely enough," failed to tell how "we may succeed in raising our own capacities to a certain pitch of elevation." And one of the most distinctive features of the Longinian system is a special version of the Roman doctrine of imitation. What Horace was content to understand as a technical imitation of classic models becomes for Longinus something far more exciting, a powerful illumination and inspiration enjoyed through submission to the ancient masters. As the Pythian priestess is impregnated with prophetic knowledge by a divine afflatus which rises through the floor of the Delphic chamber, so modern devotees of the ancient poets experience a kind of inspirational effluence from those mighty souls (XIII).

To turn our attention once again to all *five* sources of the sublime and try to see these in a single perspective: the basis of division, a logician might say, is not single. (1) and (2), thoughts and emotions, are coextensive, not co-ordinate, with (3), (4), and (5), the rhetorical features. The quintuple division does not in reality constitute a single logical classification coextensive with the sources of the sublime. The Longinian preoccupation with the genius of the poet (as it is managed in the essay alongside of the rhetorical themes) suggests a question whether the two ancient distinctions which we have considered in our last chapter, that between *poiēsis* (content) and *poiēma* (form) and that between either *poiēsis* or *poiēma* on the one hand and on the other *poiētēs* (the author), may not sometimes become confused. The more compact choice *natura . . . an 'arte* (*ingenium* or *studium?* natural gifts or studied art?) seems to be equally capable of referring either to two things in the poet, his native genius and his acquired art, or to two other things, no doubt reflections of the first, but properly enough attributed to the poem itself, its fidelity to some kind of nature and its artfulness or technique. The problem may be sketched by a table having four compartments, as follows:

	POET	POEM
NATURE	1 GENIUS	1 X SUBLIMITY, OR HIGHER REALITY, OR ANY QUALITY OF CONTENT IMPUTED TO THE POEM ITSELF
ART	2 EDUCATION	2 X TECHNIQUE

A literary psychologist or a teacher of composition might well wish to inquire whether 1 or 2 in this table is the more important for the making of a poet, and whether they produce respectively and separately 1x and 2x or (what is more plausible) combine—both causes producing each effect. But a theorist looking at literature itself may be more concerned with inquiring whether 1x and 2x can actually be distinguished within a poem, and if they can, which is the more important, and what the relation is between the two. The last question may be par excellence the question confronting the literary theorist. What it is more relevant to stress at the present moment, however, is the possibility that a theorist might slide into yet another distinction, one which seems to harbor a certain duplicity and invalidity. This might conveniently be called the "Diagonal Distinction." It is indicated by the dotted line in the table. Two distinctions in one, we may say, by which the agile theorist is able to move out of an area of difficulty and reappear in another area with a solution which does not legitimately avail for the first. As if a theoretical rhetorician on being pushed to the wall about extravagance of conceits or figures in his favorite author were to answer: "Well, I excuse them on the grounds of the author's genius, the high seriousness of his message, and his intense emotion. Lesser persons, you and I, couldn't get away with them. But he obviously can. It is because he has the ideas and passions of a great soul. He uses his figures sincerely."

IV

BUT it may be well at this point to back away and return to the *Peri Hupsous* from another angle, observing that this essay is after all a rhetorician's essay, the third and fourth sources of elevation—that is, diction and figures—filling a very large part of what survives (Chapters XVI–XL). The chapters on these two sources, much more than the casual and graceful dicta of Horace on words, require for their understanding that one remember the degree of formal codification at which Graeco-Roman rhetoric had arrived. The history of that rhetoric was one which closely paralleled the history of the Horatian genre concepts.

The victory of verbal rhetoric which we have described in an earlier chapter had not occurred without serious cost through the encouragement which it gave to a hyper-development of rhetorical machinery.
Where Isocrates had named [8] and Aristotle (*Rhetoric* III, 13) had
grudgingly accepted four main parts of a speech: *proem, narrative, proof,*
and *epilogue,* Cicero in his youthful summation of Hellenistic doctrine,
the *De Inventione,* prescribes for the custom-built speech the following
five: *exordium, narratio, argumentum, refutatio, peroratio.* The loose divisions of the art itself rather casually implied by Aristotle—*heurēsis* or
finding of arguments (Books I and II of the *Rhetoric*), *taxis* or structure
(Book III, Chapters 13–19), *lexis* or verbal style (Book III, Chapters
1–12), *hupocrisis,* acting or delivery (mentioned disrespectfully in Book
III, Chapter 1)—have become in Cicero's *De Inventione* (I, 9) the
clearly definable and formally distinct four heads: *inventio* (*heurēsis*),
dispositio (*taxis*), *elocutio* (*lexis*), and *pronuntiatio* (*hupocrisis*), and at
the same time a fifth and purely subjective head, *memoria,* has been
added between *elocutio* and *pronuntiatio.* The kind of analytic interest
shown by Aristotle in such technically namable figures as *parisōsis,*
paromoiōsis, antithesis, homōnumia, and *metaphora* [9] had blossomed by
the time of Horace into the manifold repertoire of the figures of speech
and figures of thought (*figurae verbi, figurae sententiae; schēmata
lexeōs, schēmata dianoiēs*). These were managed with diverse efforts at
precision by numerous rhetoricians, by Cicero in his *De Oratore,*[1] by his
contemporaries, the anonymous author of the Hellenistic *Ad Herennium*
and the Greek litterateur Dionysius of Halicarnassus in his *Peri Suntheseōs Onomatōn* (*On Verbal Composition*), and during the next century
by Demetrius in his *Peri Hermēneias* (*On Style*) and by Quintilian in
Books VIII and IX of his *Institutio Oratoria.* Finally, the time of Horace
and Cicero saw the firm establishment of three (or four) *kinds* of verbal
style. Aristotle had said cautiously that it might be useful to think about
three areas of prose style, appropriate more or less to the three recognized branches of oratory—forensic, deliberative, and epideictic.[2] With
far greater confidence Cicero named the three now celebrated kinds of
oratorical style: *genus vehemens, genus modicum, genus subtile* (*Orator*
XXI). The author of the *Ad Herrenium* used the approximately synonymous terms: *gravis, mediocris, extenuata.*[3] The treatise *On Verbal Com-*

---

[8] Atkins, I, 132, says that Lysias first named these parts. Cf. R. C. Jebb, *Attic
Orators from Antiphon to Isaeus* (London, 1893), II, 68.

[9] Balance of clauses, like sounds at beginning or end of clauses, antithesis, equiv-
ocation, metaphor.

[1] See *De Oratore* III, 36–54.

[2] Dionysius of Halicarnassus reports that the lost *Peri Lexeōs* of Theophrastus
alludes to a mixed or middle style (Atkins, I, 156).

[3] *Ad Herennium* IV, viii.

position of Dionysius used a slightly different three: the elegant (*sunthesis glaphura*), the middle or common (*koinē*), and the severely plain (*austēra*); and the same author's *Essay on Demosthenes*, again a different three: the lofty or "sublime" (*charaktēr hupsēlos*), the middle (*mesos*), and the plain (*ischnos*). Demetrius is the only author who distinguishes not three styles, but four: the magnificent (*charaktēr megaloprepēs*), the elegant (*glaphuros*), the plain (*ischnos*), and the forceful (*deinos*).[4]

The three styles had been linked by Cicero with three great purposes of oratory: to prove (low style), to please (middle style), and to move or persuade (vigorous or lofty style).[5] Cicero distinguished the style of oratory in general from the styles of philosophy, sophistry, history, and poetry.[6] But during later centuries the three oratorical styles would be formally appropriated to three genres of poetry: to eclogue the low, to georgic the middle, to epic the lofty.[7]

The whole Graeco-Roman system of verbal rhetoric receives its eclectic, serenely sophisticated, and classically retrospective statement about a century after Horace in Books VIII and IX of a kind of politician's and pleader's encyclopedia, the *Institutio Oratoria* in twelve books, by the lawyer and laureate rhetorician[8] Quintilian. In the century after that rhetoric moved once more, as in the century after Aristotle, with Hegesias of Magnesia, in the direction of perfumery, euphuism, Asiatic conceit. A chief authority was Hermogenes of Tarsus. The period is known to historians as the Second Sophistic.

V

THE "figures" noticed by Longinus tend to have to do with abnormalities of syntax and other peculiarities of structure: *asundeton* (absence of conjunctions), *huperbaton* (inversion), changes of number, person, tense, *periphrasis* (a roundabout way of saying something), rhetorical question. It may even seem to a modern reader something like an inversion of values to dignify these twists by the name of "figure" when the queen of figures (the chief rhetorical concern of Aristotle) metaphor, along with comparison and simile, is treated under the head of "diction." The whole distinction between the third and fourth Longinian sources

---

[4] See Charles S. Baldwin, *Ancient Rhetoric and Poetic* (New York, 1924), pp. 56–7; *Demetrius On Style*, ed. W. R. Roberts (Cambridge, 1902), p. 22; Donald Lemen Clark, "John Milton and 'the fitted stile of lofty, mean, or lowly,'" *Seventeenth-Century News*, XI (Winter, 1953), No. 4, *Milton Society Supplement*, 5–9.

[5] "*Quot sunt officia oratoris tot sunt genera dicendi: subtile in probando, modicum in delectando, vehemens in flectendo*" (*Orator* XXI).

[6] *Orator* XIX–XX.

[7] Cf. *post* Chapter 8, p. 146; Chapter 16, p. 342.

[8] Under Vespasian.

of the sublime, diction (*phrasis*) and figures (*schēmata*), is indeed one which may be difficult to explain, and its status is not improved by the nearly parallel or overlapping subdistinction which appears under the head of "figures" themselves: between those of expression (*lexis*) and those of thought (*noēsis*). A certain technical conventionalism marks the rhetorical analysis of Longinus, a limitation through dealing with inherited concepts. This can be seen too in other parts of the essay, for instance, under the head of "great thoughts," the first source of elevation, where we come upon such an anomaly as "amplification" (or padding out an idea). Nevertheless, Longinus is an extraordinary rhetorician—and for the reason that he is trying to put two sides of a problem together—one side, the technicalities and definitions of the rhetoric which was current, and the other side, a sense of something indefinable which he calls "elevation" and which he attempts actually to specify in a non-rhetorical dimension, that of the great soul and its thoughts and passions. Whether these latter are something observable in the poem itself—or something outside the poem which causes the poem—or again something which the poem causes in its audience—is not clearly indicated. At times therefore the equation between the passions of the soul and verbal rhetoric tends to take the form of a shortcircuit or, as we have suggested, a diagonal escape back and forth between tricky technique and passionate inspiration, artful poem and natural man. This is most evident in the several treatments of extravagance in figures and diction. What is it that makes us swallow a violent hyperbole (Ch. XXXVIII)? or a far-fetched metaphor (Ch. XXXII)? Nothing else but "strong and timely passion," or "deeds and passions which verge on transport." Such passion (ours or the poet's may not be clear) is a kind of lenitive and remedy (*panakeia*) for hyperbole and a palliative (*alexipharmakon*) for metaphor.[9] "Art (*technē*)," says Longinus in another place, "is perfect (*teleios*) when it seems to be nature, and nature hits the mark when she contains art hidden within her."[1] And one of the main points of apology in his opening chapters concerns the difficulty of conceiving an *art* for so natural and spontaneous a performance as the sublime (*ei estin hupsous tis ē bathous technē*). On the main premises of the essay one might well argue that works of nature are only enfeebled and wizened by rules of art (*tais technologiais kataskeleteuomena*). But Longinus undertakes precisely to defend art against such hypernaturalistic charges.

> While nature as a rule is free (*autonomon*) and independent in matters of passion and elevation, yet she is wont not to act at random and utterly without system (*amethodon*). Further, na-

[9] Cf. *alexēma* (Ch. XVI), a palliative for the figure of adjuration.
[1] Ch. XXII, on the figure of inversion or *huperbaton*.

ture is the original and vital underlying principle in all cases, but system (*methodos*) can define limits and fitting seasons, and can also contribute the safest rules for use and practice.   II

On the view suggested by such words as *panakeia* and *alexipharmakon*, however, we seem actually to have something more like nature blurring the vision, soothing our doubts and irritations, covering over and apologizing for the ineptitude of art. We may be moved to ask: What has art done for nature? Do the metaphors and hyperboles and other paraphernalia of art correspond somehow to nature in her phase of emotion? Do they provoke her emotions? Or do they express them? Longinus does not say any of these things—though to say any one of them might be a bolder critical statement than he actually makes and would reverse the direction of what actually seems to be a retreat from the analyzable rhetorical figures into a reservoir of emotive origins and effects which somewhat vaporously defies inspection.

This kind of choice appears under another form in a section of the essay which in later ages was to be among the most often echoed. Chapters XXXIII—XXXVI are a digression from the technical theme of metaphor for the sake of drawing a strong contrast between scrupulous technical correctness and a grandeur of soul which is conceived as careless.

> . . . I am well aware that lofty genius is far removed from flawlessness; for invariable accuracy incurs the risk of pettiness, and in the sublime, as in great fortunes, there must be something which is overlooked. It may be necessarily the case that low and average natures remain as a rule free from failing and in greater safety because they never run a risk or seek to scale the heights, while great endowments prove insecure because of their very greatness.

> . . . does Eratosthenes in the *Erigone* (a little poem which is altogether free from flaw) show himself a greater poet than Archilochus with the rich and disorderly abundance which follows in his train and with that outburst of the divine spirit within him which it is difficult to bring under the rules of law? Once more: in lyric poetry would you prefer to be Bacchylides rather than Pindar? And in tragedy to be Ion of Chios rather than—Sophocles?   XXXIII

> In reply . . . to the writer who maintains that the faulty Colossus is not superior to the Spearman of Polycleitus, it is obvious to remark . . . that in art the utmost exactitude is admired, but

that grandeur is admired in the works of nature; and that it is by nature that man is a being gifted with speech. XXXVI

There is an obvious truth about all this (that if a poet writes a great play, an *Oedipus* or a *Lear*, marred by a faulty line or even a faulty scene, he has achieved more than if he wrote a good sonnet, even a *very* good sonnet), but this obvious truth seems to get out of hand, in the author's enthusiasm, and to sweep him along to something very like an implication that mediocrity is on the whole apt to be flawless, and swashbuckling genius strongly, if forgivably, inclined to make mistakes. A disclaimer to the effect that the blunders of Homer, Demosthenes, and Plato add up to only "an infinitesimal fraction" of their works (XXXVI) scarcely stems the main sweep of the argument, which reaches its flood in statements such as those we have quoted, that the abundance of Archilochus is disorderly and lawless, that art and exactitude stand against grandeur and nature, that great authors despise persistent accuracy (XXXV). Two possibilities, that a mediocre writer might be full of faults and partly because of these faults might be mediocre, and that a great writer might be faultless (or rather that his greatness might be in proportion to the fewness of his faults) are scarcely given enough weight.[2] The single sublime and happy touch (XXXVI), a notion that echoes one of the original emphases of the essay,[3] plays a greater role in redeeming the mistakes of genius than any greatness or perfection achieved through a whole structure. The discussion could scarcely countenance the idea that in a large literary work (as in a large practical enterprise, say the building of a jet bomber compared to the building of a wheelbarrow) a relevant mistake—one that is really a mistake—will be the more catastrophic. If we conceive both *perfection* and *grandeur* as qualities which ought to be resident in a poem itself, the antagonism suggested by Longinus seems bound to be troublesome. It is on the whole perhaps easier to read this celebrated digression upon genius and perfection as part of the author's prevailing tendency to seek a route of escape from the technicalities of the poem itself (where his spirit withers) to the great soul of the poet (in the idea of which he rejoices). The alignment of *perfection*, not against any *grandeur* in the poem itself, but against a godlike soul or "genius" in the author, is strongly invited. At a later date, from the *Spectators* of Addison to the *Seven Lamps* of Ruskin, this antithesis, with all the ambiguity of its bearing on the actual work of art, was to enjoy, despite the protests of a few hard heads like Macaulay, a triumphant vogue in English criticism.

[2] There is indeed the statement that Lysias is inferior to Plato not only in degree of excellences but by reason of his faults (XXV).
[3] "Sublimity flashing forth at the right moment scatters everything before it like a thunderbolt" (I).

VI

ONE of the most extraordinary features of the essay on *The Sublime* is the variety of criteria, the number of approaches to poetry, which it manages to include: not only the main three, the transport of the audience, the genius of the author, the devices of rhetoric—but in passing the democratic idea that great poetry is that which pleases all and always (VII)[4] and again a further variation on the subject-object relation, the most spectacular or operatic part of the essay (in Chapters IX and XXXV), the idea of physical grandeur as the counterpart of psychic. There may be some danger of our supposing that the author means that the sublime state of soul is to be measured by the magnitude of the external objects mentioned in a poem. For instance, by the battle of the gods in *Iliad* XX and XXI:

> You see, my friend, how the earth is torn from its foundations, Tartarus itself is laid bare, the whole world is upturned and parted asunder, and all things together—heaven and hell, things mortal and things immortal—share in the conflict and the perils of that battle. IX

We are perhaps saved from an over-simple interpretation of this passage if we notice the warning that these things must be taken allegorically (*kat' allēgorian*), that Homer makes gods of men and men of gods, and that hence even superior to the battle of the gods are passages which represent the gods as pure and great and undefiled. But another and more eloquent passage, in Chapter XXXV (part of that digression on genius and accuracy), hangs out the fiery symbols more brightly and became to later ages one of the most attractive spots in the essay.

> . . . Nature has appointed us men to be no base or ignoble animals; but when she ushers us into the vast universe as into some great assembly, to be as it were spectators of the mighty whole and the keenest aspirants for honour, forthwith she implants in our souls the unconquerable love of whatever is elevated and more divine than we. Wherefore not even the entire universe suffices for the thought and contemplation within the reach of the human mind, but our imaginations often pass beyond the bounds of space, and if we survey our life on every side and see how much more it everywhere abounds in what is striking, and great, and beautiful, we shall soon discern the purpose of our birth. This is why, by a sort of natural impulse, we admire not

---

[4] Cf. XXXVI, and Atkins, II, 236. Sikes, *The Greek View of Poetry*, p. 236, quotes St. Vincent of Lerins (d. 304): *quod semper, quod ubique, quod ab omnibus.* See his *Commonitorium*, ed. R. S. Moxon (Cambridge, 1915), II, 3.

the small streams, useful and pellucid though they be, but the Nile, the Danube, or the Rhine, and still more the Ocean. Nor do we view the tiny flame of our own kindling (guarded in lasting purity as its light ever is) with greater awe than the celestial fires though they are often shrouded in darkness; nor do we deem it a greater marvel than the craters of Etna, whose eruptions throw up stones from its depths and great masses of rock, and at times pour forth rivers of pure and unmixed subterranean fire. In all such matters we may say that what is useful or necessary men regard as commonplace, while they reserve their admiration for that which is astounding.

Here, it is true, Longinus is talking a language of teleology and religious psychology. He is speaking directly about the place of man in the universe, rather than making rules for literary composition. But in the context of the whole essay the passage might easily be given a direct literary application. It has been easy to assimilate to another famous piece of first-century literary exhortation, that of the old Bohemian poet Eumolpus in the *Satyricon* of Nero's Arbiter Elegantiarum, Petronius. *Praecipitandus est liber spiritus.* This is a plea for Homeric machinery and supernatural excitement (*ambages deorumque ministeria*), after the mere military realism of Lucan's *Civil Wars.* Put Petronius and Longinus together, and you have something like the spirit with which Dryden was to defend Heroic Plays in 1672 and a little later opera. Take the Longinus of *Peri Hupsous*, Chapter XXXV, alone ("Wherefore not even the entire universe suffices for the thought and contemplation within the reach of the human mind, but our imaginations often pass beyond the bounds of space . . ."), and we have a very good start toward the "sublime" in Kant's *Critique of Judgment* in 1790.

VII

THE same quest for the indefinable, no doubt, gives the rhetorical analysis itself here and there a more subtle turn. It is the mark of a rhetorician who knows the difficulties and the limits of his metier to observe that sublimity must "leave in the mind more food for reflection than the words seem to convey" (VII), and that "the very fact that there are some elements of expression which are in the hands of nature alone, can be learned from no other source than art" (II). Among the preliminary statements of the first chapter, close to that about the "transport" of the audience, occurs a statement that "Elevation (*hupsos*) consists in a certain distinction and excellence of expression" (*akrotēs kai exochē tis logōn*).[5] The author of a recent essay on Longinus has suggested that

[5] Cf. XXX: "Beautiful words are in very truth the peculiar light of thought."

the key to understanding this "excellence" lies in the fifth source of "elevation," that is, composition (*sunthesis*), or "harmony," as the term may perhaps be translated.[6] *Sunthesis* had been distinguished by Aristotle (*Rhetoric* III, 5) from simple diction or single words, though his observations under the two heads show not much difference. *Sunthesis* seems to have been emphasized by at least one Hellenistic critic, Heracleodorus.[7] And the term, as we have seen, appears in the title of one of the best poetico-rhetorical treatises of the century preceding Longinus, the *Peri Suntheseōs Onomatōn* of Dionysius, though there it seems to have a fairly generic and perfunctory meaning, simply the "management" of words. Longinus himself devotes relatively little space, Chapters XXXIX–XL, to his fifth source, and he appears to mean by the term *sunthesis* the special feature of verbal order which is usually called *rhythm*.[8] From this alone not a great deal might be deduced, at least not a very comprehensive theory of verbal ordonnance—not very much about any indefinable exactitudes of style or dynamic interdependence between style and content. But one other and more celebrated passage of the *Peri Hupsous* may be adduced to support such an emphasis. Chapter X, on the choice and combination of striking materials, contains the passage which speaks of the dazzling intensity and complexity of Sappho's Ode to Anactoria.

> Are you not amazed how at one instant she summons, as though they were all alien from herself and dispersed, soul, body, ears, tongue, eyes, colour? She unites contradictions. She is, at one and the same time, hot and cold, in her senses and out of them. She is either terrified or at the point of death. The effect desired is that not one passion only should be seen in her, but a concourse of the passions (*pathōn de sunodos*). All such things occur in the case of lovers, but it is, as I said, the selection of the most striking of them and their combination into a single whole that has produced the singular excellence of the passage.

This is a long way from the figures of thought and diction in the *Ad Herennium* or in Book VIII of Quintilian's *Institutio* and even from the acute observations of Aristotle on metaphor and pun. It is a kind of statement which may be extrapolated in various directions—perhaps even in that suggested by another recent commentator,[9] who sees the Longinian *ekstasis* as an adjustment, harmony, or gratifying integration

---

[6] Allen Tate, "Longinus and the 'New Criticism,'" in *The Forlorn Demon* (Chicago, 1953), pp. 131–51.

[7] Atkins, I, 174.

[8] Chapter I explicitly prefers the momentary lightning flash of sublimity to the "hard-won result . . . of the whole texture of the composition" (*tou holou tōn logōn huphous molis*).

[9] T. R. Henn, *Longinus and English Criticism* (Cambridge, 1934).

of impulses, much like that to which Messrs. Ogden and Richards once gave the name of "synaesthesis." [1] In any event Longinus must be saluted as a lover of great literature who knew something about how to cope with what was for him the very palpable, in fact inescapable, barbed wire of contemporary rhetoric. As Horace had subdued the theory of poetic words to a decorum of urbanity, conversation, idiom and satire, Longinus heightened it to a decorum of transport.

SUPPLEMENT

I never got my lips in the Horse's spring, and I can remember dreaming no dreams on either peak of Parnassus—not for such reasons do I suddenly come forth a poet. The Heliconian ladies and the waters of Pirene that produce the library pallor are not my dish. I leave these to the gentlemen whose busts are graced with the ivy tendrils. I venture out among the holy professional poets like a half-citizen at a village festival. What teaches the parrot his "Polly-want-a-cracker" and the magpie to ape being a man? That master of arts, that generous dispenser of genius—the Belly. Most skilful in removing obstacles to speech! If only they could take in the lovely, meretricious flash of money, what poets and poetesses, ravens and magpies, you would hear—singing the pure Horse nectar.

—Persius, Prologue to the *Satires*

What I should like to stress is the fact that in creative intuition we have the primary rule to which, in the case of the fine arts, the whole fidelity, obedience, and heedfulness of the artist must be committed. I also should like to stress the fact that between this primary, primordial, primitive rule and all other rules of making, however indispensable they may be, there exists an essential difference, so to speak infinite, as between heaven and earth. All other rules are of the earth, they deal with particular ways of operation in the making of the work. But this primary rule is a heavenly rule, because it deals with the very conception, in the bosom of the spirit, of the work to be engendered in beauty. If creative intuition is lacking, a work can be perfectly made, and it is nothing; the artist has nothing to say. If creative intuition is present, and passes, to some extent, into the work, the work exists and speaks to us, even if it is imperfectly made and proceeds from a man

c'ha l'habito de l'arte a man che trema,

—who has the habit of art and a hand which shakes.

At the summit of artistic activity, and for one who has long traveled along the road of the rules, finally there is no longer any road. For the sons of

[1] C. K. Ogden and I. A. Richards, and James Wood, *The Foundations of Aesthetics* (New York, 1925), pp. 75–6.

God are under no law. Just as finally the unique law of the perfect soul, according to the saying of St. Augustine (not literally of him, but it does not matter), is *"ama et fac quod vis"*—love and do what you want—so the unique rule of the perfect artist is finally: "Cling to your creative intuition, and do what you want."

—Jacques Maritain, *Creative Intuition in Art and Poetry* (Bollingen Series XXXV, 1, New York, 1953), Chapter II, p. 60, by permission of Pantheon Books Inc.

But the inner and most important distinction between the Sublime and Beautiful is, certainly, as follows. (Here, as we are entitled to do, we only bring under consideration in the first instance the sublime in natural Objects; for the sublime of Art is always limited by the conditions of agreement with Nature.) Natural beauty (which is self-subsisting) brings with it a purposiveness in its form by which the object seems to be, as it were, pre-adapted to our Judgement, and thus constitutes in itself an object of satisfaction. On the other hand, that which excites in us, without any reasoning about it, but in the mere apprehension of it, the feeling of the sublime, may appear as regards its form to violate purpose in respect of the Judgement, to be unsuited to our presentative faculty, and, as it were to do violence to the Imagination; and yet it is judged to be only the more sublime.

The mind feels itself *moved* in the representation of the Sublime in nature; whilst in aesthetical judgements about the Beautiful it is in *restful* contemplation. This movement may (especially in its beginnings) be compared to a vibration, i.e. to a quickly alternating attraction towards, and repulsion from, the same Object.

Bold, overhanging, and as it were threatening, rocks; clouds piled up in the sky, moving with lightning flashes and thunder peals; volcanoes in all their violence of destruction; hurricanes with their track of devastation; the boundless ocean in a state of tumult; the lofty waterfall of a mighty river, and such like; these exhibit our faculty of resistance as insignificantly small in comparison with their might. But the sight of them is the more attractive, the more fearful it is, provided only that we are in security; and we readily call these objects sublime because they raise the energies of the soul above their accustomed height, and discover in us a faculty of resistance of a quite different kind, which gives us courage to measure ourselves against the apparent almightiness of nature.

—Immanuel Kant, *Critique of Judgement* (1790), trans. J. H. Bernard (2d ed., London, 1931), pp. 102–3, 120, 125, by permission of Macmillan & Company Ltd.

Kant wrote in terms which presaged a Wagnerian view of the Rhine on a foggy night.—Student paper, 1950

CHAPTER 7

THE NEO-PLATONIC CONCLUSION: PLOTINUS AND SOME MEDIEVAL THEMES

§ *place of Plotinus in critical history—II. the philosophy of his* Enneads, *its relevance to aesthetics: unity and being, the good and the beautiful, ugliness and evil, matter, negation, beauty and reality in* Enneads I, vi *and* V, viii—III. *problems posed by Plotinus: unity and simplicity in relation to diversity, Stoic symmetry and brightness, beauty of parts, light, vision, intelligibility, subject and object, the problem of various beautiful forms, the two pieces of stone—IV. St. Augustine,* beate contemplari, *harmony of number, "angelic imagination," unity* in spite of *diversity,* obiter dicta *suggesting the contrary, symbols in Scripture —V. Aquinas, substantive ontology and theology (conflict of neo-Platonism and Christianity), "beauty" as a Divine Name, as form and intelligence,* quae visa placent, tria requiruntur, *splendor of form, beauty distinguished from the good, aesthetic detachment, analogy, beauty a transcendental, beauty and art, poetry in relation to logic and rhetoric—VI. Neo-Platonic aesthetic through the ages, the 19th century, James Joyce, cognitive and affective axes of theory* §

HISTORY OF TASTE AND LITERARY CRITICISM HAS LITTLE TO SAY ABOUT the thinker with whom we conclude our account of classicism. He is a theorist of *to kalon* in its purest sense rather than of *mimēsis* or of the *utile* and the *dulce*. All the other classical theories which we have seen have been considered by a great modern aesthetic philosopher [1] to be less than "aesthetic," defective either through simple hedonism or through hedonism joined with didacticism; but the theory we are now to look at is considered by the same philosopher to be something *more* than aesthetic, a mystical "excess" or ascent into the boundless, beyond criticism. Not only peripatetic definition, genre, and technicality, so friendly to the comic and satiric mirror of daily life, but their source in Aristotelian realism are now of vastly diminished account. Plotinus, the founder of the Roman school of neo-Platonism, who came to Rome from the school of Alexandria in 244 and died at Rome in 270, was a man who was able to hurl back sorceries upon those of a jealous rival; his presiding spirit, evoked by an Egyptian priest in the Temple of Isis at Rome, turned out to be a divinity; and several times in his life he experienced the trance of mystic communion with the Absolute. When he was asked to sit for a portrait, he replied: "Is it not enough to have to bear the mere simulacrum (*eidōlon*) of reality in which nature has wrapped me, without consenting to perpetuate the image of an image, as if that were worth contemplating?" It is through an emphasis on divinity, on the Divine One, as the radiating source and constitutive principle of all Being, that neo-Platonism, and especially the philosophy of Plotinus, makes its peculiar contribution to aesthetics.

II

THE philosophy of Plotinus is contained in his six *Enneads,* or sets of nine essays each, which after the death of Plotinus his disciple and biographer Porphyry arranged and edited in an order of ascent from ethical and aesthetic matters up to the absolute or One. It is a philosophy of Being through emanation (*tolma*) from, and return (*epistrophē*) to, the Divine One. There is this world, an appearance, as for Plato, and there is the reality which is Yonder. The grades of a kind of trinity, Soul (*psuchē*), intelligence (*nous*), and Oneness (*to hen*), occur as microcosmic and macrocosmic counterparts: in the individual things of this world, in the whole world, and in the Yonder. (In effect a kind of stratified or hierarchical universe is projected from our introspective awareness of our own consciousness.) An analogy to the generations of the Hesiodic theogeny, the Uranian, Chronian, and Olympian, was noticed of course by Plotinus but barely countenanced. The divine soul, looking toward the world, dreams it up or creates and sustains it. Looking toward intelligence, this soul reflects the ideas of Intelligence, the forms of the world. And Intelligence, looking up toward the One, is transcended in the One, the very principle of form or Being, the first

[1] Benedetto Croce, *Aesthetic,* trans. Douglas Ainslie (London, 1922), pp. 65, 156.

thing (*to prōton*), and hence the good (*to agathon*). The One is so pure and simple and primal [2] that we ascend to a concept of it only by the way of abstraction or negation.

> But possess yourself of it by the very elimination of Being and you hold a marvel.—*Ennead* III, viii, 10 [3]

The more empirical aspects of this reasoning and its most immediate relevance to aesthetics appear in passages of the following tenor:

> It is in virtue of unity that beings are beings. This is equally true of things whose existence is primal and of all that are in any degree to be numbered among beings. What could exist at all except as one thing? Deprived of unity, a thing ceases to be what it is called: no army unless as a unity: a chorus, a flock, must be one thing. Even house and ship demand unity, one house, one ship: unity gone neither remains.
>
> Take plant and animal; the material form stands a unity; fallen from that into a litter of fragments, the things have lost their being; what was is no longer there; it is replaced by quite other things—as many others, precisely, as possess unity.
>
> —*Ennead* VI, ix, 1

> Where the Ideal-Form has entered . . . it has rallied confusion into co-operation: it has made the sum one harmonious coherence: for the Idea is a unity and what it molds must come to unity as far as multiplicity may.
>
> And on what has thus been compacted to unity, Beauty enthrones itself, giving itself to the parts as to the sum. . . . Thus for an illustration, there is the beauty conferred by craftsmanship, of all a house with all its parts, and the beauty which some natural quality may give to a single stone.—*Ennead* I, vi, 2

But if One is Being and the Good and the Beautiful, and if nothing can even be unless it is one, how do we explain the operation of an apparently contrary principle in the world of physical things with which we are most familiar? What makes so much failure, evil, and ugliness? How are such things even conceivable? Philosophers have devised three kinds of answer to this question: the dualistic or Manichaean, which says that evil is an independent, positive, active principle fighting the

---

[2] "Yet again, the One is prior to the intelligence. For the intelligence, though unmoved, is yet not unity: in knowing itself it is object to its own activity" (Proclus, *Institutio Theologica*, 20).

[3] The *Works* of Plotinus are quoted throughout this chapter from the translation of Stephen MacKenna, 5 vols., London, 1917-1930, by permission of Faber and Faber Limited and Pantheon Books Inc. Proclus is quoted from E. R. Dodds, *Select Passages Illustrating Neo-Platonism* (London, 1923), by permission of The Macmillan Company.

good (Ahriman the Persian god of darkness against Ormazd the god of light); the neutral or Spinozistic, which says that good and evil are relative to our own pleasures and sufferings only and that the substantial and ultimate reality is beyond Good and Evil; and the Neo-Platonic and Christian scholastic, which says that evil per se is really nothing, but that it manifests itself as an absence of something where something ought to be. If we conceive that the form or unity or being of a given something has to work against or upon, or dominate, something else, we may readily slip a little way toward Manichaean dualism and conceive that something else to be "matter," a kind of potentiality or thing inconceivably nothing in itself if we try to conceive it purely—but nevertheless a principle of negation and evil. This is approximately the form which the theory of evil according to Plotinus assumes. Matter (*hulē*), said Plotinus, is multiplicity, the principle of falling apart and being nothing, the negative or nothingness which the One conquers into form and being. We may conceive unity (form or reality) and its opposite, matter, to be like a pair of intersecting cones—as in the world system of W. B. Yeats.[4] Each vanishes to a point at the base of the other. Again, invoking a Plotinian metaphor of the luminous (about which we shall have more to say within a few pages), we may conceive the universe as a series of concentric rainbows, the One in the center as pure white light, radiating through circles of increasingly dark color, to blackness at the outer limit. Matter is the last, lowest, and least emanation of the creative power of the All-Soul—the fringe or fraying-out limit at which the transmission of ideas and unity and the generative power of the soul come to a halt. (In the sphere of individual moral consciousness an analogy to "matter" appears in the concept of "environment," so far as that checks our purely rational or autonomous acts.[5]) Plotinus came near to making matter a kind of recalcitrant and obstructive low-grade stuff—a clay or powder—hence a positive principle of amorphousness.

> An ugly thing is something that has not been entirely mastered
> by pattern, that is by reason, the matter not yielding at all points
> and in all respects to Ideal-form.—*Ennead* I, vi, 2

A later Athenian Neo-Platonist, Proclus (who has been called the Aristotle of the movement), was to put the doctrine of evil as negation in a safer form.

[4] "If we think of the vortex attributed to Discord by Empedocles as formed by circles diminishing until they are nothing, and of the opposing sphere attributed to Concord as forming from itself an opposing vortex, the apex of each vortex in the middle of the other's base, we have the fundamental symbol of my instructors" (William Butler Yeats, *A Vision*, London, 1937, p. 68). "My instructors used . . . a double cone or vortex, preferring to consider subjectivity and objectivity as intersecting states struggling one against the other" (p. 71).

[5] *Ennead* I, viii, 7, 15.

> If Evil be wholly independent of God, then there is plurality
> of First Principles, Good and Evil arising from two several
> sources. . . . we can neither introduce a Form of things evil,
> nor yet consider Matter to be their cause. . . . Accordingly, we
> must . . . represent them [evils] as a side-product of certain
> partial and dispersed causes. . . . If a body is infected with Evil
> it doubtless embraces diverse elements which do not observe
> their just relative proportions, and thus, because every part
> would have the mastery, distemper is generated as a side-product.
> —*In Rempublicam*, 358

We find Plotinus in the earlier of two essays which he wrote on
beauty,[6] *Ennead*, I, vi, strongly inclined, like his master Plato, to de-
preciate physical beauty, or at best to value it as an approach to the real
beauty of intelligence in the Yonder.

> He that has the strength, let him arise and withdraw into him-
> self, foregoing all that is known by the eyes, turning away
> forever from the material beauty that once made his joy. When
> he perceives those shapes of grace that show in body, let him
> not pursue: he must know them for copies, vestiges, shadows,
> and hasten away towards That they tell of. For if anyone follow
> what is like a beautiful shape playing over water—is there not
> a myth telling in symbol of such a dupe, how he sank into the
> depths of the current and was swept away to nothingness?
> —*Ennead* I, vi, 8

> Therefore the Soul must be trained—to the habit of remarking,
> first, all noble pursuits, then the works of beauty produced
> not by the labour of the arts but by the virtue of men known
> for their goodness: lastly, you must search the souls of those
> that have shared these beautiful forms.—*Ennead* I, vi, 9

This we might say is the *Symposium* of Plato revisited. Perhaps the
tone is even more lofty—and somewhat more severe. Yet it required
little more than a shift of accent for Plotinus to distinguish himself
from the Gnostic puritans of that era, the philosophers who were carrying the distinction between matter and formal reality to the point of
making apparent natural beauty an actual ugliness and evil.

[6] The identity of Being, Good, and Beauty, and of Negation, Evil and Ugliness is to be assumed throughout the discussion. "We may even say that Beauty *is*
the authentic-Existents and Ugliness is the Principle contrary to Existence: and the
Ugly is also the primal evil; therefore its contrary is at once good and beautiful, or
is Good and Beauty: and hence the one method will discover to us the Beauty-Good
and the Ugliness-Evil. . . . the Intellectual-Principle . . . is preeminently the manifestation of Beauty; through the Intellectual-Principle Soul is beautiful."—*Ennead* I,
vi, 6

Evil is not alone: by virtue of the nature of Good, the power of Good, it is not evil alone: it appears necessarily, bound around with bonds of Beauty, like some captive bound in fetters of gold.—*Ennead* I, viii, 15

What geometrician or arithmetician could fail to take pleasure in the symmetries, correspondences and principles of order observed in visible things? . . . Surely no one seeing the loveliness lavish in the world of sense—this vast orderliness, the Form which the stars even in their remoteness display—no one could be so dull-witted, so immovable, as not to be carried by all this to recollection, and gripped by reverent awe in the thought of all this, so great, sprung from that greatness.

—*Ennead* II, ix, 16

And if nature may be countenanced—as an excellent mirror or image —what of art? It would have been greatly to our discomfort had so radical a philosopher of unity and being as Plotinus not written in *Ennead* V, viii (one of his later essays if the chronology of Porphyry is correct) a defence of worldly beauty which was catholic enough to find room even for the products of art.[7] This he manages by saying that artists, far from being at a disadvantage, as on the Platonic view of double removal from reality, actually enjoy a more than usual divine radiation of *nous*, a more than usually full participation in the Divine Intelligence and realization of the beautiful reality of the Yonder. It is a simple exchange of basic analogies, and in the rarefied atmosphere of the Plotinian context it may seem almost arbitrary. But it makes the difference between two worlds of literary theory.

Still the arts are not to be slighted on the ground that they create by imitation of natural objects; for, to begin with, these natural objects are themselves imitations; then, we must recognize that they [the arts] give no bare reproduction of the thing seen but go back to the Ideas from which nature derives, and, furthermore, that much of their work is all their own; they are molders of beauty and add where nature is lacking. Thus Pheidias wrought the Zeus upon no model among things of sense but by apprehending what form Zeus must take if he chose to become manifest to sight.—*Ennead* V, viii, 1

If we are willing to give this passage the benefit of some 1,400 years' anachronism, to place it momentarily in a context shining back from, let us say, the Germany of the Schlegels and the England of Coleridge

---

[7] The concession is made more cursorily in the paragraph of II, ix from which we have just quoted.

and Shelley (and such a procedure can be by no means contrary to the spirit of a really critical and theoretical inquiry), we may agree with those historians who have already proclaimed Plotinus as the earliest systematic philosopher of the creative imagination.[8]

III

ENNEAD V, viii is a remarkable essay in general aesthetics, not only for its Platonic eloquence and lofty metaphysics, but for certain more analytic problems which it is likely to pose to a thoughtful reading. We have seen that the emphasis of the Plotinian system lies upon a kind of unity which we can conceive as the triumph of an ordering principle over multiplicity and diversity of parts. It is even difficult to conceive this triumph except as occurring through and in virtue of the diversity of the parts. The Plotinian term "simple" (*haplous*), a modern editor of Plotinus explains, may describe either *absence* of *internal differentiation* (as with the simplicity or unity of a pebble) or precisely the opposite, a high degree of *internal differentiation*—in other words, organic unity (as with the unity of a living body).[9] The kind of unity and intelligibility enjoyed by the Plotinian object of knowledge is furthermore not that of a species, but that of an individual, and of an individual so intensely organized as to be microcosmic, an implication of the whole universe.

> Each member shall remain what it is, distinctly apart; yet all is to form, as far as possible, a complete unity so that whatever comes into view shall show as it were the surface of the orb over all, bringing immediately with it the vision, on the one plane, of the sun and of all the stars with earth and sea and all living things as if exhibited upon a transparent globe.
>
> —*Ennead* V, viii, 9

Yet the system of Plotinus, in another of its emphases, transcends, as we have seen, the heterogeneity of this world in an ascent to a divine One that is so simply One as to be conceivable only by the method of abstraction and negation. As the mind turns from this abstracted and

[8] The specifically aesthetic idea and the same example occur also in the *Life of Apollonius of Tyana* written in the same century by Flavius Philostratus. "For imitation will fashion what it has seen, but imagination goes on to what it has not seen, which it will assume as the standard of reality. . . . If you have envisaged the character of Zeus, you must see him with the firmament and the seasons and the stars, as Pheidias strove to do in this statue." VI, 19. The passage is part of an argument that Greek plastic art rose above the animal symbolism of the Egyptians to an expression of divinity in the human form. Flavius Philostratus of Tarsus (c. A.D. 172–245) was a sophist who taught rhetoric at Athens and Rome.

[9] Dodds, pp. 45–6, notes to *Ennead* VI, vii, 13–15.

severe concept back to the diverse and composite world of nature and art, certain perplexities may arise.

Among the criteria of beauty known to later antiquity two of the most respected were those emphasized by Stoic philosophers and litterateurs: symmetry and brightness of color.[1] But how *could* symmetry be part of the definition of beauty? Think, says Plotinus, what that doctrine leads us to.

> Only a compound can be beautiful, never anything devoid of parts; and only a whole; the several parts will have beauty, not in themselves, but only as working together to give a comely total. Yet beauty in an aggregate demands beauty in details; it cannot be constructed out of ugliness; its law must run throughout.—*Ennead* I, vi, 1 [2]

> All the loveliness of color and even the light of the sun, being devoid of parts and so not beautiful by symmetry, must be ruled out of the realm of beauty. And how comes gold to be a beautiful thing? And lightning by night, and the stars, why are these so fair?—*Ennead* I, vi, 1

Such questions may be translated all too easily into the language of the practical literary critic. How many lines of a poem, we might ask ourselves, do we read before we begin to form some opinion of its merit? How many scenes of a play, before knowing whether we enjoy it? Certain short phrases have, or seem to have, poetic power—the sudden flashes of the sublime about which Longinus spoke—the sure "touchstones" or sovereign fragments by which Matthew Arnold in a distant post-Platonic age would propose the ordering of criticism. Our choice between a holistic view of art and a connoisseurship of the *disjecta membra* may not be able altogether to escape the fact that in one of its most natural, primitive, and perennial uses, the term *beautiful* does apply to simple and bright and smooth objects—gold rather than rusty iron, a polished topaz rather than a lump of mud. The Stoic doctrine of charming color may seem, when confronted with such examples, not very profoundly integrated with that of symmetry. If nowadays we refuse to entertain any such conception as that earlier Greek one of *kosmos*[3]—the word "purple" or the word "topaz" as a

---

[1] Cicero, *Tusculan Disputations* IV, 13. Cf. Aristotle, *Metaphysics* XIII, 3: "The essential characters composing beauty are order, symmetry, and definition."

[2] Cf. the statement of Coleridge, written not without influence of Neo-Platonic reading, but shaded too by the Kantian distinction between the beautiful and the agreeable: A poem is a species of composition which proposes "to itself such delight from the *whole*, as is compatible with a distinct gratification from each component *part*" (*Biographia Literaria*, XIV).

[3] Cf. Lane Cooper, "The Verbal 'Ornament' (KOSMOS) in Aristotle's Art of Poetry," *Classical and Mediaeval Studies in Honor of Edward Kennard Rand*, ed.

valuable ornament in a poem—or to adopt the thought of the sophist Hippias in the Platonic dialogue, "Gold is what is beautiful,"—nevertheless we do to some extent inevitably recognize the affinity between the beautiful and the brilliant. We do so, for instance, in the very metaphors we choose for commending works of art—bright or brilliant or clean or clear, we are likely to say, not muddy, or dirty or drab.

The reconciliation which Plotinus himself effects between simple brightness and complex intelligible order as criteria of beauty is based on a metaphor that runs through all Platonic philosophy, beginning with the great image of the dark cave and the fire of knowledge in the *Republic* and the analogy of sun and eyesight to truth and intelligence.

> The beauty of colour is also the outcome of a Unification. It derives from shape, from the conquest of the darkness inherent in matter by the pouring-in of light, the unembodied, which is a Rational-Principle and an Ideal-Form.
>
> Hence it is that fire itself is splendid beyond all material bodies, holding the rank of Ideal Principle to the other elements, making ever upwards, the subtlest and sprightliest of all bodies, as very near to the unembodied; itself alone admitting no other, all the others penetrated by it: for they take warmth but this is never cold; it has colour primally; they receive the Form of colour from it: hence the splendour of its light, the splendour that belongs to the Idea. And all that has resisted and is but uncertainly held by its light remains outside of beauty, as not having absorbed the plenitude of the Form or colour.—*Ennead*, I, vi, 3

In the Persian dualistic system, the god of light, Ormazd, is the principle of good; the god of darkness, Ahriman, the equally positive principle of evil. It is one of the insights of the Platonic Western mind to make darkness a negation, brightness an analogue of all that is positive—knowledge, form, being, Divinity.

> O Light eternal who only in thyself abidest, only thyself doest understand, and to thy self, self-understood, self-understanding, turnest love and smiling! [4]

L. W. Jones (New York, 1938), pp. 61–77. "Further, add words for fine raiment, as 'purple,' and armor, as 'corslet,' 'glaive,' and 'hauberk,' and all the noble names for things that delight the senses, particularly sight and hearing, as Aristotle notes, but also touch, taste, and smell, and delight the higher sensibilities, and for things with which men and women adorn themselves, their servants, their animals, their houses, public buildings, ships; 'jewel' and the names of jewels—'beryl,' 'topaz,' 'amethyst,' 'diamond,' 'coral,' 'pearl,' and 'ruby'; words for incense and perfume—'frankincense,' 'spices,' and 'myrrh'; beautiful words from music, 'music' itself, 'melody,' 'harmony,' 'choral,' 'canticle,' 'alleluia,' and the names of instruments, the harp, the flute. . . ." (pp. 70–1).

[4] *Paradiso*, XXXIII, 124–6, trans. Philip H. Wicksteed.

O luce eterna, che sola in te sidi,
sola t'intendi, e, da te intelleta
ed intendente te, ami ed arridi!

Hail holy Light, offspring of Heaven first-born,
Or of the Eternal coeternal beam.

Lo! thy dread Empire, CHAOS! is restored;
Light dies before thy uncreating word;
. . .
And universal darkness buries all.

The idea of brightness as intelligible form is closely connected with
another classical aesthetic idea—found, for instance, in Plato's *Philebus*
and *Hippias Major* and again in *Enneads* I, vi, 1—that Beauty is discerned
chiefly by the senses of sight and hearing [5]—these being the highest or
most intellectual senses and those through which we derive our most distinct ideas of pattern and, more abstractly and metaphysically, of "form."
Plotinus takes it for granted that sight comes first. "Beauty addresses itself
chiefly to sight."

Again the refined sensory experience of sight allies itself readily
with the idea that human knowledge arises from some kind of interdependence between object and organ. "Thought and thing depend upon
and correspond to each other."

Never did the eye see the sun unless it had first become Sunlike,
and never can the soul have vision of the First Beauty unless itself be beautiful.—*Enneads* I, vi, 9

Like alone sees like. Or as modern students of neo-Platonism, quoting
Blake, are likely to put it.

The sun's light when he unfolds it,
Depends on the organ that beholds it.

Or, quoting Goethe:

Did not the eye partake of sun,
Sun would be darkness to our seeing;
No splendour could from the divine be won
Were God not part of mortal being.[6]

In the higher reaches of Plotinian thought, the idea of the brilliant intelligibility of all being blends into the idea that being *is* pure intelligibility

[5] Cf. Aristotle, *Politics* VIII, 5, and *ante* Chapter 2, pp. 26–7.
[6] Ludwig Lewisohn, *Goethe: The Story of a Man* (New York, c. 1949), II, 74,
Lewisohn's translation from Goethe's *Zahme Xenien*, III, by permission of Farrar,
Straus and Cudahy, Inc.

or is composed of ideas. "It is hard to work down to crude matter beneath all that sheathing of idea." [7]

Perhaps one of the chief questions about beauty which the system of Plotinus is likely to provoke a modern reader to ask will run somewhat as follows: Are all the perfect forms (*eidē*) equally good and beautiful? And if not, how do we know which sensible forms have more beauty than others? Is a peacock more beautiful than a goose? Is a worm or a warthog more beautiful than certain objects undoubtedly lower in the hierarchy of complex unities but more usually called beautiful, say a block of lapis lazuli or even a finely cut diamond? Plotinus himself has written two contrasting passages which present the problem succinctly. One, from *Ennead* I, vi, 2, we have quoted above:

> . . . there is the beauty, conferred by craftsmanship, of all a house with all its parts, and the beauty which some natural quality may give to a single stone.

The following appears in *Ennead* V, viii, 1:

> Suppose two blocks of stone lying side by side: one is unpatterned, quite untouched by art; the other has been minutely wrought by the craftsman's hands into some statue of God or man, a Grace or a Muse, or if a human being, not a portrait but a creation in which the sculptor's art has concentrated all loveliness.
>
> Now it must be seen that the stone thus brought under the artist's hand to the beauty of form is beautiful not as stone—for so the crude stone would be as pleasant—but in virtue of the form or idea introduced by art. This form is not in the material; it is in the designer before it enters the stone.

The stone as something already existent is a being and has a form of its own, a unity and beauty. But then to expound the stamping of form on the formlessness of sheer matter, we adopt the analogy of the image finely imposed upon the simple and unadorned piece of material. Form upon form. And how beautiful was the original form? And is something of it not lost in the carving? The theory of Plotinus does not start as a theory of beauty, much less as a theory of art or poems. It is a theory of the world and God, of all being and all knowing, and only as an incident

---

[7] *Ennead* V, viii, 7. *Ennead* I, vi, 3 bears a marked resemblance to the notion of closure or psychic completion of forms found today in Gestalt psychology and in general aesthetics. "So with the perceptive faculty: discerning in certain objects the Ideal-form which has bound and controlled shapeless matter, opposed in nature to Idea, seeing further stamped upon the common shapes some shape excellent above the common, it gathers into unity what still remains fragmentary, catches it up and carries it within, no longer a thing of parts, and presents it to the Ideal-Principle. . . ."

or an analogy does it find a place for art. The opposite procedure, to start by explicitly attempting a theory of art and to move away from that to a general epistemology,—that is, to try to explain art or beauty or poetry by a principle so broad that it explains everything else too—is a reversal, or mirror imaging, of neo-Platonism which appears in some forms of modern idealism and aesthetic and perhaps testifies to the toughness of the paradox posed by Plotinus.[8]

I V

THE ideas of Plotinus, though perhaps least likely of all ideas about aesthetics to be widely known or respected today, have had their subsequent career and their analogues—especially among Christian philosophers from about the time of Plotinus himself to the late middle ages. St. Augustine for instance had read Plotinus in a Latin translation, and as he shared with Plotinus the aim of combatting the several forms of dualism and Puritanism prevalent in the third and fourth centuries (he was frequently engaged, for instance, *Contra Manichaeos*), he gives us some rather close echoes of the neo-Platonic philosopher.

> Without unity nothing could exist. To be is no other than to be one; the more unity a thing has, so much the more being does it possess . . . no material object is really one because a body as such is indefinitely divisible, potentially, if not actually.[9]

> Any beautiful object whatsoever is more worthy of praise in its totality as a whole than in any one of its parts. So great is the power of integrity and unity that what pleases as a part pleases much more as a unified whole.[1]

The Plotinian affinity between subject and object is argued by Augustine at both the sensory and spiritual levels. The senses enjoy whatever is proportioned to them by simple reason of the principle that agreement always produces pleasure.[2] And the full aesthetic pleasure of delighted contemplation (*beate contemplari*) occurs in the presence of objects which are in harmony not only with the senses but with the whole na-

---

[8] See *post* Chapter 23, Benedetto Croce.

[9] *De Moribus Ecclesiae Catholicae et de Moribus Manichaeorum* II, vi. Translations from Augustine in this paragraph are adopted from Immanuel Chapman, *Saint Augustine's Philosophy of Beauty* (New York, 1935); see esp. pp. 59, 61, 63. See the same author's "Some Aspects of St. Augustine's Philosophy of Beauty," *Journal of Aesthetics and Art Criticism*, I (Spring, 1941), 46–51. The Latin texts of St. Augustine may be consulted in J. C. Migne's *Patrologia Latina*, vols. XXXII and XXXIV (Paris, 1841, 1845).

[1] *De Genesi Contra Manichaeos* I, xxi.

[2] *De Vera Religione* I, xxxix; *De Musica* VI, xiii.

ture of man, especially with the mind as the ruler and interpreter of the senses.[3] In Augustine's treatise *De Musica* a line from a hymn by St. Ambrose, *Deus creator omnium*, furnishes the more analytic concepts— funneled as it were towards unity—of number, form, and order.[4] The heading of Book VI of the *De Musica*, "The ascent from rhythm in sense to the immortal rhythm which is in truth," [5] synopsizes the argument by which Augustine, returning to Pythagorean and Platonic ideas about number, performs for the aesthetic of sound a service analogous to that performed by Plotinus for the aesthetic of bright colors. Like Plotinus and even more like Socrates arguing the doctrine of recollection (*anamnēsis*) in the *Phaedo* and *Meno*, Augustine is at a loss to know how we derive from our actually imperfect material experiences the normative concepts of order and perfection. He maintains that we do not. Such criteria are supplied to our minds, or infused, directly by divine gift.[6]

The argument is marked by a certain etherealism, an appeal to what a modern literary critic might call the "angelic imagination." [7] The quest for beauty is rather an argument from divine postulates than an attempt to ascend from human experience. Or at any rate it is ordered by a devotion to harmony and unity which in many places seems to entertain little respect for the multiplicity and resistance of the secular principle. The supreme good of the spirit is *monas*, a state of freedom from the discords incident to human life, even from the division intrinsic to sex. Moral evil is *duas*, two-ness, the failure to submit to the power of the One.[8] From such principles it follows more or less plausibly—though perhaps not with strict necessity—that among geometrical figures an equilateral triangle is more beautiful than a scalene, a square even more beautiful than an equilateral triangle, and a circle the most beautiful figure of all.[9] One likes the doors and windows of a house to be arranged symmetrically.[1] Here is a critical spirit which if not militantly anti-dramatic seems at least largely indifferent to whatever aesthetic claims may be enjoyed by the principle of division or conflict. Like Plotinus, Augustine seems to understand beauty as arising through a unity which occurs in spite of, or aside from, the diversity of parts. Certainly this beauty does not arise *through*, or at least not in virtue of, that diversity.

It may be with some surprise that we encounter certain remarks which Augustine let fall in other connections. A work of art, he will say

[3] *De Ordine* II, xii.

[4] *De Musica* VI, ii.

[5] W. F. Jackson Knight, *St. Augustine's De Musica* (London, 1949).

[6] *De Vera Religione* I, xxx–xxxi.

[7] Allen Tate, *The Forlorn Demon* (Chicago, 1953), esp. p. 37; William F. Lynch, "Theology and the Imagination," *Thought*, XXIX (Spring, 1954), esp. p. 76.

[8] *De Ordine* II, xv–xix; Gilbert and Kuhn, pp. 133–4, citing K. Svoboda, *L'Esthétique de St. Augustine et ses Sources*, Brno, 1933.

[9] *De Quantitate Animae* I, ix.

[1] *De Ordine* II, xi.

in one place, has its own truth, and just in virtue of its being a particular species of falsehood. An artist cannot be true to himself unless he is in a sense a maker of lies.[2] Again: Rightly attuned souls will look at all things in their contexts. Beauty cannot bear scrutiny in isolation. Augustine is indeed able to countenance something very much like an artistic theory of harmony *through* contrast, beauty *in* variety: Poets use even barbarisms and solecisms to "season" their poetry; sweet music is made sweeter by the consonance of differing voices; a drama needs clowns and villains to bring out the virtue of the heroes.[3]

One problem which somewhat puzzled Augustine concerned the appearance of symbols in the Scriptures. Why was it pleasant to linger in symbols? to prefer the outer show to the inner and pure meaning? Was it commendable? The more remote or difficult the divine symbol (the lion, the panther, the bear, the worm), the more difficult perhaps the problem. Another writer of the patristic era, the Pseudo-Dionysius, speaks (almost in what nowadays we might call "metaphysical" terms) of incongruity, shock and stimulus to the mind in unravelling mystery.[4] Augustine himself engages in a meditation which comes close to stating, if not so close to solving, one of the main problems of literary criticism in every age.

> I feel greater pleasure in contemplating holy men, when I view them as the teeth of the Church, tearing men away from their errors. . . . It is with the greatest pleasure too that I recognize them under the figure of sheep that have been shorn. . . . But why I view them with greater delight under that aspect than if no such figure were drawn from the sacred books, though the fact would remain the same, is another question, and one very difficult to answer. Nobody, however, has any doubt about the facts, both that it is pleasanter in some cases to have knowledge communicated through figures, and that what is attended with difficulty in the seeking gives greater pleasure in the finding.[5]

V

NINE hundred years later than Augustine, Thomas Aquinas turned the preoccupation of Christian metaphysics from the Platonic realm yonder

---

[2] *Soliloquia* II, x. Cf. *Confessions* III, vi; Gilbert and Kuhn, p. 126.

[3] *De Ordine* II, iv. Gilbert and Kuhn, p. 138, point out that Plotinus had said: "Take away the low characters and the power of the drama is gone; they are part and parcel of it."

[4] *De Coelesti Hierarchia* II ("*Quod apte res divinae atque coelestes dissimilibus etiam signis explicentur*"), v (in *Patrologia Graeca*, ed. J. C. Migne, III, 143–6). Cf. Gilbert and Kuhn, p. 154–5.

[5] *De Doctrina Christiana* II, vi, quoted by Gilbert and Kuhn, pp. 153–4, from *Nicene and Post-Nicene Fathers*, 1st Series, II (Buffalo, 1887), 537. Cf. Migne, *Patrologia Latina*, XXXIV, 38–9.

of forms to an Aristotelian, immediately experienced world of natural substances. It was a world, however, which pointed upwards (like a cathedral, says Henry Adams) to a transcendentally substantive and personal God.[6] Between the dreaminess of Plotinian pantheistic immanence and the concrete, particular, historical claim of Christianity there was a difference which was bound to develop sooner or later theoretical differences at the aesthetic as well as at the metaphysical and theological levels. The Plotinian theory of emanation, a theory of continuity between Creator and created, a shading of values, is supplanted in the Christian Aristotelianism of Aquinas by an emphatic distinction between God and his works. Our apprehension of God, the source of the beautiful, is not by any kind of either spiritual or abstractive suffusion, as, for instance, of light from an inner stage seen through a gauze curtain, but by a clear apprehension of, and reasoning from, the separate works of His hand. The philosophy of the first ten or twelve centuries of the Christian era had been, for that matter, not only a Platonic attack on materialism (at some moments even carried to the extreme of "iconoclasm"[7]) but alternatively, in certain phases, a realistic (and in that sense a materialistic) defense of this world against the Gnostic and Manichaean rarefactions of value.[8] A certain kind of beauty, a serenely abstracted and ordered cosmos of neo-Platonism (in which abstraction itself was spirituality and divinity)—like the columns of a Greek temple distant upon a hill in a luminous mist—was cut across and wrecked by the concretely historical, bloody and suffering claim of Christianity. A fourth-century Roman philosopher, Eunapius, called it a "fabulous and formless darkness mastering the loveliness of the world."[9] And a modern Irish poet has echoed:

> The Roman Empire stood appalled:
> It dropped the reins of peace and war
> When that fierce virgin and her Star
> Out of the fabulous darkness called.[1]

Yet we may be disappointed if we look to Aquinas or to other theologians of the high Middle Ages for any new and more concrete theory of beauty, of fine art in general, or of poetry. In the aesthetic remarks of Aquinas—remarks occurring mainly at three places in his

[6] See the elaboration of this image by Henry Adams, *Mont-Saint-Michel and Chartres* (Boston, 1927), p. 382.

[7] Cf. Bosanquet, *A History of Aesthetic*, pp. 132–9.

[8] Cf. Etienne Gilson, *The Philosophy of St. Thomas Aquinas*, trans. Edward Bullough (London, 1937), Ch. 17, esp. p. 354; Thomas Gilby, *Poetic Experience* (New York, 1934), pp. 23–4.

[9] Eunapius, *Vita Maximi*, quoted by E. R. Dodds, *Select Passages Illustrating Neoplatonism* (London, 1923), p. 8.

[1] W. B. Yeats, "Two Songs from a Play," *Collected Poems* (New York, 1942), p. 246, by permission of The Macmillan Company.

Summa Theologiae[2] and in his opuscular commentary on the *Divine Names* of Dionysius—we have a discussion of "beauty" precisely as a "Divine Name." "Beauty" belongs to form and intelligence, and hence pre-eminently to the contemplative life.[3] If we try to take Aquinas in the most secular or natural way we can—looking at what he says about the objects in this world which are the analogical starting points for our knowledge of Divine beauty and at what he says about the human experience of perceiving beauty, we find a kind of tabloid and laconic, even casual, codification of the principles with which we are familiar in the earlier centuries of neo-Platonism. Beautiful things, he says, are those which are apprehended with pleasure—*quae visa placent*—and thus he parallels Augustine in giving his simplest definition of the beautiful a subjective accent. As with Augustine and Plotinus, we are once more in the presence of a basic assumption of radical harmony between man the knower and the external universe which he knows—and in some parts of which he takes a special delight. The beauty of a beautiful object consists not merely in a self-enclosed character but in a corresponding external relation of fitness to the knowing subject, a relation of knowability. All knowledge, and especially knowledge of the beautiful, and pleasure in the beautiful, arise by a kind of union between subject and object.[4]

As for that object itself, the cognitive counterpart of aesthetic pleasure, it must have three qualities (*tria requiruntur*): wholeness or perfection (*integritas sive perfectio*), due proportion or harmony (*debita proportio sive consonantia*), and brilliance (*claritas*). The term "harmony" may sound sufficiently broad, but it is worth noting that in this passage Aquinas seems to be thinking chiefly about the kind of "harmony" that obtains between an image and what it images. This requirement for beauty, he says, is found in the Son because he is the "express image of the Father" (*inquantum est imago expressa Patris*).[5] No doubt the Stoic

[2] *Summa Theologiae* I, 5, 4, ad 1m (*quae visa placent*); I, 39, 8 (*tria requiruntur*); I–II, 27, 1, ad 3m (*sensus maximi cognoscitivi*). Works of Aquinas are conveniently consulted in *Sancti Thomae Aquinatis . . . Opera Omnia*, ed. Vernon J. Bourke, vols. I–XXV (New York: Musurgia Publishers, 1948–50). This is a photographic reproduction of the edition at Parma, 1852–73.

[3] "*Et ideo in vita contemplativa, quae consistit in actu rationis, per se et essentialiter invenitur pulchritudo.*" *Summa Theologiae* II–II, 180, 2, ad 3m.

[4] "*Sensus delectantur in rebus debite proportionatis, sicut in sibi similibus. . . . Et cognitio fit per assimilationem, assimilitudo autem respicit formam*" (*Summa Theologiae* I, 5, 4, ad 1m). Concerning the peculiarly subjective and emotive kind of knowledge called by neo-Thomists "knowledge through connaturality" or "knowledge through affective connaturality," see Thomas Gilby, *Poetic Experience* (New York, 1934), p. 21; Jacques Maritain, *Creative Intuition in Art and Poetry* (New York, 1953), pp. 117–25. See de Bruyne I, 26 and III, 23 on musical and visual harmonies between man and the universe in different phases of medieval aesthetics.

[5] *Summa Theologiae* I, 39, 8. Echoing Aristotle and other ancient writers, Aquinas adds that an image is said to be beautiful if it perfectly represents even an ugly object (*Unde videmus quod aliqua imago dicitur esse pulchra, si perfecte repraesentat rem, quamvis turpem*). It is perhaps permissible to reflect further that if an image

criterion of bright color occurs to Aquinas with a special recommendation in the light of the cathedral art with which he was familiar, the Byzantine mosaic, the rose-stained glass of nave or apse,[6] the bright painting of the school of Cimabue. "Bright colored objects," remarks Aquinas, "are said to be beautiful." Yet neo-scholastic commentators hasten to assure us, and plausibly, that such *claritas* is but the accent of perfection in the structural concept. They produce from an opusculum written either by Aquinas or by his master Albertus the phrase *resplendentia formae*—"the splendor of form shining upon the proportioned parts of matter, or upon diverse powers or actions." [7] In Aquinas, as in most of the theological and aesthetic writers of his century, and notably the Franciscans, we find the Plotinian and Platonic philosophy of light more radiant than ever. *Claritas, splendor, resplendentia, fulgor, lux, lumen*—such words recur throughout theological writing with almost as much frequency as words relating to *form* itself or to unity and being.[8] And we are not surprised to read in this context, as we have read before in Plato, Plotinus, and Augustine, that sight and hearing are the senses which preeminently open on beauty, because they are the preeminently intellectual senses (*maxime cognoscitivi*).[9]

---

is proportioned to an object (even an ugly object), the image by that very fact will have its own, internal, proportion or harmony, corresponding to the degree of harmony which the object must have in order to be an object at all. See the interesting speculation of Dorothy Sayers on "Trinitarian" aspects of poetic creation, *Unpopular Opinions* (London, 1946), p. 37, "Towards a Christian Aesthetic." John A. Duffy, *A Philosophy of Poetry Based on Thomistic Principles* (Washington, D.C., 1945), pp. 28-9, lists a number of passages on beauty in which Aquinas uses such terms as *consonantia, ordo, proportio* in a more directly internal sense to mean relation or location of parts (*situs partium*).

[6] Cf. Robert Grinnell, "Iconography and Philosophy in the Crucifixion Window at Poitiers," *Art Bulletin*, XXVIII (September, 1946), 171-96.

[7] *Opusculum de Pulchro et Bono* I, 6, 2. Cf. Jacques Maritain, *Art and Scholasticism*, trans. J. F. Scanlan (New York, 1943), pp. 25, 160; Leonard Callahan, *A Theory of Esthetic, According to the Principles of St. Thomas Aquinas* (Washington, D.C., 1927), pp. 31, 89, 126, quoting *Opuscula Selecta S. Thomae Aquinatis* (Paris, 1908) XXI, *De Pulchro et de Bono*: "[Pulchrum] congregat omnia, et hoc habet ex parte formae cujus resplendentia facit pulchrum. . . . Secundum autem quod forma resplendet super partes materiae, sic est pulchrum habens rationem congregandi. . . . Ratio pulchri in universali consistit in resplendentia formae super partes materiae proportionatas, vel super diversas vires, vel actiones."

[8] Gilbert and Kuhn, p. 141. For an extended account of the pervasive 13th-century neo-Platonic and Biblical philosophy of light—an aesthetic of light, mystical, physical, and cosmological—see de Bruyne III, 3-29, "L'esthétique de la lumière." See Robert Grosseteste, *On Light*, trans. Clare C. Riedl (Milwaukee, 1942).

[9] "*Illi sensus praecipue respiciunt pulchrum qui maxime cognoscitivi sunt, scilicet visus et auditus rationi deservientes: dicimus enim pulchra visibilia et pulchros sonos; non enim dicimus pulchros sapores aut odores*" (*Summa Theologiae* I–II, 27, 1, ad 3m). The opinion of Aquinas seems, however, by no means rigid. Other passages (*Summa Theologiae* I, 91, 3, ad 3m; *In Libris Aristotelis De Coelo et Mundo Expositio* II, 14) suggest that he looked upon the human pleasure in smelling flowers as close to the beautiful when compared with an animal's pleasure in smelling food. See John A. Duffy, *A Philosophy of Beauty . . .* , p. 62.

Beauty is thought to be apprehended in a kind of reposeful contemplation (*pulchrum . . . cuius ipsa apprehensio placet*) [1] and in that sense is different from the good (*bonum*),[2] which is the object of appetite. The conception is much better known to modern aestheticians under its Kantian name of "disinterest." There may be difficulties here, relating to the fact that the very act of knowing is a kind of possessing, so that "possession" in the sense of control or ownership, though less often requisite for aesthetic knowing than for other kinds of knowing, is scarcely the crux of the argument. We know the picture that we see in the art gallery (or in our own collection), and we know the apple that we eat, and it is these two kinds of knowledge or possession that must be compared—the amorphic and even destructively internal possession of the apple and the more coolly distanced ocular union with the picture. The pleasure afforded by a thing we call beautiful—whether a natural object or a product of art—would seem to differ from other pleasures in being more steady and cumulative and more surely held by the mind, and more charged with symbolic intimations. In the case of the overtly symbolic or referential arts at least, and especially in that of verbal arts, it is easy to make a distinction between those, the rhetorical, whose end is persuasory and dynamic (to move us toward their referents) and those others, the poetic —sometimes nowadays called the "autotelic"—arts, which seem to absorb the interest of their referents and hold it in themselves by a kind of symbolic suspension.

One of the most striking technical feats of Thomist aesthetic consists in its being able to confront rather squarely that paradox of the two stones —plain beauty and excellently carved beauty—which was bequeathed by Plotinus. This is accomplished through one of the central concepts of the metaphysics, that of "analogy," the very concept by which the whole world of created reality is kept both dependent upon and apart from God. Both above and below, beauty is in everything. It is a transcendental, surpassing "all limits of kind or category." It is always relative to the individual form.[3] It is predicated differently (that is, analogously) of each beautiful object in the wide variety of objects to which we give that

---

[1] *Summa Theologiae* I–II, 271, ad 3m. Cf. *In Librum Beati Dionysii de Divinis Nominibus Expositio* IV, v, 356: "*Quamvis autem pulchrum et bonum sint idem subiecto, quia tam claritas quam consonantia sub ratione boni continentur, tamen ratione differunt: nam pulchrum addit supra bonum, ordinem ad vim cognoscitivam illud esse huiusmodi*" (ed. Fra Ceslai Pera, O.P., Turin and Rome, 1950, p. 115).

[2] Yet the distinction again is hardly rigid. *Summa Theologiae* II–II, 145, 2, "*Utrum honestum sit idem quod decorum*," argues that moral good is spiritual beauty: "*Et ideo honestum est idem spirituali decori. Unde Augustinus dicit . . . 'Honestum voco intelligibilem pulchritudinem, quam spiritualem nos proprie dicimus.'* "

[3] "*Pulchritudo quodamodo dicitur per respectum ad aliquid. Alia enim est pulchritudo spiritus et alia corporis, atque alia hujus et illius corporis*" (*In Librum Beati Dionysii de Divinis Nominibus Expositio* IV, v, 339; ed. cit., p. 113).

name. As one neo-Thomist,[4] with his eye on the logical and semantic difficulties involved, has put it: we use an ordinary, literal specific term like "man" in a way that does not admit the idea of more or less and in a way that is standard or univocal. Jack is not less a man than Jim, and each is a man in just the same way and for just the same reason. But it is clear that the contrary is true of a term like "beauty." Beauty is indeed everywhere, and it is more or less. And in each case (and most clearly in each case of expressive art) beauty is of a different kind or occurs for a different reason. The details always have to be taken into account in some special way. As another neo-Thomist has said wittily: "The lack of a head or an arm is a serious defect in a woman but of much less account in a statue—whatever disappointment M. Ravaisson may have felt at being unable to *complete* the Venus of Melos." [5]

For such reasons, the discussion of the term "beauty" in Aquinas is not closely related to, and is not at all dependent upon, the discussion of the term "art," however close or inevitable the association between the two terms may have come to seem in later times. Art in the Middle Ages is just the right way of making whatever anybody happens to be making (*recta ratio factibilium*)—each artifact according to its own plan, in a hierarchy, a cathedral being worth more than a cowshed, but each one right (and beautiful) in its own way. In this hierarchy there were, from a modern point of view, certain curious placements—painting in the same class with saddle-making, for instance, because saddles were painted.[6] The physical, servile, or mechanical arts in general (not only saddle-making and shoe-making but sculpture, architecture, and painting) were on a plane inferior to that of the seven liberal arts named in the canon of the encyclopedist Martianus Capella: grammar, rhetoric, logic, dialectic, music, arithmetic, geometry, and astronomy. And these in turn were, of course, inferior to the theological arts. The medieval conception viewed from its lower end (the root of any functionalist theory of art) has been neatly epitomized in our century by the neo-Thomist sculptor and theorist Eric Gill in the title of his book *Beauty Looks After Herself*. "To make a drain pipe," he says in another book, "is as much the work of an artist as it is to make paintings or poems." [7] Properly speaking, there are no fine arts in such a system. The neo-Thomist philosopher Jacques Maritain offers us his own version of the two stones of Plotinus when he says that what we now call the fine arts are right ways of making which are some-

---

[4] Thomas Gilby, *Barbara Celarent* (London, 1949), pp. 78-9.

[5] Jacques Maritain, *Art and Scholasticism*, trans. J. F. Scanlan (New York, 1943), p. 27. The joke is not altogether spoiled by the fact that this Hellenistic statue was not made à la Rodin, and that it *would* actually be completed by the restoration of its arms. See R. H. Wilenski, *The Meaning of Modern Sculpture* (London, c. 1933), p. 66.

[6] Gilbert and Kuhn, pp. 157-8.

[7] *Art* (London, 1935), p. 4.

how specially directed to the splendid rightness of beauty—a species is in a peculiar way turned back upon its transcendental genus.[8]

And in all this what of poetry? The literary student will by now have missed any conspicuous mention of poetry either under the Thomist head of beauty (what especially affects the senses of sight and hearing) or under that of art (a discipline of honest making). We hear that the Middle Ages, following such ancient writers as Quintilian and Augustine, were likely to treat poetry as a pendant to logic, or to rhetoric. (The Dutch Meistersingers called themselves rhetoricians, for poetry was a "secondary rhetoric.") Or in deference to Aristotle's dictum, repeated by Aquinas, that one cannot think logically without framing images, poetry might be made a propaedeutic to logic.[9] The student who inquires about poetry in the system of Aquinas himself will search the texts to find poetry treated only here and there, either as a problem in semantics—the locale of a kind of subrational metaphoric evasion (to be distinguished from theological analogy)[1]—or as an art of verbal reasoning lower even than sophistic or rhetoric (that is, at the bottom) in a scale which has Aristotelian metaphysical demonstration at the top.[2]

> Poetic knowledge concerns matters which through a deficiency in their truth cannot be laid hold of by the reason; hence the reason has to be beguiled by means of certain similitudes. Theology, on the other hand, deals with matters which are above reason. So the symbolic mode is common to both types of discourse; neither type is suited to reasoning.[3]

VI

THE train of sceptical and scientific thinking which began with Galileo and Descartes was not friendly to the kind of aesthetic we have been

---

[8] *Art and Scholasticism* (New York, 1943), pp. 33–4. See his later adjustment of this view—beauty an "end beyond the end" of "poetry," a "transcendental correlative"—in *Creative Intuition in Art and Poetry* (New York, 1951), pp. 167–71.

[9] Gilbert and Kuhn, p. 157. Cf. Aristotle, *De Anima* III, 7; Aquinas, *In Boethii de Trinitate* 6, 2, ad 5m.

[1] Cf. Walter J. Ong, "Wit and Mystery: A Revaluation," *Speculum*, XXII (1947), 324.

[2] Cf. Walter J. Ong, "The Province of Rhetoric and Poetic," *Modern Schoolman*, XIX (1942), 25, quoting Aquinas, *In I. Analytica Posteriora*, lectio 1.

[3] "*Ad tertium dicendum, quod poetica scientia est de his quae propter defectum veritatis non possunt a ratione capi; unde oportet quod quasi quibusdam similitudinibus ratio seducatur: theologia autem est de his quae sunt supra rationem; et ideo modus symbolicus utrique communis est, cum neutra rationi proportionetur.*" *Commentum in Primum Librum Sententiarum Magistri Petri Lombardi, Prologus*, q.1, a5, ad 3m. See M.-D. Chenu, O.P., *Introduction à l'Étude de Saint Thomas D'Aquin* (Montreal, 1950), pp. 93, 144, for a succinct statement of the opposition between the Aristotelian and scholastic scientific Latin style of Aquinas and the Platonic and Augustinian poetical styles of irony, metaphor, and symbol.

sketching, at least not to its ontological supports, Platonic or Thomistic. Yet as early as the late 17th century and notably in the *Monadology* and related essays and letters of Leibniz, an idealistic reaction set in which was not without affinities for neo-Platonism and which, if pursued through German aesthetics of the later 18th century to the flowering of German and English criticism,[4] would provide a chain of statements about beauty through unity and order[5] with which one might amply continue our history. The kind of "organic" unity acclaimed by Coleridge and the Germans, with its strongly pantheistic implications about the organic structure of the universe and the union in knowledge and being of subject and object, will be a part of our theme in later chapters (17 and 18). By the end of the 19th century, several forms of idealism had become available for litterateurs of a metaphysical bent. They might turn to various romantic and neo-Platonic forms—or, just after 1900, to Crocean expressionism. It was a distinct anachronism, however, that the novelist James Joyce should at about that date allow an acquaintance with scholastic philosophy gained in his school days with the Jesuits in Clongowes and Dublin to determine the character of the rather elaborate exposition of an aesthete's creed which occurs toward the end of *A Portrait of the Artist as a Young Man*.[6] An account of this retrospective and romanticized piece of scholasticism may serve appropriately as a conclusion to the present chapter and to the present section of our history. In a rather florid, even pompous, yet sufficiently accurate style of schoolroom metaphysics Stephen Dedalus expounds to his friend Lynch a series of freely rendered Thomistic theses.

> You see I use the word *arrest*. I mean that the tragic emotion is static. Or rather the dramatic emotion is. The feelings excited by improper art are kinetic, desire or loathing. . . . The arts which excite them, pornographical or didactic, are therefore improper arts. The esthetic emotion . . . is therefore static. The mind is arrested and raised above desire and loathing.—*Portrait*, p. 205

> Aquinas . . . says that is beautiful the apprehension of which pleases.   p. 207

> · · ·

[4] See a convenient summary by James Benziger, "Organic Unity: Leibniz to Coleridge," PMLA, LXVI (March, 1951), 24–48.

[5] See for instance Coleridge's three essays "On the Principles of Genial Criticism," *Biographia Literaria* (ed. J. Shawcross), II, esp. p. 239.

[6] "The lore . . . was only a garner of slender sentences from Aristotle's Poetics and Psychology and a *Synopsis Philosophiae Scholasticae ad mentem divi Thomae.*" The *Synopsis* is apparently not to be identified with any school book actually used by Joyce. The quotations from *A Portrait of the Artist* which follow in our text are from the Viking Compass Edition, New York, 1956, by permission of The Viking Press, Inc.

. . . all people who admire a beautiful object find in it certain relations which satisfy and coincide with the stages themselves of all esthetic apprehension.   p. 209

Aquinas says: *Ad pulcritudinem tria requiruntur integritas, consonantia, claritas.* . . . Do these correspond to the phases of apprehension?   p. 211

The synthesis of immediate perception is followed by the analysis of apprehension. Having first felt that it is one thing, you feel now that it is a thing. You apprehend it as complex, multiple, divisible, separable, made up of its parts, the result of its parts and their sum, harmonious. That is *consonantia.*   p. 212

. . . you make the only synthesis which is logically and esthetically permissible. You see that it is that thing which it is and no other thing. The radiance of which he speaks is the scholastic *quidditas,*[7] the *whatness* of a thing. . . . The instant wherein that supreme quality of beauty, the clear radiance of the esthetic image, is apprehended luminously by the mind which has been arrested by its wholeness and fascinated by its harmony is the luminous silent stasis of esthetic pleasure.—p. 213

We have Aquinas, we might say, with inverted emphasis, or the *tria* of required objective qualities seen upside down in the deep pool of the poet's imagination. It is an idealistic modification which rings very naturally against the background of the preceding century. The other form of idealism, the Platonic or purely symbolic, by which beauty is "a light from some other world, the idea of which matter was but the shadow," is explicitly rejected by Stephen (pp. 212–13). "That is literary talk." And to complete the account, it is worth noting that in Joyce's earlier and longer version of the *Portrait* entitled *Stephen Hero,* the idea of "claritas" has a somewhat different accent.

Claritas is *quidditas.* After the analysis which discovers the second quality the mind makes the only possible synthesis and discovers the third quality. This is the moment which I call epiphany. First we recognize that the object is *one* integral thing, then we recognize that it is an organized composite structure, a *thing* in fact: finally, when the relation of the parts is exquisite, when the parts are adjusted to the special point, we recognize that it is *that* thing which it is. Its soul, its whatness, leaps to us from the vestment of its appearance. The soul of the commonest object,

[7] As Stephen expounds the matter, this radiance is more like scholastic *haecceitas* or individuality. *Quidditas* is actually the Aristotelian specific universal, the essence of the main class to which the individual belongs. See Aquinas, *On Being and Essence,* ed. A. A. Maurer (Toronto, 1949).

the structure of which is so adjusted, seems to us radiant. The object achieves its epiphany.[8]

There is more about discovery here, less about a phase of apprehension and feeling. More about the soul of the object, less about the imagination of the artist. With its now current Joycean word *epiphany*, the passage may strike us as more clearly like Joyce himself and significantly less like Stephen Dedalus, rebellious aesthete, scribbler of *fin de siècle* verses, "priest of the eternal imagination."

Taken as a dual statement and dramatically ambiguous emphasis on the relation between object and response in the experience of the beautiful, the aesthetic of Stephen Dedalus may be thought of as epitomizing and holding unresolved a choice that has haunted not only aesthetics but general epistemology since early times. The answers we have been hearing up to now have borne far more heavily on object than on response or feeling. We have yet to hear the opposite case in any strength. By way of anticipating some of the main themes of the history which lies ahead of us and of indicating their relation to what has gone before, one might draw a diagram of two radically opposed axes of aesthetic theory, thus:

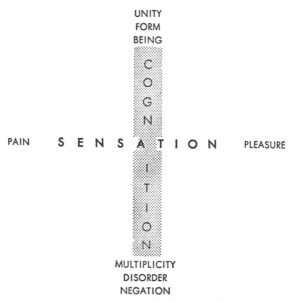

UNITY
FORM
BEING

C
O
G
N

PAIN   S E N S A T I O N   PLEASURE

I
T
I
O
N

MULTIPLICITY
DISORDER
NEGATION

The classical theories of antiquity range themselves along the vertical axis, with Plotinus one of the most systematic classical spokesmen but at the same time the most subjectively idealistic. We have had so far no instance of a theory lying simply along the horizontal axis—though the

[8] *Stephen Hero* (New York, 1944), p. 213. Copyright 1944, 1955 by New Directions and reprinted by permission of the publisher, New Directions.

affective clause—*quod placet*—is somewhat prominent with Aquinas. The era of fully horizontal theory does not appear until the 18th and 19th centuries. In the *Portrait* Stephen guards against one form of affectivism, the exclusively sensate.

> The desire and loathing excited by improper esthetic means are really not esthetic emotions not only because they are kinetic in character but also because they are not more than physical. Our flesh shrinks from what it dreads and responds to the stimulus of what it desires by a purely reflex action of the nervous system. Our eyelid closes before we are aware that the fly is about to enter our eye.—p. 241

Some of the most refined theories of aesthetic value which have appeared since the date of the *Portrait* have been attempts to raise the horizontalism of sensate and purely emotive theory into an alignment with the cognitive. Modern aesthetics may be thought of, provisionally, as operating along a line drawn at some intermediate angle of our diagram.

SUPPLEMENT

Eryximachus spoke as follows: . . . . medicine may be regarded generally as the knowledge of the loves and desires of the body, and how to satisfy them or not; and the best physician is he who is able to separate fair love from foul, or to convert one into the other; and he who knows how to eradicate and how to implant love, whichever is required, and can reconcile the most hostile elements in the constitution and make them loving friends, is a skilful practitioner. Now the most hostile are the most opposite, such as hot and cold, bitter and sweet, moist and dry, and the like. And my ancestor, Asclepius, knowing how to implant friendship and accord in these elements, was the creator of our art, as our friends the poets here tell us, and I believe them; and not only medicine in every branch, but the arts of gymnastic and husbandry are under his dominion. Any one who pays the least attention to the subject will also perceive that in music there is the same reconciliation of opposites; and I suppose that this must have been the meaning of Heracleitus, although his words are not accurate; for he says that The One is united by disunion, like the harmony of the bow and lyre. Now there is an absurdity in saying that harmony is discord or is composed of elements which are still in a state of discord. But what he probably meant was, that harmony is composed of differing notes of higher or lower pitch which disagreed once, but are now reconciled by the art of music; for if the higher and lower notes still disagreed, there could be no harmony,—clearly not. For harmony is a symphony, and symphony is an agreement; but an agreement of disagreements while they disagree there cannot be; you cannot harmonize that which disagrees. In like manner rhythm is compounded of elements short and long, once differing and now in accord; which accordance, as in the former instance, medicine, so in all these other cases, music implants, making love and unison to grow up among them; and thus music, too, is concerned with the principles of love in their application to harmony and rhythm. Again, in the essential nature of harmony and rhythm there is no difficulty in discerning love which has not yet become double. But when you want to use them in actual life, either in the composition of songs or in the correct performance of airs or metres composed already, which latter is called education, then the difficulty begins, and the good artist is needed.

—Plato, *Symposium*, 186–7, trans. Benjamin Jowett

Do love and harmony arise through diversity, or in spite of diversity?

PART TWO

CHAPTER 8

FURTHER MEDIEVAL THEMES

§ *metaphysics of beauty reviewed, harmony, light, number (the quadrivium), applications to literature, metrical discussions, Latin and vernacular* (metrum, rhythmus, rhyme)—II. *the trivium, rhetoric as verbal technique,* Martianus Capella, *dictamen,* Geoffrey of Vinsauf, "*colors,*" *Chaucer's application, importance to him of conventions*—III. *logic vs. grammar,* Servius on Vergil, *identifying the figures*—IV. *allegory, the world as God's book,* Aquinas, *symbolism of things and words, Dante's Letter, the four levels,* Fulgentius on Virgil—V. *The Owl and the Nightingale,* Chaucer on "moralitee," *Aquinas on secular literature and the Scriptures, Dante's* Convivio, *figura, the Medieval grotesque*—VI. *Boccaccio on theology and poetry, Platonism in Church Fathers, Augustine's* Confessions, *the Middle Ages devoted to theology, not literary criticism* §

O UR LAST CHAPTER HAS PICKED OUT CERTAIN POINTS OF INTEREST IN the history of a theme which runs rather evenly through a vast period of European literary history, the thousand years or more which extend from the twilight of pagan antiquity in the fifth century, A.D., to the Renaissance of antique learning in the fifteenth. That theme was the metaphysical aesthetic of beauty in unity, order, and being. It had, as we have noted briefly, two metaphoric developments: the aesthetic of Platonic and Biblical luminosity (the beauty of brightness seen as the analogue of clear knowledge and of the clearly knowable) and the aesthetic of numerical and musical harmony (the beauty of ordered sound, related to the Pythagorean and Platonic beauty of the numerically ordered

ground of being). Both these metaphoric dimensions might have been illustrated much more fully not only from scholastic metaphysicians but
from other writers more directly concerned with the liberal arts—poets,
grammarians, and rhetoricians. The aesthetic of numerical harmony, we
ought to note, is in fact involved in all four branches of the Quadrivium
or higher medieval school curriculum: arithmetic, geometry, music, and
astronomy (the last including in its purview the "music of the spheres").
This aesthetic, we are told by a recent historian,[1] reached its climax in
a very quantitatively minded 12th century. The succeeding century, more
metaphysically and qualitatively minded, was that in which Aquinas made
the remarks about integrity, harmony, and brilliance to which we have
already alluded, and in which a school of writers including Grosseteste,
Bonaventure, and the unknown author of a *De Intelligentiis*, produced a
far more pervasively physical and cosmological account of light as the
fundamental form and energy of all being, the source and form of all
beauty—from the mineral realm dull but susceptible of polish and glitter,
out through water, air, fire, the moon, and the other heavens to the
crystalline sphere and the empyrean. "Light is the most beautiful, the
most delightful, the very best of all material things." [2] Light is "the beauty
and perfection of all material things." [3]

A history of literary theory ought to *try* to discern the theoretical
working of such overall mystiques as that of light and number during the
Middle Ages in their most specific connections with literature. Such an
aim, however, may not carry very far. These philosophies were perhaps
not likely to foster any specific code of the literary man (an Horatian
Ars) or the literary philosopher (a *Poetics*). What the historian of medieval ideas may call with some justice a "collective spiritual life of gigantic
proportions" does seem to have produced during the Middle Ages, along
with the metaphysical and cosmological strains of luminist philosophy
which we have seen, an equally pronounced literary tradition. The tradition, however, is not properly a theoretical one. It is a tradition of literary
content—it can be described approximately in lists of nouns, adjectives,
and verbs referring to light and brightness and radiant beauty. The
literary historian gives us, for example, the roseate effulgence at the end
of the *Commedia*, the play of sunlight on the helms, weapons, shields and
gonfalons at Roncevalles—

> *E Durandal, cum ies et clere et blanche!*
> *Cuntre soleil si reluis et reflambes!*—

[1] De Bruyne III, 3-29, "*L'Esthétique de la Lumière.*"

[2] Bonaventure, *Commentaria in Librum Sapientiae* VII, 10 (*Opera Omnia*, 1882,
VI, 153); De Bruyne III, 23.

[3] Grosseteste, *De Luce seu de Inchoatione Formarum* (Ludwig Baur, *Die Philo-
sophischen Werke des Robert Grosseteste, Bischofs von Lincoln*, Münster, 1912,
p. 56); De Bruyne III, 28.

or the clear light of moon and stars (*"Clere est la lune, les esteiles flam-bent"*) over the same objects. He gives us of course the white skin of "Bele Erembors" or "Bele Yolanz," the golden hair, the bright eyes, the vermeil, the roses and lilies of all the other ladies, even some of the knights, in the romances.[4] But we all know that poetry, even medieval poetry, can be written about dark things too. There is nothing here relevant to a general formal principle of poetry. Perhaps the features of Gothic architecture to which we have partly alluded in Chapter 7, its *verticalisme* joined with its *luminisme*,[5] the lofty window openings and the stained glass, come closer to showing a formal relation between the medieval aesthetic of light and the working of an actual art.

The aesthetic of proportion and number, as we have perhaps already suggested, was more likely to connect with, or even to start from, technical problems of musical art. Yet even such technicalities may give us relatively thin ideas about a poetics. St. Augustine, as we have seen, derived his metaphysics of beautiful number and order from a single line of a hymn by St. Ambrose—or from his contemplation of such geometrical entities as triangle, square, and circle. In his *De Musica* we find a theology of harmonious order connected with a technical prosody written on classical quantitative principles. Boethius, the Roman senator of the early sixth century whose mournfully anti-aesthetic *De Consolatione Philosophiae* was a classic of the Middle Ages and Renaissance, was also a theorist of numerical harmony who wrote a *De Musica* and a *De Arithmetica*. In these we read once more that unity, number, and proportion are the Divine principles of all being, and that music is their universal expression, alike in the most cosmic and the most humanly technical senses. The music made by human instruments is an imitation of the music of the world, the harmony of the four elements. "How could the swift movement of that celestial machinery proceed in silence? The sound may not come to our ears—this happens for a number of reasons—but the extreme velocity with which those great bodies are whirled about cannot fail to generate some sound."[6]

Later on, metrical speculation, such as that in the letters of the Bishop Sidonius Apollinaris or that in the *Ars Metrica* of the Venerable Bede,[7] is couched in terms which were very largely decided by one of the great technical changes involved in the emergence of vernacular literature from Latin, the change from quantitative, non-accentual verse (*metrum,* or

---

[4] De Bruyne III, 11–16, citing in part Emile Legouis, *Défense de la poésie française, à l'usage des lecteurs anglais* (London, 1912).

[5] De Bruyne III, 10.

[6] *De Musica* I, ii. *"Qui enim fieri potest ut tam velox coeli machina tacito silentique cursu moveatur? Et si ad nostras aures sonus ille non pervenit, quod multis fieri de causis necesse est, non poterit tamen motus tam velocissimus ita magnorum corporum, nullos omnino sonos ciere."* The *De Musica* of Boethius may be consulted in J. C. Migne, *Patrologia Latina*, LXIII (Paris, 1847). Cf. De Bruyne I, 12–13.

[7] Saintsbury I, 384; Atkins, *English Criticism* I, 45–6.

meter proper) to accentual verse (*rhythmus*), the new form of Latin hymns and their later parodies in Goliardic songs and of vernacular poetry, both sacred and profane. The transition from Latin quantitative theory to the inductively discovered new rhythms—the new accentual swing, and the new *magic* of rhyme (curious deflection from the prose *logic* of homoioteleuton)—was doubtless a challenge of considerable gravity to theoretically minded litterateurs of those centuries. For us today, looking back from the other side of the whole vernacular and romantic diversification (both medieval and modern), it is relatively easy to see that rules of phonetic form in poetry arise in each age from the concrete nature of a spoken language. It worries us little that we have to accept somewhat different phonetic materials in our approximate scansion of Virgilian hexameter, of Chaucerian rhyme royal, of Racinian Alexandrine. The problem is one which we may well consider as subsumed under the more general conflict between neo-classic theories of decorum and romantic experimental violations—the general conflict with which the 16th century was to be engaged so busily.

II

MEDIEVAL literary criticism and theory, where it appears as such, is connected less often with the higher part of the school curriculum (the Quadrivium and its mathematical implications) than with the lower, the Trivium, the three grade-school subjects, Grammar, Logic, and Rhetoric.[8] Most obviously, and perhaps least profoundly, criticism appears all through late antiquity and the middle ages as Rhetoric. Rhetoric, as we have seen, was from the start, in the theory of Isocrates or Aristotle, concerned equally with verse and prose examples and was never far removed from the purposes of a technical poetics. If we consider style—diction, figures of syntax and word order, metaphor, and "ornament" of all kinds —in a means-end relation to the practical, hortatory purposes of forensic or parliamentary speeches, then we have "rhetoric" in the double sense— verbal artifice in the cause of legal or political results. But if we consider the same details in a part-whole relationship to the more cognitive, the more dramatic, features of a verbal composition—love, honor, war and the expression of human feeling about these things—then we have, crude or refined, what is implicitly poetics—a study of verbal meaning at its several interacting levels. The difference between the Middle Ages and Classical Antiquity in the management of such rhetorical poetics was mainly a diminution of whatever classical tendency there had been to philosophize or understand the repertory of figures and a corresponding

[8] See Paul Abelson, *The Seven Liberal Arts, A Study in Mediaeval Culture* (New York, 1906).

increase in the formalizing, stereotyping, and prescriptive tendency—a thickening of the atmosphere of artificiality, euphuism, flowers, incense, ornament. The models were for the most part late Hellenistic (like the pseudo-Ciceronian treatise *Ad Herennium*) or Second Sophistic (Latin derivations from the second-century Hermogenes). The role of Rhetoric as sweet adorner may well be illustrated from a celebrated, though perhaps to our eyes fantastically allegorical and conceited, treatise on the seven liberal arts (of Quadrivium and Trivium) which stands conveniently at the exit from antiquity. The *De Nuptiis Mercuriae et Philologiae* of the fifth-century African Martianus Capella celebrates the wedding of wit and learning—that is, of the inventive or imaginative faculty and the faculty of learning and understanding. Whatever the actual performance, the title is an epitome and promise of all that a literary scholar presumably might desire. The seven arts appear as Muses, to be recommended by Mercury to Philologia his bride. The book on Rhetoric opens with a flourish of trumpets (*Interea sonuere tubae* . . .) and Rhetoric steps forth:

> a stately woman of lofty stature, and confidence greater than common, but radiantly handsome, helmed and crowned, weaponed both for defence and with flashing arms wherewith she could smite her enemies with a thundering coruscation. Under her armpits, and thrown over her shoulder in Latian fashion, was a vest, exhibiting embroidery of all possible *figures* in varied hue, while her breast was baldricked with gems of the most exquisite colour. As she walked her arms clashed, so that you would have thought the broken levin to rattle—with explosive handclaps, like the collision of clouds, so that you might even believe her capable of wielding the thunderbolts of Jove. For it is she who, like a mighty queen of all things, can direct them whither she will and call them back whenever she chooses, and unbend men to tears or incite them to rage, and sway the minds of civic crowds as of warring armies. She brought beneath her sway the senate, the rostra, the courts at Rome.[9]

In short, rhetoric is a powerful form of incitation and subdual; it works with an armory of flashing devices. The thousand years of Medieval Europe are, as Saintsbury observes, a period of human history which has scarcely been paralleled in its cultural continuity—and especially in respect to the rhetorico-poetical tradition. The encyclopedic pageant of Martianus is an allegory which remains appropriate for the whole period. In the Carolingian age rhetoric appears notably in the service of

[9] Translated by Saintsbury I, 351–2. Cf. *De Nuptiis Philologiae et Mercurii*, V, 426 ff (Adolfus Dick, ed. *Martianus Capella*, Leipzig, 1925, pp. 211–12).

the flowery diplomacy of court letter-writing (*dictamen*) [1]—another application in the doubly "rhetorical" form of suasive verbal artifice. During the late 12th and the early 13th centuries, the poetical application, which had always been ready (and which by the end of the Middle Ages would flourish elegantly in the school of French poets called the "*Grands Rhétoriqueurs*"), broke out in a "new poetics" among French and English international scholars—in the *Ars Versificatoria* of Matthew of Vendôme, for instance, or the *Poetria Nova* and the *De Coloribus Rhetoricis* of the Norman Englishman Geoffrey of Vinsauf. The main model for these treatises was the pseudo-Ciceronian *Ad Herennium*.

The list of ornaments in Vinsauf's *Poetria* includes sixty-three, divided into difficult ornaments or tropes and easy ornaments or "colors." Colors (or figures) are in turn divided into those of speech (*figurae verborum*) and those of thought (*figurae sententiarum*). The distinctive features of the system are the formal definition of the figures, the prescription of the contexts in which each is at home, and the practical illustration. For example, "Apostrophe" is a turning toward, or address to, some absent thing or person or some abstraction personified. It is good for amplifying a theme. King Richard Coeur de Lion was mortally wounded on a Friday. To express your grief, deliver a reproachful series of addresses, to that very day Friday, to the soldier who was guilty of the blow, and so on.

> With grievous words express your hour of grief.
> . . .
> O Vendreday, O tearful, bitter blight,
> Not day but night, and Venus turned to venom.
> You gave the wound. . . .[2]

Within one figure of course others can be contained. A 13th-century manuscript of the *Poetria Nova* glosses the passage just quoted as follows:

> Note that in the expression *Venus . . . venenum* appears the verbal color known as agnomination, which may be defined as an echo of one word by another which differs only in a single letter or in certain syllables or letters. See the chapter on verbal colors.[3]

---

[1] John C. Mendenhall, *Aureate Terms* (Lancaster, 1919), p. 21.
[2] *Temporibus luctus his verbis exprime luctum:*
. . .
O Veneris lacrimosa dies! O sidus amarum!
Illa dies tua nox fuit et Venus illa venenum.
Illa dedit vulnus. . . .—ll. 368 ff.
Edmond Faral, *Les Arts Poétiques du XIIᵉ et du XIIIᵉ Siècle* (Paris, 1924), p. 208.
[3] Karl Young, "Chaucer and Geoffrey of Vinsauf," *Modern Philology*, XLI (February 1944), 175: "*Nota quod dicendo illa Venus fuit venenum utitur colore*

In the complicated and sometimes perverse history of the literary self-consciousness perhaps nothing ever goes to waste—not a vanity is given in vain—no aridity or pomposity appears which may not be ploughed under to sprout again and bloom in its own way another season. The systems of technical stereotyping, the "conventions" of rhetorical figure and of literary genre, as well as those of making love and war, which characterize the Middle Ages, may appear as simple and flat conventions in the work of one poet, but in another they may be an intricate repertory of starting points for fun and feeling. The medieval poet spoke not a dialect more restricted or jejune than that of a liberated and naturalistic age (the language of a Sandburg chanting the fog over Chicago or slabs of the sunburnt West) but on the contrary the language of a highly civilized and sophisticated living past. Chaucer, the medieval poet most familiar to modern English readers, will come readily enough to mind in his diverse dramatic adaptations of fixities—his ironically slanted portraits of superlative persons in the Canterbury Prologue, his echoes of the liturgy in the Prioress's Tale, of patristic and French satirical misogyny in the Wife of Bath's Prologue, of courtly love, of romance, of Arthurian legend, of the vulgar fabliau, of uncounted other literary and social conventions in all that he wrote. The rules of the rhetorical prescribers too afforded him many an oddly tilted detail—one of the examples most easily recognizable today being, in fact, a reference to the *New Poetry* of Vinsauf. A cock is carried off by a fox on a Friday. Now here would be a chance to illustrate the working of those rules.

> O Venus, that art goddesse of plesaunce,
> Syn that thy servant was this Chauntecleer,
> And in thy servyce dide al his poweer,
> Moore for delit than world to multiplye,
> Why woldestow suffre hym on thy day to dye?
> O Gaufred, deere maister soverayn,
> That whan thy worthy kyng Richard was slayn
> With shot, compleynedest his deethe so soore,
> Why ne hadde I now thy sentence and thy loore
> The Friday for to chide, as diden ye?

---

verborum qui dicitur anominacio, et provenit quando de nomine ad idem nomen acceditur commutacione vel addicione unius litere vel silabarum aut literarum, ut patebit in capitulo de coloribus verborum."

    Atkins, *English Criticism*, I, presents a helpful summary of Vinsauf's ornaments (pp. 201–3) and tries to disentangle the terms *trope, color,* and *figure* (pp. 108–9). A number of duplicate devices seem to occur, and the lines drawn between the main classes must seem to a modern reader tenuous in the extreme.

This is part of the history of applied rhetoric.[4] It is not a direct or sober examination of the classico-medieval rhetorical claim. In its implications, however, it may perhaps be read as a substitute for a kind of rhetorical theory which in that age does not seem to have been written.

III

THE relation of the other two parts of the medieval Trivium, Grammar and Logic, to literary criticism has been for succeeding ages far less apparent, and it was indeed more submerged even in the Middle Ages. The second part of the Trivium, Logic (or Dialectic), the methodology of metaphysics and science, may be conceived as a lurking antipoetics, the inheritor of the dialectic bias which we have noted as far back as the pre-Platonic "quarrel between the philosophers and the poets," and to which we shall turn again in a chapter on the rhetorical issues of the 17th century (Ch. 10). By the same token, medieval "Grammatica," handed down by such authorities as the late classical treatises of Donatus and Priscian and the Book on Grammar in the *Wedding* of Martianus, undoubtedly carries on, though at a level largely taken for granted be· neath tangled technicalities, the method of poetic and polysemous interpretation which we earlier noted in Stoic philosophers and Hellenistic grammarians. The late classical and medieval grammarians are on the side of the poets, but in a way which they themselves scarcely understand and which they are never concerned to argue or expound. The actual performance borrows, on its most obviously literary side, much from rhetoric—the difference being that instead of prescribing figures in advance of occasions, the grammarians, in their role as practical explicators, dissect the parts of an existing text and, with an air of justifying something, tag these parts with the names of the rhetorico-poetical repertory. Thus in the greatest Latin commentary on Virgil, that of the fifth-century variorum editor Servius, we read that when Virgil says *Arma virumque, arma*, meaning "war," is a trope called "metonymy," and the order of the two words is an inversion called "hyperbaton." When Virgil borrows and alters a phrase from Ennius, Servius points out that the figure is "acyrologia." When Virgil describes the Libyan harbor where the ships of Aeneas take refuge (*Est in secessu longo locus* . . .), the figure is not "topographia" (which is *rei verae descriptio*) but "topothesia" (*fictus secundum poeticam licentiam locus*).[5]

---

[4] See J. M. Manly, "Chaucer and the Rhetoricians," *Proceedings of the British Academy*, XII (1926), 95–113. "But that some of Chaucer's freest and most delightful work should contain twice as much rhetoric as some of his least inspired compositions is a puzzle that demands investigation" (p. 108). ". . . he came more and more to make only a dramatic use of these rhetorical elements" (p. 110).

[5] Saintsbury I, 334–9. See p. 340 for Servius on the three styles.

IV

WHERE grammar came closest to an adequate rationale of literary criticism was not, however, in such feats of technical classification but in a somewhat differently slanted, though also anciently inherited, conception: namely, that allegorical and etymological meanings were naturally present in poetic texts and deserved explication. For here grammar was allied as a method to a view which we have already noted in ancient philosophers, in Church fathers as exegetes of the Scriptures, and in medieval theologians, the view according to which the created world in its radiant order and hierarchy is God's symbolic book. The world is the shell or cover (*cortex*) of an inner meaning (*nucleus*), the veil over a hidden meaning, the entrance to such a meaning, the lower symbol of a higher meaning.[6] Or, as the Franciscan St. Bonaventure put it, in a union of symbolist theory with the aesthetic of the luminous:

> It is clear that the whole world is like a mirror, bright with reflected light of the divine wisdom; it is like a great coal radiant with light.[7]

If all this was true, if the world was God's book, the objects which composed the world were a kind of dictionary of God's meanings, and when God himself wrote a verbal book (the Bible), He would write not only a word language but the directly symbolic language of the objects which He mentioned. Thus St. Thomas Aquinas near the outset of his *Summa Theologiae*:

> The author of Holy Scripture is God, in Whose power it is to signify His meaning, not by words only (as man also can do), but also by things themselves. So, whereas in every other science things are signified by words, this science has the property that the things signified by the words have themselves also a signification. Therefore the first signification whereby words signify things belongs to the first sense, the historical or literal. That signification whereby things signified by words have themselves also a signification is called the spiritual sense, which is based on the literal, and presupposes it.[8]

[6] Gilbert and Kuhn, pp. 147–50; D. W. Robertson, Jr., "Historical Criticism," *English Institute Essays 1950* (New York, 1951), pp. 10–13; E. R. Curtius, *European Literature and the Latin Middle Ages,* trans. W. R. Trask (New York, 1953), pp. 319 ff.

[7] "*Et sic patet quod totus mundus est sicut unum speculum plenum luminibus praestantibus divinam sapientam, et sicut carbo effundens lucem.*" Etienne Gilson, *The Philosophy of St. Bonaventure* (New York, 1938), pp. 229–30.

[8] *Summa Theologiae,* I, q.1, art. 10, ad 3m., trans. Anton Pegis, in *The Basic Writings of St. Thomas Aquinas* (New York, 1945), I, 16, by permission of Random House, Inc. The article goes on to name the three kinds of spiritual sense, allegorical, moral, and anagogical.

There is some serious concern here, with Aquinas as with other school-men, about a natural and proper revelatory symbolism of objects (water, the sun, Jerusalem) as distinct from the mere symbolism of words and their metaphoric manipulation—the latter department (if we may antici-pate a more modern emphasis) being in a special way the concern of poetry. But one may say that the recognition of symbolism in general was a strain of medieval thinking (grammatical, aesthetic, and theological) which, without much advertisement as such, had deep, if ambiguous, im-plications for the theory of poetry. The classic appearance of symbolistic doctrine in medieval writing upon a literary subject is that in Dante's Letter to Can Grande della Scala (prefixed to the *Paradiso*),[9] in which he is concerned explicitly to set forth the levels of meaning in his own *Commedia*. Following the lead of the Scriptural exegetes, he finds in, or has put into, his own works not only a literal meaning, the story of his journey with Virgil through Hell and Purgatory and his ascent with Beatrice through the Heavenly spheres, but three higher levels of mean-ing, the allegorical (or worldly symbolic meanings), the anagogical (or other-worldly), and the tropological (or personal and moral). This we might say is Scriptural method put to the explication and vindication of religious poetry written by natural inspiration. With more difficulty the same thing could be done for fully secular and even for pagan poetry. As in Platonic times and earlier the defenders of Homer had invoked the allegorical way (often extravagantly and pedantically, but by a ra-tionale basically correct), so late classical and medieval defenders of pagan fable, and especially of Virgil's *Aeneid*, relied largely on that way—with the support where possible of the subsidiary way of etymol-ogy. Thus the *Expositio Virgiliana*, written probably in the sixth century by the African grammarian Fulgentius, finds Virgil in his *Eclogues* a prophet, priest, musician, physiologist, and botanist, in his *Georgics* an astrologer, haruspex, physiognomist, and physician, and in his *Aeneid* something like a universal philosopher. The *Aeneid* is an allegory of the course of human life: the wanderings of the first three books are the tales that amuse childhood; the love affair of the fourth and the athletic exercises of the fifth typify phases of youth; the descent into Hades of the sixth is a profound study of the whole nature of things; the rest is the contest of active life. In the same way words and syllables are pressed to yield their meanings allegorical and etymological. *Achates* is "Graece quasi *aconetos* id est tristitiae consuetudo." In a *Mythologiae* attributed to the same author, *Teiresias* is derived from the Greek *theros* and *aeon*,

---

[9] The authorship of the Epistle to Can Grande has been questioned by mod-ern scholars, apparently on plausible grounds (see Helmut Hatzfeld, "Modern Literary Scholarship as Reflected in Dante Criticism," *Comparative Literature*, III (Fall, 1951), 296, citing Luigi Pietrobono, "*L'Epistola a Can Grande*," *Giornale Dan-tesco*, XL (1937), 1–51. For the purpose of our argument, it is not essential that the epistle should have been written by Dante.

meaning "eternal summer," and *Ulixes* is "quasi-*olon xenos* id est omnium peregrinus." [1]

V

IN A 13th-century vernacular poem which has been called the earliest literary criticism in English, the allegorical *conflictus* entitled *The Owl and the Nightingale*, the case for didactic aims in poetry (the hidden moral and religious lessons in the symbolic husk) can no doubt be heard, at least by an interested ear, as the owl argues the merits of his own austere song; at the same time the hedonistic argument for the new kind of Troubadour love lyric seems audible in the nightingale's counter plea.[2] Toward the end of the next century, Chaucer, in the same varied burlesque of medieval stereotypes (the tale of the cock and the fox) where he makes the notable use of Vinsauf's rhetoric which we have seen, is slyly scanning didactic ambitions when he has the Nun's Priest conclude with the excellent advice:

> Now, goode men, I prey yow herkneth alle:
> Lo, how Fortune turneth sodeynly
> The hope and pryde eek of hir enemy!
> . . . .
> . . . .
>   Lo, swich it is for to be recchelees
> And necligent, and truste on flaterye.
>   But ye that holden this tale a folye,
> As of a fox, or of a cok and hen,
> Taketh the moralite, goode men.
> For seint Paul seith that all that writen is,
> To oure doctrine it is ywrite, ywis;
> Taketh the fruyt, and lat the chaf be stille.

The medieval schoolmen themselves were likely to make an emphatic distinction between secular literature and the Scriptures. Modern students of medieval poetic theory have perhaps not taken seriously enough such a passage as that in his *Quaestiones Quodlibetales* where Aquinas says in effect that it is wrong to look in secular poetry for any allegorical, any tropological, any anagogical meanings. The only kind of meaning to be found in secular poetry is literal meaning. *In nulla scientia, humana industria inventa, proprie loquendo, potest inveniri nisi*

---

[1] Saintsbury I, 392–5; Smith and Parks, 130–2. Cf. *Fabii Planciadis Fulgentii V.C. Opera*, ed. Rudolfus Helm (Leipsic, 1898), pp. 44, 48, 83–4, 92.

[2] This interpretation, at any rate, is plausibly urged by Atkins. See *English Criticism* I, 143–5, and Atkins's edition of the poem, 1922.

litteralis sensus; sed solum in ista Scriptura cujus Spiritus sanctus est auctor, homo vero instrumentum.[3] This may sound forbidding. It may at first sound like an oppressively simple view of the whole nature of poetry. It may indeed run counter to the aspirations of a certain modern kind of historical rereading of medieval poems.[4] On the other hand it might be argued that the dictum of Aquinas fits, or at least is adaptable to, the needs of a strictly critical historicism very well. It must be clear for one thing that by the term *literal* in this passage the medieval philosopher did not mean to rule out of secular poetry the range of natural metaphoric and analogical meanings which are obviously there. (The places where Aquinas speaks of metaphor in poetry and compares it to metaphor in Scripture have been often enough quoted by recent students.) *Literal* in this passage of scholastic philosophy seems to be opposed quite strictly to the other three, divinely intended, levels, the allegorical, the tropological, and the anagogical. Human poetry might very well *refer* to these levels of meaning, or point to them, and in some way involve them. Dante and many other medieval poets would show that this could be done, and would easily theorize around any difficulties. But the human poet, not being at the divine level, could hardly speak down from it with a real message about divine meaning.

If we take the passage about the four meanings in Dante's *Letter to Can Grande* along with an earlier passage, in his *Convivio* (or *Banquet*), on kinds of meaning and kinds of allegory, we find that he wished to distinguish the thing he attempted in the *Convivio*, a mere "allegory of poets," abstractive, didactic, and platonically thin, from what he attempted in the *Commedia*, an "allegory of theologians," or at least something like that, a more concrete and historically dramatic kind of allegorizing, which by the use of individually named historical figures (Beatrice rather than Lady Philosophy) turned the methods of the inspired Scriptures into a special kind of secular poetry. Without forgetting the objection of Aquinas, and without overlooking the fact that Dante's poem is not after all a history but a fiction (a *bella menzogna*), we may yet conceive that his theorizing corresponds approximately to a certain contribution which the poets of the Middle Ages, and especially Dante, made to the technique of realistic narrative. In the Scriptural situation known to exegetes as *figura* or typology, an individual historical person or thing of the Old Testament (Adam, Rahab, or Jerusalem) is seen as standing for or prophesying an individual person or thing in the

---

[3] *Quaestiones Quodlibetales* VII, q.6, a.16; cf. the answer to the second objection to this article.

[4] See, for instance, H. Flanders Dunbar, *Symbolism in Medieval Thought* (New Haven, 1929), p. 20 ("Every symbol should be understood at one and the same time in all of these significations") and p. 459, the poem as "cryptographic code"; D. W. Robertson, Jr. and Bernard F. Huppé, *Piers Plowman and Scriptural Tradition* (Princeton, 1951), e.g. pp. 5–6, 240.

New Testament (Christ, or the Christian Church). An eminent modern authority on medieval literature has seen a profound difference between such "figurism and other similar forms of thinking" such as "allegorism or symbolism." In the other forms, "at least one of the two elements combined is a pure sign" (that is, a fictitious thing, a rose or a lady, supposedly valued only in as much as it stands for something else, love or wisdom). "But in a figural relation both the signifying and the signified" are "real and concrete historical" things.[5] And in Dante's *Commedia* something like a fictitious parallel to this incarnational figurative meaning may perhaps be observed. The realism of his persons as he makes them appear to exist in the places of the other world sets up strangely solid fields of relational meaning between these translated souls and the persons they have been in secular history and the Bible. The Old Testament persons appear as acted out analogies or concrete realizations of figurisms traditionally attached to them.

Under a related aspect, the whole exegetical tradition had the effect of strongly promoting the downfall of the classically separate decora of comedy and tragedy.[6] The grotesquerie, the mingling of the sublime with the low and the funny, of which we find representative examples in the *Comedy* of Dante or in miracle and mystery plays and in cathedral architecture, expressed a spirit and rationale which are close to the Scriptural interpretations of which we have been speaking—the hospitable harlot Rahab seen as a type of the Christian Church, the scarlet thread which she lets down from the window seen as a type of Christ's blood. In virtue of such occasional literary pronouncements as those of Dante and the theological pronouncements that stand behind them, the literary situation in the Middle Ages—the unique poetic achievement— has at least an implicitly shadowed, and a profound, relation to the history of literary theory.

VI

THE strain of theological criticism which we have been describing appears most boldly perhaps in Boccaccio's extended defense of poetry

---

[5] Erich Auerbach, "Typological Symbolism in Medieval Literature," *Yale French Studies*, No. 9 (Spring, 1952), p. 6. Cf. the same author's *Mimesis*, trans. Willard R. Trask (Princeton, 1953), pp. 73, 195, 201. Cf. Charles S. Singleton, "Dante's Allegory," *Speculum*, XXV (January, 1950), 79–83 (reprinted in his *Dante Studies 1, Commedia, Elements of Structure*, Cambridge, Mass., 1954).

[6] The medieval lack of interest in these classical genres and their norms is clear, for instance, in a formula for tragedy starkly simplified from the Aristotelian. "Tragedie," says Chaucer's Monk, "is to seyn a certeyn storie, As olde bookes maken us memorie, Of hym that stood in greet prosperitee, And is yfallen out of Heigh degree Into myserie, and endeth wrecchedly. And they been versified communely Of six feet, which men clepen *exametron.*"

in the fourteenth and fifteenth books of his *De Genealogia Deorum*, a work of which the very title sufficiently suggests the symbolist and allegorical contents, and in a passage of his *Trattatello* or short *Life of Dante* which 19th-century professors, W. J. Courthope in his *Life of Alexander Pope* (*Works*, V, 50) and Saintsbury in the first volume of his *History of Criticism* (p. 457) pounce upon as showing "the very head and front of that Renaissance side of him which is so undeniable."

> I say that theology and poetry can be called almost the same thing, when they have the same subject; I even say that theology is none other than the poetry of God. What else is it than a poetic fiction when the Scripture in one place calls Christ a lion, in another a lamb, and in another a worm, here a dragon and here a rock, and many other things that I omit for the sake of brevity? What else do the words of Our Savior in the Gospels come to if not a sermon that does not signify what it appears to? It is what we call—to use a well-known term—allegory. Then it plainly appears that not merely is poetry theology but that theology is poetry. And surely if in so important a matter my words deserve little reliance, I am not disturbed by it; for I put my trust in Aristotle, an excellent authority in any important matter, who affirms he found that the poets were the first to write theology.—Chapter xxii [7]

Saintsbury is surely correct in his insistence that this is not the main and not the authorized voice of Christian medievalism. This and the Virgilian allegorical defences are to be looked on rather as recurrent efforts of humanism to save secular poetry from a neglect and even disapproval which after all was a plausible enough accompaniment of the Christian Church's struggle with the classical pagan world and the surrounding barbaric world of the Middle Ages. Along with much else that the Church Fathers owe to Plato there are not a few passages which show the accent of Book X of the *Republic*. The following from St. Augustine's *Confessions* are eloquent instances.

> I was forced [by the so-called grammarians] to learn the wanderings of one Aeneas, forgetful of my own, and to weep for dead Dido, because she killed herself for love; the while with

---

[7] Gilbert, p. 211, his translation emended in one phrase. Cf. Charles G. Osgood, *Boccaccio on Poetry, being the Preface and the Fourteenth and Fifteenth Books of Boccaccio's "Genealogia Deorum Gentilium"* (Princeton, 1930). The reference to Aristotle is not to his *Poetics* but to his *Metaphysics* III, 4. Saintsbury compares Boccaccio to Maximus Tyrius as expounded *supra* in the same volume, *History of Criticism* I, 117. Cf. Tasso on theology and poetry, in Gilbert, p. 476.

Allan H. Gilbert's translations from Italian critics are quoted here and in the next chapter from his *Literary Criticism Plato to Dryden*, New York, 1940, by permission of the American Book Company.

dry eyes, I endured my miserable self dying among these things, far from Thee, O God my life.—I, 13

Did I not read . . . of Jove the thunderer and the adulterer? both, doubtless, he could not be; but so the feigned thunder might countenance and pander to real adultery. . . . As if we should have never known such words as "golden shower," "lap," "beguile" . . . or others in that passage, unless Terence had brought a lewd youth upon the stage, setting up Jupiter as his example of seduction. . . . And then mark how he excites himself to lust as by celestial authority. . . . Not one whit more easily are the words learnt for all this vileness; but by their means the vileness is committed with less shame. Not that I blame the words, being, as it were, choice and precious vessels; but that wine of error which is proffered us in them by intoxicated teachers.—I, 16

To Carthage I came, where there sang all around me in my ears a cauldron of unholy loves. . . . Stage-plays also carried me away, full of images of my miseries, and of fuel to my fire. Why is it, that man desires to be made sad, beholding doleful and tragical things, which yet himself would by no means suffer? yet he desires as a spectator to feel sorrow at them, and this very sorrow is his pleasure. What is this but a miserable madness? for a man is the more affected with these actions, the less free he is from such affections.—III, 1–2

And now I was chief in the rhetoric school, whereat I joyed proudly, and I swelled with arrogancy. . . . in that unsettled age of mine, learned I books of eloquence, wherein I desired to be eminent, out of a damnable and vainglorious end, a joy in human vanity.—III, 3–4 [8]

At the same time, a second point, made implicitly in the *Confessions*, and noted by Saintsbury in his *History of Literary Criticism*, seems worth repeating here. The seductions of secular literature were far from being the most dangerous which a St. Augustine had to think about. We shall not get from him or from his age the grounds of a literary theory such as may be found in so systematic an attack on literature as that of Plato—the philosopher of an age when other disciplines, notably poetry and sophistry, made not only practical but serious theoretical claims to the office of *paideia*. Book Ten of St. Augustine's *Confessions* closes with a discourse on worldly pleasures which contains not a single reference to literature. The pleasures of literature are

[8] *The Confessions of St. Augustine*, revised from a former translation by the Rev. E. B. Pusey, D.D. (Oxford, 1838).

apparently not important enough to be named in a list of either the main sensory or the main intellectual temptations. "The boy had been charmed by Virgil and Terence—wicked charms he acknowledges—but the man, though he certainly does not mean to deny their wickedness, has simply put them away as childish things." [9]

Let us say, in summation, that the Middle Ages—where we have lingered not long and over no single important critical figure—were not in fact ages of literary theory or criticism. They were ages indeed of great literary creativity, when romance and the lyric of both secular and religious love were born, when drama was reborn, when fable, satire, fairy tale, allegory and narrative in a dozen other forms flourished, enriching the ground for a luxuriant future criticism. But the direction of theoretical thinking in these ages was elsewhere—to the metaphysical as that leads to speculative theology or joins with Scriptural revelation. In short it was an age of theological thinking in a theologically oriented and theocratic society. Such a society does not characteristically promote the essentially humanistic activity of literary criticism—an activity which we may describe provisionally and in this context as the self-conscious discipline of man's verbal imagination, of his achievements in rhythmic and metaphoric expression, of his natural inventions in the sphere of ethical and religious symbol.

---

[9] Saintsbury I, 380. For similarly rigorous views of secular literature (*daemonum cibus*) on the part of Tertullian (*De Spectaculis*), Jerome, and Gregory, see Gilbert and Kuhn, pp. 120–3; Atkins, *English Criticism*, I, 17. See the following page of Atkins for examples of a contrary or more liberal attitude, especially on the part of the Greek Fathers Origen, Clement, and Basil.

CHAPTER 9

THE SIXTEENTH CENTURY

§ *Italian editing of classic texts, four other kinds of critical work—II. lines of speculation: justification of vernaculars, poetic diction, quantitative meters, attack on rhyme—III. more substantive problems: rules of Aristotle vs. romance materials, unities of action, time and place, Scaliger, Castelvetro, Virgil-worship—IV. Gothic innovations, defences by Cinthio and others, Minturno on "errant" poetry, problem of mixed genres—V. Tasso and Mazzoni on the fantastic, allegorical theory, mythology, the supernatural, forward glance at Boileau and Granville—VI. the moral status of poetry debated, Gosson's attack, Sidney's Defense, its style and sources, main features: Horatian, Aristotelian, Platonic, opinions of English literature, ambiguous solution of the moral problem, statements about creative imagination in Shakespeare, Bacon, Sidney* §

LITERARY THEORY AND CRITICISM RECEIVED A NEW EMPHASIS IN ITALY during that phase of the general Renaissance which was speeded by the western movement of Byzantine manuscripts after the fall of Constantinople (1453) and the multiplication of texts after the invention of printing. The *Ars Poetica* of Horace had been more or less known throughout the Middle Ages.[1] But the *Poetics* of Aristotle (master document of the theorizing which was to come in the 16th century) had lain, even in the later Middle Ages,[2] almost unknown in Latin translations from the abridged Arabic version of Averroes. And so we mark

[1] It is mentioned, for instance, in the sixth century by Isidore of Seville, in the 12th by John of Salisbury (in his humanistic treatise the *Polycraticus* I, 8), and in the 13th by Dante.

[2] It had been for that matter little known in antiquity. It is not mentioned by Horace, Cicero, or Quintilian. Aristotelian literary ideas in later antiquity were Peripatetic and Hellenistic.

with interest the first complete Latin translation, by Giorgio Valla, at Venice in 1498; the first Greek text, in the Aldine *Rhetores Graeci*, in 1508; the first juxtaposition of Latin and Greek texts, by Alessandro de' Pazzi, in 1536; the first critical edition (with a Latin commentary) by Francisco Robortello, in 1548; and the first Italian translation, by Bernardo Segni, in 1549. A text "abandoned and neglected for a long time," said Segni. "Buried for a long time in the obscure shadows of ignorance," wrote Bernardo Tasso, the father of the epic poet. And Robortello in the edition of 1548: "*Jacuit liber hic neglectus, ad nostra fere haec usque tempora.*" [3] A few years after his edition of the *Poetics*, Robortello brought out his equally celebrated first edition of the Longinian *Peri Hupsous* (1554)—the Greek text with a Latin commentary. The *Institutio Oratoria* or rhetorical and literary encyclopedia of Quintilian had been known to literary men during the Middle Ages only in fragmentary versions. But the complete text had been rediscovered by the famous literary detective Poggio at the monastery of St. Gall in 1417 and had been edited by Cardinal Campano in 1470. [4] Editions such as these and larger editions of classic philosophers and poets, such as the Aldine editions at Venice of Homer, Plato, Aristotle, and the *Rhetores Graeci*, helped to bring on a Renaissance of furious theoretical activity, an era of criticism which remains one of the most conspicuous in literary history. Yet for several reasons—the difficulty of the Italian and Latin texts, the often very local emphasis of the controversies, and the derivative and authoritarian character of the critical principles invoked—the writings of the era have long been only obscurely known to the student of English poetry and poetics.

In addition to such critically edited classical texts as we have just noted, there were four other main genres in which the critical writing of the Italian Renaissance luxuriated. (1) There was the poetic or versified *Art* (in the manner of Horace), of which the best known example is the Latin *De Arte Poetica* in three books pub'ished in 1527 by the Italian Bishop Marco Girolamo Vida—to be far outshone in the later 17th century by the French *Art Poétique* of Boileau (1674) and in the early 18th century by the English *Essay on Criticism* of Alexander Pope (1711). (2) There was the deliberately scientific and ambitiously professed treatise on poetics (in the manner of what Aristotle's notes might be thought to represent): for example, the Latin *De Poeta Libri Sex* published in 1559 by the Bishop of Ugento Antonio Minturno and later (1564) supplemented by his Italian *L'Arte Poetica;* or—most massive, most celebrated, and most reactionary, of all such treatises—the *Poetices Libri Septem* of the Frenchman Julius Caesar Scaliger, published posthumously in 1561. (3) There was the apologetic essay, either

---

[3] Spingarn, pp. 11–18.
[4] J. E. Sandys, *A History of Classical Scholarship* (Oxford, 1891), II, 103.

specifically directed against purists and classicists, and in the cause of a vernacular literature, like the *Deffence et Illustration de la Langue Francoyse* of Joachim du Bellay in 1549; or generally directed against moralists and other main enemies of poetry, like a youthful oration of Scaliger's, *Contra Poetices Calumniatores Declamatio*,[5] or the much better known English epitome of Renaissance poetics, the *Defense of Poesie* or *Apologie for Poetrie*, by Sir Philip Sidney, published in 1595. (4) There was the preface or special treatise in retort to classical objections against some particular romantic form or vernacular style—for example, Giraldi Cinthio's defence of his own tragedy *Orbecche* (1541) and of Ariosto's romance epic (1549), Tasso's *Discorsi* (1594) in defence of his *Gerusalemme Liberata*, Mazzoni's two defences of the *Divina Commedia* (1572 and 1587), and Guarini's *Compendio della Poesia Tragicomica* (1601). Italian apologetics of this species found echoes in such English prefaces as that of Sir John Harington prefixed to his translation of Ariosto (1591) and that of George Chapman prefixed to the *Seven Books* of his *Iliad* (1598).

II

SOME of the most important and persistent preoccupations of the 16th-century literary theorists have perhaps been suggested even in the enumeration of types which we have just made. Beginning with the most local and concrete critical issues and moving towards those of more general import, let us now venture to set forth briefly certain main lines of Renaissance literary speculation. One of the most local and special issues had received its classic treatment as early as about 1300 in Dante's Latin essay defending vernacular poetry, the *De Vulgari Eloquentia*. As the earlier Middle Ages had needed a revision in prosodic theory to meet the fact of the shift from quantitative, classical meters to the accentual rhythms of hymn and song, so the later Middle Ages faced a broader revision in theory to justify the increasingly palpable fact of the vernacular literatures. And long after the fact had been accomplished, theoretical scruples could be revived by professors of newly discovered classical theory and could be given new twists which corresponded to changes of balance in the classical-vernacular relationship. Where Dante is concerned mainly to assert the dignity and poetic availability of the emergent vernacular, and to distinguish certain more refined classes of words within it, in the mid-16th century the *Deffence* of Du Bellay leans heavily upon the possibility that the vernacular may be enriched by plunder and adaptation of all the finest vocabulary of the classics. "Visit the ancients

[5] In his *Epistolae et Orationes*, 1600; see Vernon Hall, "Scaliger's Defense of Poetry," *PMLA*, LXIII (December, 1948), 1125-30.

and strip them of their wealth," Vida had said repetitiously, in each part of his *De Arte Poetica*,[6] developing the late classical doctrine about the imitation of models in a direction of which we shall have more to say in Chapter 10. In the next generation, however, the distinguishing feature of an English defense of vernacular, E. K.'s Epistle prefixed to the *Shepheardes Calender*, is a reversal of Du Bellay's thesis in that E. K. applauds the Spenserian enrichment of the language from native, if rustic, dialect sources, rather than from the "inkhorns" of humanistic pedants who were practising the theory of Du Bellay with all too great a will. These shifts in the argument about vernacular show its tendency to be refined into an argument essentially about what came within a few centuries to be known as "poetic diction"—a tendency strongly manifest even in Dante's *De Vulgari Eloquentia* as he divides the noble "courtly" and "curial" vernacular into words *childish* (too simple), *feminine* (too soft), and *manly*, and then subdivides the *manly* into the *sylvan* (too rough) and the *urban*, and then again subdivides the *urban* into the *combed out* and the *shaggy* (which are grand) and the *glossy* and rumpled (which have a superfluity of the proper qualities). The *combed out* and the *shaggy* alone are fit for the illustrious tragic style.[7] At this level (that concerning "poetic diction" rather than the rights of vernacular and classic) the debate is perennial. It is one to which we shall return (Chapter 16) at the Wordsworthian crisis in the history of English poetic diction.

It remains to round off our present topic by observing that the earlier medieval contest between classical and vernacular prosodies had an aftermath during the 16th century in a succession of misguided attempts by Italian, French, and English litterateurs to cultivate quantitative vernacular meters.[8] (In England the "rules" of Drant preceded the experiments of Harvey and Spenser, and of the "Areopagus," Dyer and Sidney.) It is difficult to imagine anything more thoroughly self-refuting than the example of this workmanship offered by Webbe in his *Discourse of Poesie* (1586), the song in Spenser's Fourth Eclogue turned into sapphics.[9] A related phenomenon was the classically-minded attack on rhyme (as a "monkish" and "beggarly" barbarism) which extended

---

[6] I, 409; II, 542 ff (... *te plurima Achivos Consulere hortamur veteres, Argivaque regna Explorare oculis, et opimam avertere gazam In Latium*); III, 244 (*passimque avertite praedam*).

[7] *De Vulgari Eloquentia*, ed: Aristide Marigo (Firenze, 1938), I, xvii–xix; II, iv. Cf. Alfred Ewert, "Dante's Theory of Diction," *M.H.R.A.*, No. 31 (November, 1959), pp. 15–30. Dante's theorizing is made comprehensible by the fact that he has in mind the lyrics of his *Vita Nuova* and not the mixed vocabulary of his later *Commedia*. Cf. Erich Auerbach, *Mimesis*, trans. Willard Trask (Princeton, 1953), pp. 185–7.

[8] Saintsbury II, 46, sees "the beginning of that pestilent heresy" in the *Versi e Regole della Nuova Poesia Toscana* of Claudio Tolomei, 1539.

[9] Smith, *Elizabethan Essays*, I, 286 ff. Cf. G. L. Hendrickson, "Elizabethan Quantitative Hexameters," *Philological Quarterly*, XXVIII (1949), 298 ff.

from the later 16th century even into the early 18th, many years after the structural triumph of rhyme in the Augustan couplet. The reasons for the success and necessity of English rhyme, especially in lyric and in witty satirical verse, lie in such practical differences between the vernacular and the classical languages as that between stress and quantity, and in the absence from the vernacular of the classical morphology and hence the relative ease of avoiding the logical (and antimetrical) figure of *homoioteleuton* (similar endings). Yet an age which theorized with the classical part of its mind was bound to find fault with a difficult and often cramping technique which had indeed flourished first in the "monkish" ages, and to dream of a return to a supposed classic state of majesty—plain and regular, like the columns of the Greek temples. Rhyme, says George Puttenham, a courtier theorist in the great age of Elizabeth, "is all the sweetness and harmony of our vulgar poesie." [1] But at the same time he says it was brought into Greek and Latin by "barbarous souldiers out of the Campe." This was typical and casual enough. The better known and more deliberate attacks are that of Campion in his *Observations in the Art of English Poesie* (1602) (answered by Daniel in *A Defence of Rhyme*, 1603?) and the later note prefixed by Milton to *Paradise Lost*—perhaps at the request of a publisher apprehensive about the side-effect of a current courtly controversy in which rhyme had so able a defender as John Dryden. Milton avoided the difficulty of carrying rhyme through the vast, discursive effort of his epic. A "troublesome and modern bondage" he called it, used by some poets "much to their own vexation, hindrance, and constraint to express many things otherwise, and for the most part worse than else they would have expressed them." The court controversy concerned drama, perhaps the weakest ground on which a champion of rhyme could choose to stand. Yet this controversy had, as we shall note later on,[2] a special theoretical interest in connection with the larger Renaissance issue of dramatic verisimilitude.

III

MORE substantive problems too—of genres, of decorum and rules— were from the beginning the characteristic concern of the 16th-century critics. The world of medieval and early Renaissance fable, romance,

[1] Puttenham's *Arte of English Poesie* (1589) is a neo-rhetorical treatise characterized by the flamboyance of its diagrams of "figure" poems and by its quaintly native reduction of the classical figure terminology (*antitheton*, the "quarreller"; *traductio*, the "tranlacer"; *paradoxon*, the "wonderer"; *micterismus*, the "fleering frumpe"). Book I, Chapters V–VII and Book II, Chapters V–IX, contain his comments on rhyme. See the edition by Gladys D. Willcock and Alice Wallser (Cambridge, 1936), pp. 10–15, 76–84.

[2] Chapter 10, pp. 188–90.

and burlesque lay between the classic age and the new poets and theorizers. If they undertook to write the old forms (tragedy, or comedy, or
Virgilian epic), it was difficult not to find the new materials (Christian,
feudal, Gothic, romantic, in a word, "European") equally with the new
vernacular media, an obstacle to a perfect return. How strictly interpret
the rules of Aristotle? How far stretch or relax them? How far improve
or tighten them up? Such are the issues which inspire Giraldi Cinthio's
Address to the Reader defending his own *Tragedy of Orbecche*, 1541,
his *Apology* for his tragedy *Dido*, 1543, his treatise *On the Composition of Comedies and Tragedies*, 1543, or Giangiorgio Trissino's *Poetica*,
1529–1563, a work in part apologetic for his own epic *Italy Liberated
from the Goths* and for his tragedy *Sofonisba*. In somewhat the same
vein with these instances of special pleading appear the treatises of Antonio Minturno, his *De Poeta*, 1559, and *L'Arte Poetica*, 1564. All these
works and many others reexamine—without special illumination—such
prime Aristotelian and Horatian topics as character and plot in tragedy,
the difference between tragedy and comedy, happy and unhappy conclusions, the *deus ex machina*, pity and fear, purgation. The most signal
victory for the Aristotelian rules—or the greatest extension of their authority and increase in their stringency—was that by which the unity
of action so much stressed by Aristotle and the unity of time to which
he undoubtedly alluded (in his phrase *hupo mian periodon hēliou*) became the now famous three unities of action, time, and place, the *unités
Scaligeriennes* of French classical drama in the next century. Sufficiently
indicated by Scaliger in his *Poetics* of 1561, they were hammered home
by Lodovico Castelvetro in his *Poetica D'Aristotele Vulgarizzata et
Sposta* of 1570 (the Greek text translated and heavily annotated in Italian).[3] Castelvetro, a progressive critic who kept stage and audience firmly
in mind, argued with admirable practical solicitude that unity of time, the
limitation of the drama to one day, was a necessity by reason of the
bodily needs of the audience. (. . . *il quale io no veggo che possa passare
il giro del sole, siccome dice Aristotele, cioè ore dodici, conciosiacosaché
per le necessità del corpo, come è mangiare, bere, disporre i superflui pesi
del ventre e della vesica, dormire e per altre necessità, non possa il popolo
continuare oltre il predetto termine così fatta dimora in teatro.*)[4] This
kind of time, we may observe in passing, external or theater time, rather
than internal or plot time, was not really what Aristotle had in mind (a
matter for scene shifters only, he said—and the Greek tragedies came
three to a day, with a satyr play afterwards). The problem of internal

---

[3] See H. B. Charlton, *Castelvetro's Theory of Poetry* (Manchester, 1913); F. M.
Padelford, *Select Translations from Scaliger's Poetics* (New York, 1905).

[4] Quoted by H. Breitinger, "*Un passage de Castelvetro sur l'unité de lieu*,"
Revue Critique d'Histoire et de Littérature, Nouvelle Série, VII (27 December, 1879),
478–80. Cf. Castelvetro, *Poetica D'Aristotele*, Basel, 1576, p. 109 (II, 7). Breitinger
quotes the edition of Vienna, 1570, p. 60.

unity of time—how far it is entailed by unity of action and how far in turn it entails unity of place—is a real critical problem to which we shall have good occasion (Chapter 10) to return.

Such was the more reactionary outcome of the conflict between Aristotle and modernity—the outcome for which 16th-century literary criticism has been best known and least liked. Everyone knows about the neo-classic deference to authority and prescription and the concurrently wholehearted acceptance of the classical code for the imitation of the best models. In the words of Saintsbury's convenient simplification:

> The poet is to look first, midmost, and last to the practice of the ancients. . . . The ancients have anticipated almost everything, and in everything that they have anticipated have done so well that the best chance of success is simply to imitate them. The detailed precepts of Horace are never to be neglected; if supplemented, they must be supplemented in the same sense.[5]

What is called "Virgil Worship," the elevation of Virgil over Homer or the narrowing of the epic model to Virgil alone—flagrant instances of which appear in Vida's verse *Art* and, perhaps the most notorious, in Scaliger's *Poetics*—was a nationalistic, rather than a strictly critical, phenomenon. Still the resulting debate lasted long, in England for instance, from Chapman's Preface to the *Iliad* in 1598 (defending Homer against Scaliger of course) to the essays and clubbable conversations of the 18th century—where we find Dr. Samuel Johnson also on the side of Homer.

I V

BUT criticism in the 16th century might be at many moments uneasy in its submission—it might be even energetic in stretching, rather than tightening, the rules—and this especially when it had to say something about the undoubted (if irregular) masterpieces which were being contrived during that era in the Gothic mode: romantic and heroic epics (with tinges of burlesque), modifications of pastoral, and other hybrids of classical and medieval decora. Pronounced instances of a critical trend may be seen in the defence of Ariosto's "variety" by Cinthio in his treatise *On the Composition of Romances* (1549), in Tasso's *Discourses on the Heroic Poem* (1594) written to defend the theme of love in his own *Jerusalem Delivered*, in Mazzoni's two discourses (1572, 1587) defending the delightful "teaching" of Dante's mixed poetry and politics in the *Comedy*, and in Guarini's *Compendium of Tragicomic Poetry* (1601) written to defend his own "Pastoral Tragicomedy" *Il Pastor Fido*. ("Pastoral tragi-

[5] Saintsbury II, 217.

comedy purges with pleasure the sadness of the hearers.") [6] One of the happiest instances (through a sort of metaphoric argument about content and form which it contains) is a defence of Ariosto epitomized for the unfriendly purpose of refutation by Antonio Minturno in his *L'Arte Poetica* of 1564.[7]

VESPASIANO: Since we have gone so far in our reasoning, just what is the romance?

MINTURNO: I shall not deny that it is an imitation of great and illustrious actions that are worthy of epic poetry. But certainly the word is strange, and in the Spanish as well as in the Provençal I believe it refers to the vulgar tongue. . . . because they dealt in that language with the actions and the loves of knights more than with any other subject, the compositions made on that theme were called romances. The same word passed into Italy, because our writers began to imitate the romantic and classical compositions of the barbarians. And since our authors, as Cicero teaches us, always improve what they find in others, they make also the poetry of the romances more graceful and beautiful, if in truth it is to be called poetry.

VESPASIANO: Why is it not worthy of this name? Is not M. Ludovico Ariosto a most excellent poet, as he is a most noble writer of romance?

MINTURNO: Yes, indeed, nor do I judge that a lower estimate should be made of him. But I cannot affirm that his romances and those of others contain the kind of poetry that Aristotle and Horace taught us.

VESPASIANO: Of what consequence is it that the romance is not such poetry but another kind taken over from the Ultramontanes and made more splendid and more beautiful by the Italians, if the world is pleased with it and accepts and receives it with delight?

MINTURNO: I do not wonder about the common crowd. . . . But I cannot but be greatly astonished that there are some learned men, well versed in good literature and of excellent abilities, who (as I understand) acknowledge that there is not in the ro-

[6] Gilbert, pp. 262, 373-4, 378, 381, 484, 524.
[7] A treatise *Della Toscana Poesia*, written as a complement of his earlier Latin work on the poet in six books.

> mances the form and the rule that Homer and
> Vergil follow, and that Aristotle and Horace
> command as appropriate, and who nevertheless
> labor to defend this error. Nay more, since that
> sort of composition gives the deeds of *errant
> knights*, they obstinately affirm not merely that
> it is not fitting to write poetry in the manner of
> Vergil and Homer, but even that it is desirable
> that *poetry* also should be *errant*, passing from
> one manner to another, and binding various things
> in one bundle.[8]

Erratic form to express erratic materials. If we think of the classical
genres and their corollary rules of decorum as the patterns according to
which poetry was supposed to succeed in being like the several most
important kinds of reality, we may say that in all the ramifications of
their manifold debate over Aristotelianism—down to the articles concerning rhyme and meter—the theorizers of the 16th century were debating
(by a highly codified and rather crabbed convention) nothing else than
the degree of correspondence which should obtain between art and reality. Is a mixed genre (let us say tragicomedy) an offence against reality?
Certainly not in one sense: it is not an offense against realism or naturalism, because events in life do tend to occur mixed, the sad and the happy
and funny close together. But if we are willing to speak of such occurrences with an accent on our responses to them—if we confer on "reality"
something of an implication of ideality in its easiest sense—we may arrive
at a situation where in a very crude and preliminary way we have to say
that to mix tears and laughter is unreal. In real life a sad event tends to
concentrate or purify our sad feelings to the point where we either do
not notice, or may even resent, anything gay or hilarious. If such mix-
tures or alterations are to be received kindly on the stage, clearly some
sophistication must be at work—ideality at a special remove. On this
point no very explicit theory appears to have been entertained during the
period of which we speak. But about the ideality of poetry in still a third
sense (fairly broad and obvious)—the sense of poetic fantasy and invention in contrast to the ordinariness of actual life—there are some more
or less enlightened Aristotelian and Platonic speculations.

V

Tasso, for instance, in his *Discourses* of 1594, though he avers that poetry
should be true (*icastic*), not false (*phantastic*), and that the "marvelous"

---

[8] Gilbert, pp. 277-8, translating Minturno, *L'Arte Poetica* (Naples, 1725), Book I,
p. 26a–b. The italics are ours.

should be "credible," says at the same time that poetry is not the piddling truth of particular facts, but is something which is *like* the truth of the universal.[9] Even the opposite emphasis, the full plea for invention, might appear. Thus, for instance, Mazzoni in his treatise *On the Defense of the Comedy* (1587):

> . . . poetry, because of paying more attention to the credible than to the true, ought to be classed as a subdivision of the rational faculty, called by the ancients sophistic.

> . . . phantasy is the true power over poetic fables, since she alone is capable of those fictions which we of ourselves are able to feign and put together. From this of necessity it follows that poetry is made up of things feigned and imagined, because it is founded on phantasy.

The metaphysics of Mazzoni's view of art appears (though somewhat obscurely) in this passage of his Introduction:

> Those arts that have as their object the image, or idol, have an object for the construction of which there is no other end than to represent and to imitate; hence they are properly called imitative. . . . they are distinguished from the other arts that are not called imitative in that the latter have objects that are good for some other use and some other end. . . . when we concluded above that the image is the object of the imitative arts we did not mean that sort of image that comes into being without human artistic activity . . . but that which has its origin from our art, which usually springs from our phantasy and our intellect by means of our choice and will, as an image in pictorial art or in sculpture. . . . this species of image is that which is an adequate object of human imitation, and . . . when Aristotle said in the beginning of the *Poetics* that all the species of poetry were imitative, he meant that imitation which has for its object the image that springs entirely from human artifice. . . . Plato in the *Sophist* has left a statement that imitation is of two sorts. One of these he has named icastic; it represents things that are truly derived from some work already existing. . . . The other, which he called phantastic, is exemplified in pictures that are made by the caprice of the artist.[1]

Allow for a certain blurring of Platonic terminology here, a double (or triple) service for the word *image*, to mean both object in nature (the

---

[9] Gilbert, pp. 477, 479, 494.

[1] Gilbert, pp. 359, 360, 367, 387. Mazzoni's *Della Difesa della "Commedia" di Dante* (Books I–III published in 1587, Books IV–VII, in 1688) appears actually to have been composed by Tuccio dal Corno from materials supplied by Mazzoni.

image of a divine idea) and object in our fancy, made manifest only in the external imitation (which is a third sort of image), and we have a defense of fantasy thoroughly grounded in a transvalued Platonic theory of imitation. Not that poetry *must* be false in the factual, historical sense, but that it may be, and that even when it is false it has its peculiar kind of truth.

Such a defense of poetry was highly compatible with another, which we have already observed in the Middle Ages, the allegorical defense of pagan fables. And we must suppose this latter (or rather the whole issue of the relation of theology and poetry, as we have noted it in Boccaccio's *Life of Dante* and *De Genealogia Deorum*) to have been always close to the critical consciousness of the later age. Harington's *Apologie* prefixed to his Ariosto is an English text which names the "literal," "moral," and "allegorical" levels of poetic meaning—applying these to the myth of Perseus and Andromeda in a passage for which modern scholarship has shown the direct source to be the neo-Platonic philosopher Leo Ebreo's *Dialoghi d'Amore*.[2] One of the most radical 16th-century pleas, much like the earlier one of Boccaccio, appears in the *Discourses* of Tasso.

> . . . it is not strange that the poet should be almost the same as the theologian and the dialectician . . . . divine philosophy, or theology as we prefer to call it, has two parts, and each of them is adapted and fitted to one part of our mind, which is composed of the divisible and the indivisible, not merely according to the opinion of Plato and of Aristotle, but of the Areopagite, who wrote in the epistles to Pope Titus in the *Mystic Theology*, and elsewhere, that that part of occult theology that is contained in the signs, and has the power of making one perfect, is fitting to the indivisible part of our soul, which is the intellect at its purest. The other, eager for wisdom, which brings proofs, he attributes to the divisible part of the soul, much less noble than the indivisible. Thence it leads to the contemplation of divine things; and to move readers in this way with images, as do the mystic theologian and the poet, is a much more noble work than to teach by means of demonstration, which is the function of the scholastic theologian. The mystic theologian and the poet, then, are far more noble than any of the others, even though Saint Thomas in the first part of the *Summa* put poetry in the lowest order of teaching.[3]

[2] See the text in Smith II, 201-2; and cf. Douglas Bush, *Mythology and the Renaissance Tradition in English Poetry* (1932), p. 70; R. Elbrodt, "Sir John Harington and Leone Ebreo," *MLN*, LXV (1950), 109-10; Margret G. Trotter, *TLS*, December 30, 1944, p. 631.

[3] Gilbert, p. 476, from *Discourses on the Heroic Poem*, Book II, [10]. Gilbert quotes Aquinas, *Summa Theologiae* I, 1, 9: "It is objected that sacred teaching should not use metaphors. . . . to proceed by various similitudes and representations

As the age of scientific reason succeeded to that of humanistic imagination, and the standard of measured literalness to that of analogical insight, such allegorical defenses were to fall more and more below the critical horizon. Even Tasso argued against the intrusion of classical mythology in modern poems, on the ground that it jarred with verisimilitude.

> . . . if we . . . have recourse to the same ones as were invoked by the ancients, by that plan we are deprived of the probable and the credible. . . . I speak of the enchanted rings, the flying horses, the ships turned into nymphs, the ghosts that interfere in battles, the burning sword, the garland of flowers, the forbidden chamber . . . . if these miracles, or prodigies rather, cannot be brought about by the power of nature, it is necessary that the cause be some supernatural force or some diabolical power, and if we turn to the deities of the pagans, we for the most part give up the lifelike and the probable, or rather I would say the credible . . . . but in the ancient poets these things should be read in another frame of mind and with another taste, as it were, not merely as things received by the people but as those approved by their religion.[4]

In the next century, Boileau in his *Art Poétique*, written just a few years after the publication of Milton's *Paradise Lost*, came to a conclusion in one sense opposite to that of Tasso, yet inspired by a similar latent critical principle. Boileau argued that the one form of supernaturalism to be avoided by the epic poet was the Christian, for spiritual truth was bound to be so deformed by imagistic embodiment as to lack conviction. (And despite the signal instance of Milton, the history of Christian epic poetry in the 17th century, both French and English, largely substantiates the apprehension of Boileau.) During the rather brief 17th-century defense of "heroic" drama, the supernatural is justified, with quotations from Petronius and Longinus, largely in terms of the power to amaze and shock. After that, the theoretical contest between realism and the fantastic-supernatural flutters down progressively to the criterion of this-world naturalism. A degenerate phase of the controversy may be illustrated from a note to the poem called *An Essay on Unnatural Flights in Poetry* (1701) by Pope's friend George Granville.

> The Poetic World is nothing but Fiction; Pernassus, Pegasus, and the Muses, pure imagination and Chimaera. But being, however, a system universally agreed on, all that shall be contriv'd

is proper to poetry, which is the humblest branch of knowledge. . . . I answer that it is proper for Sacred Scripture to set forth in metaphors divine and spiritual things under the similitude of corporeal things." Cf. *ante* Ch. 7, p. 131; Ch. 8, pp. 147–8, 150.
    [4] Gilbert, p. 479; *Discourses*, II, [13].

or invented upon this Foundation according to Nature shall be reputed as truth: But what so ever shall diminish from, or exceed, the just proportion of Nature, shall be rejected as False, and pass for extravagance, as Dwarfs and Gyaunts for Monsters.[5]

That is to say: the poetic world is a classical canon of fantasy which is agreed to be according to nature because it is a classical canon—Pegasus and the Muses, not romantic Dwarfs and Gyaunts. This may not seem a great improvement over the more scholastic arguments from the principle of analogy relied on by Boccaccio and Tasso.

VI

WE MAY add one more theme—that concerning the moral status of poetry—to our account of poetics in the 16th century, and at the same time bring this account to an appropriate conclusion, if we refer now to an essay, the *Defence of Poesie* by Sir Philip Sidney, which is both the English locus of closest contact with Italian criticism and a brilliant epitome of what was best in the spirit of that criticism. The utilitarian defense of poetry by an Englishman appears quite early in the century with Sir Thomas Elyot's *Boke of the Governour*, 1530, in which chapters X and XII of Book I (the education of a public servant described by a public servant) maintain that Homer and Virgil can teach the young man not only moral lessons but arms, politics, and horse-breeding.[6] (The pre-Platonic directness of this apology—as if the rhapsode Ion were speaking —was perhaps possible only because it came before the great vogue of Aristotle's *Poetics*.) A less pragmatic idea about the civilizing value of literature was one of the basic premises of Renaissance humanism and of the Renaissance theory of education—in the *Adagia* of Erasmus, for instance, or the treatises of Ludovicus Vives.[7] Throughout Italian criticism of the century (in Trissino, Minturno, Cinthio, Mazzoni, for instance, and in almost all other writers) the accepted formula is morally didactic, the Horatio-Aristotelian instruction and pleasure,[8] with countless inconclusive variations on the relation between the two. (Castelvetro, with a practical concern for the recreation of the common spectator, was one of the earliest to make an emphatic disavowal of the didactic view—a dis-

---

[5] Cf. *post* Chapter 15, pp. 335–6.

[6] Gilbert, pp. 234, 236.

[7] A symptomatic though decidedly minor instance may be cited for English humanism in the treatise *De fructu qui ex doctrina percipitur* by Henry VIII's officer Richard Pace.

[8] Cf. Marvin T. Herrick, *The Fusion of Horatian and Aristotelian Literary Criticism, 1531–1555* (Urbana, 1946). Ch. IV, "The Function of Poetry."

avowal that would gain ground with French 17th-century critics.[9]) At the same time the Platonic charge of immorality might readily enough be brought against poetry—especially when English moralists (for example, Roger Ascham in his *Scholemaster*) associated poetry with Italianate license in manners or dress, or when Puritan writers turned their attention to the theater. One of the most pungent of the latter—and today one of the best known of all those who engaged in the long pamphlet war that began in England shortly after the start of the London professional theater in 1571—was Stephen Gosson, by turns a writer for the theater himself, a student at a Catholic seminary in Rome, and an Anglican clergyman, parson at Great Wigborow in Essex and at St. Botolph's, Bishopsgate. The gist of his rattling, tart, Euphuistic double protest, against the moral influence of plays themselves and of the deplorable bordello company which flocked to the theater, may be told almost sufficiently in the garrulous title of his *School of Abuse: Containing a pleasant invective against Poets, Pipers, Players, Jesters, and such like Caterpillars of a Commonwealth: Setting up the Flag of Defiance to their mischievous exercise, and overthrowing their Bulwarks, by Prophane Writers, Natural Reason, and common experience: A Discourse as Pleasant for them that favor learning, as profitable for all that will follow virtue.* "Because I have been matriculated myself in the school where so many abuses flourish," writes Gosson in one of his characteristically eloquent passages, "I will imitate the dogs of Egypt, which coming to the banks of Nilus to quench their thirst, sip and away, drink running, lest they be snapped short for a prey to crocodiles."

> . . . you are no sooner entered but liberty looseth the reins and gives you head, placing you with poetrie in the lowest form, when his skill is shown to make his scholar as good as ever twanged: he prefers you to piping, from piping to playing, from play to pleasure, from pleasure to sloth, from sloth to sleep, from sleep to sin, from sin to death, from death to the Devil, if you take your learning apace, and pass through every form without revolting.[1]

This pamphlet appeared in 1579, with a dedication "To the right noble Gentleman, Master Philip Sidney, Esquire." It was a moment when Sidney, returned from his educational travels in Switzerland and Italy, standing loosely attached to Elizabeth's court under the patronage of Leicester, and in companionable relation to Spenser and other gentlemen

---

[9] See, for instance, the Abbé d'Aubignac, Corneille in his *Discours de l'utilité . . . du poème dramatique*, and Saint-Evremond. Their ideas may be looked on as embryonic of far later theories of aesthetic autonomy. Cf. René Bray, *La formation de la doctrine classique en France* (Dijon, 1926), p. 727.

[1] (London: The Shakespeare Society, 1841), p. 14. We have modernized the spelling.

of like spirit, was engaged in the literary occupations, his sonnets to Stella and his romance *Arcadia*, by which in the short time that remained before his death at Zutphen he became the brilliant symbol of the courtly literary spirit of England. Largely from Gosson's dedication and from an allusion to this by Spenser in a letter dated from Leicester House to the Cambridge scholar Gabriel Harvey, but in part also from certain moments in Sidney's argument and certain snatches of parodied Euphuistic style which seem echoes of Gosson,[2] Sidney's *Defence of Poesie*, though written perhaps as late as 1585, has been traditionally considered a retort to Gosson. It circulated in manuscript among the literati during Sidney's life and was soon quoted in the best critical places—in Puttenham's *Arte* of 1589, in Harington's *Apologie* of 1591. In the year 1595 it had the advantage of being published simultaneously by two printers, Ponsonby and Olney, under two titles, *The Defence of Poesie* and *An Apologie for Poetrie*. It is a kind of formal beginning of literary theorizing by the English man of letters, and a brilliant enough one—written in the high, enthusiastic, occasionally a-syntactic style of the gifted amateur champion, headlong to outdazzle the lowness and myopia of professional moral grumblers. The essay reflects and telescopes not only the continental criticism of the century but a certain amount of classical Greek and Roman as well. Passages have been assigned to Minturno, Scaliger, and Castelvetro. And latterly the original sources of neo-classic criticism and anti-criticism, Aristotle's *Poetics* and Plato's *Republic*, Book X (perhaps in Latin translations such as Pazzi's of Aristotle and Ficino's of Plato), have been urged as the true fountains of Sidney's learning.[3] It is certain that he read little Greek, and it appears likely to us that he was better acquainted with contemporary interpretations of classical criticism than with the latter itself. But it all matters little. Sidney wrote, not a pedant's encyclopedia, but a gentleman's essay.

High points of interest in the essay include a preliminary double definition of poetry, from Aristotle and from Horace, a now famous statement that the poet's tale "holds" children from play and old men from the chimney-corner,[4] an adaptation of Aristotelian doctrine making poetry a union of philosophy and history and giving it the highest literary palm after the *Scriptures*, an invocation of Plato as a witness for poetry (following so reputable an authority as Scaliger, Sidney overrates the Socratic concessions to poetic frenzy in the *Ion*), and a section where Sidney ap-

---

[2] The opposition between Sidney's simplified Ramist rhetoric and the parody of patristic symbol-reading in the Euphuism of Gosson is part of a theme which we develop in Chapter 12.

[3] Cornell March Dowlin, "Sidney's Two Definitions of Poetry," in *MLQ*, III, (December, 1942), 573–81.

[4] "With a tale, forsooth, he cometh unto you, with a tale which holdeth children from play, and old men from the chimney-corner" (ed. A. S. Cook, Boston, 1890, p. 23). This passage is borrowed from Sidney by Harington.

plies Scaligerian and Horatian norms to English poetry. He protests against the slack unity of academic tragedies (excepting *Gorboduc*) and the clatter of wooden swords in battle endings. He mentions Spenser's *Shepheardes Calender* with respect, admits the stirring of his heart at the old ballad of Chevy Chase, and looks back with wistful respect and wonder at Chaucer—"that he in that misty time could see so clearly." We may look on these latter details of Sidney's *Defence* as constituting an early landmark in the progress of English literary self-consciousness and literary history—a topic to which we shall have occasion to return in later chapters.[5]

To look a little more closely at the theoretic content of Sidney's moral defense of poetry: one should note in the first place that the second of Sidney's preliminary definitions is such as to make the moral *content* of poetry (that is, vices and virtues correctly evaluated) a part of its essential requirement—as indeed his first definition names the purpose of poetry explicitly as teaching.

> Poesy, therefore, is an art of imitation, for so Aristotle termeth it in his word *mimēsis*, that is to say, a representing, counterfeiting, or figuring forth; to speak metaphorically, a speaking picture, with this end,—to teach and delight.[6]

> . . . it is not riming and versing that maketh a poet . . . but it is that feigning notable images of virtues, vices, or what else, with that delightful teaching, which must be the right describing note to know a poet by.[7]

Yet in the second place, at a much later point in the essay, when he is facing Platonic objections and is hence forced into reasoning about the moral requirement and how to reconcile it with the stark fact that much fine poetry is immoral, Sidney says something different: The phenomenon of immoral poetry ("amorous conceits," "lust," "vanity," "scurrility" in poetry) means "not . . . that poetry abuseth man's wit, but that man's wit abuseth poetry." He could have said (though to say so would have contradicted easily observable facts, and he did not say it) that immoral poetry was, by his earlier definition, no poetry at all. He preferred to raise the question how poetry, which is defined as something moral, can be *in fact* either moral or immoral. His answer—in terms of the ideal conceived as what is most real—should not be dismissed too lightly, though it perhaps gives mere logic some difficulty.

> Nay, truly, though I yield that poesy may not only be abused, but that by being abused, by the reason of his sweet charming force, it can do more hurt than any other army of words, yet

[5] See especially Chapters 11 and 24.
[6] Cook, p. 9.
[7] Cook, p. 11.

shall it be so far from concluding that the abuse should give reproach to the abused, that contrariwise it is a good reason, that whatsoever, being abused, doth most harm, being rightly used—and upon the right use each thing receiveth his title—doth most good.[8]

Many volumes of subsequent debate have perhaps not adjusted this delicate conflict of values any more satisfactorily. One might summarize the problem by saying that Sidney, like most of those who have maintained that poetry is (and ought to be) moral, has not been able to resolve an ambiguity of the word *ought* as used in the formula. Is this a poetic "ought," or is it in fact only a moral "ought"? In the second sense "ought to be moral" is a tautology—since moral is what all our works ought to be. Is the thesis about the morality of poetry a truism in the realm of morals, or does it lie actually in the realm of poetics? Does it actually relate to the poet's craft?

But it is when we back off from the too explicit question about morals posed by the uncomfortable Gosson and allow ourselves to hear Sidney echoing some of those safer, because more generalized, Renaissance doctrines of ideality to which we have lately referred, that we have the Sidney who is dearest to the English literary tradition. In late antiquity, we remember, there had appeared the Plotinian doctrine of the poet's intimate access to the transcendent forms, and the example of the divinely conceived Phidian Zeus, which Plotinus shared with the *Vita Apollonii* of Philostratus. These approaches to a theory of creative imagination have their notable counterparts in Renaissance English. There is, for example, that passage in Shakespeare's *A Midsummer Night's Dream* where the "poet's eye, in a fine frenzy rolling, Doth glance from heaven to earth, from earth to heaven, ... the poet's pen . . . gives to airy nothing A local habitation and a name." [9] There is that in Bacon's *Proficience and Advancement of Learning* where "reason doth buckle and bowe the mind unto the Nature of things," poetry "doth raise and erect the Minde, by submitting the shewes of things to the desires of the mind." "Therefore it was ever thought to have some participation of divinesse." [1] And Sidney himself contributes two of the brightest in our florilegium of such sententiae: the brief refutation of a stock charge, ". . . the poet . . . nothing affirmeth, and therefore never lieth," and a metaphor of the zodiac's range and fire, which, framed in its needed context, we present as the tailpiece and conclusion of our procession from antiquity to the earliest flourishing of English critical self-consciousness.

[8] Cook, p. 38.
[9] In the context (*Midsummer Night's Dream*, V, i, 1–28), where the poet is grouped with the lunatic and the lover, these words are perhaps not to be taken quite so solemnly as they often have been.
[1] *Proficience and Advancement of Learning*, Book II, paragraph 43.

There is no art delivered unto mankind that hath not the works of nature for his principal object. . . . Only the poet, disdaining to be tied to any such subjection, lifted up with the vigor of his own invention, doth grow, in effect, into another nature, in making things either better than nature bringeth forth, or, quite anew, forms such as never were in nature, as the heroes, demigods, cyclops, chimeras, furies, and such like; so as he goeth hand in hand with nature, not enclosed within the narrow warrant of her gifts, but freely ranging within the zodiac of his own wit. Nature never set forth the earth in so rich tapestry as divers poets have done; neither with pleasant rivers, fruitful trees, sweet-smelling flowers, nor whatsoever else may make the too-much-loved earth more lovely; her world is brazen, the poets only deliver a golden.[2]

SUPPLEMENT

The error here lies obviously in applying to these verses a rhythm which, if it lay not wholly outside the consciousness of their composers, at all events lay quite outside their habit and intention. A more reasonable procedure in the face of such grotesque effects would have been to hazard the query, whether such a reading or pronunciation can possibly have been contemplated by Sidney, Harvey, and the rest. An approach to such an inquiry was made by McKerrow, who asked "what is the rhythm of a hexameter?" but unfortunately he did not pursue his quest farther, and replied with the acquiescent words, "I doubt not that they read hexameters then as they are read in schools now, 'árma virúmque canó, Trojaé qui etc.'," that is with scansion rhythm. But this throws us back to the point of view of Southey, Ellis, Saintsbury and the rest, the improbability of which we have observed.

But let us reverse the procedure and see where it leaves Virgil and Ovid and Lucan on this same charge of false accents with respect to their own language. For if it is a sound conclusion that Sidney, in order to obtain hexameter rhythm, must have intended his line "núrs inwárd maladíes" to be read with distorted accents as marked, then it is equally true that Virgil made the same demand of his Roman readers in writing *Italiám fató profugús*, in defiance of the Latin rule, that no word, unless followed by an enclitic, may be accented on the last syllable. The conclusion to which such a comparison leads scarcely requires the specific formulation, that neither the Roman nor the English poet intended or entertained any thought that his verses should be read otherwise than with natural accents proper to his own language.

Where, then, unless a well defined metrical ictus is observed, is the rhythm, the characteristic beat of the hexameter? In the case of the English example

[2] Cook, pp. 7–8.

we may well ask. As for the Virgilian line the answer is easier. The poet himself and the reader whom he contemplates, possessing by nature and by training from earlier poetry a feeling for syllabic quantity, would recognize from the mere succession of long and short syllables the underlying rhythm, undisturbed by the true accents of the several words. The English reader of Sidney's day on the other hand, reproducing by artifice what the ancient reader possessed by birth, and untrained by any past usage to recognize long and short syllables, can scarcely have felt any discernible rhythm in the vague and uncertain quantities of many lines which Sidney or Stanyhurst presented to the readers of their day as quantitative hexameters.

Neither the Elizabethan composer nor his reader approached the hexameter with a preconceived notion of, or feeling for, the rhythmical movement of the whole line, or of that "tune" so to speak, which in the modern hexameter, of Longfellow for example, is so familiar. "Scanning" of course was known and practiced for the instruction of schoolboys and for "proving" their compositions, but it was not then or later looked upon as a legitimate literary rendering of the line. To be sure a good many verses occur in the compositions of Sidney and Harvey which correspond more or less accurately to the scanning scheme of dactyls and spondees, but, as we shall see, they occur rather by accident than by design. The only fixed rhythmical feature of the Latin hexameter line in agreement with the scanning pattern was the accentual cadence of the last two feet *primus ab oris* (-uu/-u), in which word accent and syllabic quantity usually coincide. This regular recurrent cadence became from an early time so fixed a mark of the verse, that in crude popular epitaphs and in late and medieval verses it is often the index of an author's intention or ambition to construct a hexameter, when little else corresponds to the requirements of the classical verse.

But this general absence of a well defined rhythmical movement throughout the verse was not missed either by the composer or by his reader. Both had inherited the century old habit of reading Latin verse simply by the word accents, and they carried this usage over naturally from Latin into the new English counterpart. The poet himself was of course conscious of his painstaking and orderly sequence of dactyls and spondees, and in the privacy of his closet may well have "scanned and proved" their correctness; but surely it was no part of his purpose that his readers should share that consciousness.

—G. L. Hendrickson, "Elizabethan Quantitative Hexameters," *Philological Quarterly*, XXXVIII (April, 1949), 241–3, by permission of the editors

Professor Hendrickson's thesis, that the quantitative pattern of the experimental verse written by Sidney and other Elizabethans was not expected either to conform to or to twist out of shape the natural English accentual rhythm, seems unquestionable and is a valuable clarification. The aesthetic problem which remains might be put thus: In what way were the English readers expected to be conscious of the quantitative dactyls and spondees? In what way did Latin readers of Virgil feel "from the mere succession of long and short syllables the underlying rhythm, undisturbed by the true accents of the several words?"

CHAPTER 10

ENGLISH NEO-CLASSICISM: JONSON AND DRYDEN

§ *Jonson as playwright: humours, characters, satire, moral intent—II. Jonson's* Timber, *its sources, its literary ideas—III. the imitation of classical models distinguished from plagiarism and illustrated, Jonson's classicism summarized—IV. French neo-classicism, Corneille's essays on drama—V. Sorbière's attack on England, Dryden's* Essay of Dramatic Poesy: *the setting, the identity and stances of the four speakers, Neander's radicalism, his Examen of Jonson's* Epicoene*—VI. the argument about rhyme, its relation to verisimilitude and the unities, rhyme in English drama and in French, Dryden's conversion to Shakespearian blank verse, the unities of different types of stages—VII. contrast between Dryden and Corneille, Dryden's gentlemanly dialectic, varieties of scepticism in his day, his probabilism* §

T HE SOURCES OF SIDNEY'S "DEFENCE" WERE CLASSICAL, BUT THE SPIRIT was not very sternly classical. Sidney sends up the joyous fireworks of the Italianate Renaissance. His colors are enthusiastic, neo-Platonic, ideal purple and gold. The motion is soaring. He is essentially a theorist of the exuberant imagination. A far more severe classicism, squared off on the norms of objective ethical imitation, may be observed in Ben Jonson, next in line of the English men of letters who have had notably critical preoccupations. Jonson was a man of the public theaters whose genius lay in the salty, astringent, and prickly comico-satiric department of classicism. He wrote middling classical tragedies (*Sejanus, Catiline*) but rubbed both the city and general humanity down well with salt in comedies either native or Italian in setting (*Every Man in his Humour, Bartholomew Fair, Volpone*). These he planted solidly on the classical unities, and in their ethical technique he united the medieval physiological heritage, the simplified character as a "humour," or an affectation of "humour," [1] with the Plautine label type (a braggart soldier, a clever servant, an avaricious and jealous husband, a gay young man, a town gull, a country gull). He showed withal a strong trace of the Theophrastan "character," a genre newly restored to the tradition by the editing of the continental scholar Isaac Casaubon, in 1592 and 1598, and appearing, simultaneously with Jonson's plays, in the English *Characterisms* (1608) of Bishop Joseph Hall and *Characters* (1614) of Sir Thomas Overbury.

Jonson wrote a kind of native [2] classicism which it has been difficult for any audience since the mid-18th century really to enjoy—obscene yet moralizing, caustic, thorny, vulgar, immediate, Londinian and topical (and so now obscure). It was Roman satiric technique applied to London vice, and a solid instance of the Augustan principle of "imitation" or recreation of the classic model. This was a time when London, the manifold and sophisticated metropolis, was producing a mushroom growth of social literature. The epigram, little known in the West since the time of Martial and imperial Rome, was now cultivated again, and so was Juvenalian satire. As Sophocles and Aristophanes had been followed by Theophrastus and his pupil Menander, Shakespeare was followed by Jonson and by Hall.[3]

The theory that comic and satiric literature has a moral rather than a libelous intent (a theory which perhaps to some extent actually guided Jonson's comic performance) often breaks out explicitly in his Prologue, Epilogue, or Induction, or in editorializing speeches by his characters. Cicero, says the Moderator Cordatus in *Every Man out of His Humour* (III, i), would have a comedy to be:

> *Imitatio vitae, Speculum Consuetudinis, Imago veritatis,*[4] a thing throughout pleasant and ridiculous, and accommodated to the correction of manners.

[1] Henry L. Snuggs, "The Comic Humours: A New Interpretation," *PMLA*, LXII (March, 1947), 114–22, argues convincingly that the comic humours of Jonsonian drama were not actually the temperaments defined in the physico-psychological tradition but the pseudo-humours of affected eccentricity.

[2]
> Our scene is London, 'cause we would make known,
> No country's mirth is better than our own;
> No clime breeds better for your whore,
> Bawd, squire, imposter, many persons more,
> Whose manners, now call'd humours, feed the stage.
>   —Prologue to *The Alchemist*

Here is an early phase in the development of a kind of national pride upon which we shall have occasion for further comment in Chapter 11.

[3] E. C. Baldwin, "Ben Jonson's Indebtedness to the Greek Character-Sketch," *MLN*, XVI (1901), 385–96.

[4] Henry L. Snuggs, "The Source of Jonson's Definition of Comedy," *MLN*, LXV (1950), 543–4, shows an intermediate source in Minturno, *De Poeta*. Cf. *ante* Chapter 5, p. 89.

Along with this comfortable view of the comic purpose went the self-righteous confidence of the author in his own character,[5] something which had come down from Aristotelian instructions to the orator about self-advertisement, from the dictum of Cato that a good orator has to be not only skilled in speaking but a good man (*vir bonus dicendi peritus*),[6] and from the Horatian portrait of the upright satirist. As Milton would put it in the *Apology for Smectymnuus:*

> He who would not be frustrate of his hope to write well here-after in laudable things, ought himself to be a true poem.[7]

II

Jonson's more formal critical utterances included an indifferent blank verse translation of Horace's *Ars Poetica*, an *Ars* of his own which may have been lost when his library burned in 1623,[8] a few pungent *obiter dicta* upon English contemporaries (as "that Donne for not keep-ing of accent deserved hanging") made when he walked to Scotland in 1619 and conversed with the poet Drummond, and one other thing—most important by far of all. This is the book published posthumously in the 1641 folio of the *Works* and given the title *Timber: or, Dis-coveries; Made upon Men and Matter: As they have flow'd out of his daily Reading; or had their reflux to his peculiar Notion of the Times.* As the title suggests, the work is a stock book of established classical ideas collected and translated, somewhat at random, by a practising man of letters for his several purposes. The resemblance between a few of the passages and certain passages of Jonson's verse [9] points toward one of these purposes. A group of essays in the political vein looks like materials for a letter to the king on the regal function. Certain passages of literary satire are the kind a man might copy or translate to soothe his own ran-cor at the stupidity of his enemies. Several other sections, the most con-tinuously developed and the most directly concerned with literature, have somewhat the look of lecture notes, and the recent discovery of a

[5] Cf. Eugene M. Waith, "The Poet's Morals in Jonson's *Poetaster*," *MLR*, XII (March, 1951), 13–19.

[6] Atkins, II, 16.

[7] *The Student's Milton*, ed. Frank A. Patterson (New York, 1941), p. 549. The dramatic application of this doctrine and hence its real critical significance are hand-somely illustrated in the biographical prefaces at the start of Books III, VII, and IX of *Paradise Lost* (cf. John S. Diekhoff, "The Function of the Prologues in *Paradise Lost*," *PMLA*, LVII, September, 1942, 696–704) and again in Alexander Pope's apol-ogies for his satiric career, especially in the *Epistle to Arbuthnot*.

[8] Cf. Leah Jonas, *The Divine Science* (New York, 1940), p. 16.

[9] Cf. No. 101, "*Amor nummi*," and No. 103 with *The Staple of News*, III, ii, and III, i; *Discoveries A Critical Edition*, ed. Maurice Castelain (Paris, 1906), pp. XXII–XXIII. Jonson told Drummond that his method of composing was to write out his thoughts first in prose and then translate them.

legal document which seems to show Jonson's residence about 1623 to have been Gresham College has led to the plausible speculation that he exercised the deputy function of Professor of Rhetoric in that College.[1] Modern scholarship has discovered classical and Renaissance sources (in Cicero, Petronius, Quintilian, and the two Senecas, in Erasmus, Machiavelli, Vives, Bacon and a host of others) for about four-fifths of the material which makes up Jonson's *Timber*. The most sustained classical literary discussion is that on poetry, tragedy, and comedy, which runs through the last eleven numbers.[2] The second half of this, on tragedy and comedy, is mostly derived, not from the Italian sources upon which Sidney had relied, but from more northern ones, from the *De Tragoediae Constitutione* and the *Ad Horatii de Plauto et Terentino Judicium Dissertatio* of the Dutch professor Daniel Heinsius and from the Bohemian Jesuit Jacobus Pontanus.[3] One longish part on prose style and letter writing (Nos. 124–126) is taken directly from an English rhetorical treatise then circulating in manuscript among the cognoscenti, the *Directions for Speech and Style* of the diplomatist John Hoskins.[4] Those parts of Jonson's *Timber* which are concerned with literary criticism constitute about two thirds of the whole. Shall we argue that these, by the simple fact of their having been chosen and put together by Jonson, represent his critical inclinations and hence may be discussed as if they were his own? Perhaps we may. At any rate, here we have a good anthology of classical and Renaissance doctrine reduced to pithy Senecan English:[5] that "ready writing makes not good writing; but good writing brings on ready writing" (No. 115); that poetry (*poesis*) requires not only "goodness of natural wit" but "exercise," "imitation," "study," and "art" (No. 130); that comic poetry[6] is nearest to oratory because most variously gifted to portray and to stir the "affections of the mind" (No. 130); that "the Episodes, and digressions in a Fable, are the same that housestuffe, and other furniture are in a house" (No. 134). Except for the last solid section (Nos. 127–136) of poetic and dramatic theory, the emphasis of *Timber* is on epistolary and oratorical style, on the manly virtues of brevity, perspicuity, vigor, discretion (No. 125), on

---

[1] C. J. Sisson, "Ben Jonson of Gresham College," *TLS*, September 21, 1951, p. 604; and the comment of George B. Johnston, *TLS*, December 28, 1951, p. 837. See Ralph Walker's rearranged edition, *Discoveries* (Syracuse, 1953).

[2] The numbers 1–137 were inserted by Gollancz (1898) and are retained by Castelain.

[3] J. E. Spingarn, "The Source of Jonson's Discoveries," *MP*, II (April, 1903), 1–10; Allan H. Gilbert and Henry L. Snuggs, "On the Relations of Horace to Aristotle in Literary Criticism," *JEGP*, XLVI (July, 1947), 240–4.

[4] John Hoskins, *Directions for Speech and Style*, ed. Hoyt H. Hudson (Princeton, 1935), pp. xxvii–xxviii.

[5] Jonson expresses his admiration of Bacon's style in Nos. 71 and 72. Swinburne, rediscovering *Timber* in 1889, rated its style better than that of Bacon.

[6] We shall have occasion in the next chapter to quote what must seem to modern ears the curious treatment of comedy in No. 131.

the author's practical problems and the rules of thumb which a veteran practitioner has found useful, on *poeta* rather than on *poema*. A few opinions about English writers form a notable incident in the early history of English literary self-consciousness.

> As *Livy* before *Salust*, *Sydney* before *Donne;* and beware of letting them taste *Gower*, or *Chaucer* at first, lest falling too much in love with Antiquity, and not apprehending the weight, they grow rough and barren in language onely. . . . *Spencer*, in affecting the Ancients, writ no Language: Yet I would have him read for his matter.—No. 116

> *Lucretius* is scabrous and rough in these; hee seekes 'hem: As some do *Chaucerismes* with us, which were better expung'd and banish'd.—No. 119 [7]

III

PROBABLY the classical doctrine which Jonson's *Timber* most illuminates is that concerning the imitation of models. That the exuberance and invention of the English Renaissance was consistent with a steady interest in classic models is a fact of which we may remind ourselves by thinking simply about such well-known phenomena as the sources of Shakespeare's plays and the numerous translations produced by the Englishmen of that age (Golding's *Ovid*, Harington's *Ariosto*, Chapman's *Homer*, Fairfax's *Tasso*, Florio's *Montaigne*, the works of the "Translator General" Philemon Holland).[8] Jonson's *Timber* relates to this spirit of the age in two ways—both through precept, and, as we have already more than hinted, very notably through example. Perhaps some of the precepts may seem in conflict with others. One of the five main ways to *poesis*, as we have noted, is "imitation."

> . . . to bee able to convert the substance or Riches of another *Poet*, to his owne use. To make choise of one excellent man above the rest, and so to follow him, till he grow very Hee; or so like him, as the Copie may be mistaken for the Principall.
> —No. 130

At the same time Jonson's *Timber* contains a number of severe animadversions regarding servile prostration before the ancients ("Nothing is

---

[7] See No. 64, on Shakespeare, quoted *post*, p. 180. (Jonson's statements about Shakespeare's "small Latin and less Greek" and his being "not of an age, but for all time" appear in the commendatory poem prefixed to the First Folio; that Shakespeare "wanted art" appears in the *Conversations with Drummond*.)

[8] Cf. F. O. Matthiessen, *Translation An Elizabethan Art* (Cambridge, Mass., 1931).

more ridiculous, then to make an Author a *Dictator* as the schools have done Aristotle." "Whiche of the Greekelings durst ever give precepts to Demosthenes?").[9] And like his ancient models Horace and Martial, Jonson has a stern sense of indignation at the kind of literary imitation which may be called robbery.[1] It was Martial who had introduced the term *plagiarius* (kidnaper) into Latin literature. Jonson in his *Poetaster* (1601) and Bishop Hall in his *Satires* (1608) use "plagiary."[2] Jonson himself, Dryden was to say,[3] is a "learned plagiary." But this phrase, applied to Jonson's acknowledged use of ancient sources, was a joke, for the concept of plagiarism was an ethical and social one, concerned with stealing another man's fame and profit. It was not a critical concept, as it has nearly become for a later age which has merged patent office legalism with aesthetic standards of inspiration and voyantism. "Plagiarism," one of Jonson's editors has remarked, "is an invention of the 19th century."[4]

The borrowed and translated fragments of Jonson's *Timber* exhibit as much care, force, and accuracy of style as if they had been his own most preciously individual thoughts. The reason is that he did not make a distinction of literary value in favor of his own thoughts and *against* those which he found in Quintilian and Cicero. Literary work was not primarily personal expression but objective imitation, either of nature straight or of nature through the model. And the use of models entailed their assimilation and invited their improvement.

> Not, as a Creature, that swallowes, what it takes in, crude, raw, or undigested; but, that feeds with an Appetite, and hath a Stomacke to concoct, devide, and turne all into nourishment. Not, to imitate servilely, as *Horace* saith . . . but to draw forth out of the best, and choisest flowers, with the Bee, and turne all into Honey.—No. 130[5]

The following passage of *Timber* on the subject of memory might surely be said to have the ring of intimate self-revelation.

> *Memory* of all the *powers* of the mind, is the most *delicate* and *fraile*; it is the first of our *faculties* that Age invades. *Seneca*,

[9] Nos. 123, 130.

[1] Writers who refuse the help of imitation (No. 65) include not only those who despise models but those who steal without acknowledgment and those who steal and protest originality—making a "false venditation of their own naturals." "Such are all the Essayists, even their master Mountaigne."

[2] Harold O. White, *Plagiarism and Imitation during the English Renaissance* (Cambridge, 1935), pp. 120-1, 133-4. Cf. Austin Warren, *Crashaw* (Baton Rouge, 1939), pp. 102-3.

[3] *Essay of Dramatic Poesy*, in *Essays*, ed. W. P. Ker, I, 43.

[4] Schelling, quoted by Castelain, p. XXIII.

[5] Cf. *post* p. 218-20 the use made by Swift of the symbol of the bee and the spider in expounding the difference between "ancients" and "moderns."

the father, the *Rhetorician*, confesseth of himselfe, hee had a miraculous one; not only to receive but to hold. I my selfe could in my youth, have repeated all, that ever I had made; and so continued, till I was past fortie; Since, it is much decay'd in me. . . . Whatsoever I pawn'd with it, while I was young, and a boy, it offers me readily, and without stops: but what I trust to it now, or have done of later yeares, it layes up more negligently, and oftentimes loses.—No. 56

Yet Jonson is here following rather closely the passage in Seneca the Elder to which he alludes.[6] (Perhaps because it fitted his own case literally, perhaps because by intimations in his own experience he saw a general truthfulness in it.) Or take one of the best known paragraphs in *Timber*, the sketch of Shakespeare.

DE SHAKE-
SPEARE
NOSTRATI.

I remember, the Players have often mentioned it as an honour to *Shakespeare*, that in his writing (whatsoever he penn'd) hee never blotted out line. My answer hath beene, would he had blotted a thousand. Which they thought a malevolent speech. I had not told posterity this, but for their ignorance, who choose that circumstance to commend their friend by, wherein he most faulted. And to justifie mine owne candor, (for I lov'd the man, and doe honour his memory (on this side Idolatry) as much as any). Hee was (indeed) honest, and of an open, and free nature; had an excellent *Phantsie*; brave notions, and

AUGUSTUS
IN HAT.

gentle expressions: wherein hee flowed with that facility, that sometime it was necessary he should be stop'd: "*Sufflaminandus erat*," as Augustus said of Haterius. His wit was in his owne power; would the rule of it had beene so too. Many times hee fell into those things, could not escape laughter: as when he said in the person of *Caesar*, one speaking to him; "*Caesar, thou dost me wrong.*" Hee replyed, "*Caesar did never wrong, but with just cause;*" and such like, which were ridiculous. But hee redeemed his vices, with his vertues. There was ever more in him to be praysed, then to be pardoned.—No. 64

Here Jonson advises us that a source for at least some of his phrasing is Seneca—a passage in the *Controversiae* (IV, Preface, 7–11) of Seneca the Elder concerning a poet named Haterius. But would we think that the part about inspiration and control—which is fitted so neatly into the context, framing the illustration from Shakespeare's *Julius Caesar*

[6] *Controversiae, Liber* I, 2–3.

—had been written originally sixteen hundred years earlier, about a minuscule Latin poet?

> *In sua potestate habebat ingenium, in aliena modum. . . . saepe incidebat in ea, quae derisum effugere non possent. . . . Redimebat tamen vitia virtutibus et persaepe plus habebat quod laudares quam cui ignosceres.*

To the neo-classical mind the earlier discovery of this individual reality seemed not to diminish its fitness for the case of a contemporary. Nor did earlier exploitation of a general truth preclude its genuine and living modern realization.[7]

Jonson's stout and craftsmanly common sense about imitation, shown even more convincingly in his practice than in his precepts, may be taken as the key to a theory of poetry which stressed hard work—imitation, practice, study, art (and with these but one poor pennyworth of *ingenium*)—a theory too which stressed poems squared off by the norm of reality. This theory celebrated the mobility and power of poetry, but it included no hymn to spontaneity or to what today we think of as the creative imagination. It included no statement even remotely parallel to that of Sidney about the free range of wit within its zodiac or that of Bacon about poetry submitting the shows of reality to the desires of the mind. Some deviation or wavering from the classic norm may appear in Jonson's treatment of such a minor article as that prescribing the unity of place—and we have seen that he is guilty of defying the authority of the antique critics. But he is the first English man of letters to exhibit a nearly complete and consistent neo-classicism. His historical importance is that he throws out a vigorous announcement of the rule from which in the next generation Dryden is to be engaged in politely rationalized recessions. One basic problem which Jonson leaves us pondering (the same as that posed implicitly once before, by a strong appreciator of poetic inspiration, Longinus) might be formulated as follows: Does an aesthetic norm of objective reality entail a *genetic* theory of conscious and strenuous artistic effort? If a poet is to give us a truthful account of general human nature, does this poet have to be a learned consumer of midnight oil, a graduate in grammar, logic, and rhetoric, and in the higher liberal disciplines? Or on the other hand: Does an aesthetic norm of personal expression entail a genetic theory of untrammeled and unstudied inspiration? If a poet is to tell the truth as he himself most really and deeply experiences it, does he have to be a rebel against tradition and conventional education, a Bohemian, long-haired, and unwashed, a defiler of ancestral ashes?[8]

---

[7] Cf. *Timber* No. 116 ("If you powre a glut of water . . .") with Quintilian, *Institute* I, ii, 26; and *Timber* No. 11 ("What a deale of cold business . . .") with Quintilian XII, xi, 18.

[8] Cf. Horace, *Ad Pisones*, 296–7, 470.

IV

DURING the time between Sidney's *Defence of Poesie* and the beginning of John Dryden's long critical career (with the Dedication of his tragi-comedy *The Rival Ladies* in 1664) the seat of continental critical authority shifted from Italy to France. In the Frenchified courtly literary circle of Restoration England, 1660–1688, the most effective outside influence was contemporary French classicism—the spirit which reached its zenith in the dramas of Corneille and Racine. One difference between this French classicism and the earlier Italian classicism was that the best creative works associated with the earlier movement were those written without concern for the code, or at least in expansion of it (*Orlando Furioso, Gerusalemme Liberata, Il Pastor Fido*), whereas the best French classicism seemed actually the product of the code or at least a conscientious attempt to demonstrate it. Neo-classicism in 17th-century French poetry was apparently a dynamic and generative force. At the same time its critical utterances tended to be cranky. Corneille's first masterpiece, *Le Cid* (1637), was a remarkably classical play, a close realization, for instance, of the three *unités Scaligeriennes* (henceforth *Corneliennes*). Yet he himself came to look on it as one of his more relaxed efforts.[9] *Le Cid* was meanly disparaged in the *Observations* of Scudéry and in Chapelain's *Sentiments de l'Académie* during the notorious imbroglio known to French historians as *La Querelle du Cid*. In the Abbé d'Aubignac's *Pratique du théâtre*, 1657, Corneille was treated to a fine blend of censure and faint praise. Corneille's own critical defenses appear in the *Examens* which he prefixed to each of his plays in the collected edition of 1660 and in the three *Discours* contained in the same volumes, *De l'Utilité et des Parties du Poëme Dramatique, De la Tragédie et des Moyens de la Traiter selon le Vraisemblable ou le Nécessaire,* and *Des Trois Unités*. These documents show the neo-classic conscience torturing itself and explaining its lapses in a way that is scarcely urbane and when seen from outside may look even a little comic.[1]

When Aristotle says the plot must be constructed *kata to eikos ē to anagkaion* (according to probability or necessity), he means, thinks Corneille, either probability of versimilitude (the way things are likely to work in nature) or—in case that is inconvenient—the "necessity"

---

[9] *"Bien que ce soit celui de tous mes ouvrages réguliers où je me suis permis le plus de licence, il passe encore pour le plus beau auprès de ceux qui ne s'attachent pas à la dernière sévérité des règles"* (*Examen* of *Le Cid, Oeuvres,* ed. Charles Marty-Laveaux, 1862, III, 91).

[1] Cf. Pierre Legouis, "Corneille and Dryden as Dramatic Critics," in *Seventeenth Century Studies Presented to Sir Herbert Grierson* (Oxford, 1938), pp. 269–78.

imposed by dramatic requirements, the exaction of the rules. Improbable that Don Rodrigue could fight two mortal combats of honor and a battle against the Moors in the space of twenty-four hours or a little more—but necessary to the economy of Corneille's classic design in the *Cid* (*c'est l'incommodité de la règle*).[2] Was unity of place really plausible (verisimilitudinous) in the *Cid* if the Moors had to be supposed invading Seville on a high tide when in fact the Guadalquivir perhaps had no such tide? The French audience would not object to this disregard of geographical truth, since they could at least conceive the phenomenon from their experience of the Seine at Paris.[3] There was a more legitimate subtlety in Corneille's explanation of his abstract or unspecified treatment of locality (*le lieu théâtral*), a vague neutral ground, an antechamber into which apartments of divers inmates of the same palace open, or even a kind of unidentified space where actors by taking only a few steps move from one part of a city to another.[4] And there was no doubt a great measure of truth in his contention that one formal "embellishment" in which he specialized, the *liaison des scènes* (whereby each group of characters, within an act, supplied some for the next group, or scene, so that the stage was never vacant), had been increasingly dictated by his own successful practice and by the steadily more finical taste of the audience themselves, rather than by ancient authority or by *a priori* theoretical conceptions. In any case, however, freedom was quickly narrowing in "from precedent to precedent." The *Discourses* and *Examens* of Corneille represent a very advanced state of neo-classic exactitude and ingenuity.

V

IT HAPPENED that in the year 1663 a Frenchman named Samuel Sorbière visited England on some sort of quasi-diplomatic or journalistic mission and on returning to France did the undiplomatic thing of publishing an account of his *Voyage*[5] in which he made highly uncomplimentary remarks about English science and about the English stage.

[2] For the sake of compactness we here conflate general principles from Corneille's *Discours* on tragedy and specific instances from his *Examen* of *Le Cid*.

[3] *Examen* of *Le Cid*, *Oeuvres*, III, 97–8.

[4] "*Ainsi, par une fiction de théatre, on peut s'imaginer que don Diègue et le Comte, sortant du palais du Roi, avancent toujours en se querellant, et sont arrivés devant la maison de ce premier lorsqu'il recoit le soufflet qui l'oblige à y entrer pour y chercher du secours*" (*Examen* of *Le Cid*, *Oeuvres*, III, 100).

[5] *Relation d'un Voyage en Angleterre où sont touchées plusieurs choses qui regardent l'état des Sciences, et de la Religion, et autres matières curieuses* (Paris, 1664). See George Williamson, "The Occasion of 'An Essay of Dramatic Poesy,'" *MP*, XLIV (August, 1946), 1–9.

These comedies of theirs would not be received quite so well in France. Their poets play hob with the unity of place and the rule of twenty-four hours. Their comic plots run for twenty-five years. The first act gives you the marriage of a Prince, and immediately afterwards come the travels and exploits of his son.[6]

Sorbière succeeded in provoking one reply, both on scientific and on literary grounds, from the historian of the English Royal Society, Thomas Sprat. And it was not long after the incident that John Dryden, courtly poet and dramatist,[7] having apparently stocked his mind with the critiques of Corneille, retired to the country during the plague years of 1665 and 1666 and wrote his dialogue published in 1668, *An Essay of Dramatic Poesy*,[8] the most ambitiously constructed critical document of his career and the most important for general literary theory.

Taking advantage of one of the most notable international relations of the day, the naval battle fought in the Channel between the British and the Dutch on June 3, 1665, Dryden imagines the four gentlemanly and witty interlocutors of his dialogue as drifting in a barge softly down the Thames past Greenwich (for the sake of better hearing the guns). The literary discussion in which they find themselves soon involved (an international engagement at another level)[9] comes about at random through some remarks about certain extravagant Clevelandish poems which have recently appeared in celebration of public events. As the conversation progresses, an interest in two somewhat similar oppositions, that between classicism and modernity and that between the Elizabethan generation (the "last age") in English letters and the present, tends to entangle and temporarily to obscure the lines of the argument.

---

[6] *"Mais les Comedies n'auroient pas en France toute l'approbation qu'elles ont en Angleterre. Les Poëtes se mocquent de l'uniformité du lieu, & de la regle des vingt-quatre heurs. Ils font des comedies de vingt-cinq ans, & apres avoir representé au premier acte le mariage d'un Prince, ils representent toute d'une suite les belles Actions de son fils, & luy font voir bien du pays"* (*Relation*, Cologne, 1669, p. 129, quoted by Williamson, p. 2).

[7] He became Poet Laureate in 1668 and Historiographer Royal in 1670 (D. Nichol Smith, *John Dryden*, Cambridge, 1950, p. 11).

[8] Dryden's *Essay of Dramatic Poesy* makes about a dozen direct allusions to Corneille's criticism, all but one or two apparently to the *Discours des Trois Unités*. The *Essay* shows also a considerable debt to Ben Jonson, as will be in part suggested during the course of our discussion. Lord Bolingbroke was to tell Joseph Spence that Dryden said he had got more from the Spanish critics than from the Italians and French and all others together (Saintsbury II, 332; Ker I, lxvi), but the meaning of this remains doubtful. For more detailed accounts, see Ker I, 288 ff and Amanda M. Ellis, "Horace's Influence on Dryden," *PQ*, IV (January, 1925), 39–60; Frank L. Huntley, *On Dryden's "Essay of Dramatic Poesy"* (University of Michigan Press, 1951), pp. 2–6. Dryden's *Essays*, ed. W. P. Ker, 2 vols., Oxford, 1926.

[9] Cf. Charles Kaplan, in *The Explicator*, VIII (March, 1950), No. 36.

But in the main: the speaker who first develops his view at length, Crites (standing perhaps for Dryden's brother-in-law Sir Robert Howard,[1] a dramatic collaborator with Dryden and one who had already published arguments on rhyme in drama and the unities), expounds the extreme classic view, that the Greeks and Romans fully discovered and illustrated those reasonable and perennial rules to which the modern drama can do no better than conform. In the really minor issue between the "last age" and the present in England, he maintains the superiority of the "last age" in making plays but is nearly ready to recognize the new degree of correctness in versification achieved by Waller and Denham. The recent advance of English versification to a state of nearly classic perfection is an assumption so solidly established for the other speakers in the dialogue as not to be of main moment to the argument. The second person to speak at length, Eugenius (plausibly to be taken as Dryden's friend Charles Sackville, Lord Buckhurst,[2] great-grandson of that Thomas Sackville who was co-author of *Gorboduc*, the first "regular" English tragedy in 1561), takes the negative position that the ancient poets failed badly in their illustration of the rules prescribed by their critics. The implication is that the moderns [3] have actually best illustrated the rules —but there is little effort to adduce positive evidence for this view. Then thirdly, Lisideius (whose name seems like an anagram of Sidleius, or Sir Charles Sedley,[4] a younger wit of the day), accepting the same premises as Crites and Eugenius, that the classical rules for decorous imitation of nature are indeed the fundamentals of correct dramatic creation, advances the argument by finding the locus of perfect realization not in the contemporary English drama (as may have been implied by Eugenius) but in the French. Thus Dryden gives preliminary free rein to three leading kinds of classicism, letting them talk themselves out, and it is not until this late point in the *Essay* that the main pivot of the argument occurs—with the entrance of Neander (the new man, Dryden of course, whose name so nearly makes a convenient anagram). A definition of a play to which all four speakers have agreed has been formulated at the outset by Lisideius:

---

[1] But see *post* p. 188; G. R. Noyes, "Crites in Dryden's *Essay of Dramatic Poesy*," *MLN*, XXVIII (June, 1923), 333 ff; and Frank L. Huntley, "On the Persons of Dryden's *Essay of Dramatic Poesy*," *MLN*, LXIII (1948), 88–95.

[2] Despite the actual historical presence of this nobleman in the fleet fighting the Dutch and the song "To all you ladies now at land" which he wrote on board his ship.

[3] Eugenius is a new thinker, a scientist. "If natural causes be more known now than in the time of Aristotle, . . . it follows that poesy and other arts may, with the same pains, arrive still nearer to perfection" (Ker I, 44).

[4] Dryden dedicated *The Assignation* to him in 1673, calling him the Tibullus of his age. Huntley, *On Dryden's "Essay . . . ,"* p. 11, suggests that "Lisideius" may be a play on an Anglicized pronounciation of *Le Cid*.

> A just and lively image of human nature, representing its pas-
> sions and humours, and the changes of fortune to which it is
> subject, for the delight and instruction of mankind.[5]

The other arguments have all rested on the first term in this definition,
the word "just." That is, they have all tried to set a value on drama according to the degree of its versimilitude. The strategy of Neander (the
champion of the English against the French) is now to redirect the argument toward the idea of liveliness and toward humours and passions.
He pushes the argument in such a way as to raise a question about the
relation of the term "justice" to the second term of the definition—*liveliness*. He asks, in effect, whether justice in an imitation of human life
can occur at all unless through liveliness—that is, through lifelikeness.

> 'Tis true, those beauties of the French poesy are such as will
> raise perfection higher where it is, but are not sufficient to give
> it where it is not: they are indeed the beauties of a statue, but
> not of a man, because not animated with the soul of Poesy,
> which is imitation of humour and passions.[6]

Dryden has some fun here with the French unity of place (where the
characters stand still and "the street, the window, the house, and the
closet, are made to walk about" [7]), and with the French declamatory
speeches. (Frenchmen are more frivolous and airy and need to be sobered
by their theatre; the English, more sullen, need entertainment.) One of
Corneille's statements in favor of practice at the expense of the rules is
quoted with approval. "Il est facile aux speculatifs d'estre severes."
Neander is willing to come out for the more unkempt, boyish, and
rowdy features of English drama—the roll of drums and clash of swords
at the finale which Sir Philip Sidney in one of the stern moments of his
Defence had ridiculed (*Quodcumque ostendis mihi sic, incredulus odi*)
and which had been a joke to Ben Jonson:

> with three rusty swords,
> And help of some few foot-and half-foot words,
> Fight over *Yorke* and *Lancaster's* long jars.
> —Prologue to *Every Man in his Humour*

"Whether custom has so insinuated itself into our countrymen, or nature has so formed them to fierceness," says Neander, "I know not; but
they will scarcely suffer combats and other objects of horror to be taken
from them."[8]

"The great work of Dryden in criticism," says T. S. Eliot, "is that
at the right moment he became conscious of the necessity of affirming

---

[5] Ker I, 36.   [7] Ker I, 77.
[6] Ker I, 68.   [8] Ker I, 74.

the native element in literature." [9] And at least he did succeed in blending an English accent with the French accent which had for the time being become a necessity.

> He who writ this, not without pains and thought,
> From *French* and *English* theatres has brought
> Th' exactest rules, by which a play is wrought.
>
> The Unities of Action, Place, and Time;
> The scenes unbroken; and a mingled chime
> Of *Johnson's* humour, with *Corneille's* rhyme.
> —Prologue to *Secret Love*, 1668

The sketches of the dramatists of the "last age" in Dryden's *Essay* are among the dearest moments in the history of national self-appreciation.

> [Shakespeare] was the man who of all modern, and perhaps ancient poets, had the largest and most comprehensive soul. . . . when he describes any thing, you more than see it, you feel it too. Those who accuse him to have wanted learning, give him the greater commendation: he was naturally learn'd.

> [Beaumont and Fletcher] understood and imitated the conversation of gentlemen much better; whose wild debaucheries, and quickness of wit in repartees, no poet can ever paint as they have done.

> [Ben Jonson was] the most learned and judicious writer which any theatre ever had. . . . If I would compare him with Shakespeare, I must acknowledge him the more correct poet, but Shakespeare the greater wit. Shakespeare was the Homer, or father of our dramatic poets; Johnson was the Virgil, the pattern of elaborate writing; I admire him, but I love Shakespeare.[1]

To show that classical rules, so far as they may be convenient, can be and have been cherished by the English, Neander chooses for an extended *Examen* one of the most regular plays of Ben Jonson, *Epicoene or the Silent Woman*. The comic action of this play occurs in two houses (actually four houses and an alley) in London and all within a few hours (between the late rising of gallants and an afternoon dinner party) and on "a signal and long-expected day." The main character, or humour (Morose, a rich old uncle, who cannot tolerate noise), is both delightful

---

[9] *Use of Poetry*, p. 14.

[1] Ker I, 79–83. "The account of Shakespeare may stand as a perpetual model of encomiastick criticism" (Samuel Johnson, *Life of Dryden, Works*, 1787, II, 378). Johnson, says D. Nichol Smith, "knew the pedigree of his own preface. Dryden's *Essay* had struck the note and set the method of the best criticism of Shakespeare for the next hundred years" (*John Dryden*, Cambridge, 1950, p. 20).

and plausible [2] (and besides, Jonson had known such a man—here the rationale teeters). And the "intrigue" (the marrying of the Morose uncle to a Silent Woman who at the wedding party becomes a chatterbox and after due torture of Morose is next discovered to be a boy—whereby Sir Dauphine releases his uncle and is rewarded with a fortune), the "intrigue," says Neander, is "the greatest and most noble of any pure unmixed comedy in any language." If we could fully understand that word "noble," we might understand much which is perhaps now obscure to us in the neo-classic view of comedy.[3]

VI

FINALLY, Dryden's *Essay*, with Neander still in charge, veers off toward its conclusion with a protracted wrangle over a question which both Dryden and his brother-in-law had before this argued in print. (On him incidentally Dryden now plays a mean trick, for Crites, whom we may plausibly accept as Howard, is made to argue Howard's real life view that rhyme is not appropriate in serious plays and is made by Neander to seem wrong, but at the same time he has in the first part of the *Essay* been assigned the losing view that the ancients surpassed the moderns—which was not Howard's view in real life.) The dispute was to be continued in the following year in a Preface by Howard and in Dryden's *Defence of an Essay of Dramatic Poesy*. Only the main lines are of interest—but they are curiously so. Howard argued against rhyme in the dialogue of serious plays on the ground that rhyme was unreal, not the way people really talk. And Dryden argued for it on the ground that:

> A serious play . . . is indeed the representation of Nature, but 'tis Nature wrought up to an higher pitch.[4]

> A play is supposed to be [not "a composition of several persons speaking ex tempore," but] the work of the poet.[5]

---

[2] Dryden here makes an attempt to explain the variety in unity of so complex a "humour" as Shakespeare's Falstaff. "I need but tell them, that humour is the ridiculous extravagance of conversation, wherein one man differs from all others. . . . As for Falstaff, he is not properly one humour, but a miscellany of humours or images, drawn from so many several men: that wherein he is singular in his wit. . . . among the English . . . by humour is meant some extravagant habit, passion, or affection, particular . . . to some one person, by the oddness of which, he is immediately distinguished from the rest of men" (Ker I, 84–5). Cf. *post* Chapter 11, p. 205.

[3] See *post* Chapter 11, pp. 204–13. See *OED*, "noble," A. II 8.

[4] Ker I, 100 (*Essay of Dramatic Poesy*).

[5] Ker I, 114 (*Defence*).

At the same time, however, and in the same documents Howard was pooh-poohing the unities of time and place on the ground that they aimed at an impossible verisimilitude through exact coincidence of theater time and space with plot time and space. The argument is a rather full anticipation (wrapped though it is in Howard's bungling manner) of a far more celebrated instance which was to appear a hundred years later, in Samuel Johnson's *Preface to Shakespeare.*

> He that can take the stage at one time for the palace of the *Ptolemies,* may take it in half an hour for the promontory of *Actium.* Delusion, if delusion be admitted, has no certain limitation. . . . Time is, of all modes of existence, most obsequious to the imagination; a lapse of years is as easily conceived as a passage of hours.[6]

Dryden argued the opposite: he upheld the unities because he thought they tended, successfully enough, toward verisimilitude. We have then an odd opposition in which Howard rejects rhyme because it is further from reality than blank verse but rejects the unities because they are only a pointless approximation to a reality which cannot be attained— whereas Dryden upholds the unities for their verisimilitude but upholds rhyme for its transcendence of a verisimilitude which is not the real aim of the drama. The tastes of both Howard and Dryden may perhaps be made consistent if one suggests for each a different, though not explicitly entertained, general principle. Howard, that is, apparently desired a relaxation of formalities (and hence, though he may not have known it, of dramatic intensity). Dryden on the contrary desired to maintain the formalities. And each was misled in his theorizing by the then current but partly irrelevant issue of verisimilitude.

What degree of formality, and what kind, is possible for a given theater in a given language? The history of the 17th-century drama in France and England shows that certain qualities of the French language, its relative absence of tonic stress and its undulatory long Alexandrine, made possible for Corneille a certain style which the accentuated English language and its pentameter made at least exceedingly difficult for Dryden. The English rhymed heroic couplet was to have its successes, but not in heroic drama. The rhetorical declamations of Dryden's plays were moving toward an idiom of epigrammatic, moral and reflective poetry; the movement was towards satire and Popean epistle. Among the several conversions for which Dryden's career is noted was one *from* rhyme and *to* blank verse in his later serious dramas. In the Prologue to the last of his heroic dramas, *Aurengzebe,* 1675, "Our Author. . . . to confess a truth (though out of time) Grows weary of his long-lov'd Mistress, Rhyme." And the style of the best of his serious

[6] *Works* (1787), IX, 259–60.

plays, *All for Love*, 1677, is blank verse, as nearly on the Shakespearian model as his genius and his classical inclinations would permit. "In my style," he writes in the Preface, "I have professed to imitate the divine Shakespeare; which that I might perform more freely, I have disencumbered myself from rhyme." [7]

As for the unities, it is to be observed that the peculiarities of the French stage in the time of Corneille and those of the English stage in the time of Shakespeare and again in that of Dryden go a long way to determine the argument. Every stage is both one place and several places —one sitting room with several corners or groups of chairs (more or less set off as separate places according to the needs of the action), or one city square or street with several houses. The stage designer's problem of unity (before it is complicated by a temporal succession of scenes on the same stage) is a problem of the relation between an overall space and its components. How abstract and conventional (and hence how flexible), or how concrete and natural (and hence how inflexible) shall this be?

The three arches of the Hellenistic arcade stage, representing formally and hence freely three entrances from three places at indeterminate distances apart, was a medium decor from which one might diverge in several directions—toward the advanced abstraction or formal freedom of the Elizabethan architectural and symbolic façade (something arrived at apparently through the influence of other visual arts—the monument and the tableau) or at the other extreme toward the highly illusionistic Vitruvian perspective contrived by wings and painted backdrops on the Italian stage during the 16th century. The latter was a very reasoned attempt to make the several places which were simultaneously present (and successively needed for the action) appear as parts of one larger outdoor place—typically a city street or square—one place in the sense that in nature it could really all be seen at once by a human eye.[8] And then, thirdly, there was a kind of stage which had departed wildly and naively from such norms, toward a simultaneous ocular realization of several places widely distant on the earth's surface and beyond—the *maisons* (mansions) of the French medieval mystery stage: Paradise, Nazareth, the Temple, Jerusalem, the Palace, the Golden Gate, the sea of Galilee, Limbo and Hell.

By an inopportune anachronism the theater of the Hôtel de Bourgogne, at which the classical plays of Corneille and his early contemporaries were acted, had inherited the machinery of the medieval dramatic organization which was known as the Confrérie de la Passion. As a

---

[7] "Not that I condemn my former way, but that this is more proper to my present purpose" (Ker I, 200).

[8] See George R. Kernodle. *From Art to Theatre, Form and Convention in the Renaissance* (University of Chicago Press, 1944), esp. Chaps. IV, V, VI, VIII.

result the evolution of stage and plot toward the perspective ideal and its companion classical unities produced some curious intermediate phases.[9] Imagine, for instance, two towns or even two distant quarters of the same town joined in a kind of perspective synthesis. Corneille's free treatment of such paradoxes under the rubric of the indeterminate place, or *lieu theatral*, was in effect a movement toward something like the fluid or merely geometric space of the Elizabethan façade and apron, with its entrance right and left, its balcony representing anything above, its curtained recess representing anything within or discoverable. With an increased use of the *ferme* or movable shutter on the French stage and at the same time the moving forward and enlargement of the proscenium, the theater of the later 17th century developed toward the more complicated realism of successive different scenes—though not toward the dispersion of these in time and space such as may be found in Shakespeare's *Antony and Cleopatra* and other global or cosmic Elizabethan plays. The French ideal of concentration was fully achieved perhaps once, a few years after Dryden's *Essay*, in Racine's *Bérénice*, 1670, where the whole action (summed up by Racine in the words of Suetonius: *Titus Reginam Berenicen dimisit invitus invitam*) takes place during about two hours and a half in one small chamber. This ideal, or its approximation, is what has actually prevailed in the modern European theater, where today an *Antony and Cleopatra* or a *Marco's Millions* is an anomalous intrusion of a structure more familiar in the novel.

As for the unity of time, two inversely proportional verisimilitudes seem always to have troubled the dramatist. If the play's plot time is compressed into the Aristotelian single day or into Racine's even smaller compass, thus approaching or attaining the verisimilitude of the actual two hours of the theater, this achievement is likely to impair the plausibility of the strenuous series of exertions and the reversal of fortune required for a dramatic action[1]—the several armed conflicts of Don Rodrigue, or the firm faith and sudden suspicion of Othello. On the other hand, the extension of time and space required to accommodate a large and various action moves inevitably away from the verisimilitude of the theatrical two hours. A concentration of psychological effort within a vaguely defined period has been found on the whole a smaller affront to our sense of the real than the jamming together of many visible acts of violence during a period so sharply defined as a day or a little more.

---

[9] Ker I, xlv.

[1] "If a Tragedy is to be composed from the last story [that of Ceyx and Alcyone] it should not begin with the departure of Ceyx, for as the whole time for stage-representation is only six or eight hours, it is not true to life to have a storm arise, and the ship founder, in a part of the sea from which no land is visible" (Scaliger, *Poetics*, III, 97). In an era where air travel from Paris to London in a time much shorter than one "period" of the sun is an everyday matter, requirements for unity of space on the stage may well be expected to undergo some change.

VII

NEANDER and his three friends at the end of the *Essay of Dramatic Poesy* come quietly to shore at the foot of Somerset Stairs and, having amicably agreed on hardly anything, part with mutual courtesy for their several destinations. One of the chief contributions of Dryden to English criticism is the conversational pace, the gentlemanly tone (though it sometimes masks ironic mayhem), the cool and judicial posture. Corneille wrote lofty and fiery tragedies of honor but attached to them quibbling criticisms—crabbed vindications of literary honor. Dryden's plays, produced for the most part in the pragmatic, craftsmanly spirit of one who aims to hit the public taste or who is satisfied that he has "swept the stakes," (or who will even cynically confess: "I knew they were bad enough to please" [2]) are less impressive, but in their very defects they were the occasions for the casually graceful causerie of his Prefaces, Dedications, and other defences. The *Essay of Dramatic Poesy* exemplifies that kind of pseudo-Platonic dialogue which during the next seventy-five years became one of the most prevalent neo-classic forms in England.[3] Neander, however, differs from Socrates in having not only less dialectical tenacity and subtlety but also less triumphant pugnacity. Neander is Socrates become a gentleman, an *honnête homme*. His opponents have their say at length, and his own replies, though wittily pointed, are not insistent or humiliating. A remarkable feature of Dryden's critical mind is his capacity to retain, along with a steady concern for the reasoned justification of taste, an openness to contrary argument almost approaching scepticism. Among several somewhat different principles of scepticism prevalent in Dryden's day, one was scientific and positivistic, what we find in the work of Hobbes and in the activities of the Royal Society, of which Dryden himself, with other literary men, was for a time a member.[4] Another principle—a form of reaction to the scientific —was Pyrrhonist, antirational, fideist. Dryden apparently cultivated in himself a degree of resemblance to the more fashionable modes of doubt. In the *Defence of the Essay*, for instance, he says:

> My whole discourse was sceptical, according to that way of reasoning which was used by Socrates, Plato, and all the Academics of old, . . . and which is imitated in the modest inquisitions of the Royal Society. . . . You see it is a dialogue sus-

[2] Dedication of *The Spanish Friar*, 1681 (Ker I, 246).

[3] Eugene R. Purpus, "The Plain, Easy, and Familiar Way: the Dialogue in English Literature 1660–1725," *ELH*, XVII (March, 1950), 47–58.

[4] See Louis I. Bredvold, *The Intellectual Milieu of John Dryden* (Ann Arbor, 1934), Chaps. II and III; R. F. Jones, "Science and Criticism in the Neo-Classical Age of English Literature," *JHI*, I (October, 1940), 387–8; H. O. White, "Dryden and Descartes," *TLS*, December 19, 1929, p. 1081; cf. *TLS*, January 2, 1930, p. 12.

tained by persons of several opinions, all of them left doubtful, to be determined by the readers in general.[5]

Dryden's basic critical attitude, nevertheless, would seem to have been not so much scepticism as a kind of reaction to scepticism which we may call "probabilism," the source of which, transmitted in certain contemporary treatises of logic, was the Aristotelian way of practical reasoning to which we have referred in an earlier chapter. It is the mark of an educated man, Aristotle had said, to seek in each field of knowledge the degree of precision which is available there. In the practical sciences, ethical and political, and in the practical art of rhetoric, knowledge is not of the same sort as in the demonstrations of physics, metaphysics, and mathematics. It is this distinction which Dryden apparently wishes to give us in the following passage of his *Defence of the Essay.*

> Hitherto I have proceeded by demonstration; . . . having laid down, that Nature is to be imitated, and that proposition proving the next, that then there are means which conduce to the imitating of Nature, I dare proceed no further positively; but have only laid down some opinions of the Ancients and Moderns, and of my own . . . which I thought probable.[6]

SUPPLEMENT

Seen from the perspective of a brief jaunt around Western Europe, that good old proscenium arch seems in general to be mighty small—and shrinking. Everywhere you see or hear about open stages. Everywhere, at least during the summer, the theatre leaves the darkness of the picture frame and moves outside into the sunlight—in front of palaces, into church courtyards, in village squares, on hillsides. It seems to be searching by instinct if not by design for the kind of stage it had in periods of greatest achievement: a platform in space.

And what of the proscenium? It remains, but perhaps a little less sure of itself. So recently a liberal, it has in the normal course of events become a conservative. Once so obviously the normal relation between actor and audience, it has become one of many norms, many relationships. Hardy the architect who would today design a theatre without adequate provision for varying, enlarging, breaking through—if not entirely eliminating—that artificial dam through which the theatre tends to spill.

· · ·

[5] Ker I, 124.
[6] Ker I, 123. See the lucid statement of Dryden's probabilism by Hoyt Trowbridge, "The Place of the Rules in Dryden's Criticism," *MP*, XLIV (November, 1946), 84–96.

Granted that something magical is missing when there is no red velour curtain, no background splendor or technical virtuosity. But there is some other kind of magic lurking about these actors who have three dimensions and not two-and-a-half; Prospero would have liked this island that appears and disappears in space.

Someone is always asking: What about their backs? The questioner is the same fellow who, when the movie close-up was invented, prophesied that women and children would scream when they saw their decapitated heroes before them. With equal logic, what about their faces? Is a face per se necessarily more interesting or revealing than a back? Would Phidias agree? Or Michelangelo?

The open stage, four-sided or three-sided, or in a corner of a room, is no passing fancy. It represents for the theatre the same search, the same tendencies which have taken place in the past half-century in the arts of sculpture, painting and architecture and which we have termed "modern." Like the other arts, the theatre sometimes turns to simplicity, to essentials, to the primitive. Like the other arts, it tries to extend itself beyond rigid framework; it looks for fluidity and freedom; it gropes for organic form just as much as does the Lever House, a Finnish armchair, or a Fourth Street ashtray. Between Frank Lloyd Wright and Stanislavsky, after all, there is not so much difference. The key to both lies in their faith that inner life dictates outer form.

Most specifically, the theatre's continuing experiment with the open stage represents, alongside the other arts, a concern with revealing and utilizing instead of concealing the nature of its material.

A theatre building lasts longer than an ashtray or a chair. But is that any reason why it should be any less "modern"?

No one tears down theatres for esthetic reasons, only for parking lots. So that good old proscenium arch remains—a respectable though illegitimate grandchild of Renaissance painting and Baroque elegance. Not exactly crumbling either. But—watch out for falling plaster.

—Alan Schneider, "Shrinking Arch," *The New York Times,* Sunday, July 25, 1954, Section 2, Drama . . . , by permission of the author and *The New York Times.* Mr. Schneider was Artistic Director of Arena Stage, Washington, D.C., 1952–54

Discovery in the Works Accounts of the startling evidence that Shakespeare's stage at Court was placed *in the middle of the Hall* has established a novel and revealing point. Not only was his platform not provided with a front curtain: it was moreover not set against any scenic wall or background whatever. With this plastic rather than pictorial kind of stage, the only fluent method of production feasible is that of the traditional "multiple" or "simultaneous" setting of fixed "mansions" or "scenes" common to the European stage of the Renaissance.

Hardest perhaps for our modern minds to give up is the preconception of a backdrop: to realize, instead, that spectators were *behind* the stage, on the fourth side, as in a circus. But now we *know* that at Court Shakespeare's plays were produced completely "in the round." What then of the production at the public theaters such as the Globe? Were they utterly different? Or has our fixed modern idea of a "background" blinded us to the fact that here too there was no "scenic wall," that the Globe productions also were completely "in the round"?

Once we lay preconception aside, it is curious to see how the proof that the public stage, like that at Court, was a complete circus stage has been staring us in the face unregarded. The De Witt drawing has always shown spectators on the fourth side, behind the stage. As W. J. Lawrence pointed out, "Of the four known views of early non-scenic theatres, three show incontestably that spectators sat in elevated boxes at the back of the stage"—a position from which it is physically impossible to see the "inner stage" of the theorists. Henslowe at the Rose Playhouse mentioned "the room over the tire-house," and contemporary references to this "lords' room" for spectators at centre-back "over the stage" are common. This audience on the fourth side refuses to be argued out of existence to make hypothetical and remote inner and upper stages possible. It is a fact, as it is at Whitehall. Clearly, the Elizabethans meant what they said when they called their playhouses "amphitheatres," when they spoke of the "cirque" and "the Globe's fair Ring," and when they imagined "lines drawn from the circumference of so many ears, whiles the Actor is the Center."

Those responsible for the theory of an inner stage have managed to close their eyes not only to Shakespeare's common sense as a producer and to the undeniable presence of high-paying spectators behind the stage, but also to the economics of the theatre. A theory which would tuck crucial action away in a recess beyond the sight-line both of the lords' room and of the adjacent arcs of "this wooden O," "this throngèd round, . . . this fair-fill'd Globe," ignores the all-important box-office. The "inner stage" proposition would receive short shrift from any business manager. His advice would be, "Don't be foolish. Keep the action out on the stage, as it is shown in the De Witt picture, where it can be seen from all the surrounding galleries. The only way to make money is to fill the house."

—Leslie Hotson, "Shakespeare's Arena," *The Sewanee Review*, LXI (Summer, 1953), 356–7, by permission of *The Sewanee Review*

CHAPTER II

DRYDEN AND SOME LATER SEVENTEENTH-CENTURY THEMES

§ *the heroic norm, English heroic plays, Dryden's theory, burlesque resistance—II. courtly wit vs. "mechanic humour,"* Epilogue to Conquest of Granada, *comic theory,* Preface to An Evening's Love, *shift from "humour" to manners, the conversational norm, "fallacy of imitative form," passage from Virginia Woolf's* Orlando—*III. aim of comedy, delight vs. instruction, Poetic Justice, French influences, Dryden, Rymer, Dennis, Addison's* Cato, *poetic injustice, Rapin and catharsis sentimentalized—IV. satire as painless execution, the classical defence of satire and comedy: agelastic (Sidney and Jonson), urbane (Molière and Pope), problem of moral aim vs. libel, general vs. local truth—V. Molière's refinement, English "humours," Jonson to Sterne, Temple's* Of Poetry, *a 19th-century reaction, Meredith's lecture on the* Comic, *relation of the comic to the serious in the classical tradition, Fielding's* Covent Garden Journal—*VI. Dryden's later years, translation, his view of Chaucer, Augustan sense of superiority, ancients vs. moderns, progress and cycles, Latin vs. English, translation and imitation, Pope, principle of allusion and burlesque* §

AT ABOUT THE SAME TIME AS HE WAS WRITING HIS *Essay of Dramatic Poesy* Dryden signed a contract with the King's Theater to write three plays a year. Shortly afterwards he became Poet Laureate and Historiographer Royal and entered upon the palmiest phase of his career. In a critical sense this phase had two main features: it was heroic and it was courtly, and in neither of these ways was it modest.

Both the theory and to some extent the practice of heroic poetry were the outcome of a theory of ideal literary genre which had waxed in the later 16th century.[1] Thus Sir Philip Sidney:

> There rests the heroical, whose very name, I think, should daunt all backbiters. For by what conceit can a tongue be directed to speak evil of that which draweth with it no less champions than Achilles, Cyrus, Aeneas, Turnus, Tydeus, Rinaldo? who doth not only reach and move to truth, but teacheth and moveth to the most high and excellent truth; . . . But if anything be already said in the defense of sweet poetry, all concurreth to the maintaining the heroical, which is not only a kind, but the best and most accomplished kind of poetry. For, as the image of each action stirreth and instructeth the mind, so the lofty image of such worthies most inflameth the mind with desire to be worthy, and informs with counsel how to be worthy.[2]

The term "poem" (which since the time of Wordsworth and Keats has meant for us a short piece of verse, characteristically, let us say, an ode or sonnet) meant in Dryden's time par excellence a long story in verse (an epic or heroic poem) or a drama like an epic. (D'Avenant argued that the epic should be fashioned after the drama in five main parts;[3] Dryden argued that the narrative epic was the correct model for the mighty drama.) A shorter poem was likely to be dubbed a "paper of verses."[4] Nobody in Dryden's day would have understood (or at least nobody would have admitted understanding) Edgar Allan Poe's typically romantic thesis that a long poem is a contradiction in terms and that such an apparently successful long poem as Milton's *Paradise Lost* is really a collection of short poems, intense moments, held together by prose.[5] As tragedy was the norm of Aristotle's theory, and epistolary

[1] The theory begins at least as early as Vida's *De Arte Poetica*. See B. J. Pendlebury, *Dryden's Heroic Plays* (London, 1913), pp. 9 ff; C. V. Deane, *Dramatic Theory and the Heroic Play* (London, 1930).

[2] *A Defense of Poesy*, ed. A. S. Cook (Boston, 1890), p. 30. Cf. Scaliger, *Poetics* III, 96: "In epic poetry, which describes the descent, life, and deeds of heroes, all other kinds of poetry have . . . a norm, so that to it they turn for their regulative principles."

[3] Letter to Hobbes prefixed to *Gondibert*, 1651. D'Avenant's letter and Hobbes's answer, the earliest full-bloom pronouncements in English of heroic theory, first appeared, together, at Paris in 1650.

[4] See Howard, Preface to *Four Plays* (D. D. Arundell, *Dryden and Howard*, Cambridge, 1929, p. 8) and Dryden, *Essay of Dramatic Poesy:* "Blank verse is acknowledged to be too low for a poem, nay more, for a paper of verses; but if too low for an ordinary sonnet, how much more for Tragedy, which is by Aristotle, in the dispute betwixt the epic poesy and the dramatic, for many reasons he there alleges, ranked above it?" (Ker I, 101).

[5] But cf. Dryden's opinion: Milton "runs into a flat of thought, sometimes for a hundred lines together . . ." (*Original and Progress of Satire*, Ker II, 29); and cf. *post* Chapter 20.

satire implicitly that of Horace's best insights, so the heroic epic was the more or less explicit norm of poetry in the latter part of the 17th century (and was a rather unhappily dilated focus for critical theory). Witness not only the numerous original epic attempts and the epic translations of the century but the epic straining of even such a topical poem as Dryden's *Annus Mirabilis* and the dreams of strong poets like Dryden and Pope about writing a British epic. Heroic poets, says the Earl of Mulgrave in his *Essay upon Poetry*, 1682, are "gigantic souls;" the heroic poem is the "chief effort of human sense." And Dryden was sure that the heroic poem not only always had been but always would be "esteemed . . . the greatest work of human nature." [6] As late in his career as 1697 (long after the passion for heroic *drama* had cooled) he opened the Dedication of his translated *Aeneis* with the sentence: "A HEROIC POEM, truly such, is undoubtedly the greatest work which the soul of man is capable to perform."

Partly as a result of such ideas, partly as a result of grandiose political trends (which doubtless underlay the literary doctrine), and in some small part through the Puritan interdict of the stage which drove the poet Davenant in 1656 to adopt in lieu of a real play the expedient of a musical and recitative spectacle (*The Siege of Rhodes*), the English heroical play was born. At its most glorious the heroical play was an amalgam of Marlovian and Cornelian passion drama, of Fletcherian romantic melodrama, of French nine-volume pastoral romance, of masque and Italian opera. It was Homeric and Aristotelian in its aim at action, largeness, and elevation; it was Virgilian and Heliodoran [7] in its tender concern for the union of a pair of lovers and the founding of an illustrious house. It urged the themes of love, honor, and civic virtue, in high places, and with furious confusion and rivalry, before an exotic and pseudo-historical setting, to the continuous fanfare of trumpets and clash of arms on nearby plains.

The English heroic drama consisted most conspicuously of Dryden's five plays of this kind, from *The Indian Queen*, written in collaboration with Howard and produced in 1664, to *Aurengzebe*, produced in 1677. Heroic theory, Dryden's justification for the magnitude, the uproar, and the constant oratorical altitude at which he found himself moving, appears in his *Essay of Heroic Plays*, prefixed to his two-part heroic play *The Conquest of Granada*, 1672, and in his *Apology for Heroic Poetry and Poetic Licence* prefixed to his operatic rhymed rendition of Milton's *Paradise Lost, The State of Innocence and the Fall of Man*, a work printed in 1677, though never acted. Heroic theory was a coarse

---

[6] *Apology for Heroic Poetry and Poetic Licence*, Ker I, 181.
[7] See Sidney's and Scaliger's statements about the *Theagenes and Chariclea* of Heliodorus compared by Cornell M. Dowlin, "Sidney and Other Men's Thoughts," *RES*, XX (October, 1944), pp. 257–71.

parody of Aristotelian epic theory: the Homeric hero inflated to a colossus and paragon of prowess, honor, and passion, the element of the wonderful (*to thaumaston*) magnified both in the direction of the amazing and in that of the admirable, and the element of fear, in the direction of terror. Withal a dash of Longinianism and Petronianism[8] was convenient to justify the liberal introduction of the supernatural (ghosts and heavenly signs) to the main end of hair-raising. Were it not for Dryden's unparalleled aplomb, which makes him at all times amusing, it might be a sorry shock to find his hand lent to this task.

> But I have already swept the stakes; and, with the common good
> fortune of prosperous gamesters, can be content to sit quietly;
> to hear my fortune cursed by some, and my faults arraigned by
> others, and to suffer both without reply.[9]

Critical resistance to heroic insensibility in England was furnished not so much by reasoned argument as by ruthless burlesque, the first effort being that of Buckingham and his friends in *The Rehearsal*, 1671, which hit Dryden himself and may in part have provoked his defences. Later, came the retrospective sortie of Fielding, *The Tragedy of Tragedies; or the Life and Death of Tom Thumb the Great*, 1731, which parodies every element of inflation in English drama from Shakespeare to Addison.[1]

II

THE second main character of Dryden's thinking in this period, his standard of courtly wit, though it merged easily with the heroic, yields perhaps a nicer critical question—a question about reality, and about ideality and imitation, as these grow out of a social circumstance. This standard has to do mainly with comedy rather than with heroics, but as even in his heroic plays Dryden aimed at and even achieved the refinement of wit, and as his complacency about the heroic plays was closely bound up with his successful arrival in the court circle, it happens that his most blatant pronouncement on the courtly theme (and the most succinctly turned, because in verse) is attached to the Second Part of *The Conquest of Granada* in the form of an Epilogue. We quote this admirably conceited poem in its entirety.

> They, who have best succeeded on the stage,
> Have still conform'd their genius to their age.

[8] Petronius is quoted in *Of Heroic Plays* (Ker I, 152); Longinus is cited in the *Apology for Heroic Poetry and Poetic Licence* (Ker I, 181).
[9] *Of Heroic Plays*, Ker I, 159.
[1] And later still (1779) *The Critic* of Sheridan.

Thus *Johnson* did mechanic humour show,
When men were dull, and conversation low.
Then, *Comedy* was faultless, but 'twas coarse:
Cobb's tankard was a jest, and *Otter's* horse.[2]
And, as their *Comedy*, their love was mean;
Except, by chance, in some one labour'd scene,
Which must atone for an ill-written play:
They rose, but at their height could seldom stay.
Fame then was cheap, and the first comer sped;
And they have kept it since, by being dead.
But, were they now to write, when critics weigh
Each line, and ev'ry word, throughout a play,
None of them, no, not *Johnson* in his height,
Could pass, without allowing grains for weight.
Think it not envy, that these truths are told;
Our poet's not malicious, though he's bold.
'Tis not to brand 'em that their faults are shown,
But, by their errors, to excuse his own.
If *Love* and *Honour* now are higher rais'd,
'Tis not the poet, but the age is prais'd.
Wit's now arriv'd to a more high degree;
Our native language more refin'd and free.
Our ladies and our men now speak more wit
In conversation, than those poets writ.
Then, one of these is, consequently, true;
That what this poet writes comes short of you,
And imitates you ill (which most he fears),
Or else his writing is not worse than theirs.
Yet, though you judge (as sure the critics will),
That some before him writ with greater skill,
In this one praise he has their fame surpast,
To please an age more gallant than the last.

Or, as Dryden found himself compelled to put it in his immediately subsequent prose *Defence* of this Epilogue:

Now, if they ask me, whence it is that our conversation is so much refined? I must freely, and without flattery, ascribe it to the court; and, in it, particularly to the King, whose example gives a law to it. His own misfortunes, and the nation's, afforded him an opportunity, which is rarely allowed to sovereign princes,

---

[2] Cobb is a poor water-carrier in Jonson's *Every Man in his Humour*; Otter is a braggart but hen-pecked captain in Jonson's *Epicoene*, who has a favorite tankard named "Horse."

I mean of travelling, and being conversant in the most polished courts of Europe.

Gentlemen will now be entertained with the follies of each other.[3]

The application of this taste to a theory of the comic appears in the Preface prefixed by Dryden in 1671 to his comedy *An Evening's Love* but actually representative of the more refined concept of comedy which by 1671 he was able to embody in his best comic effort *Marriage-à-la-Mode*. The burden of the argument is that Ben Jonson was good at the realism of humours but was unequal to wit. Jonson's technique consisted in the faithful imitation of low-grade material, "the natural imitation of folly." This required some "judgment," to be sure, in order to tell when folly was faithfully imitated, but no creative wit. The new way of comedy, that which Dryden would illustrate, was to be a "mixed way," part humours, part wit, with an accent on the pleasant theme of amorous intrigue. The repartee of witty gentlemen was a department in which Dryden specially plumed himself—though modesty devised the compensatory confession that he found himself lacking in the "judgment" necessary to follow Jonson's way of the humour. An insistence that wit could not, as might be sometimes thought, transcend the principle of propriety inherent in the humour—that is, that various kinds of witty characters must be fitted with variously appropriate kinds of witty speech—may be said to have turned somewhat the edge of the argument which Dryden was urging.[4]

---

[3] Ker I, 176-7. The servility that at moments accompanied this view may be sampled in Dryden's motto to *Marriage-à-la-Mode* ("*Quicquid ego sum . . . . tamen me cum magnis vixisse, invita fatebitur usque invidia*") and in the Dedication of that play to Rochester: "I am sure, if there be anything in this play, wherein I have raised myself beyond the ordinary lowness of my comedies, I ought wholly to acknowledge it to the favour of being admitted into your lordship's conversation. . . . Wit seems to have lodged itself more nobly in this age, than in any of the former; and people of my mean condition are only writers, because some of the nobility, and your lordship in the first place, are above the narrow praises which poesy could give you. . . . Your lordship has but another step to make, and from the patron of wit, you may become its tyrant."

The readiness of such talk to collapse into irony may be seen in the opening paragraphs of the mock-modest debate about rhyme with Sir Robert Howard in Dryden's *Defence of an Essay* and (after his being slighted by Rochester) in the passage on gentleman wits in the Preface to *All for Love*, 1678. "And is not this a wretched affectation, not to be contented with what fortune has done for them, and sit down quietly with their estates, but they must call their wits in questions, and needlessly expose their nakedness to public view?" (Ker I, 196).

[4] The transition from the English comedy of humours to the comedy of manners involved among other critical problems that concerning the difference between the supposed individuality of the humour (asserted by Dryden in his discussions of Falstaff; see *ante* Chapter 10) and the social or class implications of the "manners," and that concerning the difference between an opaque butt or target of ridicule (the

The social influences at work in Dryden's theory, the snobbery and complacence of the courtier poet, the dawning signs of linguistic Augustanism, the character of Dryden's actual comic production (a mélange of Fletcherian romance, humor of courtly affectation, and wit of bawdy lovemaking), markedly inferior to the best of Ben Jonson—these should not obscure for us the quite basic critical issue involved in the shift from the comedy of Jonsonian humors toward the comedy of Restoration manners, and in Dryden's rationalization of his part in this. Throughout the English Augustan age, from Dryden to Samuel Johnson, a certain kind of ease and naturalness in writing, partly initiated by Dryden himself in his critical discourses (but so various a thing as to include the coffee-house pace of Defoe, the green-room frippery of Cibber, the affable chatter of Addison) is supposed by historians to have run parallel with an ideal of correctness and elegance that was being cultivated in the actual conversation of cultured society. Literary historians have been inclined, in effect, to agree with Dryden, that English written prose during the period in question improved greatly through the imitation of English conversation. But what shall our theory be? If naturalness is desirable in a novel or play, why is a novel or a play preferable to the daily run of natural conversation? Was Lord Chesterfield or Bishop Atterbury a model talker because he sounded like Addison? Or was Addison a good essayist because he sounded like Chesterfield or Atterbury, or like what one heard everyday in the boudoir or coffee-house? Low realism ("mechanic humour"), we may suppose, is less difficult to write than high realism (the wit of Benedick and Beatrice, Millamant and Mirabell, Diana of the Crossways). Drab realism may be at times merely neutral, but it has at least a tendency toward the formless and subrational, and hence toward producing the problem for criticism which one 20th-century American critic has sharply focussed in the phrase "fallacy of imitative form." If a fullness of imitative embodiment is what poetry must achieve, and that through its form, can this form survive the imitation of negative or formless materials? [5] So far as concerns social conversation and its imitation in literature, a conclusion which to the present writers seems eminently plausible has been dramatized as follows by Virginia Woolf in a passage of her fantastic history of modern English literary taste, *Orlando*.

> About the third time Orlando went . . . [to one of Lady
> R.'s assemblies] a certain incident occurred. She was still under

---

Jonsonian humour) and the witty character *with* whom the audience laughs. The latter question is nearer to Dryden's drift in the Preface to *An Evening's Love*. The more delicate situation which arises when two main characters are reciprocally partial butts and partial wits has been alluded to *ante* Chapter 3.

[5] On the other hand, of course, stands the question: Can the fullness of this form, its quality of embodiment, survive the imitation of the highly rational, the scientific or metaphysical?

the illusion that she was listening to the most brilliant epigrams in the world, though, as a matter of fact, old General C. was only saying at some length, how the gout had left his left leg and gone to his right, while Mr. L. interrupted when any proper name was mentioned. "R.? Oh! I know Billy R. as well as I know myself. S.? My dearest friend. T.? Stayed with him a fortnight in Yorkshire"—which, such is the force of illusion, sounded like the wittiest repartee, the most searching comment upon human life, and kept the company in a roar; when the door opened and a little gentleman entered whose name Orlando did not catch. Soon a curiously disagreeable sensation came over her. To judge from their faces, the rest began to feel it as well. One gentleman said there was a draught. The Marchioness of C. feared a cat must be under the sofa. It was as if their eyes were being slowly opened after a pleasant dream and nothing met them but a cheap washstand and a dirty counterpane. It was as if the fumes of some delicious wine were slowly leaving them. Still the General talked and still Mr. L. remembered. But it became more and more apparent how red the General's neck was, how bald Mr. L.'s head was. As for what they said—nothing more tedious and trivial could be imagined. Everybody fidgeted and those who had fans yawned behind them. At last Lady R. rapped with hers upon the arm of her great chair. Both gentlemen stopped talking.

Then the little gentleman said.

He said next.

He said finally.*

Here, it cannot be denied, was true wit, true wisdom, true profundity. The company was thrown into complete dismay. One such saying was bad enough; but three, one after another, on the same evening! No society could survive it.

"Mr. Pope," said old Lady R. in a voice trembling with sarcastic fury, "you are pleased to be witty." Mr. Pope flushed red. Nobody spoke a word. They sat in dead silence some twenty minutes. Then, one by one, they rose and slunk from the room. That they would ever come back after such an experience was doubtful.[6]

* These sayings are too well known to require repetition, and besides they are all to be found in his published works.

In Dryden's day the matter was put as follows by Congreve in his Letter to Dennis *Concerning Humour in Comedy*, 1695.

[6] Virginia Woolf, *Orlando* (New York: Harcourt, Brace and Company, Inc., 1928), Chapter IV, pp. 200–2. By permission of Harcourt, Brace and Company, Inc., and Leonard Woolf.

If this Exactness . . . were to be observed in Wit as some would
have it in Humour, what would become of those Characters
that are design'd for men of Wit? I believe if a Poet should
steal a dialogue of any Length from the Extempore discourse
of the two Wittiest Men upon Earth, he would find the Scene
but coldly receiv'd by the Town.[7]

III

DRYDEN was inclined to take the aim of comedy not very seriously.
Comedy, he observed, begets "malicious pleasure," testified by laughter.[8] "The chief end of it is divertisement and delight. . . . the first
end . . . is delight, and instruction only the second." [9] And he was inclined to wink at—nay participate cheerfully in—the obscenity [1] of the
Restoration comedy of manners. He drew a rather sharp distinction between the moral responsibility of comedy and that of tragedy, especially
in the matter of instruction through the spectacle of rewards and punishment.

Comedy is not so much obliged to the punishment of faults
which it represents, as Tragedy. For the persons in Comedy
are of a lower quality, the action is little, and the faults and
vices are but the sallies of youth, and the frailties of human
nature, and not premeditated crimes.[2]

With regard to serious drama Dryden was already in tune with a latter-
day species of classical didacticism which became a fixation toward the
end of the century.

The theme of "Poetic Justice" [3] begins to appear in Dryden's critical
defences of the late 1670's: his *Apology for Heroic Poetry*, 1677, his
Preface to *All for Love*, 1678, and that to his improved version of *Troilus
and Cressida*, 1679. In these essays Dryden exhibits the influence of cer-

[7] Spingarn III, 247.
[8] *Essay of Dramatic Poesy*, Ker I, 85.
[9] *Preface to An Evening's Love*, Ker I, 143.
[1] A quality which at the end of his life, after the storm raised by Jeremy Col-
lier, he could recognize and even connect with one of its main causes, the Stuart
court.

> But sure a banished court, with lewdness fraught,
> The seeds of open vice returning brought. . . .
> The poets, who must live by courts or starve,
> Were proud, so good a government to serve;
> And mixing with buffoons and pimps profane,
> Tainted the stage for some small snip of gain.
> —Epilogue to Beaumont and Fletcher's *Pilgrim*, 1700

[2] Preface to *An Evening's Love*, Ker I, 143.
[3] On the general question whether poetry should mainly teach or mainly please,
Dryden's varied career exhibits all the usual Renaissance devices and modifications.
See, for instance, Ker I, 113, 142, 196, 209; II, 128.

tain French critics who had recently published notable works: Boileau, whose Horatian *Art Poétique* and translation of Longinus had both appeared in 1674; René Rapin, whose *Réflexions sur la Poétique d'Aristote* appeared in the same year and was translated by an English critic of a fanatically classic temper, Thomas Rymer; and René le Bossu ("the best of modern critics," says Dryden), whose *Traité du Poëme épique*, 1675, was the most authoritative summation of 17th-century epic theory, a kind of dried essence of epic, as a romantic historian has termed it, or recipe for epic *in vacuo*. French influence meant a tightening of Dryden's classicism all along the line. It meant far less indulgence of the English foibles and irregularities than we saw in the *Essay of Dramatic Poesy*, and, along with a continuing expression of esteem for the "divine Shakespeare" (especially in the matter of his characterizations),[4] a complacent opinion that Dryden himself was improving upon Shakespeare in language, in regularity of plot, and in the administration of "justice." In the story of Antony and Cleopatra both Dryden and Shakespeare had enjoyed a great initial advantage.

> I mean the excellency of the moral: for the chief persons represented were famous patterns of unlawful love; and their end accordingly was unfortunate. All reasonable men have long since concluded, that the hero of the poem ought not to be a character of perfect virtue, for then he could not, without injustice, be made unhappy.[5]

But the end of the chief persons in the story of Troilus and Cressida, as Shakespeare managed it, had been not so felicitously "unfortunate." "The chief persons, who give name to the tragedy," complains Dryden, "are left alive; Cressida is false, and is not punished." It is later in the same Preface that he uses the full term "poetical justice," [6] introduced by Rymer the year before in his *Tragedies of the Last Age,* and soon to become a commonplace of criticism.[7] In the closing scenes of Dry-

---

[4] The appreciation of the brutish character of Caliban (Preface to *Troilus and Cressida,* Ker I, 219) is a classic spot of 17th-century Shakespeare criticism. And the effort to reconcile Falstaff's complexity with the canon of consistency in character-drawing (I, 215) is a marked advance in theoretical precision over the account of the same character in the *Essay of Dramatic Poesy.* Cf. *ante* Chapter 10, p. 188.

[5] Preface to *All for Love,* Ker I, 191. ". . . nor yet altogether wicked," continues Dryden, "because he could not then be pitied. I have therefore steered the middle course; and have drawn the character of Antony as favourably as Plutarch, Appian, and Dion Cassius would give me leave."

[6] Preface to *Troilus and Cressida,* Ker I, 203, 210.

[7] The conception, always a dangerous likelihood in the Aristotelian poetic tradition (especially in view of the adjacent doctrine of distributive justice in Aristotle's *Ethics*), may be found adumbrated in many earlier authors—in Jonson, for instance, and Sidney. M. A. Quinlan, *Poetic Justice in the Drama* (Notre Dame, 1912) quotes the Parliamentary Act of 1543 tolerating only such plays as presented "the rebuking and reproaching of vices and the setting forth of virtue." Cf. Spingarn, *Essays* I, lxxiii, lxxxvi.

den's *Troilus and Cressida,* Cressida stabs herself, Troilus kills Diomede, and Achilles, coming along with his Myrmidons, kills Troilus—a far enough cry from the cynical half-light of Shakespeare's closing scenes, where Ulysses and Thersites lead Troilus beside a tent and he overhears the conversation in which Cressida gives Diomede the sleeve. It was not Dryden, however, nor even Thomas Rymer, but in the next generation Pope's antagonist John Dennis, of the neo-Longinian sensibility, who raised the loudest voice for Poetic Justice—in a controversy which reached its climax over the suicide of Addison's patriotic protagonist Cato.[8]

Poetic Justice was an exaggeration of the Aristotelian punishment of the flaw in the character of the tragic protagonist. But the doctrine could thrive only through a certain lack of interest in what Aristotle said about the greatness of the protagonist and about the infelicity of distributive justice, or the mixed ending, in tragedy—punishment for the wicked, reward for the just. A conspicuous exhibit in the history of Poetic Justice is Nahum Tate's mixed ending for *King Lear,* in which Cordelia marries Edgar. Yet, like most other moral conceptions of poetry, Poetic Justice is not adequately treated by a summary dismissal. The question is at least a complicated one, for it concerns not only evil and punishment but virtuous inclinations and sympathy, and conflict of sympathies. "Though I might use the privilege of a poet," says Dryden, "to introduce . . . [Octavia] into Alexandria, yet I had not enough considered, that the compassion she moved to herself and children was destructive to that which I reserved for Antony and Cleopatra." [9] Even in Shakespeare's version of the story, the casual and gross injustice with which Antony treats Octavia may somewhat obstruct our view of Antony as a protagonist worthy of tragic sympathy. And then on the other hand there is such a case as that of Addison's Cato. It is not easy to argue, against Dennis, that the Stoic death of the champion of republican virtue is really the downfall of a tragically erring figure. Innocent suffering, or poetic injustice, as it appears in *Cato* and is defended by Addison in advance in *Spectator* 40, has a close relation to the tide of generally tender feelings, the commiseration and compassion, that would run so strong through the whole of the 18th century. The intensity of the neo-classic crusade to see that the sinful protagonist suffered the death-penalty— and that no innocent character did—may obscure for us a reactionary but equally simplistic trend of that time toward the luxury of pity for innocence injured. The cases had much in common, for in either the Aristotelian tension was resolved. And in either the Aristotelian catharsis

---

[8] See *Spectators* 39 and 40, by Addison, and 548, attributed to Addison, and the several replies of Dennis including his *Remarks upon Cato, a Tragedy,* 1713 (*Works,* ed. E. N. Hooker, Baltimore, 1939-1943, I, 40; II, 7, 19, 49, 435-42, 446-57).

[9] Ker I, 192.

of undesirably soft emotions (pity and fear) slides conveniently into a new and sentimentalized version of catharsis—such as that which Dryden in the Preface to his *Troilus and Cressida* adapts from Rapin: not catharsis (or "abatement") of fear and pity, but abatement of such aggressive and evil emotions as pride and anger through the *feeding and watering* of the soft-hearted emotions of fear and pity.[1] Thus the most nearly amenable classic doctrine became, by a sufficient deflection, an authority on the side of the coming ethics of benevolent feeling.[2]

IV

It is one of Dryden's claims to an urbane, if at times rather faltering, good sense that he was not one of the most earnest promoters of Poetic Justice—like Rymer or Dennis. He only lent himself to it. As we have already observed, he took his comic art even more lightly, resting his apologia on the easy grounds of pleasure and diversion. As for his burlesque and hurting satires, *MacFlecknoe* and *Absalom and Achitophel*, he doubtless looked on them honestly as what they were—masterly exhibitions of the art of personal assault and partisan politics. His theory of satire appears later, in the long essay entitled *The Origin and Progress of Satire* prefixed to his translation of Juvenal and Persius in 1693.

> . . . the nicest and most delicate touches of satire consist in fine raillery. . . . How easy it is to call rogue and villain, and that wittily! But how hard to make a man appear a fool, a blockhead, or a knave, without using any of those opprobrious terms!. . . . Neither is it true, that this fineness of raillery is offensive. A witty man is tickled while he is hurt in this manner, and a fool feels it not. . . . there is . . . a vast difference betwixt the slovenly butchering of a man, and the fineness of a stroke that separates the head from the body, and leaves it standing in its place. A man may be capable, as Jack Ketch's wife said of his servant, of a plain piece of work, a bare hanging; but to make a malefactor die sweetly was only belonging to her husband.[3]

This view of fine satire as a form of painless execution could doubtless be shown to have its resemblance to Dryden's idea of the comic. In the

[1] "Rapin, a judicious critic, has observed from Aristotle, that pride and want of commiseration are the most predominant vices of mankind; therefore, to cure us of these two, the inventors of Tragedy have chosen to work upon two other passions, which are fear and pity" (Ker I, 210). Cf. Baxter Hathaway, "John Dryden and the Function of Tragedy," *PMLA*, LVIII (September, 1943), 665–73.

[2] See *post* Chapter 14.

[3] Ker II, 92–3.

relaxed theory of comedy which we have already noted, Dryden stood even further apart from his age than in his relative casualness about Poetic Justice.

Dryden's views are hardly the ideal ground from which to launch a discussion of English neo-classic theory. Yet because there is no other single theorist of the period who provides that ground, we choose to enter here upon the following brief elaboration. Other comic writers and other satirists, from Ben Jonson to Pope and Fielding, were mightily preoccupied with a kind of satirist's apology which we have already noted in Jonson. We may summarize it roughly as follows: The satirist meant to hurt nobody, least of all any innocent person; he named nobody, but aimed at the universal; his charter was to lash vice and folly, to correct manners, to uphold morality. In times so low that men were not afraid to be known as knaves, they were yet ashamed to be laughed at as fools. Hence the satirist's special power and opportunity—in fact his duty—which he performed with an obvious gusto. In tragic justice grand crimes were punished by death. In comic and satiric justice mean vices and the folly which went with them were punished by scornful ridicule.

There is some evidence from the earlier part of this period that the view of comedy as a moral agent may have been quite grim. Thus Sir Philip Sidney in his *Defence:*

> I speak to this purpose, that all the end of the comical part be not upon such scornful matters as stir laughter only, but mixed with it that delightful teaching which is the end of poesy. And the great fault, even in that point of laughter, and forbidden plainly by Aristotle, is that they stir laughter in sinful things, which are rather execrable than ridiculous; or in miserable, which are rather to be pitied than scorned.[4]

And Ben Jonson in a passage of his *Timber* translated from an agelastic interpretation of Aristotle's *Poetics* by the Dutch theorist Heinsius:

> Nor is the moving of laughter alwaies the end of *Comedy,* that is rather a fowling for the peoples delight, or their fooling. For, as *Aristotle* saies rightly, the moving of laughter is a fault in Comedie, a kind of turpitude, that depraves some part of a man's nature without a disease. As a wry face without paine moves laughter, or a deformed vizard.—No. 131 [5]

[4] *Defense of Poesy*, ed. A. S. Cook, p. 51.
[5] Compare Heinsius: "*Nec movere risum sane constituit Comoediam, sed plebis aucupium est, et abusus. Nam Ridiculum, ut recte Aristoteles, vitium est et foeditas, doloris expers; quae partem in homine aliquam corrumpit absque morbo. Sicut foeda et detorta facies, si nullo cum dolore id fiat, risum movet*" (*Ad Horatii de Plauto et Terentino judicium*, quoted in *Timber*, ed. Castelain, pp. 133-4). And compare Aristotle, *Poetics* V. The fault in human nature which Aristotle took as the object

Jonson must have made his audience laugh, in order to make his living. Yet the starkness of his plays, the saltiness and grit, a certain holystoning of the sensibility often quite distressing even if funny, doubtless might be argued to show some correspondence to the version of Aristotle which he chose to adopt from Heinsius.

Later on, the tone of the comic writer's apology is more easy. He admits being funny and claims laughter as his moral technique. Molière, even though under official censure for the immorality of *Tartuffe*, Pope, though beset by Grubstreet in a war of libels, conduct their self-defenses with urbanity and wit. The satire so obviously rejoices in the skilful administration of punishment that it is difficult to accept with complete seriousness the concern avowed for "healing." These ideas, like so many others of the age, were epitomized often and neatly by Alexander Pope— sometimes with casual aplomb, as in his *Epistle to Augustus*, where paraphrasing the Horatian thumbnail history of poetry, he slips in the couplet:

> Hence Satire rose, that just the medium hit,
> And heals with Morals what it hurts with Wit.

Sometimes with feelings of tender self-regard, as in his *Epistle to Arbuthnot*, where he brings in his filial piety and the good influence of his parents. And once, with fierce conviction and political self-righteousness, in the *Epilogue* to his *Satires*.

> Yes, I am proud; I must be proud to see
> Men not afraid of God, afraid of me:
> Safe from the Bar, the Pulpit, and the Throne,
> Yet touched and shamed by Ridicule alone.
> O sacred weapon! left for Truth's defence,
> Sole Dread of Folly, Vice, and Insolence!

The special élan of Pope's *Epistle to Arbuthnot* arises in large part from the ironic alternations of slaughterous portraiture with the author's professions of childlike innocence.

> Yet soft by nature, more a dupe than wit,
> *Sappho* can tell you how this man was bit.

One may observe in passing that the neo-classic satirist's protestation of moral, and denial of slanderous, intent, poses very vividly the Aristotelian distinction between general poetic meaning and historical particularity. Although Pope and Warburton maintained that the names in the *Dunciad* did not matter, because the types were perennial,[6] the

---

to be imitated in comedy (the ridiculous, *to geloion*) is taken by Heinsius as a fault in comedy itself, the laughable, *ridiculum*. Jonson heavily underscores this interpretation with the phrase "the moving of laughter is a fault in Comedie."

[6] Cf. Fielding, *Joseph Andrews*, Bk. III, Ch. 1.

fact that Grubstreet was then and there swarming with dunces was what provoked the poem, and living dunces were hit—some less fairly than others. It was surely not immoral for Molière to satirize the pious fraud (*faux dévot*), but then Molière could scarcely help implying something about the prevalence of frauds among pious persons in the France of Louis XIV. The practical truth and moral value of all such implicit indictments (or their untruth and immoral libel) depended on statistical factors which lay outside the scope of literary criticism and of moral philosophy too.

V

THE kind of generalized moral criticism which was the professed aim of 17th-century comedy and satire is to be found at its most refined in a few plays of Molière—*Le Tartuffe, Le Bourgeois Gentilhomme, L'Avare*, and above all *Le Misanthrope*. English comedy of manners along the same lines—and sometimes it was copied rather closely from Molière—suffers from two main defects, the Horneresque indecency which later elicited Lamb's defence [7] and Macaulay's censure, and the English fondness for the "humour," a kind of bumptiousness which was never completely sophisticated even in the smartest Restoration comedies. Toward the end of the century this very indigenous form of the laughable settled into a national institution, a phenomenon of actual English life, a supposedly superior source of comedy, and a matter of national pride. Thus Temple in his essay *Of Poetry*, 1690:

> . . . our English [comedy] has . . . excelled both the modern and the Ancient, . . . by Force of a Vein Natural perhaps to our Country, and which with us is called . . . Humour, a Word peculiar to our Language too, and hard to be expressed in any other. . . . This may proceed from the Native Plenty of our Soyl, the unequalness of our Clymat, as well as the Ease of our Government, and the Liberty of Professing Opinions and Factions. . . . Thus we come to have more Originals, and more than appear what they are; we have more Humour, because every Man follows his own, and takes a Pleasure, perhaps a Pride, to shew it. . . . We are not only more unlike one another than any Nation I know but we are more unlike our selves too at several times. . . . our Country must be confest to be what a great Foreign Physitian called it, The Region of Spleen, which may arise a good deal from the great uncertainty and many suddain changes of our Weather in all Seasons of the Year. . . .

[7] By a theory which posited a more than Kantian degree of detachment in our experience of such comedy.

There are no where so many Disputers upon Religion, so many Reasoners upon Government, so many Refiners in Politicks, so many Curious Inquisitives, so many Pretenders to Business and State-Imployments, greater Porers upon Books, nor Plodders after Wealth. And yet no where more Abandoned Libertines, more refined Luxurists, Extravagant Debauchees, Conceited Gallants, more Dabblers in Poetry as well as Politicks, in Philosophy, and in Chymistry. I have had several Servants far gone in Divinity, others in Poetry; have known, in the Families of some Friends, a Keeper deep in the *Rosycrucia Principles*, and a Laundress firm in those of *Epicurus*.[8]

The English "humour" was softening. What had been in the plays of Ben Jonson prickly, gross, and smelly now became quaint, merely eccentric, cozy, a harmless or lovable tendency of national character. A tribe of "originals" flourished: the bluff squire, the angular and brambly spinster, the cove, the codger, the dodger, Uncle Toby with his hobby horse, Aunt Betsey Trotwood, Mr. Micawber. Without passing judgment on this art of comfortable caricature, we may observe that along with the Augustan trend toward burlesque (of which we must say more before the end of this chapter) this kind of comic art was mainly to blame for the fact that the most brilliant essay in English on the ethical value of comedy was to be written only in the latter 19th century as an expression of classical reaction against what its author considered the hoydenish parochialism of English laughter. George Meredith's lecture *On the Idea of the Comic and the Uses of the Comic Spirit in Literature*[9] was delivered in 1877, and except for the fact that it relates closely to a concept of comedy both expounded and to some extent illustrated in several of his own novels (*The Ordeal of Richard Feverel*, *The Egoist*, *Diana of the Crossways*),[1] it was an anachronism—an unlimited celebration of French classical comedy and something like a master statement of the values achieved in that form.

There are, announces Meredith, two extreme spirits which are anti-comic—that of the Puritanical enemies of Comedy, the non-laughers or *agelasts* (here conceivably one might have to place Heinsius and the Ben Jonson of *Timber*) but no less that of the bellyshaking *hypergelasts*, the riotous Bacchanalians. (In Aristotle's *Ethics* indeed one found the boorish enemy of fun and the buffoonish and chronic fun-maker set on each side of the gentlemanly and discreetly ready wit. Meredith's terms, aside from their etymology, have a clear classical coloration.) Within the area of the literary laughable he distinguishes from comedy both satire

[8] Spingarn III, 103–6. Cf. Congreve, Letter to Dennis *Concerning Humour in Comedy* (Spingarn, III, 252); E. N. Hooker, "Humour in the Age of Pope," *Huntington Library Quarterly*, XI (August, 1948), 361–85.
[9] See the edition by Lane Cooper, *An Essay on Comedy* (New York, 1918).
[1] See J. W. Beach, *The Comic Spirit in George Meredith* (New York, 1911).

(prideful, egoistic, self-vindicatory, sentimental, working on a storage tank of bile) and humour, so beloved of the British (bumptious and cheerful, "laughter holding both his sides," comforting his victim with the hearty slap on the back). Meredith's lecture is a plea for the corrective and civilizing agency of wit and especially of feminine wit.[2] Shrewdly he read a tribute to the saving grace of woman's charity and laughter in even such minor fragments of the plays of Menander as were then known. He traced the same theme in the Roman echoes of Terence's she-comedies, *The Mother-in-Law*, and *The Woman of Andros*, then in the comedies of Molière and par excellence in *The Misanthrope*—where the heroine Célimène, coquette and gossip, sweetheart and foil to the cynical Alceste, soars in the end as the sweetly transcendent critic of his surliness, his self-gratulatory spirit of satire, and his morose impulse to retirement. English plays which attempted to follow this chastely tempered pattern of bitter-sweet, sad-and-funny—Wycherley's *Plain Dealer*, for instance, with its theme of gross infidelity, its tarpaulin-and-brandy-smelling hero, its farrago of irrelevant humours and *Twelfth Night* girl in boy's clothes—pointed all too readily the contrast which Meredith was interested to draw at the expense of his countrymen. Such a view of comedy had some difficulty in the accommodation of irregular or romantic comic geniuses like Aristophanes, Rabelais, and Shakespeare—a feat accomplished only by local brilliance of phrasing and at the cost of some inconsistency in Meredith's total argument. But in his main stress he comes as close as anyone ever has to laying out a definition of high and quintessential comedy as a literary genre—a golden center of the comic target, the kind of moral and social quality, non-didactic, non-satiric if one insists, sympathetic, yet clearly critical, which had been the province of the most exquisite in the classical way of comedy.[3]

The rather severe and ethically serious theory of comedy to be traced from Aristotle to Meredith did not often if ever reach the point of saying that comedy is a strangely chameleon obverse, or mocking counterpart, of the tragic. The theory did not notably seek to associate comedy with the peripeteia and its complement of verbal irony so conspicuous in Sophoclean tragedy, nor did it make much of the insight hinted in Aristotle's analogous use of the terms *hamartia* and *hamartēma* in his definitions of the tragic and the laughable. Still the low style, the *genus tenue* of comedy and of Horatian epistle and satire, was not conceived as something merely frivolous or frolicsome. In our next chapter

[2] Compare the following by Lord Chesterfield: ". . . the conversations of our mixed companies here . . . if they happen to rise above bragg and whist, infallibly stop short of everything either pleasing or instructive. I take the reason of this to be, that (as women generally give the tone of conversation) our English women are not near so well informed and cultivated as the French; besides that they are naturally more serious and silent" (*Letters*, January 23, 1752).

[3] See the classical vein admirably renewed in our own day by L. J. Potts, *Comedy*, London: Hutchinson's University Library, 1949.

we shall have something to say about the role played in the theory of this era by the ambiguous native term "wit." At this point, we may relevantly remark that the double orientation of this term was toward the two poles of the smartly amusing and the imaginatively creative. It would be somewhat of a simplification, but not a grossly unfair one, to say that the main effort of the "wits" of Pope's age, so far as it was a theoretical effort, was directed to asserting the serious value of the laughable. The point was made by Swift and Pope but perhaps never so explicitly as by their successor Henry Fielding (the last of the English comic wits in the classical tradition) in a passage of his *Covent Garden Journal* with which we may conclude this section of our history.

> It is from a very common but a very false Opinion, that we constantly mix the Idea of Levity with those of Wit and Humour. The gravest of Men have often possessed these qualities [of Wit and Humour] in a very eminent Degree, and have exerted them on the most solemn Subjects with very eminent Success. These are to be found in many Places in the most serious Works of Plato and Aristotle, of Cicero and Seneca. Not only Swift, but South hath used them on the highest and most important of all subjects. In the sermons of the Latter, there is perhaps more Wit, than in the Comedies of Congreve.—No. 18, March 3, 1752 [4]

VI

THE last twenty years of Dryden's long career were devoted increasingly to translation and to critical writing apropos of his translation. And so at the close of the 17th century Dryden brings us back again to an emphasis upon which we dwelt at the beginning, with Ben Jonson, that on the imitation of classical models. Dryden produced translations of Ovid's *Epistles*, 1680, of the *Satires* of Juvenal and Persius, 1693, of the French painter Du Fresnoy's *De Arte Graphica*, 1695, of Virgil's *Eclogues*, *Georgics*, and *Aeneid*, 1697, and of selections from Homer, Ovid,

[4] A complementary Augustan insight was that dulness could appear in the form of smartness or frivolity. Fielding continues: "True indeed it is that Dulness appears in her own Form, and in her proper Dress, when she walks abroad in some critical Essay on a grave Subject; and many millions of Reams have in all Ages been sacrificed to her by her Votaries in this Manner; but she doth not always preserve this solemn Air. She often appears in public in Essays of Entertainment . . . and sometimes in Print, as well as on the Stage, disguises herself in a Jack-pudding Coat, and condescends to divert her good Friends with sundry Feats of Dexterity and Grimace. The late ingenious Dr. Swift . . . likens these two different Appearances of Dulness to the different Qualities of small Beer in the Barrel, and small Beer in the Bottle. The former of which is well known of all Things the most vapid, insipid and heavy; but the latter is altogether as airy, frothy, brisk and bouncing." Cf. *Dunciad* IV, 239–40: "Ah, think not. Mistress! more true Dulness lies In Folly's Cap, than Wisdom's grave disguise."

Boccaccio, and Chaucer which in the last year of his life, 1700, he published under the title of *Fables*.

Perhaps the best known of the critical essays attached to these translations, the last and one of the mellowest expressions of Dryden's fluent old age, is the Preface to the *Fables*. And the most notable feature of this is the generous appreciation of Chaucer which Dryden managed in spite of a quaintly confident inability to scan his verses. Chaucer is "the father of English poetry," "a perpetual fountain of good sense." Yet his verses have only the "rude sweetness of a Scotch tune;" "some thousands" of them are "lame for want of half a foot." He lived "in the infancy of our poetry." [5] Here we have both a milestone in one kind of Augustanism, the superior notion that the rudeness of the past ought to be translated into the elegance of the present, and at the same time a very sympathetic reading of an archaic idiom, an outstanding exercise of what today is likely to be called the "historic sense." Dryden, let us reflect, was writing six years after the publication of the following lines by Addison in the *Sixth Miscellany*.

> . . . Chaucer first, a merry bard, arose,
> And many a story told in rhyme and prose,
> But age has rusted what the poet writ,
> Worn out his language and obscur'd his wit:
> In vain he jests in his unpolish'd strain,
> And tries to make his readers laugh in vain.
> —*Account of the Greatest English Poets*, 1694

And thirty-seven years before Pope's *Epistle to Augustus:*

> Chaucer's worst ribaldry is learn'd by rote,
> And Beastly Skelton Heads of houses quote.

Dryden and Pope's translations from Chaucer and Pope's *Satires of Dr. Donne Versified* illustrate this side of Augustanism. The Augustan feeling of superiority to archaic English poetry sat comfortably enough with respectful submission to the classical ancients. "Still green with bays each ancient Altar stands." And hence Augustanism was at odds with the kind of scientific or Royal Society modernism which often (as in the argument of Eugenius in Dryden's *Essay*) came over into the literary battle between the Ancients and Moderns. This battle,[6] translated

[5] Ker II, 257-9. Cf. Edmund Waller, *Of English Verse:* "Chaucer his sense can only boast; The glory of his numbers lost!" The correct versification of Waller in English was made parallel to that of Malherbe in French when Dryden chose the English equivalents for French examples in Soames's translation of Boileau's *L'Art poétique*, 1683. In the Preface to the 1690 edition of Waller's *Poems*, his claims were stated in an extravagant way by Francis Atterbury. Waller became the "parent of English verse and the first that showed our Tongue had Beauty and Numbers in it." Wellek, *Rise*, pp. 35-6.

[6] See R. F. Jones, *Ancients and Moderns: a Study of the Background of the "Battle of the Books,"* St. Louis, 1936; Wellek, *Rise*, pp. 39 ff.

from France to England in a series of attacks and counterattacks, from Temple's *Essay Upon the Ancient and Modern Learning*, 1690, to Swift's *Battle of the Books*, 1704, was an intricate confusion of several issues, among them these two: (1) whether there is progress in literature, as in science; (2) whether, if there is progress, it is continuous from antiquity steadily onward, or is cyclical,[7] through alternate ages of barbarism and polished Augustanism. A belief in cycles was not inconsistent with a belief in the overall decline of poetry from antiquity to modern times— a progress from Ennius to Virgil and Horace, from Chaucer to Dryden, but the old height not to be reached again. In part this was due to the rapidity of the shifts in the linguistic ground under one's feet. Bacon had written his important works in Latin or translated them into Latin or let somebody else do it. Most English poems of great repute in this age and of convenient length (and some much longer) [8] were translated by somebody into Latin. And as late as the time of Pope it made good sense to lament the insubstantiality of the idiom upon which one had to rely.

> Poets that lasting marble seek
> Must carve in Latin or in Greek;
> We write in sand. . . .[9]

Marble, let it be understood (this seems a legitimate implication of the argument all along), is better for sculpture than sand for two reasons: not only does it wear better but one can do more with it to begin with. And thus arises the need not only to bring the archaic and ragged English writers (Chaucer and Donne) into line with whatever Augustan perfection of form has been achieved in English but also (and this is the heroic task) to translate the more monumental values of antique literature into the modern idiom—not only in order that the less learned may read more readily, but also in order that the more learned may have the pleasure of following the translator in the course of his creative analogizing. The translations from the classics in the era of Dryden and Pope would seem to have been directed by a conjunction of two literary theories: one, as we have seen, that heroic poetry is the most desirable kind (though apparently an almost impossible feat in the modern age of decline); and the other, that translation and "imitation" are quite possible in such and such ways.

Dryden's role in the history of English translation was described in the next century by Samuel Johnson as follows:

[7] Cycles of culture are discussed in Bouhours' *Entretiens*, 1671, and Fontenelle's *Dialogue des morts*, 1683.

[8] Sir Francis Kynaston translated the first two books of Chaucer's *Troilus and Criseyde* into rhymed Latin: *Amorum Troili et Creseidae Libri Duo Priores Anglico-Latini*, Oxford, 1635. Christopher Smart's *Poems on Several Occasions* (London, 1752) includes *De Arte Critica; a Latin Version of Mr. Pope's "Essay on Criticism."*

[9] Waller, *Of English Verse*. Cf. Pope, Preface to *Works*, 1717.

Dryden saw very early that closeness best preserved an author's sense, and that freedom best exhibited his spirit; he therefore will deserve the highest praise, who can give a representation at once faithful and pleasing, who can convey the same thoughts with the same graces, and who when he translates changes nothing but the language.—*Idler* 69, 1759

Dryden himself in one of his early statements on the subject, the Preface to his *Ovid*, had distinguished grades of translation thus:

All translation, I suppose, may be reduced to these three heads.

First, that of metaphrase, or turning an author word by word, and line by line, from one language into another. . . . The second way is that of paraphrase, or translation with latitude, where the author is kept in view by the translator, so as never to be lost, but his words are not so strictly followed as his sense; and that too is admitted to be amplified, but not altered. . . . The third way is that of imitation, where the translator (if now he has not lost that name) assumes the liberty, not only to vary from the words and sense, but to forsake them both as he sees occasion; and taking only some general hints from the original, to run division on the groundwork, as he pleases.[1]

Dryden announces as his own standard the mean, "paraphrase," but he confesses that he may sometimes have taken more liberty. Both the theory and the practice of Dryden presage something which is far more plainly legible in the first half of the next century in the Horatian imitations of Pope and the Juvenalian imitations of Samuel Johnson. To take but one instance, Pope's *Epistle to Augustus* is an imitation of the corresponding Horatian epistle in a sense quite far advanced beyond that in which Ben Jonson's character of Shakespeare in *Timber* is an imitation of the happy model which he had found in Seneca's sketch of Haterius. With Jonson the parallel between Haterius and Shakespeare is of small consequence. If we attend to it at all, it is only a small joke, almost irrelevant to the tone and pattern of Jonson's sketch. But with Pope not only parallel, but adaptation, and even recognizable deviation are the essential techniques. It is a technique of discrepant or ironic analogy—Augustan London matched fairly enough against Augustan Rome, but George Augustus II matched lamely and insultingly against Oc-

---

[1] Ker I, 237. Similar distinctions may be found in English writing of an earlier date—as far back, for instance, as the *Scholemaster* of Roger Ascham. Dryden takes the term "imitation" in the special sense in question from Cowley. He notes the practice of this kind of translation in Cowley's Pindaric and Horatian Odes and in Denham's Second *Aeneid*.

tavius Augustus—ridicule accomplished by eulogy. "A vile Encomium doubly ridicules: There's nothing blackens like the ink of fools." In short the difference between the Jonsonian and the Popean stages of classical imitation is that between mere borrowing from a source and the strategy of allusion, a difference of all the more theoretical import if we consider the pervasive and Protean role of allusion in the poetry of all sophisticated ages.

The aesthetic of imitation in the age of Dryden and Pope merges with another principle, that of parody and burlesque—forms of literature which were at the same time techniques of intricate allusion and symptoms of decline from the heroic. They were symptoms too of the freedom of the poetic spirit even when it appears most dedicated to the rules.[2] If it was not possible to be the English Homer or the English Virgil or even adequately to translate the highly serious works of those authors, it was both possible and delightful to use their range of meaning and the mammoth authority of their very presence in the mind of the age to construct smaller but brightly reflecting models, either in the mode of rococo delicacy or in that of the harrowing grotesque. It may have been play—the elevated person putting on the mask for the visit to the bazaar of ordinary life—but it was crafty and potent play. In these modes of composition the poet enjoyed all the advantages which "imitation" can afford. He was an objective imitator in the fullest way—in a way, however, which during every age lies at least latent in the triangular relationship of poet, contemporary world, and literary past.

SUPPLEMENT

The work by Mr. Pound which has laid itself most open to this kind of attack, *Homage to Sextus Propertius*, is not included in the volume under consideration here. At the same time, though it is strictly not a translation of Propertius so much as what a Restoration poet would have called an "Allusion to Propertius" or "Imitations of Propertius," it perhaps provides the best starting-point for a general consideration of Mr. Pound's achievement as a verse translator. The academic critics of this poem are right, of course, in dis-

[2] Cf. Austin Warren, "The Mask of Pope," *Sewanee Review*, LIV (Winter, 1946), 19–33. Fielding in his Preface to *Joseph Andrews* finds it incumbent upon him to distinguish between mere burlesque and the truly comic imitation of nature which he professes. For about seventy-five years various forms of play and irresponsibility may have been a chief outlet for the poetic impulse—not only the burlesques of Pope, Swift, and Fielding, but the Spenserian parody of Shenstone (increasingly tender in its revisions), Smart's whimsical mad play with the Scriptures, Percy's condescension to the ballads, Chatterton's forged medievalism. Cf. R. D. Havens, "Assumed Personality, Insanity, and Poetry," *Review of English Studies*, New Series, IV (January, 1953), 26–37.

covering howlers in it. They could discover comparable howlers in Marlowe's very beautiful versions of Ovid, and it may be admitted that Mr. Pound's knowledge of Latin is nearer to that of an eager undergraduate (an undergraduate impatient with grammar and in love with the *idea* of poetry) than to that of a university lecturer. At the same time, the academic critics of *Homage to Sextus Propertius* have largely missed Mr. Pound's point. We can see what he is doing in this poem most clearly if we look at passages where there are no howlers, but where, for the sake of bringing out a latent irony in Propertius, Mr. Pound deliberately distorts his strict sense. Thus the elegiac couplet,

> *a valeat, Phoebum quicumque moratur in armis!*
> *exactus tenui pumice versus eat,* [*Elegies* III, i, 7–8]

which is literally, in Butler's version, "Away with the man who keeps Phoebus tarrying among the weapons of war! Let verse run smoothly, polished with fine pumice," becomes in Mr. Pound's variation:

> Out-weariers of Apollo will, as we know, continue their Martian generalities.
>   We have kept our erasers in order.

Mr. Pound obviously here does understand the literal sense of the Latin. But for his own purposes, he is "pointing up" that sense. He is not using Propertius as a *mere* stalking-horse. He is, in the lines just quoted, striving by a slight distortion of the literal sense of his original to bring over much more vividly than Butler does its tone and feeling. He brings in "Martian" to remind us that after all it is a Latin poet he is starting from. On the other hand, he brings in the modern word "generalities" and the word "erasers" (which probably suggests typewriter erasers to us more immediately than fine pumice) to remind us that the reason why he is imitating, or alluding to, Propertius, is that Propertius has contemporary relevance. We are to reflect not only that Propertius did not want to write war-poetry but that Mr. Pound did not fancy himself as a poet of the school of Newbolt and Kipling.

> —"The Poet as Translator," review of *The Translations of Ezra Pound*, with an Introduction by Hugh Kenner (London, 1953) in *Times Literary Supplement*, London, September 18, 1953, p. 596, by permission of *The Times*

    Upon the highest corner of a large window, there dwelt a certain spider, swollen up to the first magnitude by the destruction of infinite numbers of flies, whose spoils lay scattered before the gates of his palace, like human bones before the cave of some giant. The avenues to his castle were guarded with turnpikes and palisadoes, all after the modern way of fortification. . . . it was the pleasure of fortune to conduct thither a wandering bee, to whose curiosity a broken pane in the glass had discovered itself, and in he went; where, expatiating a while, he at last happened to alight upon one of the outward walls of the spider's citadel; which, yielding to the unequal weight, sunk down to the very foundation. . . . the bee had acquitted himself of his toils, and, posted securely at some distance, was employed in cleansing his wings, and disengaging them from the ragged remnants of the cobweb. By this time the spider was adventured out, when, beholding the chasms, the ruins, and dilapidations of his fortress, he was very near his wit's end; he stormed and swore like a madman, and swelled till he was ready to burst.

'Not to disparage myself,' said he, 'by the comparison with such a rascal, what art thou but a vagabond without house or home, without stock or inheritance, born to no possession of your own, but a pair of wings and a drone-pipe? Your livelihood is an universal plunder upon nature; a freebooter over fields and gardens; and, for the sake of stealing, will rob a nettle as easily as a violet. Whereas I am a domestic animal, furnished with a native stock within myself. This large castle (to show my improvements in the mathematics) is all built with my own hands, and the materials extracted altogether out of my own person.'

'I am glad,' answered the bee, 'to hear you grant at least that I am come honestly by my wings and my voice; for then, it seems, I am obliged to Heaven alone for my flights and my music; and Providence would never have bestowed on me two such gifts, without designing them for the noblest ends. I visit indeed all the flowers and blossoms of the field and the garden; but whatever I collect thence enriches myself, without the least injury to their beauty, their smell, or their taste. Now, for you and your skill in architecture and other mathematics, I have little to say: in that building of yours there might, for aught I know, have been labour and method enough; but, by woeful experience for us both, 'tis too plain, the materials are naught, and I hope you will henceforth take warning, and consider duration and matter as well as method and art. You boast, indeed, of being obliged to no other creature, but of drawing and spinning out all from yourself; that is to say, if we may judge of the liquor in the vessel by what issues out, you possess a good plentiful store of dirt and poison in your breast; and, though I would by no means lessen or disparage your genuine stock of either, yet I doubt you are somewhat obliged, for an increase of both, to a little foreign assistance. Your inherent portion of dirt does not fail of acquisitions, by sweepings exhaled from below; and one insect furnishes you with a share of poison to destroy another. So that, in short, the question comes all to this— Whether is the nobler being of the two, that which, by a lazy contemplation of four inches round, by an overweening pride, feeding and engendering on itself, turns all into excrement and venom, producing nothing at all, but flybane and a cobweb; or that which, by an universal range, with long search, much study, true judgement, and distinction of things, brings home honey and wax.'

This dispute was managed with such eagerness, clamour, and warmth, that the two parties of books, in arms below stood silent a while, waiting in suspense what would be the issue, which was not long undetermined: for the bee, grown impatient at so much loss of time, fled straight away to a bed of roses, without looking for a reply, and left the spider like an orator, collected in himself and just prepared to burst out.

It happened upon this emergency, that Aesop broke silence first. . . . he . . . swore in the loudest key, that in all his life he had never known two cases so parallel and adapt to each other, as that in the window, and this upon the shelves. . . . 'For, pray, gentlemen, was ever anything so modern as the spider, in his air, his turns, and his paradoxes? He argues in the behalf of you his brethren and himself, with many boastings of his native stock and great genius, that he spins and spits wholly from himself, and scorns to own any obligation or assistance from without. Then he displays to you his great skill in architecture, and improvement in the mathematics. To all this the bee, as an advocate retained by us the Ancients, thinks fit to answer—that, if one may judge of the great genius or inventions of the Moderns by what they have produced, you will hardly have countenance to bear you out in boasting of either. Erect your schemes with as much method and skill as you please; yet if the materials be nothing but dirt, spun out of your own entrails (the guts of modern brains), the edifice will conclude at last in a cobweb, the duration of which, like that of other spiders' webs, may be imputed to their being forgotten, or neglected, or hid in a corner. For anything else of genuine that the Moderns may pretend to, I cannot recollect; unless it be a large vein of wrangling and satire, much of a nature and substance with the spider's poison; which, however, they pretend to spit wholly out of themselves, is improved by the same arts, by feeding upon the insects and vermin of the age. As for us the Ancients, we are content with the bee to pretend to nothing of our own, beyond our wings and our voice, that is to say, our flights and our language. For the rest, whatever we have got, has been by infinite labour and search, and ranging through every corner of nature; the difference is that, instead of dirt and poison, we have rather chosen to fill our hives with honey and wax, thus furnishing mankind with the two noblest of things, which are sweetness and light.'

—Jonathan Swift, *The Battle of the Books*, 1704

CHAPTER 12

RHETORIC AND NEO-CLASSIC WIT

§ *Crocean view of 17th-century rhetoric,* Ramus *and* Talon: *rearrangement of rhetoric and dialectic, relation of poetry to dialectic and rhetoric, Arcadian Rhetoric, euphuism, ambiguous import of Ramism, Cicero and Professor Howell—II. scientific plain style in England, Glanville,* The Royal Society, *Wilkins and Sprat, Swift's satire —III. "wit" vs. "judgment," Dryden, Hobbes, Locke, Addison ("mixt wit"), Augustan vs. metaphysical poetry, lag between poetry and theory, Puttenham's figures—IV. Alexander Pope,* Essay on Criticism, *classical "imitation" again, literary theory as influence, content, and norm, Vida, Boileau, the mob of English gentlemen, synopsis of Pope's Essay—V. Pope's ideas: "Nature" universal and social, reason and authority, rhetorical rules, "representative" verse, Pope's tour de force, diction, Horace's rule of idiom vs. poetic diction—VI. "wit" again, a genteel slang word, Pope's artful use of its meanings, the norm of salon conversation, a social question, Tories and high churchmen vs. middle-class dissenters, Blackmore, "wit," "nature," and "dress," the inevitable residuum, Samuel Johnson's retrospect, "familiarity" and "surprise," "sheer wit" and repartee, Corbyn Morris—VII. the 17th-century double shift, in style and theory, ambiguity of theory, Sprat, Pascal, Swift, Newman; Pope, Dryden, Gildon, Blackmore—VIII. end of ancient rhetorical tradition in 18th century, simultaneous new concept, Giambattista Vico died 1744, contrasted to Hobbes, Pope's* Dunciad IV, *1743, negative celebration of the "word"* §

THE STRONGLY BIASED SURVEY OF CRITICAL HISTORY WHICH FORMS THE second part of Benedetto Croce's *Aesthetic* probably did a great deal to establish the 17th century in the mind of the early 20th as the moment of a rhetorical event that had been long overdue—the breakdown of the elaborate system of verbal artifice which had endured under the name of "rhetoric" from classical times into the Renaissance. According to this view, the last and most preposterous phase of classical rhetoric occurs during the early 17th century in such baroque developments as Gongorism and Marinism on the continent and in the English parallel known as "metaphysical wit," the extravagant ingenuity in metaphor, pun, and paradoxical conceit attained by the poets Donne, Herbert, and Crashaw, and by such sermon writers as Donne and Andrewes. After this phase there was no further scope for the elaboration of ornamental rhetoric. The system collapsed.

Subsequent research has produced a good deal of evidence tending to show the part played in England by post-Baconian science and the Puritan spirit of economic and practical tidiness in clearing the ground for what was conceived as a desirable unification of language and real knowledge. Whatever the justice of the Crocean evaluation, it is safe to say that the 17th century was a critical period in the long struggle—more or less continuous since pre-Platonic times—between the custodians of pure idea and pure fact, dialecticians and scientists, on the one hand, and on the other, the custodians of the riches of the "word," grammarians, rhetoricians, critics, exegetes.

A preliminary *cause célèbre*, though probably more symptomatic of the main unrest of the age than a sufficient or even a necessary influence for the rhetorical events which followed, had been the educational reform promoted by the French logician Peter Ramus, whose life work was a sustained attack on what he considered the perversions of latter-day Aristotelianism. His program included a broad revision of the traditional rhetoric, carried out with the assistance of his colleague and special authority in that department, Omer Talon. Among the most influential books during the later 16th century and the first half of the 17th century in France and England were undoubtedly the now little-known *Dialectique* (1555) and *Dialecticae Libri Duo* (1556) of Ramus and the companion *Institutiones Oratoriae* (1544), in a later version entitled *Rhetorica*, of Talon.[1] Ancient Stoic philosophers had made a distinction be-

---

[1] See Wilbur Samuel Howell, "Ramus and English Rhetoric," *Quarterly Journal of Speech*, XXXVII (October, 1951), 301-2. The date of Talon's subsidiary work is to be explained by the fact that both the *Dialectique* and *Dialecticae Libri Duo* were condensations of earlier works by Ramus. His *Dialecticae Institutiones* or *Dialecticae Partitiones* and his *Aristotelicae Animadversiones* appeared in 1543. See also

tween the "closed fist" of dialectic and the "open palm" of rhetoric.[2]
With Ramus and with his English followers of the 17th century, both
dialectic and rhetoric came heavily under the "clunchfist"[3] of method.

One of the first principles of Ramist reasoning was a clean separation
of each liberal discipline from every other—with no overlapping. Ramus
could not tolerate, for instance, the fact that the intellectual activities of
"invention" and "disposition" had traditionally appeared not only in dialectic (or logic) but in rhetoric. His revision of the art of rhetoric began
with a radical reassignment of the anciently established five parts of the
art of rhetoric—Invention, Disposition, Elocution, Memory, and Delivery. He took invention, disposition, and memory[4] away from rhetoric
and gave them securely and univocally to dialectic, leaving to rhetoric
proper only elocution (that is, style) and delivery. Since the last of
these is a matter of externalization (the actor's part), rhetoric proper
might be conceived as consisting only of style. And that, furthermore,
was to be a relatively simple style. For everywhere Ramus was a purist
and simplist. In dialectic he reduced the traditional complexities of "invention" to ten topics or commonplaces of argument, and (under the
head of distribution) he treated the syllogism only in its most elementary
forms.[5] In rhetoric he treated style as a repertory of "tropes" and "figures," with greater emphasis on the latter. "Tropes" included what we
today might call the metaphoric and the ironic qualities of meaning—
what medieval rhetoricians called "difficult" ornaments. "Figures" were
various artful or unusual ways of expression—apostrophe, exclamation,
hesitation, concession, understatement and the like, and also various repetitive or echoing patterns of words ("turns," as Dryden would later call
them)—all these being the "easy" ornaments of the medieval rhetorician.
There were (and are) of course rather close ties—of ironic and metaphoric insinuation—between the "tropes" of such a system and the "figures." But Ramist rhetoric did not reach the levels of analysis where
such connections might have been discussed.

One striking feature of this rhetorical situation lay in the close relation of *poetry*, as Ramus saw it, both to rhetoric and to dialectic. The
Ramist dialectic was implicitly the Platonic anti-rhetoric of the *Phaedrus*
returning against the long successful Aristotelian answer. The main plea
was for a revitalized dialectic, a more direct and intuitive union of mind

P. A. Duhamel, "The Logic and Rhetoric of Peter Ramus," *Modern Philology*, XLVI
(February, 1949), 163–171.

[2] Cicero, *Orator* XXXII. "*Zeno quidem ille a quo disciplina Stoicorum est manu
demonstrare solebat quid inter has artis interesset; nam cum compresserat digitos
pugnumque fecerat, dialecticam aiebat eiusmodi esse; cum autem deduxerat et
manum dilataverat, palmae illius similem eloquentiam esse dicebat.*" Cf. *ante* Chapter 4.

[3] See *Oxford English Dictionary*, s.v. *clunchfist*: "1662 Fuller *Worthies* I, 189,
The Clunch-fist of Logick (good to knock a man down at a blow)."

[4] Duhamel, *loc. cit.*, p. 164, n. 12.

[5] Duhamel, pp. 166, 169.

with "argument," the steady unfolding of natural and concrete implications and of necessary and logically compelling dichotomies—without the interference of deductive abstraction (the "false secondary power by which we multiply distinctions").[6] Ramism had a strong leaning toward the immediacy and warmth of the poetic argument. It conceived an "argument" not as a statement or series of statements, but simply as any term, idea, image, or quality—any *thing*, in short, when seen in the light of some significance.[7] The system was strongly "practical" in that it stressed example more than theory. Both in their dialectical and in their rhetorical works the Ramists freely adduced examples from the poets. *The Lawiers Logike* (1588) of Abraham Fraunce, translated and digested from Ramus's *Dialecticae Libri Duo*, uses, side by side, illustrations from English law and from Spenser's *Shepheardes Calendar*. A companion volume, Fraunce's *Arcadian Rhetorike*, translated from Talon's *Rhetorica*, is in effect a rich anthology of examples from Homer, Virgil, Sidney, Spenser, Tasso, Du Bartas, and other continental poets.[8] Sidney's Arcadian figures became standard Ramist rhetorical illustrations in England.

Sidney's Arcadian rhetoric is likely to seem florid enough to a 20th-century reader. A recent close analysis of this rhetoric has, however, suggested its rather heavy dependence on certain devices of word order (*figures* or *schemes*—such as isocolon, parenthesis, anaphora, antithesis) rather than on the metaphoric and ironic range of the *tropes*. In short, Sidney's rhetoric was what would have been called by a medieval writer in the *Ad Herennium* tradition a rhetoric of "easy ornaments."[9] Another Elizabethan style which would have been called "easy" in the same tradition was that of Lyly in his *Euphues*, no matter how great its modern reputation for artificiality. The dominant artifice of Euphuism was structural (in parallel, antithesis, and transverse alliteration), and its numerous images, far fetched though they were from natural history and myth, were seldom truly metaphoric, seldom ironic or in any way subtle. The fact that Stephen Gosson (the Puritan enemy of poetry) wrote in a Euphuistic style which was more elaborate than that of the courtier Sidney, who was provoked, perhaps by Gosson himself, to the *Defence of Poesie*, constitutes a paradoxical crisscross which well illustrates the concrete complexity of the historic situation.[1] But this is perhaps only a

---

[6] Wordsworth, *Prelude* II, 214-17.

[7] P. A. Duhamel, "Milton's Alleged Ramism," *PMLA*, LXVII (December, 1952), 1035-53. Cf. Rosemond Tuve, "Imagery and Logic: Ramus and Metaphysical Poetics," *JHI*, III (October, 1942), 383-4.

[8] Howell, *loc. cit.*, p. 305. See *The Arcadian Rhetorike by Abraham Fraunce*, ed. E. Seaton, Oxford, 1950. Cf. Thomas Blount, *Academie of Eloquence*, 1654.

[9] P. A. Duhamel, "Sidney's *Arcadia* and Elizabethan Rhetoric," *SP*, XLV (April, 1948), 134-150.

[1] Comparable crosscurrents appear in antiquity. Stoics of the third century B.C. hold the doctrine of the *logos*, the creative word, yet favor plain style, the closed fist. Seneca the Younger champions philosophy but holds for the union of eloquence

facet of the larger paradox that the technically simplified rhetoric promoted by Ramus and Talon, the "Arcadian" rhetoric, should soon come
to be taken as the very embodiment of rhetorical floridity.[2] The explanation of this latter fact lies in the principle that a pure rhetoric (that is,
a rhetoric of elocution detached from invention and disposition—of style
detached from sense), no matter how simplified or restricted, is inevitably an excessive and artificial rhetoric. Far more "difficult" writers
than either Lyly or Sidney—Shakespeare, for instance, or Donne—
employ the whole range of both figures and tropes without being
"flowery."

The Ramist reshuffling of the three intrinsic parts of ancient rhetoric—invention, disposition, and elocution—that is, the translation of
the term "rhetoric" from a name embracing all three of these parts to a
name of merely the third, was a procedure of highly ambiguous import.
It might mean, on the one hand, that a person decided: "Invention and
disposition, the two substantial sinews of argument, are really parts of
logic. Rhetoric in fact is mainly logic. What good rhetoric wants is a
severe and honest style of adherence to argument. The elocution is the
trimmings—or the clippings. Save them who will." This in fact was the
kind of 17th-century thinking represented in the aphorism of Pascal,
"*La vraie éloquence se moque de l'éloquence,*"[3] and no less in the plainish, anti-metaphysical, anti-baroque style which in England during the
third quarter of the century would appear in pulpit eloquence, in the
scientific writing of the Royal Society, and even in literary prose, for
instance, in the lucidly conversational idiom of Dryden.

But at the same time, a person caught in the consequences of the
Ramist rhetoric and logic might conceivably entertain a different train
of reflections, somewhat as follows: "The art of rhetoric, as distinct
from philosophy and science, has after all been always a matter essentially of style. Leaving the content and structure of argument, therefore,
to the logician, the scientist, the theologian, let me discuss rhetoric in its
pure form, that of the figures and tropes and of external pronunciation."
And this in fact is what may be heard in many places. Professor Perry
Miller quotes the following Commencement theses on rhetoric proposed
at Harvard College during the latter part of the 17th century.

---

and wisdom. Quintilian champions rhetoric against philosophy, but writes, and
argues for, a plainish style. The same ambiguous allegiance in the contest between
rhetoric and thinking is shown in the Ciceronian mean between Asianism and At-
ticism and the later development of the Silver Latin or Senecan curtly brilliant
artifice. Cf. *ante* Chapter 4.

[2] Cf. *ante* Chapter 6, p. 103, n. 4.

[3] *Pensées* VII, 34. Cf. Montaigne, "*Le parler que j'aime, c'est un parler simple
et naïf, tel sur le papier qu'à la bouche . . .*" (*Essais*, I, xxvi). Cf. the statements
of Nashe, Puttenham and Jonson, quoted by F. W. Bateson, *English Poetry and the
English Language* (Oxford, 1934), p. 39.

Rhetoric differs as a species from logic.

The principal constituents of rhetoric are elocution and pronunciation.

Elocution is the place of the flowers of rhetoric, pronunciation
the expiration of the odors.[4]

Whichever way one interpreted the Ramist mandate, a serious cleavage
in the art of verbal expression was the result. The new Platonic philosophy, like the old, was the enemy of a kind of verbal power which,
whatever its relation to science or philosophy, is close to the interests of
both oratory and poetry. In Roman classical times the complaint of
Cicero, the champion of eloquence, against Socrates, the dialectician, was
that the latter had succeeded in dividing the mind and the tongue, the
man who knew from the man who spoke. In a strikingly parallel fashion
a modern professor of public speaking (Professor Wilbur S. Howell of
Princeton) looks back on the reform effected by Ramus and reports:
". . . it tended to separate the investigative responsibilities of speakers
and writers from their presentational responsibilities . . . as if one set
of men could do the thinking for society, and quite another set, the
speaking." [5]

II

During the latter half of the 17th century, re-enforcements to plain-style
philosophy from Cartesian and empirically scientific quarters largely
took over the program. At least it is true that in England the scientific
was the most obvious influence upon literary men and is the most easily
described. The contrast between the baroque, Brownian way of writing
and the new severe scientific style may be conveniently shown in a passage which Joseph Glanvill, author of the Cartesian and anti-Aristotelian *Vanity of Dogmatizing*, 1661, revised for a version of that work
which appeared after his admission to the Royal Society. In 1661 Glanville was no doubt proud of the following:

[4] Perry Miller, *The New England Mind* (New York, 1939), p. 323.

[5] W. S. Howell, *loc. cit.*, pp. 309–10. Professor Howell adds that at that moment
in history "social pressures were at work to bring these responsibilities together."
"Talaeus's rhetoric, with its exclusive emphasis upon these routines [tropes and
figures, voice and gesture], had increasingly less and less to say to the brave young
science of the seventeenth century, whereas that science meanwhile wanted nothing
so much as a theory of communication suitable to the transfer of experimental
knowledge from scientist to scientist and from scientist to public." For the reasons
indicated above, we suggest that the system of Ramus taken as a whole made its
own contribution toward the development of the plain scientific style and even
more toward that of the plain preaching style. Cf. Miller, *op. cit.*, Ch. XII, "The
Plain Style;" Walter J. Ong, "Peter Ramus and the Naming of Methodism," *JHI*,
XIV, 2 (April 1953), pp. 235–48.

If after a decoction of *hearbs* in a Winter-night, we expose the
liquor to the frigid air; we may observe in the morning under
a crust of Ice, the perfect appearance both in *figure*, and *colour*,
of the *Plants* that were taken from it. But if we break the *aque-
ous Crystal*, those pretty images dis-appear and are present[ly]
dissolved. Now these *airy Vegetables* are presumed to have
been made, by the reliques of these *plantal emissions* whose
avolation was prevented by the *condensed inclosure*. And therefore playing up and down for a while within their liquid prison,
they at last settle together in their natural order, and the *Atomes*
of each part finding out their proper place, at length rest in
their methodical Situation, till by breaking the *Ice* they are disturbed, and those counterfeit *compositions* are scatter'd into
their first Indivisibles.[6]

But in 1676:

. . . after a decoction of Herbs in a frosty Night, the shape of
the Plants will appear under the Ice in the Morning: which
Images are supposed to be made by the congregated *Effluvia* of
the Plants themselves, which loosly wandring up and down in
the Water, at last settle in their natural place and order, and so
make up an appearance of the Herbs from whence they were
emitted.[7]

The Royal Society too inspired the most resolute effort of the age to
reduce natural language to the abstractness, regularity, and reliability of
mathematical symbols, a basic English and symbolic logic of that age.
This was Bishop John Wilkins' *Essay Towards a Real Character and a
Philosophical Language*, 1668—a system of "integral" and "particle"
shorthand that proved far too cryptic to be manageable.[8] And again, the
Royal Society, in its *History* (1667), written by a literary and religious
man, the biographer of the poet Cowley, Bishop Thomas Sprat, gives
us one of the age's most unvarnished statements concerning what was
conceived as the ideal relation between things and words:

[6] *Vanity of Dogmatizing*, 1661, p. 46. Cf. R. F. Jones et al., *The Seventeenth
Century* (Stanford, 1951), pp. 89–93. The five essays of Professor Jones reprinted in
this volume are pioneer investigations of first importance to the theme pursued in
this chapter.
[7] *Essays*, 1676, p. 11. The second and largely unrevised edition of Glanville's
Vanity, published in 1664 and entitled *Scepsis Scientifica*, contains a dedicatory
"Address to the Royal Society" in which he makes an advance announcement of
his change of heart about style. In his *Essay Concerning Preaching*, 1688, he was to
say: "Plainness is a character of great latitude and stands in opposition, First to *hard
words*: Secondly, to *deep and mysterious notions*: Thirdly, to *affected Rhetoricians*:
and Fourthly, to *Phantastical Phrases*" (Spingarn, II, 273).
[8] Cf. Francis Christensen, "John Wilkins and the Royal Society's Reform of
Prose Style," *MLQ*, VII (1946), 179–87, 279–90.

They have therefore been most rigorous in putting in execution, the only Remedy, that can be found for this *extravagance:*
and that has been, a constant Resolution, to reject all the ampli-
fications, digressions, and swellings of style: to return back to
the primitive purity, and shortness, when *men* deliver'd so
many *things*, almost in an equal number of *words*. They have
exacted from all their members, a close, naked, natural way of
speaking: positive expressions; clear senses; a native easiness:
bringing all things as near the Mathematical plainess, as they
can.[9]

The later burlesque version of this ideal, in the Third Book of *Gulliver's
Travels*, during the visit to the scientific Academy of Lagado, conveys
very well the implications to which a literary man was bound to object.

The other project was a scheme for entirely abolishing all
words whatsoever, and this was urged as a great advantage in
point of health as well as brevity. . . . An expedient was therefore offered, that since words are only names for things, it
would be more convenient for all men to carry about them such
things as were necessary to express the particular business they
are to discourse on. . . . many of the most learned and wise
adhere to the new scheme of expressing themselves by things.[1]

Words and things, *res et verba*, was a theme which had come echoing
down rhetorical corridors since the days of the Ciceronian *ratio et oratio*
and Quintilian's *Curam ergo verborum rerum volo solicitudinem esse.*[2]
But the 17th-century preoccupation with the theme laid a new emphasis
on the naked "thing." The words they would somehow get around.
"Few words are best when once we go a-Maying."

III

SUCH depreciation of the word had intimate connections with a simultaneous decline in respect for something which was then usually called
"wit," and which we may describe approximately as the inventive or
imaginative side either of poetic writing or of pulpit eloquence. (In the
latter sphere, the root of the matter was supposed to be the religious
quality of "enthusiasm." This inspired vain imagination and was

[9] *History of the Royal Society*, 1667, p. 112. ". . . and preferring the language
of Artizans, Countryman, and Merchants, before that, of Wits, or Scholars." Contrast the views of Dryden described *ante* Chapter 11.
[1] *Gulliver's Travels*, Book Three, Chapter 5, Section 4.
[2] See the excellent discussion of the 17th-century situation by A. C. Howell,
"*Res et Verba:* Words and Things," *ELH*, XIII (June, 1946), 131-42.

equally to be mistrusted.[3]) The history of the highly indigenous term and concept "wit" in 17th-century England was a disguised double progress, both a shifting in the value normally attributed to poetry and an accommodative shifting in the definition of a term so rich with value associations that it could only by a violent wrench of speaking habits have been abandoned. Let us conceive "wit," [4] a term which etymologically means the faculty of knowing in general (with either mind or senses) and which about the time of Shakespeare comes to mean smart knowing, joking, or repartee, invention or ingenuity, and even poetic keenness or fancy. Then, as the idea of ingenuity, the metaphysical *discordia concors*, becomes for a time more firmly attached to the idea of poetry, "wit" in the days of Cowley and the youthful Dryden comes to be almost equivalent to poetry itself or to the main principle of poetry. It is almost synonymous with "imagination" and "fancy." It is defined analytically as the faculty of seeing difficult resemblances between largely unlike objects—and in practice it is the enforcement of such resemblances by all the verbal resources available. At this juncture, however, arises the complication of a growing philosophical and scientific stress on the desirability, not of conceiving resemblances between things (too much of that, on slender grounds, in the poets and orators already), but of discerning differences. In short, an emphasis on analysis rather than synthesis. And the faculty of analysis is called, in distinction from "wit," "judgment." Classical notions of decorum and fitness to nature are highly compatible with this philosophic "judgment." For a time philosophy (or science) and neo-classical humanism walk evenly together.

Bacon had described the two powers—that of perceiving resemblances and that of perceiving differences—in the Latin of his *Novum Organum* (I, 55) without recourse to either of the terms "wit" or "judgment." And it may be well if we try to think of those powers, or the concepts of them, taken neutrally, as relatively stable concepts behind a considerable activity of the term "wit," an effort as it were on the part of that agile term to keep up with the center of value which not only in philosophy but in poetry was shifting from the pole of imagination or seeing resemblances to that of judgment or seeing differences. "Imagination" and "fancy" had to stay more or less on one side of the polarity, and so did "judgment." But "wit," because of its near synonymity with "poetry," had to move as the implicit concept of good poetry moved. It is only thus that one can explain, from

[3] Donald F. Bond, " 'Distrust' of Imagination in English Neo-Classicism," *PQ*, XIV (1935), 54–69; George Williamson, "The Restoration Revolt Against Enthusiasm," *SP*, XXX (October, 1933), 571–603.

[4] See W. L. Ustick and H. H. Hudson, "Wit, 'Mixt Wit,' and the Bee in Amber," *Huntington Library Bulletin*, VIII (October, 1935), 103–30; Murray W. Bundy, "Wit," in *Dictionary of World Literature*, ed. Joseph T. Shipley (New York, 1943).

the inside as it were, the successive uses of the term "wit" by single writers, like Dryden or Hobbes. In the Preface to his *Annus Mirabilis*, 1666, Dryden says:

> *Wit writing* . . . is no other than the faculty of imagination in the writer, which, like a nimble spaniel, beats over and ranges through the field of memory . . . , *Wit written is* . . . the happy result of thought, or product of imagination.[5]

In his *Defence of the Epilogue*, 1672, we find him canvassing a double definition of "wit." There is "wit in the stricter sense, that is, sharpness of conceit," a thing which Ben Jonson's comedy of "humour" does not have. At the same time:

> Ben Johnson . . . always writ properly, and as the character required; and I will not contest farther with my friends who call that wit; it being very certain, that even folly itself, well represented, is wit in a larger signification.[6]

Then later, in the *Apology for Heroic Poetry*, 1677, we find Dryden completely embracing the tamer alternative.

> . . . the definition of Wit . . . is only this: that it is a propriety of thoughts and words; or, in other terms, thought and words elegantly adapted to the subject.[7]

As Dryden's courtly friend the Earl of Mulgrave put it in his *Essay Upon Poetry*, 1682:

> 'tis the top of wit
> T'express agreeably a thing that's fit.[8]

The epistemological groundswell which accounts for this dancing of the literary coracles may be seen very well in the philosophers Hobbes and Locke. Chapter VIII of Hobbes's *Leviathan* furnishes the following complicated, if not self-contradictory, instance of the mid-century commotion among the ideas associated with the term "wit." To make it easier to trace the activity of the term in this passage, we present what appear to be the crucial statements in a numbered list:

---

[5] Ker I, 14. Even at this date, Dryden, who had already outgrown his own metaphysical period (that of the verses lamenting the death of Lord Hastings), was inclined to view imagination as a faculty that needed restraint. Cf. the parallel image of the spaniel in the Epistle Dedicatory of *The Rival Ladies*, 1664. "For imagination in a poet is a faculty so wild and lawless that like an high-ranging spaniel, it must have clogs tied to it, lest it outrun the judgment" (Ker I, 8).

[6] Ker I, 172.

[7] Ker I, 190.

[8] Spingarn II, 294.

1. Naturall Wit, consisteth principally in two things; *Celerity of Imagining*, (that is, swift succession of one thought to another;) and *steddy direction* to some approved end. . . .

2. Those that observe their similitudes, in case they be such as are but rarely observed by others, are sayd to have a *Good Wit*; by which, in this occasion, is meant a *Good Fancy*. But they that observe their differences, and dissimilitudes; which is called *Distinguishing*, and *Discerning*, and *Judging* between thing and thing; in case such discerning be not easie, are said to have *good Judgement*. . . .

3. In a good Poem, whether it be *Epique* or *Dramatique;* as also in *Sonnets, Epigrams*, and other Pieces, both Judgement and Fancy are required: But the Fancy must be more eminent; because they please for the Extravagancy; but ought not to displease by Indiscretion.

4. In a good History, the Judgement must be eminent. . . . Fancy has no place, but onely in adorning the stile. In Orations of Prayse, and in Invectives, the Fancy is praedominant. . . .

5. And in any Discourse whatsoever, if the defect of Discretion be apparent, how extravagant soever the Fancy be, the whole discourse will be taken for a signe of want of wit; and so will it never when the Discretion is manifest, though the Fancy be never so ordinary. . . .

6. Judgement therefore without Fancy is Wit, but Fancy without Judgement not.

In the following passages from Locke's *Essay Concerning Human Understanding* (1690) the clear reference of the term "wit" to a faculty of seeing resemblances is a reversion to earlier usage, but the spirit is none the less Hobbesian and anti-rhetorical; the role assigned to "wit" is not complimentary.

For *wit* lying most in the assemblage of ideas, and putting those together with quickness and variety, wherein can be found any resemblance or congruity, thereby to make up pleasant pictures and agreeable visions in the fancy; *judgment*, on the contrary, lies quite on the other side, in separating carefully, one from another, ideas wherein can be found the least difference, thereby to avoid being misled by similitude.—II, xi

Since wit and fancy find easier entertainment in the world than dry truth and real knowledge, figurative speeches and allusion in language will hardly be admitted as an imperfection or abuse of it. I confess, in discourses where we seek rather pleasure and delight than information and improvement, such ornaments as are borrowed from them can scarce pass for faults. But yet if we would speak of things as they are, we must allow that all the art of rhetoric, besides order and clearness; all the artificial and figurative application of words eloquence hath invented, are for nothing else but to insinuate wrong ideas, move the passions, and thereby mislead the judgment; and so indeed are perfect cheats. . . . —III, x

In one of his *Spectator* essays on "wit," No. 62, Joseph Addison, making some parade of acquaintance with the first of these passages from Locke, is confident that this, rather than Dryden's later equation of wit with propriety, is the correct account. Unlike Locke, Addison starts with the assumption that "wit" is a term of honor, but his approval is ingeniously qualified. With his introduction of the categories "False Wit" (consisting merely in resemblance between words—as in puns, anagrams, rhymes, acrostics, figure poems and the like) and "Mixed Wit" (consisting partly in resemblance between words and partly in resemblance between ideas—as, for example, in the "flames" and "ardors" of love in Cowley's *Mistress* [9]) Addison leans very heavily toward the side of "judgment." He gives us, within a metaphysical and neoclassical frame of reference, a shrewd enough anticipation of a technical question that in our own day has been much more urgently brought to the fore: To what extent and in what way is the auditory intimation of metaphoric insight a respectable poetic procedure? More directly: Isn't it true that poetry flourishes on puns? And how can this be defended?

The 17th-century campaign against imagination is sometimes said to have been directed against the extravagant or licentious use of that faculty or only against its use in certain places—in sermons, for example, or in scientific papers. And often enough attacks on imagination did include provisos that the author did not mean to censure the appearance of imagination in poetry, its native and appropriate place. The passage which we have quoted above from Hobbes might be put under this head.

---

[9] The conceits in Cowley's *Mistress* to which Addison refers—the cold eyes of the mistress as burning glasses, the secret message read by the flame of love—may well strike a modern reader as less clear examples of the pun than many in Donne or Herbert. We suggest that the punning effect of the Cowleyan conceit comes about as follows: An expression at some time metaphorical, such as "flame" of love, lapses into cliché; it becomes an entrenched and firmly authorized—though not an intensely realized—meaning. In a final stage, "flame" of love comes to mean something quite unrelated to "flame" of combustion, and one need not think at all of the latter when referring to the former. Then occurs the extravagant re-realization or galvanization of the original metaphoric sense through the Cowleyan conceit (reading a message by the flame of love), and the very extravagance of the realization, or testing, of the dormant metaphor suggests that Cowley has taken unfair advantage of an authoritative cliché metaphor—or perhaps of a mere phonetic accident—"flame[1]" and "flame[2]."

There were even active defenses of poetic imagination by literary men.[1] But so pervasive a change in epistemological assumptions and in norms of prose communication as that which we have been discussing could scarcely take place without affecting the adjacent art of poetry. Even nowadays, with all our revival of respect for Augustan English poetry, we hardly dispute the view that this was more regularly ordered, more restrained, decorous, and *prima facie* a more prosaic, mode of composition than Metaphysical or Elizabethan poetry. There is that much truth in the now discredited statement of Matthew Arnold that "Dryden and Pope are classics of our prose."

On the other hand, there is a peculiar sense in which Augustan practice, more than theory, escaped the rigor of the scientific mood. The achievement of Dryden and Pope was that they used the guise of an apparently level and rationalized, even prosaic, discourse to accomplish poetic expression of a certain character. Though Pope's imaginative forces may seem somewhat soberly drawn up and cautiously limited to the obvious, the ordered parallels and contrasts of his verse have their own way of framing and forcing implicit metaphoric alignments and ironic confrontations. Pope and Dryden and no less Swift (whose insidiously plain prose may be taken as a counterpart of the Augustan prosaic verse) are the grand rhetoriqueurs of the close of an age of rhetoric that had its antecedents in classical antiquity. Pope's verse stands near the end of the tradition, not as an instance of decline, but as the most intense neo-classic realization of the verbal artifice described in Aristotle's *Rhetoric* [2] and the socially idiomatic nicety intimated by Horace.

The age of Pope witnessed a strange lag between poetry and theory—a success for poetry which consisted in its being a hundred years behind the most advanced theory. The numerous and varied figures (mixed wit and false wit), antithesis, metaphor, pun and quasi-pun, Gothic rhyme, alliteration, turn, tranlacer, and agnomination, which actually mark the highly artful poetry of Alexander Pope, are scarcely alluded to in the reigning poetic treatise of his day, the *Art of Poetry* by Edward Bysshe.[3] In his burlesque critical work *Peri Bathous, or of the Art of Sinking in Poetry*, Pope himself betrays a decided relish for ridiculing the figures. For an enthusiastic account of many of the Popean figures and the specific recommendation of them as poetic techniques we must go back as far as the Elizabethans, to Fraunce's *Arcadian Rhetorike*, for instance, or to Puttenham's quaintly phrased repertoire:

[1] See the articles by Donald F. Bond and George Williamson cited *ante* p. 229.

[2] Cf. *ante* Chapter 4, p. 70. For an account of the rhetoric involved in Pope's "poetry of statement," see Maynard Mack, "Wit and Poetry and Pope: Some Observations on His Imagery," in *Pope and his Contemporaries, Essays Presented to George Sherburn* (Oxford, 1949), pp. 20–40.

[3] Bysshe's *Art* appeared first in 1701 and went through numerous editions during Pope's lifetime.

Mezozeugma, or the Middlemarcher
Sillepsis, or the double supply
Parison, or the figure of even
Traductio, or the tranlacer
Antitheton, or the quareller
Ploche, or the doubler
Ironia, or the drie mock
Meiosis, or the disabler
Micterismus, or the fleering frumpe
Charientismus, or the privie nippe
    ("These be souldiers to the figure *allegoria*
      and fight under the banner of dissimu-
      lation.")
Paradoxon, or the wonderer
Synecdoche, or the figure of quick conceit
Noema, or the figure of close conceit [4]

But even Puttenham, with his uneven collection of jokes and conceits and the theoretical hints which he musters to introduce them, falls far short of providing anything like an adequate rationale of either Renaissance or Augustan poems of any sort. The significance of Puttenham is that he testifies to a climate of ideas in which the poetic relevance of these rhetorical and conversational, ironic and jesting, artifices was safely to be assumed.

I V

BUT we have reached a point in our account of wit and rhetoric in the neo-classic age where some expansion of that theme is needed. A consideration of so important a figure as Alexander Pope requires, for one thing, the re-introduction into our argument and the reaccentuation of the theme of classical "imitation." Pope's most ambitious critical work, his verse *Essay on Criticism*, is written squarely in the tradition of the Horatian *Ars Poetica*. It is thus an "imitation" of a literary genre complicated by the fact that literary theory itself is the theme of the work to be executed. Let us dwell on this point momentarily by asserting that a literary theory which operates as an influence on the writing of a poem ought to be distinguished more often than perhaps it is from a literary theory which manages to appear in the poem itself. And both of these ought to be distinguished from yet a third thing, the theory which is unified with a work by being really exemplified or carried out in that work. Pope's *Essay* shows marked relations to the literary theory in all

[4] Atkins, *English Criticism*, II, 157, believes that the extensive treatment of the figures in Puttenham's *Arte* argues a date of composition before 1570.

three ways. He is not only influenced by the tradition and clearly enough
bent on talking *about* the tradition, but he is at the same time exemplifying
it—for he is writing a classical poem, an example of the Horatian *Ars*,
and an example which succeeds by its classical brilliance. The reason
for the relative inferiority of the most celebrated 16th-century Italian
re-enactment of Horace, the *De Arte Poetica* of Vida, is that Vida was
not enough of a poet to bring it off. He knew the rules very well, but
apparently not what they meant. And so his poem is memorable mostly
for a few of its echoes of Horace [5] and for its forthright nationalistic advice about plundering the Greek classics and worshiping Virgil.[6] Boileau's
Art Poétique, 1674, had been a far more amusing expansion of Aristotle
and Horace to encompass the several genres—epic, tragedy, comedy, pastoral, elegy, ode, sonnet, epigram, rondeau, ballade, madrigal, satire,
"vaudeville"—which were countenanced by French classicism. This poem
exhibited a certain interesting Gallic bias, as of classicism nationalized, and
a nicely reasonable wit. The clean Horatian and Aristotelian ring of
Boileau's formulas and their occasional satiric sting created his own kind
of authority.

La montagne en travail enfante une souris. III, 274

Qu'en savantes leçons votre muse fertile
Partout joigne au plaisant le solide et l'utile. IV, 87-8

Pour me tirer des pleurs, il faut que vous pleuriez. III, 142

Mais dans l'art dangereux de rimer et d'écrire,
Il n'est point de degrés du médiocre au pire. IV, 31-2

Toutefois aux grands coeurs donnez quelques foiblesses.
  III, 104

Conservez à chacun son propre caractère. III, 112

Il n'est point de serpent ni de monstre odieux,
Qui, par l'art imité, ne puisse plaire aux yeux. III, 1

*Aimez donc la raison—*I, 37

Que la nature donc soit votre étude unique,
Auteurs qui prétendez aux honneurs du comique. III, 359

Quelque sujet qu'on traite, ou plaisant, ou sublime,
Que toujours le bon sens s'accorde avec la rime. I, 27-8

Un sot trouve toujours un plus sot qui l'admire. I, 232

---

[5] See, for instance, I, 40 (*Atque tuis prudens genus elige viribus aptum*); III,
459-60 (*Non totam subito praeceps secura per urbem Carmina vulgabit*).
[6] Cf. *ante* Chapter 9, p. 161.

The highly finished resumés of classical norms, the jokes against the universal enemy, stupidity, the keen moral maxims, are bound to elicit admiration. Boileau's flash was followed within a few years by a series of similar efforts on the part of the English courtly critics, the "mob of gentlemen who wrote with ease"; Rochester's *Allusion to the Tenth Satire of Horace* (in which Dryden is treated like the archaic crude poet Lucilius), 1680; Mulgrave's *Essay upon Poetry*, 1682; and Roscommon's translation of Horace's *Ars* and his *Essay on Translated Verse*, 1684. In Pope's day appeared the *Essay on Unnatural Flights in Poetry* by George Granville, 1701, Samuel Wesley's *Epistle to a Friend*, 1700, and other more or less lame instances of the genre. After Pope's precocious summation had appeared in 1711 there was nothing further for Englishmen to say in this area. By the title of this poem, not *An Essay on Poetry* but *An Essay on Criticism*, Pope appears to stand apart from the tradition in a new perspective. He appears to be raising the Art of Poetry to the second power. In actuality the notion of "criticism," when scrutinized, very readily becomes transparent, focussing telescopically on the more concrete matter of poetry itself, so that much of what Pope says is actually *De Arte Poetica*. At the same time his poem is never without the interest of a certain shimmer upon the surface through the implied dimension of criticism of criticism. The First Part of the poem, after the introductory wit, making the critic's job no less risky, responsible, and comically vulnerable than the poet's,

> 'Tis hard to say, if greater want of skill
> Appear in writing or in judging ill,   1–2

dwells on the theme of universal nature and the ancient models, sliding from that easily at the end to social observation upon the deplorable license of the last age. The Second Part enumerates causes of bad criticism, of which the greatest number are moral and psychological—pride, partisanship, snobbery, fashion, and the like ("Whatever nature has in worth denied, She gives in large recruits of needful pride"). But one of these causes—the bad habit of judging mere details, wit, diction, and verse, instead of whole poetic achievements—is of a very technical and objective sort. The discussion of it contains the heart of practical criticism in the *Essay*. The Third Part of the *Essay* is a history of the norms reflected in the first two parts, a recital of the great names of criticism—Aristotle, Horace, Quintilian, Longinus (who "is himself the great sublime he draws"), Boileau, Roscommon, and lastly, with a concluding dedication, Pope's boyhood monitor and promoter, the English gentleman critic, William Walsh. It was he who had repeatedly given Pope the advice that the last accomplishment left for an English poet was to be not only "great" but "correct."

V

THE theme of the present chapter is verbal rhetoric, but another theme of Pope's *Essay*, the prominent if elusive idea of "nature," claims some emphasis here, for Pope's main statement about rhetoric will turn out to be a prescription for some kind of improving conjunction or complementary interaction between the "wit" of rhetoric and the "nature" it deals with.

"Nature" (the object of artistic imitation) has for Pope three main features. First, Nature is a Platonic and Stoic universal order and superior reality:

> First follow Nature, and your judgment frame
> By her just standard, which is still the same.
> Unerring NATURE, still divinely bright,
> One clear, unchang'd, and universal light.
>
> —68–71

Secondly, Nature, the universal order, assimilates readily with man's effort to enforce or increase that order in his own affairs—that is, with his civilization and all its parts, his cities, institutions, businesses, and recreations. Pope's nature is the nature not only of Windsor Forest but of Hampton, Stowe, Twickenham, Drury Lane, Button's, and Grubstreet. It is the nature of socially ordered human conduct. Its antithesis is eccentricity or hyper-individualism. Another kind of nature, that known best to Rousseau and Wordsworth ("I heard a thousand blended notes, while in a grove I sate reclined . . .") was, to be sure, already well on the way in Pope's age. There are traces of it, primitivistic gleams, in Pope's *Essay on Man*. But it was not yet an open standard for poetry. That standard, and with it a hostile spotlight on the contrary element of civilization, was to come only after Pope's day—though not long after. Pope "stuck to describing *modern manners*," wrote Joseph Warton in 1782, "but these *manners*, because they are *familiar, uniform, artificial,* and *polished*, are, in their very nature unfit for any lofty effort of the Muse." [7]

Thirdly, Pope's idea of nature has the distinction of residing in a state of great harmony with the idea of the classical models. No other poet or theorist has expressed the reconciliation of these threateningly twin standards [8]—the rivals, modern reason and classic authority—with such persuasive aplomb.

---

[7] *Essay on the Genius and Writings of Pope* (London, 1808), II, 401–3.

[8] Homage to classical models, as we have already noticed, did not disable the theory of cultural cycles among the Augustans—that as Roman literature had been

Nature and Homer were, he found, the same.—135

Those RULES of old discover'd, not devis'd,
Are Nature still, but Nature methodiz'd.—88–9

Still green with bays each ancient Altar stands,
Above the reach of sacrilegious hands.—181–2

But to turn now to the rhetorical part of Pope's *Essay*, that concerning the technical reasons for bad criticism: it may be observed first that Pope seems guilty of a certain shifting between two pairs of coordinates, part-whole and aim-effect (or means-end).

In ev'ry work regard the writer's End,
Since none can compass more than they intend.—255–6

Survey the WHOLE, nor seek slight faults to find.—235

Here is an alternation of concepts which has often been paralleled—in certain 20th-century criticism, for instance, written along lines very much different from Pope's.[9] But the confusion straightens out in the ensuing passage on "wit," "diction," and "verse." The last of these topics is the occasion for a brilliant display of literary theory under two complementary aspects which we have mentioned above—that of assertion and that of exemplification. In a criticism preoccupied with the idea that poetry is an imitation of nature (and a loving if superior sister of other imitative arts—music and painting)[1]—it was reasonable to bestow a close attention on any poetic feature which could be shown to be not merely statement about nature but in some peculiar way direct imitation. The theme of "representative" verse, as Samuel Johnson was to term it, was a native of the classical climate. In his *Spectator* No. 253, reviewing Pope's *Essay*, Addison quotes the best-known antique locus, the passage by Dionysius of Halicarnassus praising the artful reality—the heavy labor and the sudden drop—of Homer's verses in which Sisyphus rolls up hill the continually relapsing stone. One of the most original passages in Vida's *De Arte Poetica* was a repetitive demonstration of six main metrically imitative effects: heavy, light, slow, fast, rough, smooth. The

refined from Naevius to Virgil, so English, from Chaucer to Dryden. Pope was on defensible, if somewhat ambiguous, ground when in the maturity of his satirical *Epistle to Augustus* he imitated Horace:
    Had ancient times conspir'd to disallow
    What then was new, what had been ancient now?   135–6
    [9] See *post*, Chapter 27 pp. 624–5, comment on I. A. Richards' *Principles of Literary Criticism*.
    [1] See *post* p. 274 and Robert J. Allen, "Pope and the Sister Arts," in *Pope and his Contemporaries, Essays Presented to George Sherburn* (Oxford, 1949). The passage on representative verse in the *Essay on Criticism* has a counterpart on music in *Dunciad* IV, 63–70, where Pope defends Handel's supposed mimetic re-enforcement of his chorus by cannon. "But soon, ah soon, Rebellion will commence, If music meanly borrows aid from sense."

parallel passage by Pope is much more economical and pointed. In a space of 29 lines Pope simultaneously states and illustrates some nine prosodic principles. Thus, the fault of hiatus, three times in one line:

> Tho' oft the ear the open vowels tire. . . . 345

(where just the opposite of Milton's natural rule of elision is called for in order to have enough syllables for the pentameter). Or the atomically structured monosyllabic line:

> And ten low words oft creep in one dull line.—347

Or stereotyped rhymes:

> Where-e'er you find "the cooling western breeze,"
> In the next line, it "whispers thro' the trees:"
> When crystal streams "with pleasing murmurs creep,"
> The reader's threaten'd (not in vain) with "sleep."—350-3

And then that attractive matter of "representation," comprising the last six of Pope's principles:

> 'Tis not enough no harshness gives offence,
> The sound must seem an Echo to the sense.—364-5

The "hoarse rough verse" for the "roaring torrent," the "smoother numbers" in which the "smooth stream flows," the heavy labor of Ajax ("The line too labors, and the words move slow"), and, most striking of all, the contrasting hexameters, one off-beat, spondaic, and slow, the other precisely and elliptically fast.

> A needless Alexandrine ends the song,
> That, like a wounded snake, drags its slow length along.—356-7

> Not so, when swift Camilla scours the plain,
> Flies o'er th' unbending corn, and skims along the main.—372-3

In a series of shrewd *Rambler* inquiries into metrical realism, Samuel Johnson was to indulge in too much skepticism about this Popean *tour de force*. There can scarcely be any question that Pope here demonstrates how the Alexandrine (so often used, along with the triplet, for special purposes in the narrative verse of Dryden [2]) is capable of exactly contrasting effects. It is no refutation of his doctrine to observe that such effects are always highly generic or schematic, taking their specific feel from the sense of the lines, as the chameleon takes its color from the grass. The precise limits of metrical imitation and the wider range of phonetic properties or "orchestrations" distinguished by modern schol-

---

[2] Cf. Pope's *Epistle to Augustus*, ll. 267-9: "Waller was smooth; but Dryden taught to join . . . The long majestic March, and Energy divine."

ars[3] (and indeed recognized in the repertory of Renaissance figures) would be an inquiry of more technical nicety than is needed for the present argument.

Concerning the second of the three technical details named above—"diction"—Pope's formula in the *Essay on Criticism* is a neat approximation to the Horatian rule of idiom which we have already quoted in Pope's words, in our chapter on Horace.[4] Be neither archaic nor new-fangled, use the living language of your day, avoid both the flat and the highfalutin. Some further specifications but also some complications appear when we explore other statements by Pope. "Shut, shut the door, good John! fatigu'd I said, Tye up the knocker, say I'm sick, I'm dead." The opening of the *Epistle to Arbuthnot* is a neat complement to one of the burlesque rules of the *Peri-Bathous*, that for "the Buskin or stately" style: "Will not every true lover of the Profound be delighted to behold the most vulgar and low actions of life exalted. . . ?" Instead of "Shut the Door," say "The wooden guardian of our privacy quick on its axle turn." On the other hand there are Pope's *Pastorals* and his Homer and the whole matter of "poetic diction." As Isaac Watts said and Samuel Johnson was to repeat, there was "scarcely a happy combination of words or a phrase poetically elegant in the English language" which Pope was not skilful enough to "insert" in his Homer.

VI

To come then to the last, and most important, of our three technical details,—that is to say, "wit"—Alexander Pope's *Essay on Criticism*, if we view it in the perspective of 17th-century history already outlined in this chapter, is remarkable less for any theoretical contribution to the problem of "wit" than for his artful management of the large repertory of intimations which the term "wit" had acquired by his time. Poet, critic, salon joker—mind, thinking, speech—what is brilliant, inventive, poetic—what is critical, mocking, affected, specious, frivolous—such gradations and oppositions of meaning play in and out of the 46 occurrences of the key term "wit" in Pope's *Essay*.

For wit and judgment often are at strife,
Tho' meant each other's aid like man and wife.—82–3

Nay wits had pensions, and young Lords had wit.—539

Some have at first for Wits, then Poets past,
Turn'd Critics next, and prov'd plain fools at last.—36–7

Pleas'd with a work where nothing's just or fit;
One glaring Chaos and wild heap of wit.—291–2

---

[3] Wellek and Warren, pp. 164 ff.   [4] See *ante* Chapter 5, pp. 87–8.

True wit is Nature to advantage dress'd;
What oft was thought, but ne'er so well express'd.—297–8

"Wit" is a kind of genteel slang word in Pope's day—a handy instrument
of "complex structure" capable of being managed so as to intimate a
number of "equations" between the ideas which it implicates.[5] At the
sociocritical level, Pope is slyly urging (though with all kinds of momentary ironies and reversals) the case for the aristocratic wit which Dryden
had announced in the essays of his most courtly phase. The witty man
of the salon, the master of elegance in conversation, gives us the best idea
of what an appreciator and critic of poetry ought to be, and this composite figure, the salon conversationalist and critic, provides us in turn
with our paradigm of the poet or at least of the gifts and outlook the
poet ought to have. As the Tory gentlemen and high churchmen who
constituted the party of wit in Pope's day were the political opponents
and social superiors of the rising generation of middle-class dissenters,
so the gentlemanly standard of wit aroused the partizans of middle-class
sobriety and "good sense" to violent resentment.[6] Sir Richard Blackmore
(Homer of the modern profound) published, among other attacks on
"wit," his *Satyr Against Wit* in 1699. He was promptly answered by a
combination of wits in the scurrilous volume entitled *Commendatory
Verses* and was defended by his friends in a retaliation entitled *Discom-
mendatory Verses*. The squabble was mean on both sides, but the main
ideas of Blackmore are worth noticing. Wit as Blackmore saw it was not,
as in the later phrase of Johnson, a principle of "vitality," but actually
a principle of universal corruption. The influence of Will's Coffee House
—"Dryden and his crew"—was debauching not only literature but all
virtue, public and private,—business, arts, the church, the legal profession.
Wit was soft, loose, degenerate, insane, it wanted the traditional "noble
roughness" of the British temper.

> Felonious *G*[*arth*] pursuing this Design,
> Smuggles *French* Wit, as others Silks and Wine.

The rhetoric of the remedy proposed was founded on images of solid
commercial virtue.

> If once the Muses Chequer would deny
> To take false Wit, 'twould lose its currency.

Let Congreve, Southerne, Wycherley, and especially Dryden, be melted
down and coined into new, sound wit (good sense) and a safe national
balance be deposited in a new Bank of Wit administered by Sheffield and
other more conservative lords.

[5] William Empson, " 'Wit' in the *Essay on Criticism*," *Hudson Review*, II (Winter 1950), 559–77.
[6] Robert M. Krapp, "Class Analysis of a Literary Controversy, Wit and Sense
in Seventeenth-Century English Literature," *Science & Society*, X (Winter 1946),
80–92.

These are good men, in whom we all agree,
Their Notes for Wit are good Security.[7]

So a form of rhetoric had a social tone and implied a social content. The deepest matter and meaning of Pope's poems was tied in to what was considered by the bourgeois men of sense as the frivolity and immorality of a brilliant form. And this depth of correspondence is what we should hope to find in any period where we could sample first-class literature. But here we have more to do with Pope's expressed theory. The last quotation in the series from Pope above is his famous definition of "wit" and hence of poetry, his epigrammatic reconciliation of the terms "wit" and "nature" by the mediation of the third term "dress," a reconciliation which may be said to resound with all the social implications of the view of nature which Pope entertained. This aphorism no more describes the "meaning" of Pope's own poetry in its fullness than the phrase "emotion recollected in tranquillity" does that of Wordsworth. But since a conspicuous part of Pope's meaning does lie in a high degree of verbal brilliance (a feature perfectly in keeping with and indeed impossible without an internal or abstract meaning of a certain witty sort), the aphorism has seemed to the post-romantic mind an all-too-apt expression of the superficiality of neo-classic rhetorical practice. The statement, both as specific theory of Augustan poetry and as general theory, is in fact disappointing. It is a kind of minimum classical stand, a last-ditch defense of wit-theory after a century more or less of the empirical assault. It is the wittily summarized dilemma of the classic mind in confrontation with the scientific, a reflection of the tightened poetic defense, the apparently prosaic and stripped-down wit of the neo-classic retreat from the metaphysical.

To give Pope's aphorism its due, on the other hand, one can hardly pretend that it does not offer us a sort of token, or temporary expression, for a paradoxical idea which is always residual in attempts to rationalize poetry—the ultimate surrender of theory in its attempt to reduce poetic meaning to the kinds of rational or philosophic meaning on which in some sense and in part it does depend. The element of "dress" (so repugnant under that figure to the romantic mind) is never quite squeezed out of poetic theory except by a rigorous extreme of idealistic symbolism. Samuel Johnson was to object that Pope's definition of wit depressed it "below its natural dignity," "reduced it from strength of thought to happiness of language." But Johnson himself, suffering along with the rest of his generation from an even more advanced phase of the scientific division between argument and elocution (and so rejecting energetically the metaphysical *discordia concors*), could offer as substitute only a defi-

[7] Richard Boys, *Sir Richard Blackmore and the Wits* (Ann Arbor, 1949), pp. 7-13.

nition close to the terms of "familiarity" and "surprise" provided by the psychological aesthetics of the century. He found "more noble and adequate" than Pope's view the compromise view of wit as "that which though not obvious is, upon its first production, acknowledged to be just." [8]

In Johnson's day the word "wit" was well on the way to becoming only a relic of serious criticism. Johnson was writing in retrospect. The ambiguous reference to the poetically imaginative and the nimbly amusing which "wit" had enjoyed from Elizabethan times was split during the neo-classic age into the meaning of "propriety" which we have observed and a second and lighter meaning of "sheer wit" or repartee in comedy.[9] As the wit which was equated with poetry (the respectable wit of propriety) sank before certain kinds of pre-romantic imagination, the wit of the comic became associated with more disagreeable and trivial forms of laughter, with raillery, ridicule, and nasty satire. (Satiric criticism, as we have suggested in Chapter 11, was at the same time softening into the roly-poly kind of "humour.") During the 18th century such associations seem to have gained ground, until the term "wit" assumed something like the vague and degraded meaning which is still popular in the 20th century—a form of the ludicrous more smart than humour. The definition framed by the literary gentleman Corbyn Morris in his *Essay Towards Fixing the True Standards of Wit, Humour, Raillery, Satire, and Ridicule,* 1744, might seem not unpromising:

> Wit is the Lustre resulting from the quick Elucidation of one Subject, by a just and unexpected Arrangement of it with another Subject.—p. 1

But it soon appears (pp. 3–4) that the quality of being "quick" and "unexpected" is what distinguishes "wit" from both "simile" and "metaphor," and then come the examples.

> Upon the Restoration Mr. Waller presented a congratulatory Copy of Verses to King Charles; His Majesty, after reading them, said,—Mr. Waller, these are very good, but not so fine as you made upon the PROTECTOR:—to which Mr. Waller return'd,—Your Majesty will please to recollect that we Poets always write best upon FICTIONS.—p. 7

In short, wit appears as joke or repartee.

---

[8] Johnson minimizes the Addisonian idea of surprise, yet relies on it. See his *Life of Cowley,* in *Lives of the Poets,* ed. G. B. Hill (Oxford, 1905), I, 19–20 and Appendix F. In the couplet following that to which Johnson objected Pope had written: "Something, whose truth convinc'd at sight we find, That gives us back the image of our mind."

[9] Spingarn, *Essays* I, lviii.

VII

To RETURN to Pope: the fact that neo-classic performance itself remained more complicated than the neo-classic theoretical assertion points up a principle which we may now urge a little more insistently than earlier in this chapter: namely, that in the 17th-century decline of rhetoric celebrated by Croce, at least two main things took place. (1) There was a shift in *theory* of style from the extravagance of Renaissance Aristotelianism and Ciceronianism to the theory of the Royal-Society era that words should be strictly tied down to things. And (2) at the same time there was a shift from certain Baroque forms of flamboyance (as in the actual prose of Browne or the verse of Donne) either to a fully plain form (like the scientific prose of the Royal Society) or to a superficially plain form (like the conversational verse of Dryden and Pope). It is of great importance to note that these two shifts (one of theory and one of performance) were not identical, nor even inevitably tied together, nor in a step-for-step relation—especially if we take the theoretical shift broadly as a shift from a theory of ornamentalism to a theory of stylistic integration. Within certain limits it has been possible, at various times in literary history, for either kind of theory (ornamental or integrational) to refer to either kind of style (flamboyant or simple). Most obviously, it has been possible for one of the theories, that of integrated style, to have a very wide range of applications. When Sprat in his *History of the Royal Society* spoke of "so many things almost in an equal number of words," he had in mind a use of words so severely limited to a certain kind of human experience (the scientifically factual) that he was content to make no demand whatever on a considerable range of important linguistic powers—the metaphysical, the moral, the poetic, the rhetorical. Such levels of meaning were inevitably irrelevant and merely ornamental in the program of research and reporting which the Royal Society was mapping out for itself. Sprat, that is, hardly meant the same thing as Pascal (a scientist of different affiliations) when the latter said, "*La vraie éloquence se moque de l'éloquence.*" Again, Sprat hardly meant the same thing as Swift (the satirist of Royal-Society thing-speech) when the latter wrote, "Proper words in proper places, makes the true definition of a style." [1] And again, probably neither Pascal nor Swift had arrived at the advanced stage of expressionism which in the 19th century permitted so traditionally minded and patristically eloquent a writer as Cardinal Newman to write:

> Thought and meaning are inseparable from each other. Matter and expression are parts of one: style is a thinking out into lan-

[1] *A Letter to a Young Gentleman, Lately Entered into Holy Orders*, 1721.

guage. . . . When we can separate light and illumination, life
and motion, the convex and the concave of a curve . . . then
will it be conceivable that the . . . intellect should renounce its
own double.[2]

To explore the issue for a moment in the opposite direction: it may
be worth while to compare the turn and emphasis of Pope's couplet definition of wit with certain more awkward betrayals. That of Dryden,
for instance, in the Preface to his *Fables:*

> Words are the colouring of the work, which, in the order of
> nature, is last to be considered. The design, the disposition, the
> manners, and the thoughts, are all before it.[3]

Or that of Gildon in his *Complete Art of Poetry,* 1718:

> As for your Ladyship's *fine Things,* and *fine Language,* to pre-
> fer them to more charming, and more essential excellencies,
> wou'd be as ridiculous, as to prefer your Ladyship's *Dress* to
> your *Person.*[4]

Or the debasing definition of the anti-wit Blackmore:

> Wit is a Qualification of the Mind, that rises and enlivens cold
> Sentiments and plain Propositions, by giving them an elegant and
> Surprising Turn.[5]

An expression of ornamentalist theory when it takes a form like Pope's
couplet means something a little different from what a less guarded expression means. And the general theory of ornamentalism means one
thing when applied to the verse of Blackmore and another when applied to that of Pope himself.

VIII

THE large part of a century that follows the effort of Pope, before the
rise of romantic theory, produces, as we have already suggested, only a
more or less dismal continuation of the ornamentalist view concerning

---

[2] "Literature, a Lecture in the School of Philosophy and Letters," 1858, in *The
Idea of a University* (London, 1907), pp. 276–7.

[3] Ker II, 252. L. I. Bredvold, *Selected Poems of Alexander Pope* (New York,
1926), pp. xvi–xvii, quotes the opinion of the French academician LeBrun that "design imitates all *real* things, whereas color only imitates that which is accidental."
Cf. *post,* Chapter 13, p. 264.

[4] Durham, p. 36. Cf. Samuel Wesley, *Epistle to a Friend* (London 1700), p. 15:
"Style is the dress of thought."

[5] *Essay upon Wit,* in *Essays Upon Several Subjects,* 1716, p. 191, quoted by
Boys, *op. cit.,* p. 10. Cf. the edition of Blackmore's *Essay* by Boys (Ann Arbor, 1946).

metaphor and related figures. The ancient defense of the dignity of verbal powers was slowing to a standstill. At the same time, let us note it here, a new concept of verbal power was in the early phases of development, although this concept, because of geographical and cultural distances, seems to have had for about a hundred years no direct influence upon any English man of letters. Modern scholarship has been interested to discover in certain late 17th-century Italian criticism antecedents of "pre-romantic" ideas which appeared during the 18th century in England. In a broader perspective, the most important new critical idea of the early eighteenth century was that concerning metaphor and its relation to the rise of human institutions which was announced in the *New Science* of the Neapolitan professor Giambattista Vico, published first in 1725. Vico was a reactionary against 17th-century rationalism. Where the English empiricist Hobbes imagined primitive man as thinking just like Hobbes himself (in a scientifically calculating way) and coming to abstract conclusions about the desirability of social conventions, and where Sprat, as we have seen, believed in a "primitive purity and shortness," by which words matched things in a terse economy, the Italian jurisconsult and rhetorician conceived man in the early phases of human culture, the patriarchal and the heroic, as groping dimly and imaginatively, through symbols, myths, and nascent metaphors, toward the abstract speculations which in later phases of civilization bring on the anemia of spirit and decrepitudes which we know. It was a form of primitivism and a theory of history which not only for 19th-century historiographers but for neo-idealist philosophers and theorists of poetic imagination was to seem increasingly important in retrospect.

Vico died in 1744 at about the age of 74. It is a less striking coincidence that his younger but rhetorically archaic British contemporary Alexander Pope should have died in the same year than that in 1743 Pope should have published his Greater *Dunciad*. The revised Fourth Book of the *Dunciad*, especially in its sublimely chaotic and profoundly dark conclusion, is a burlesque celebration of the "word," so radical, so metaphysical, Platonic, and Patristic, that it goes far to return the neo-classic argument to a place in its history where it connects with the remote sources of Vichian and romantic symbolism. The Fourth *Dunciad*, a climactic afterthought to the rest of the poem (and a grand climax to Pope's whole career) presents a vast levee of courtiers before the throne of Dulness, "bard and blockhead side by side," a throng of crank patrons, virtuosos, pedagogues, scholars, tutors, and publicists, all the false educators by whom the mind of youth and that of more mature imbecility are formed. Even at the outset the event is made safe by the knockout and imprisonment of two ancient guardians of sense (members of the classical trivium).

> There foam'd rebellious *Logic*, gagg'd and bound,
> There, stript, fair *Rhet'ric* languish'd on the ground;
> His blunted Arms by *Sophistry* are born,
> And shameless *Billingsgate* her Robes adorn.

In the chiaroscuro nightmare which follows, as the champions advance to the throne, they repeat no theme more often than that of the "word" and its abuses.

> . . . Since Man from beast by Words is known,
> Words are Man's province, Words we teach alone.   149–50

> Confine the thought, to exercise the breath;
> And keep them in the pale of Words till death.   159–60

> Give law to Words, or war with Words alone.   178

> 'Tis true, on Words is still our whole debate.   219

> First slave to Words, then vassal to a Name.   501

The concluding crescendo of the poem is an extraordinary recapitulation in negative of the rhetorico-metaphysical tradition.

> *Wit* shoots in vain its momentary fires,

> *Art* after *Art* goes out, and all is Night.

> *Physic* of *Metaphysic* begs defence,
> And *Metaphysic* calls for aid on *Sense!*

The last lines reach out for the utmost metaphysical and theological implications of the "word," not only the human but the divine creative act, the "logos." Not only grammarian, rhetorician, and poet, but Academician, Church Father, neo-Platonist, scholastic theologian, and aesthetician of "light," have contributed to the edifice of humanistic intelligence which appears in the darkly brilliant subverted image of this denouement.

> Lo! thy dread Empire, CHAOS! is restor'd;
> Light dies before thy uncreating word.

SUPPLEMENT

But in order to discover with perfect clearness and precision the importance of literature, both in its original destination, and in the power which it certainly exerts on the worth and welfare of nations, let us for a moment consider it under both of these aspects. And, in the first place, let us regard the true nature and object, the wide extent, and original dignity of literature. Under this name, then, I comprehend all those arts and sciences, and all those mental exertions which have human life, and man himself, for their object; but which, manifesting themselves in no external effect, energise only in thought and speech, and without requiring any corporeal matter on which to operate, display intellect as embodied in written language. Under this are included, first, the art of poetry, and the kindred art of narration or history; next, all those higher exertions of pure reason and intellect which have human life and man himself for their object, and which have influence upon both; and, last of all, eloquence and wit, whenever these do not escape in the fleeting vehicle of oral communication, but remain displayed in the more substantial and lasting form of written productions. And when I have enumerated these, I imagine I have comprehended almost everything which can enter into the composition of the intellectual life of man.—With the single exception of reason,—and even reason can scarcely operate without the intervention of language—is there anything more important to man, more peculiar to him, or more inseparable from his nature than speech? Nature indeed could not have bestowed on us a gift more precious than the human voice, which, possessing sounds for the expression of every feeling, and being capable of distinctions as minute, and combinations as intricate, as the most complex instrument of music, is thus enabled to furnish materials so admirable for the formation of artificial language. The greatest and most important discovery of human ingenuity is writing; there is no impiety in saying that it was scarcely in the power of the Deity to confer on man a more glorious present than LANGUAGE, by the medium of which he himself has been revealed to us, and which affords at once the strongest bond of union, and the best instrument of communication. So inseparable indeed are mind and language, so identically one are thought and speech, that although we must always hold reason to be the great characteristic and peculiar attribute of man, yet language also, when we regard its original object and intrinsic dignity, is well entitled to be considered as a component part of the intellectual structure of our being. And although, in strict application and rigid expression, thought and speech always are, and always must be regarded as two things metaphysically distinct,—yet there only can we find these two elements in disunion, where one or both have been employed imperfectly or amiss. Nay, such is the effect of the original union or identity that, in their most extensive varieties of application, they can never be totally disunited, but must always remain inseparable, and every where be exerted in combination.

However greatly both of these high gifts, which are so essentially the same,—these, the proudest distinctions of human nature, which have made man what he is, may be in many instances misdirected and abused; still our innate and indestructible sense of the original dignity of speech and language, is sufficiently manifest, from the importance which we attach to them, in the formation of all our particular judgments and opinions. What influence the art of speaking has upon our judgment in the affairs of active life, and in all the relations of society,—what power the force of expression every where exerts over our thoughts, it would be superfluous to detail. The same considerations which govern us in our judgment of individuals, determine us also in our opinions concerning nations; and we are at once disposed to look upon that people as the most enlightened and the most polished, which makes use of the most clear, precise, appropriate, and agreeable medium of expression: insomuch, that we not unfrequently allow ourselves to be biassed even to weakness by the external advantage of diction and utterance, and pay more attention to the vehicle than to the intrinsic value of the thoughts themselves, or the moral character of those from whom they proceed.

—Friedrich von Schlegel, *Lectures on the History of Literature, Ancient and Modern* (1811), trans. J. G. Lockhart (Philadelphia, 1818), I, 10–13, Lecture I.

Because of its peculiar insistence on remaining concreted within the act of apprehension itself, a poem resists the very abstraction by which we would understand it. Abstraction, in one way or another, destroys it, dissolves it away. So we must content ourselves largely with simply apprehending the poem by reading or hearing it read, and as for any strict understanding of a poem, we must content ourselves with thinking and talking *around* it. Thomas does not put it in exactly the same words, but when he speaks of its 'deficiency of truth,' he is concerned with the same thing about a poem which prompts Mr. Archibald MacLeish to observe that 'A poem should not mean/ But be.'

Yet it would be inaccurate to say that we have no understanding at all of poetry. We do find ourselves able to think about it, which means that some-how or other our understanding is concerned with it. What we are doing is approaching it by a kind of indirection—this fact is attested to by the constant resort to metaphor which the most rigorous discussion of poetry seems inex-orably to demand. A poem seems unable to forego this minimum of concre-tion even in being discussed. And in so far as it will not submit fully to abstrac-tion but must retain the concretion of metaphor, it escapes reason. Not that it is against reason, anti-rational. Reason is an imperfect way of getting at a thing: it implies a special approach, it produces understanding only under cer-tain conditions, and those things which are not amenable to these conditions simply escape it.

Hence poetry really demands too much of the reason in its insistence both that it be understood, and that it be understood somehow without resort to abstractions. From this fact arises the strain, which Thomas supposes as a matter of common observation, the state of tension in which poetry leaves reason. Plato had some warrant, after all, for barring poets from his republic: they do violence to and unsettle the reason on which his political order was to have been based.

In this connection Thomas says nothing specifically about the use of con-ceit. But the implications of his view are plain. If poetry implies a sort of rational derangement, an unmanagableness, a non-integration on the rational level in the face of a unity perceptible in other ways (the unity of impression, the unity of perception in a poem), *the superlative derangement inherent in the conceit,* which by operating through devices such as paradox maintains a sense of order in disorder and disorder in order, *stands as a kind of paragon of procedure in a poetic economy.*

Perhaps the most familiar instance of wit in St Thomas Aquinas's poetry is a couplet in the vesper hymm *Pange Lingua* written for the office of Corpus Christi, where it still occurs in the Roman breviary:

> *Verbum caro panem verum*
> *Verbo carnem efficit.*

This multi-dimensional conceit is a variant of one of the paradoxes consequent upon the Incarnation of the Word of God, and in availing himself of it, Thomas is tapping a source which lies at the innermost heart of Christian doctrine. . . . This is the same theology of the Word which has proved a limitless source of conceits not only for mediaeval theologians but also for patristic rhetoricians, for seventeenth-century Englishmen, and for contemporary poets interested in the metaphysical tradition. St Thomas is moving over ground to which wit poetry has never relinquished its claim. One conceit, for instance, is to be found in all the three groups of writers just mentioned. St Augustine uses in a sermon the paradox of the *Verbum infans*, Who was not only the infant Word, the child Jesus, but, to take the Latin *infans* in its full etymological force, the unspeaking Word. A strange and startling paradox, but an unmistakable dogmatic fact, that the Word of God initiates His personal mission among men in the inarticulate role of a child. The identical paradox is remarked later by Lancelot Andrewes in a sermon on the Incarnation: 'What, *Verbum infans*, the Word of an infant? The Word, and not to be able to speak a word.' And from Andrewes' world, that of the English 'metaphysicals,' the same conceit makes its way into Mr. T. S. Eliot's *Geronion.*

> —Walter J. Ong, "Wit and Mystery: A Revaluation in Mediaeval Hymnody," *Speculum*, XXII (July, 1947), 326–7, 316–17, by permission of the author and The Mediaeval Academy of America

As the art of discourse or speaking, or of teaching, dialectic or logic had a definite connection with the audile and with words as sounds, with the definite personalist and existentialist implications which attach to a world of voices. Ramus arrives on the scene at the time this dialectic is being "simplified" in an operation which is among the most complicated and critical and central in the whole history of the human mind and out of which grows preoccupation with method and the whole modern mechanistic-minded world, for it must not be forgotten that, in theory and to a great extent in fact, dialectic or logic controlled all the other arts or sciences or curriculum subjects. This simplification of logic is connected with the humanists' determination to provide something adapted to the capacities of children, for humanism is pupil-centered, whereas the northern universities, essentially teachers' unions, were teacher-centered, tending to see their pupils not in terms of the pupils' capacities here and now, but as aspirant pedagogues. But the simplification is even more deeply related to a widespread and mysterious shift from the audile to the visile in the whole way of thinking about cognition and the nature of man. At the end of this shift, by the eighteenth century, God will become in the minds of many curiously mute, and by that fact depersonalized, a mere mechanic, a celestial architect, a mason, whose laws concern not the human consciousness but the ranging of objects in space. Man's notion of what he himself is will undergo a corresponding shift in emphasis.

Ramism is above all, although not exclusively, a manifestation of the subtle and apparently irresistible shift sacrificing auditorily oriented concepts for visually oriented ones which sets in with medieval scholasticism and on which most of the characteristic manifestations of the modern as against the ancient world depend. This shift is intimately connected with the scholastic emphasis on a logic which, as against more purely Aristotelian logic, was a kind of logistic, and on physics—a bad physics, but physics nevertheless, taught to millions of schoolboys from the thirteenth to the sixteenth century and later on a scale the ancient world had never even approximated. The shift is equally connected with the scholastic build-up of the teaching profession. It is connected with the invention of printing, with the emergence of book titles in their postincunabular form, with the development of a sense of format for communication encouraged by printing, with the humanists' attitude toward language—a thing controlled by the *written* word, the word committed to space, not by *living* speech—as well as with the belief that all revelation was contained in a book.

The shift manifests itself in Ramism particularly in Ramus's complete divorce between dialectic and rhetoric. For Ramus appears on the scene just when dialectic (or logic) was shifting from an art of discourse, as Cicero had had it and as Ramus's Latin definitions nominally have it, to an art of thinking or reasoning. As an art of discourse, dialectic had suggested an interplay of personalities, a give and take in an existentialist situation. As an art of thinking, it was carried on in the privacy of one's own head and in a fashion more and more diagrammatic, with greater and greater reliance on spatial analogies and a more or less overt desire to dispense with words as words, since these annoyingly hint that in some mysterious way thinking itself is always carried on in the presence—at least implicit—of another. The meaning of the well-known Ramist tables of dichotomies is to be sought here in the drift toward spatial analogies of any and all sorts. With dialectic separated from rhetoric as a kind of intellectual diagrammatics, rhetoric is left in absolute control of the world of sound as sound. But even here, the spatial imagination gains control, and rhetoric comes to be described as a kind of ornament conceivable in mechanico-spatial terms.

—Walter J. Ong, "Ramus and the Transit to the Modern Mind," *The Modern Schoolman*, XXXII (May, 1955), 307–9, copyrighted. By permission of the author and *The Modern Schoolman*.

CHAPTER 13

ADDISON AND LESSING: POETRY AS PICTURES

§ *philosophy of sensation, Hobbes, Locke—II. Addison,* Spectators *on imagination, a medley of themes: art and nature, pleasant and unpleasant, primary and secondary, imagination and wit, ease and difficulty, nature's wit, notion of sight compared with the neo-Platonic, lower senses and the understanding—III. the rationalist alternative, Cartesianism,* esprit géométrique, *seeing the world as it really is, without colors, guaranteed external causes of beauty, gross or corpuscular, Burke, Lord Kames, the sublime, immediacy and compulsion, Abbé Dubos on the merits of a stew, Leibniz, Baumgarten, clear though confused ideas (sensuous), the* je-ne-sais-quoi, *internal aesthetic sense, Hutcheson—IV. "aesthetic," the "fine arts," Batteux and the Encyclopedists, parallels between the arts, ancient hints: Aristotle, Simonides, Cicero, Horace, Du Fresnoy's* De Arte Graphica, *two meanings of* ut pictura poesis, *literary influence on painting, Aristotelian critique of Poussin's "Fall of Manna," painting the passions, painterly influence on literature, toward sensation and landscape, Claude and Rosa, James Thomson, landscape gardening—V. virtuoso and Hellenizing trends, Spence's* Polymetis, Count Caylus, Winckelmann, *Lessing's* Laokoon, *the sculptural group and Virgil, difference between painting and poetry before Lessing, time and space, actions and objects, 18th-century nature poetry, Lessing's insight, Goethe's praise, limitations of Lessing, moving pictures,* enargeia, *artificial and natural signs, drama, Homeric lines on Agamemnon's sceptre—VI. poetry and music, the 16th century academies, music serves poetry: Campion, Milton and Lawes, poetry serves music: operas, Dryden, Tate, Purcell, the era of the music odes, Dryden's*

odes for St. Cecilia's Day, Handel's setting, Pope, Collins,
Gray, burlesques, English theory in the 18th century,
Avison et al., three-fold resemblance between music and
poetry, musical "puns," the imitative norm—VII. general
assimilation and mélange of the arts during the 19th cen-
tury, The New Laokoon (1910), arts as geometry—VIII.
systems of the arts, Batteux, Herder, Sulzer, Kant and
after, what is meant by classifying the arts, irrelevance to
literary criticism, yet merit in the exercise §

ONE OF THE CRITICAL CATCHWORDS MOST OFTEN REPEATED IN OUR
time has been "dissociation of sensibility," a term adapted from
Remy de Gourmont [1] by T. S. Eliot in 1921 and used by Mr.
Eliot to describe the aesthetic frame of mind which he believed to have developed in the latter half of the 17th century with the lapse of metaphysical poetry and the rise of rationalism and prosaism, and, at a later stage,
of sentimentalism. In some areas the "dissociation" may be noted more
easily than in others. Something like it perhaps appears, for instance,
in the drama, that is, in the ethical declamatory and heroic tendencies
of neo-classic tragedy and in the attendant decline of what is today
called poetic imagery. On the other hand, the kind of witty discursive
poetry and the burlesque narrative developed by Dryden and Pope were
forms of seeming acquiescence in the laws of prose which actually
sustained, as we have suggested in our last chapter, a peculiar kind of
poetic interest. The full effects of 17th-century philosophy on creative
writing, and especially on verse writing, were not felt until the mid-
18th century. In the early part of the century perhaps the effects may
be most readily observed in the areas of epistemology and aesthetic
theory. It would appear that in this age both feeling and the act of
valuing were theoretically detached from a certain something—an Aristotelian structure of ideas, a substantive belief about God, man, and
the universe—and were either left floating free of reference or were
attached to another area of experience provided or newly emphasized
in another vision of reality—the new vision of the empirical and sensational.

One of the most convenient concentrations of the new epistemology in its British beginnings is that very opening section of Hobbes'
Leviathan, the eighth chapter of which we have already quoted for

[1] Cf. F. W. Bateson in *Essays in Criticism*, I (1951) 302–12. Bateson argues persuasively that Eliot himself meant by the term "sensibility," not emotion, but sensation and at the same time, a union of thought and sensation. Later writers have taken
"dissociation of sensibility" to mean a split between thought and emotion. "The
sentimental age" is on Eliot's view a second stage.

the sake of the somewhat confused semantics of its dealings with "wit." In his first and second chapters Hobbes states with an appropriate forthrightness the simple epistemological grounds of his world view.

> Chapter I. *Of* SENSE. . . . The cause of Sense, is the Externall Body, or Object, which presseth the organ proper to each Sense, either immediatly, as in the Tast and Touch; or mediately, as in Seeing, Hearing, and Smelling. . . . All which qualities called *Sensible*, are in the object that causeth them, but so many several motions of the matter, by which it presseth our organs diversely. Neither in us that are pressed, are they anything else, but divers motions. . . . But their apparance to us is Fancy, the same waking, that dreaming. . . . Sense in all cases, is nothing els but original fancy.
>
> Chapter II. *Of* IMAGINATION. . . . after the object is removed, or the eye shut, wee still retain an image of the thing seen, though more obscure than when we see it. And this is it, the Latines call *Imagination*, from the image made in seeing; and apply the same, though improperly, to all the other senses. But the Greeks call it *Fancy*. . . . IMAGINATION therefore is nothing but *decaying sense;* and is found in men, and many other living Creatures, as well sleeping, as waking.
>
> . . . when we would express the *decay*, and signifie that the Sense is fading, old, and past, it is called *Memory*. So that *Imagination* and *Memory*, are but one thing, which for divers considerations hath divers names.

There is not much to add to this. Later on, Locke's *Essay Concerning Human Understanding*, 1690, urged the distinction between the primary qualities of our sensory experience (those that were really *in* things—bulk, shape, and movement) and the "secondary" (those that were only in our eyes, noses, and ears—color, smell, and sound). In this way, Locke greatly furthered the subjective and phenomenalistic drift of the sensationalist philosophy. Even more than Hobbes, Locke broke down the metaphysical rallying point of substance, and provided the complete set-up for the startling coup of Berkeley—the merging of primary and secondary qualities in the same status (*esse* is *percipi*), by which, overnight, sensationalism was inverted into idealism.

II

IN A celebrated series of *Spectator*[2] papers *On the Pleasures of the Imagination* (Nos. 411–421, appearing in June and July of 1712) Joseph

[2] Joseph Addison, *The Spectator*, ed. Henry Morley, 3 vols. (London, 1883).

Addison made his acknowledgement (as he had done in his paper on "mixed wit") to the *Essay* of Mr. Locke. The *term* "imagination" in Locke's *Essay* had, as we have seen, largely the pejorative sense associated with the malefactor "wit." Nevertheless, the newly brightened *meaning* of "imagination" as that term appears in Addison's *Spectators* is to a large extent determined by the sensationalism of Hobbes and Locke.

The ten *Spectator* papers on the imagination present some difficulties to exposition largely through their complicated inconsistency, the medley of aesthetic theses which they complacently recite. In Nos. 414 and 418, for instance, we discover in effect the following account of the pleasures of artistic *imitation*. Artistic imitation is more pleasant the more it resembles nature, but at the same time nature is more pleasant the more it resembles art—as when clouds or veins of marble display the shape of trees or other objects. Art improves on nature, though at the same time it cannot compete with nature. Artistic imitation is the more pleasant if it contains a touch of emotion—as when a portrait of a beautiful human countenance shows a melancholy cast. But in this miscellany of observations, nothing is so typical of the contemporary aesthetic trend as Addison's distinction between pleasant and unpleasant objects of imitation. Artistic imitation, even of an unsavory object like a dunghill, gives pleasure through fidelity of resemblance.[3] But, all other things being equal (complete fidelity of imitation, that is, obtaining), an imitation of a pleasing object is more pleasing than an imitation of an unpleasing object. Thus: the bowers and fruits and sweet gales in Book IV of *Paradise Lost* are a more pleasing poetic imitation than the brimstone and pitchy fires of Hell in Book I. This statement is central. It develops in all literalness the implications of Addison's first paper of the series (No. 411), in which the "primary" pleasures of the imagination are defined as simply those experienced upon our actually seeing certain natural objects,[4] and the "secondary" pleasures are defined as those experienced in our seeing good representations (surrogates) of the same kinds of objects.[5] Addison's theory of the secondary pictorial imagination is the clas-

[3] As Aristotle, Plutarch, Aquinas and others had observed.

[4] The thesis holds also for certain artificial objects, like architecture, as appears later (No. 415).

[5] The three kinds of natural objects which qualify for the definition are, let us note in passing, the beautiful, the great, and the uncommon, approximate types of the three aesthetic genres more distinctly discriminated later in the century, the beautiful, the sublime, and the picturesque. The third of these, the "uncommon" (the "novel" or "surprising" in Addison's definition of "wit") is a detail which has a strong affinity for more overt forms of 18th-century affectivism.

The terms "primary" and "secondary" of Addison's distinction, though apparently inspired by the Lockean distinction between the "primary" and the "secondary" qualities of our general experience, exhibit no very closely analogous meaning.

sical theory of imitation reduced to its most stark and literal form, the imitative object or ikon performing its most servile and secondary role —that of the photograph on the bureau which reminds the lonely student of the distant sweetheart. If we compare Addison's *Spectators* on the imagination with his earlier series on "wit," especially No. 62, on "wit," "mixt wit," and "false wit," we can observe the rising new "imagination" and the declining old "wit" moving for a moment in conjunction, though in opposite directions. The series on imagination deals with a resemblance between art objects and extrinsic nature. The series on wit deals with a kind of resemblance which is internal to a poetic composition—a resemblance between two parts of a metaphor, between two ideas or two word sounds. A literary student might well attempt an inquiry whether there is any rationale by which the two kinds of resemblance (internal and external to the poem) may be approximated to each other. If the structure of a poem is such that we may look on the whole (a kind of reflecting structure of metaphorically arranged parts) as a tacit larger metaphor or symbol of other areas of reality than those explicitly mentioned in the poem, then Addison's remarks on the secondary or imitative imagination may invite being subsumed (and to some extent tested) under the general head of "wit."

One of the reasons why Addison praises the pleasures of the secondary imagination (and we shall develop this idea further in a few pages) is the easiness and persuasiveness of these pleasures—no cudgelling of the brain needed to respond to a picture of a flower or of a beautiful flower girl, or to notice a camel in the clouds. At the same time (even though Addison sets some store by the element of surprise in almost any kind of artistic pleasure),[6] the main burden of the papers on wit is a protest that some forms of wit—the mixed and the false—are fantastic, far-fetched, over-ingenious. It would seem to be not only the purely verbal trick but the difficult metaphysical trick —the metaphors yoked together by violence—which Addison dislikes.[7] "The pleasures of the fancy are more conducive to health, than those of the understanding, which are worked out by dint of thinking, and attended with too violent a labour of the brain" (No. 411). The examples of "mixt wit" (the message writ in juice of lemon read by the heat of love's flames, the lady's eyes felt as burning glasses of ice) which Addison adduces from Cowley's *Mistress* will perhaps be more readily seen as instances of extravagant metaphorical conceit than as the partial puns which Addison himself professes to see.[8] The contrast, though it is not overtly developed, between the two kinds of resem-

[6] Cf. Clarence D. Thorpe, "Addison and Some of his Predecessors on 'Novelty,'" *PMLA*, LII (December, 1937), 1114–29.

[7] Cf. Robert L. Morris, "Addison's *Mixt Wit*," *MLN*, LVI (December, 1942), 666–8.

[8] See *ante* Chapter 12, p. 232.

blance, the metaphoric, intellective, difficult metaphysical, and the literal, pictorial, easy "imaginative," invites us to look on the latter as the wit of the new epistemology—nature's wit in shaping a cloud like a camel, the artist's wit in making a portrait remind us of a lovely girl.[9]

Addison's argument in *Spectator* No. 411 that the sense of sight is by far the most richly dowered in pleasures of the imagination is almost a metaphysical argument (almost neo-Platonic and scholastic). But the margin by which it fails to be such an argument is important. The older argument for the aesthetic superiority of sight, and of hearing (the *sensus maxime cognoscitivi*), worked (through analogy) in the direction of form and intelligibility. The new argument worked (literally) in the direction of diversified pleasurable excitements. A medieval theorist would have said, for instance, that the art of painting looked (through the analogy of brilliance) toward the mind. A later 18th-century literary theorist, writing in a highly Addisonian vein, would propose explicitly: "the Poet writes principally to the eye." [1] The sense of sight (aside from the fact that in the Lockean and Addisonian system it enjoyed only a secondary and subjective status) suffered the limitation of being but another sense of touch—long-range and hypersensitive, "more delicate and diffusive." Addison's main thesis, unmistakable despite the cul-de-sacs with which his papers are amusingly varied, is that the pleasures of the imagination are the pleasurable sensations stimulated in ourselves directly by certain external causes or indirectly by reasonably close imitations of or substitutes for such causes.[2] "The Pleasures of the Imagination, taken in the full Extent," explains Addison, "are not so gross as those of Sense, nor so refined as those of the Understanding" (No. 411). But the word "sense" in this sentence has abruptly acquired the special meaning of "lower sense" (touch, taste, or smell presumably), for nothing in Addison's system can be clearer than that the pleasures of the imagination all proceed from the sight, and that sight is a "sense."

[9] In *Spectator* No. 62 Addison includes "external mimicry" among the forms of false wit. In No. 416 the secondary pleasures of imitative art are explained as arising from the exercise of our faculty of comparing and are explicitly associated with wit. In No. 418 the pleasure arising from the description of an unpleasant object like a dunghill is said to be "more properly called a pleasure of the understanding than of the fancy."

[1] Erasmus Darwin, *The Botanic Garden* (London, 1791), Part II, p. 48 (Interlude to Canto I, *The Loves of the Plants*). And a German theorist Wilhelm Heinse (1746–1804) would say: "Painting and sculpture serve first of all lust." Gilbert and Kuhn, p. 311.

[2] "My Design being first of all to Discourse of those Primary Pleasures of the Imagination, which entirely proceed from such Objects as are before our Eyes; and in the next place to speak of those Secondary Pleasures of the Imagination which flow from the Ideas of visible Objects, when the Objects are not actually before the Eye, but are called up into our Memories, or formed into agreeable Visions of Things that are either absent or Fictitious" (No. 411).

III

Yet not "so refined" in its pleasures as the Understanding. And not so difficult. The main reason for the new sensationalist trend in theory of the arts (the heavy investment in sweet and grand stimulations) lay, as we have already suggested, in the fact that the other side of contemporary philosophy, its rationalistic and supposedly superior side, was too sterile and discouraging. The same Hobbes who had laid out the easy definition of "imagination" as decaying sense had also said this:

> We must consider that although sense and memory of things, which are common to man and all living creatures, be knowledge, yet because they are given us immediately by nature, and not gotten by ratiocination, they are not philosophy.[3]

It was of course possible for a literary theorist to pursue not the Addisonian alternative but actually this rational line. It was done less in England than in Cartesian France, where some critics of Addison's day had the disillusioning candor to style themselves *géomètres*, or to boast of their *esprit géométrique*. Consider, for instance, the statement of the Homeric critic Terrasson:

> The way to think about a literary problem is that pointed out by Descartes for problems of physical science. A critic who tries any other way is not worthy to be living in the present century. There is nothing better than mathematics as a propaedeutic for literary criticism.[4]

For the literary man of the other temper, the British empiricist, the threat of that cold mathematical realm of reality—the "unearthly ballet of bloodless categories"—was all too imminent—the tissue of colorful ocular pleasures by which he protected himself all too flimsy. Addison himself, in *Spectator* No. 413, on final causes, the reasons why God has made the world beautiful, writes a passage which reveals with shocking clarity how forcefully the Lockean epistemology of subjective secondary qualities, and the Newtonian corpuscular universe which causes the experience of such qualities by its incessant bombardment

---

[3] *Elements of Philosophy*, I, i, 2, quoted by D. G. James, *The Life of Reason* (London, 1949), pp. 54–5.

[4] *Dissertation Critique sur L'Iliade d'Homère*, 1715, Preface, p. 65. "*Toutes les critiques que Perrault, Fontenelle, La Motte dirigent contre les Oeuvres particulières des anciens sont fondées sur ce principe. Ce que je ne comprends pas ne saurait être raisonnable*" (Gustave Lanson, "*Sur l'Influence de la Philosophie Cartesienne sur la Littérature Française*," *Revue de Metaphysique et Morale*, IV, 517–50, quoted by Austin Warren, *Alexander Pope as Critic and Humanist* [Princeton, 1929] p. 17).

of our sensoriums, had laid hold of the "imagination" of the age. Suppose we had to *see* the world as it *really* is—without its colors.

> Things would make but a poor Appearance to the Eye, if we saw them only in their proper Figures and Motions: And what Reason can we assign for their exciting in us many of those Ideas which are different from any thing that exists in the Objects themselves, (for such are Light and Colours) were it not to add Supernumerary Ornaments to the Universe, and make it more agreeable to the Imagination? . . . what a rough and unsightly Sketch of Nature should we be entertained with, did all her Colouring disappear, and the several Distinctions of Light and Shade vanish.[5]

British critics, on the whole, escaped the geometric urge. They did exhibit nevertheless a strong desire to account for aesthetic experience by fixed external *causes,* either grossly observable, or corpuscular. As Burke was to put it in his youthful *A Philosophical Inquiry into the Origin of Our Ideas of the Sublime and Beautiful* (1757):[6] "Beautiful objects" are "small," "smooth," gently curved, "delicate," "clean and fair" (III, xiii–xviii).[7] "Beauty is, for the greater part, some quality in bodies acting mechanically upon the human mind by the intervention of the senses" (III, xii). "Beauty acts by relaxing the solids of the whole system" (IV, xix). With a more pictorial emphasis on the observed object, Henry Home, Lord Kames, would write in his *Elements of Criticism* (1762):

> Such is our nature, that, upon perceiving certain external objects, we are instantaneously conscious of pleasure or pain: a gently-flowing river, a smooth extended plain, a spreading oak, a towering hill, are objects of sight that raise pleasant emotions: a barren heath, a dirty marsh, a rotten carcase, raise painful emotions.

> Elevation touches the mind no less than grandeur doth; and, in raising the mind to elevated objects, there is a sensible pleasure: the course of nature, however, hath still a greater influence than elevation; and therefore, the pleasure of falling with rain, and descending gradually with a river, prevails over that

[5] Addison refers to the Eighth Chapter of the Second Book of Mr. Locke's *Essay.*

[6] "Second Edition with an Introductory Discourse concerning Taste, and Several Other Additions," 1759. We quote the edition of Glasgow, 1818.

[7] "Observe that part of a beautiful woman, where she is, perhaps, the most beautiful, about the neck and breasts; the smoothness; the softness; the easy and insensible swell; the variety of the surface, which is never, for the smallest space, the same; the deceitful maze, through which the unsteady eye slides giddily, without knowing where to fix, or whither it is carried" (III, xv). "An air of robustness and strength is very prejudicial to beauty" (III, xvi).

of mounting upward. But where the course of nature is joined with elevation, the effect must be delightful: and hence the singular beauty of smoke ascending in a calm morning.[8]

The sublime, as it had been hinted long ago by Longinus and recently developed in a trend of criticism to be noticed further in our next chapter, was particularly susceptible to this kind of causative explanation. "The noise of vast cataracts," says Burke, "raging storms, thunder, or artillery, awakes a great and awful sensation in the mind." "A low, tremulous, intermitting sound . . . is productive of the sublime" (II, xvii, xix).[9] The philosophy of the aesthetic according to its guaranteed external causes was perhaps not very unfairly summarized in a joke recorded by A. W. Schlegel: According to Burke, "the Beautiful is a tolerably pretty strumpet, and the Sublime is a grenadier with a big moustache."[1]

Such a definitive location of aesthetic objects allied itself quite readily with a concept of sensational immediacy and compulsion—a stage beyond the mere idea of easiness. "Of the emotions thus produced," said Kames, "we inquire for no other cause but merely the presence of the object."
And Addison:

> It is but opening the Eye, and the Scene enters. The Colours paint themselves on the Fancy, with very little Attention of Thought or Application of Mind in the Beholder. We are struck, we know not how, with the Symmetry of any thing we see, and immediately assent to the Beauty of an Object, without enquiring into the particular Causes and Occasions of it.[2]

And Burke:

> The appearance of beauty as effectively causes some degree of love in us, as the application of ice or fire produces ideas of heat or cold.—*Enquiry* III, ii

[8] *Elements of Criticism,* 1805, I, 30 (Chap. 2); I, 22 (Chap. 1). Compare Mark Akenside's didactic blank verse poem, *The Pleasures of Imagination,* 1744.
[9] The list extends through Sections iii–xx. John Dennis, *The Grounds of Criticism in Poetry,* 1704, draws up a similar list of objects which inspire the lofty emotion of terror: Gods, Daemons, Hell, Spirits, and Souls of Men, Miracles, Prodigies, Enchantments, Witchcraft, Thunder, Tempests, Raging Seas, Inundations, Torrents, Earthquakes, Volcanoes, Monsters, Serpents, Lions, Tygers, Fire, War, Pestilence, Famine.
[1] A. W. Schlegel, *Vorlesungen über Schöne Litteratur und Kunst* (Heilbronn, 1884), I, 63: "*Man hat ganz treffend eingewandt: nach Burke sey eine nur leidlich artige Buhlerin schön, und ein Grenadier mit einem grossen Schnurrbarte erhaben.*" The translation, perhaps a slight improvement on the original, is Saintsbury's, III, 400.
[2] *Spectator* No. 411. No. 409 compares a taste in writing to a taste in tea.

The Abbé J. B. Du Bos in his *Réflexions critiques sur la poésie et sur la peinture*, 1719, drew a parallel between the pleasures of the aesthetic taste and those of cookery.

> Do we stop to reason about the merit of a stew? Do we appeal
> to geometric principles of flavor, or attempt a scientific descrip-
> tion of ingredients, or debate about their proportion—before
> we decide if the stew is good or bad? [3]

Do we indeed? The force of such a question was one powerful per-
suader to a strictly sensuous theory of the aesthetic.

Continental philosophers in the Cartesian heritage, Leibniz in his
Meditationes de Cognitione, Veritate, et Ideis, 1684, and Baumgarten,
in his *Philosophical Thoughts on Matters Connected with Poetry*, 1735,[4]
made a special contribution to the dissociation of sensibility when they
formulated the theory that beauty is experienced not in Cartesian clear
and distinct ideas, but in ideas that are clear though *confused*, that is,
in "sensuous" ideas (images). Clear but confusedly sensuous ideas (that
is, ideas which are distinguishable from one another but not internally
analyzable) constitute one form of the ineffable. The theory of the
ineffable, the nameless object of "taste" (the Leibnizian *je-ne-sais-quoi*,
in more amateurish terms the "grace beyond the reach of art") [5] is
strongly in the ascendant at the birth of modern aesthetics, and along
with it, let us add, the theory of an "internal" aesthetic "Sense," no
less simple and ultimate than the external senses, no less autonomous,
no less infallible. "Nor does there seem any thing more difficult in this
matter, than that the Mind should be always determin'd to receive the
Idea of *Sweet*, when Particles of such a Form enter the Pores of the
Tongue." [6]

IV

THE term "aesthetic," which has been creeping into our discussion of
the last few pages, can be justified here in part by its etymology and
its Platonic meaning of a sheerly sensate, phenomenal or phantasmal,
kind of experience. A poetics of sensational pleasure is, in that simple
sense, necessarily an "aesthetic." But there is another and a more precisely historical sense which does much to justify the use of the term

---

[3] *Réflexions* II, xxii.

[4] See *Reflections on Poetry, Alexander Gottlieb Baumgarten's Meditationes philosophicae de nonnullis ad poema pertinentibus*, trans. Karl Aschenbrenner and William B. Holther (Berkeley and Los Angeles, 1954).

[5] Samuel H. Monk, "A Grace Beyond the Reach of Art," *JHI*, V (1944), 131-50.

[6] Francis Hutcheson, *An Inquiry into the Original of our Ideas of Beauty and Virtue*, 1725, VI, x. Cf. Clarence D. Thorpe, "Addison and Hutcheson on the Imagination," *ELH*, II (1925), 222-9.

"aesthetic" in referring to the poetics conditioned for Addison by the epistemology of Locke and Hobbes. During this age, as we have remarked a few lines above, arose the modern concept of general "aesthetics," the general philosophy of the higher arts. Poetry, as we have seen, had been discussed in antiquity at times under the rubric of the fine or the beautiful (*to kalon*), but more readily, along with rhetoric, under the rubric of art or technique (*technē*), and again in the Middle Ages chiefly under the latter. It remained for the Renaissance, with the aid of a neo-Platonic historical appeal, to shift the emphasis in speaking of the arts very pronouncedly toward the concept of the fine, the ideal, the beautiful, and at the same time to begin viewing several of the "imitative" arts as members of one general and literally unified category. A medieval accent on the intellectuality of such verbal arts as poetry and rhetoric (and along with them music, because of its mathematical component) was in the Renaissance gradually modified so as to admit to equal standing visual arts such as painting and sculpture. These had once been looked on as lower, because they were physical arts, manual or handicraft, like shoemaking. We find Italian painters of the 16th century, for instance, much concerned to argue that the manual character of their effort was outweighed by the intellectual. Painting demanded a knowledge of mathematics, especially in perspective, and of other sciences. Like poetry, it could achieve a moral end, for it could show human gesture and facial expression.[7] The argument could also become comic. Leonardo, in his comments *Della Pittura*, makes an invidious distinction between the art of the sculptor (laborious, with sweat and fatigue, and covered with stone dust) and that of the painter (elegantly and easily at work in his studio with brush and colors).[8]

During the 16th and 17th centuries appear various momentary and partial alignments of arts and sciences according to one principle or another. A sharp differentiation between arts and sciences appears to have been an event that had to wait on the late 17th-century quarrel between Ancients and Moderns. Meanwhile, however, in Italy during the 16th century had arisen the term *Arti del Disegno* and in France during the 17th century the corresponding term *Beaux Arts*, both terms meaning in the main the newly unified and newly respected arts of visual appeal, painting, sculpture and architecture—though sometimes poetry and music were included. By the early 18th century, habits of thinking about groups of the "imitative" and idealizing arts were closely approaching the concept of the "Fine Arts" which was to become so widely honored and so much taken for granted during the 19th and

---

[7] Thomas Munro, *The Arts and Their Interrelations*, p. 32.

[8] Munro, pp. 32–3, citing J. P. Richter, *The Literary Works of Leonardo da Vinci* (London, 1880), Vol. I, No. 654. See a longer quotation by Jacques Maritain, *Art and Scholasticism* (New York, 1942), p. 156.

20th centuries. The Abbé Du Bos' *Réflexions critiques sur la poésie et sur la peinture* of 1719 says a good deal not only about painting and poetry but also about sculpture, engraving and music, and in the English translation of this work in 1748 the word *Music* is added to the title. This was one milestone. But to the Abbé Charles Batteux, in his *Les beaux arts réduits à un même principe* of 1746, seems to go the credit of having first defined and rationalized almost exactly the modern category. The common principle was "imitation of beautiful nature," and the arts included were music, poetry, painting, sculpture, and the dance. Succeeding writers, notably the encyclopedists (Montesquieu, Diderot, D'Alembert) took up and broadcast the ideas of Batteux, substituting for the dance architecture—and the grouping most often encountered today was established.[9] Meanwhile, the German Leibnizian philosopher Alexander von Baumgarten, whose early work on *Poetry* we have already mentioned, had constructed the first sensuous philosophy of the fine arts and had given it the name *Aesthetics*.[1]

Such broadly inclusive theorizing came accompanied by a new kind of urge to draw parallels between the arts and to describe and criticize one art in terms of another. A visually centered sensationalist aesthetic such as we have noted in Addison's *Spectators* might plausibly enough promote a discussion of poetry in terms taken from sculpture or painting. And it happened too that antiquity provided a few hints for such a parallelism:—the equal mention in Aristotle's *Poetics* of music, dancing, and painting as forms of *mimēsis;* an even more ancient *mot* of Simonides, repeated by Plutarch (that painting is mute poetry, poetry a speaking picture); the general defence of the arts by Cicero in his speech for a poet threatened with banishment (*habent omnes artes quoddam commune vinculum*); and most persuasive of all the three words of Horace—so easily taken out of context[2] and then so easily misinterpreted: *ut pictura poesis*.[3] By the latter half of the 17th century the phrases of Horace and Simonides had accumulated through repetition

---

[9] Paul O. Kristeller, "The Modern System of the Arts: A Study in the History of Aesthetics," *JHI*, XII (October, 1951), 496–527; XIII (January, 1952), 17–46. See esp. XII, 497–524 ("Beaux Arts"), 525–7 (Ancients and Moderns); XIII, 18–23 (Du Bos and Batteux and the Encyclopedists).·D'Alembert's *Discours préliminaire* to the *Enyclopédie* I (1751), 117, makes the substitution of architecture for the dance: "*La peinture, la sculpture, l'architecture, la poésie, la musique et leurs differentes divisions component la troisième distribution générale, qui naît de l'imagination et dont les parties sont comprises sous le nom de beaux-arts*" (Kristeller, XIII, 23)·.

[1] His work of that title appeared in 1750.

[2] *Ut pictura poesis: erit quae, si propius stes, te capiat magis, et quaedam, si longius abstes* (ll. 361–2). That is, *some pictures are murals, and some miniatures— and so with poems.*

[3] The authority of the phrase had perhaps always threatened. Saintsbury (I, 398) points out that Venantius Fortunatus in an epistle to Syagrius of Autun introduces an elaborate "shaped" poem and argues for this combination of visual and verbal art "by a twist of the Horatian tag."

and debate a considerable weight of authority. Thus in the opening lines of a popular poetical treatise (paralleling Horace's *Ars Poetica* and Boileau's *Art Poétique*) the *De Arte Graphica* by the French painter Charles Alphonse Du Fresnoy:

> *Ut pictura poesis erit; similisque Poesi*
> *Sit Pictura;* . . . .
>
>   *. . . . muta Poesis*
> *Dicitur haec, Pictura loquens solet illa vocari.*

> A poem is like a picture; so a picture ought to try to be like a poem. . . . a picture is often called silent poetry; and poetry a speaking picture.

This poem was translated into English by no less a man of letters than Dryden in 1695 and given a lengthy theoretical Preface containing a "Parallel Between Poetry and Painting." The plot of a poem, for instance, is, as Aristotle had suggested, like the line drawing or sketch for a painting. The diction and imagery are like the colors (the outline "to advantage" filled).[4]

The theory in the phrase *ut pictura poesis* worked in complementary directions between the arts of painting and poetry: It worked for a literary influence on painting and a judgment of painting in literary terms; and at the same time for a painterly influence on literature and a corresponding kind of judgment.[5] The first of these influences is not directly a matter of literary criticism; but it may be examined as a highly instructive parallel. For the theory was not only technical (concerned with colors, outlines, ways of painting clouds, shadows, and light, and of grouping figures) but very broadly humanistic—historical and heroic. That is, both poetry and painting were said to aim at imitation: the most proper subject of imitation was human nature, and not ordinary but ideal or heroic human nature. The models for either painting or poetry might be found alike in the classics. More precisely, the

---

[4] Cf. *ante* Chapter 12, p. 245. When Augustan theorists took an anti-rhetorical stand, that is, when they wished to stress their dedication to the main design or grand total meaning and their relative contempt for the stylistic niceties, they found this analogy convenient.

"The words are the colouring of the work, which, in the order of nature, is last to be considered. The design, the disposition, the manners, and the thoughts, are all before it. . . . Words, indeed, like glaring colours, are the first beauties that arise and strike the sight; but, if the draught be false or lame . . . then the finest colours are but daubing."—Dryden, Preface to *Fables*, 1700 (*Essays*, ed. Ker, II, 252–253)

Cf. L. I. Bredvold, *Selected Poems of Alexander Pope* (New York, 1926), pp. xvi–xvii, parallel quotations from the French academicians Félibien and Le Brun and from Gildon and Pope. The Lockean assignment of color to the subjective secondary status worked in fairly close harmony with Platonic neo-classic tendencies toward the abstract universal. Cf. *post* Chapter 15.

[5] William G. Howard, "*Ut Pictura Poesis*," *PMLA*, XXIV (1909), 46–123; Cicely Davies, "*Ut Pictura Poesis*," *MLR*, XXX (1935), 159–69.

models for historical, or narrative, painting (the highest genre, as epic was the highest in poetry) might be found in the literary classics. The painter had to be not only accomplished in his technique of color and shape, but "learned" in the important subject matters—classical mythology and Christian Scriptures. A critique of Nicolas Poussin's Biblical painting "The Fall of Manna in the Desert" by the French Academicians is a remarkable illustration. Here was the graphic telling of an action, single, of sufficient size and completeness, in a mode highly compatible with the rules laid down in Aristotle's *Poetics*. It had a beginning (the downcast state of those Israelites who had not yet noticed the manna), a middle, with a peripeteia or turning point (the descent of the manna and the looking up of certain Israelites to see it), an end or denouement (the gathering and eating of the manna by certain others). So the element of time was caught and rendered in space, and so were cause and effect, the reasons for emotions and the expression of them.[6]

Another highly developed part of humanistic painting theory, one to which we have alluded briefly at the opening of this chapter, related precisely to the visual symptoms by which human emotion is betrayed. The French Academicians in general made this their concern, but none more systematically than the official painter to Louis XIV, Charles Le Brun, in his treatise entitled *Expression des passions*. As a recent writer has happily phrased it, this work put "Descartes' psychology . . . virtually on the tip of the young painters' brushes."[7] A translation of the work that appeared in London as late as 1813, with twenty copper engravings, gives, for example, the following caption for the picture of "Sadness."

> The dejection that is produced by sadness makes the Eye brows rise towards the middle of the forehead more than towards the Cheeks; the Eye ball appears full of perturbation; the white of the Eye is Yellow, the Eye lids are drawn down and a little swell'd; all about the Eyes is livid; the Nostrils are drawn downward; the Mouth is held open and the corners are drawn down; the head carelessly leaning on One of the Shoulder[s]; the face is of a lead Colour the lips of pale.[8]

[6] Rensselaer W. Lee, "Ut Pictura Poesis: The Humanistic Theory of Painting," *The Art Bulletin*, XXII (December, 1940), esp. 223–5.

[7] Brewster Rogerson, "The Art of Painting the Passions," *JHI*, XIV (January, 1953), 75. Rogerson's account (pp. 68–94) extends to the arts in general—for not only painting but all such visual and auditory arts as poetry, oratory, acting, and music were arts of "painting" the passions. He points out that the theory of expressive signs involved runs back through the Renaissance, appearing prominently, for instance, in Leonardo's remarks on painting and in Lomazzo's handbook of 1585, and that it finds its classical authority in Aristotle's *Rhetoric* III, 1 and 7, and in Quintilian's *Institutes* XI, iii, 61 ff.

[8] Rogerson, *loc. cit.*, p. 76. Cf. Edmund Burke's account of what beauty does to the beholder, quoted *post* Chapter 14, p. 299.

We are now in a position to notice a curious contrast between the influence of literary norms on painting and the influence of painting norms on literature. Whereas the influence of literature on painting was broadly intellectual and humanistic, the reciprocal influence of painting on literature was in the long run if not anti-intellectual and anti-humanistic at least markedly non-humanistic and sensational. At its best, the new influence was part of a blandly urged general movement of human nature (toward landscape) which was in progress throughout the 18th century, a substitution of landscape for the older ethical structure of values as the objective counterpart of human emotions.[9] It was not in the heroic historical pictures of French and Italian painters that the poets had a great deal to learn (the historical pictures were learned from poetry itself), but in pictures where the painters were not so closely rivaling earlier poets, that is, in landscapes—the serenely classical ones by Claude (with their human elements static and remote—a group of fishing peasants by a stream, a boat in a bay, a shepherd with his flock, the porticos of temples on hilltops rising out of valley mists) or the wild and ragged ones by Salvator Rosa (the crags, the brown and blasted heaths and twisted trees, the torrents, and the ruined Gothic arch or tower). A distinct reflection of these painting styles appears throughout English topographical and descriptive poetry of the 18th century.[1] On the theoretical side, the classic quotation is from James Thomson's allegorical, Spenserian description of the castle of Indolence.

> Sometimes the Pencil in cool airy Halls
> Bade the gay Bloom of vernal Landskips rise,
> Or Autumn's varied Shades imbrown the Walls:
> Now the black Tempest strikes the astonish'd Eyes;
> Now down the Steep the flashing Torrent flies;
> The trembling Sun now plays o'er Ocean blue,
> And now rude Mountains frown amid the Skies;
> Whate'er *Lorrain* light-touched with softening Hue,
> Or savage *Rosa* dash'd, or learned *Poussin* drew.
>   —I, xxxviii

A fair example of the execution, the actual significance for poetry of the liaison with painting, is this Claudian perspective across the landscaped estate of Hagley Park—from the last edition of Thomson's *Spring* during his lifetime (1744):

> Meantime you gain the Height, from whose fair Brow
> The bursting Prospect spreads immense around;

---

[9] Cf. H. M. McLuhan, "Tennyson and the Analogy of the Picturesque," *Essays in Criticism*, I (July, 1951), 262–82.

[1] See Elizabeth W. Manwaring, *Italian Landscape in Eighteenth Century England* (London, 1927).

And snatch'd o'er Hill and Dale, and Wood, and Lawn
And verdant Field, and darkening Heath between,
And Villages embosom'd soft in Trees,
And spiry Towns by dusky Columns mark'd
Of rising Smoak, your Eye excursive roams . . .
To where the broken Landskip, by degrees,
Ascending, roughens into ridgy Hills;
O'er which the *Cambrian* Mountains, like far Clouds
That Skirt the blue Horizon, doubtful, rise.—ll. 950–62

Modern scholarship has labored the point that Italian and French painting affected the actual landscaping of 18th-century English gardens and parks, an outdoor movement in which not only Lyttelton, the owner of Hagley, but Alexander Pope and other poets took an important part.

V

FRIENDLY relations between poetry and the visual arts were also much assisted during the 18th century by antiquarian, virtuoso, and Hellenizing trends of the day. One of these was the "illustration" of classical literature by classical sculpture, reliefs, and medals—as in the encyclopedic dialogue *Polymetis*, 1747, the work of the Oxford Professor of Poetry and friend of Pope, Joseph Spence. There was also the fresh illustration of classical poetry by living draughtsmen and at least an implicit judgment in favor of this poetry according to its capacity to inspire such illustration—as in the Count Caylus' *Tableaux Tirés de l'Iliade, de l'Odysée de Homère et de l'Enéide de Virgile*, 1754–1758. Such matters were the theme of the archeologist Winckelmann's *Gedanken über die Nachahmung der griechischen Werke in der Malerei und Bildhauerkunst*, 1755. The instructive frontispiece of this book, in an edition of 1756, shows the learned painter at work on a sacrifice of Iphigenia, Agamemnon holding his cloak to his eyes; on the ground at the painter's feet are scrolls bearing versions of the story by Sophocles and Aeschylus, and in the painter's left hand is the play by Euripides at the passage: "Putting his cloak before his eyes" (*ommatōn peplon protheis*). The appearance of the three books just mentioned precipitated in 1766 the most notable act of theorizing upon our theme to occur during the 18th century, the *Laokoon* [2] of G. E. Lessing.

The German critic's protest against the extravagance of the humanistic *ut pictura poesis* gets under way with some bickering about a Hellenistic sculptural group dug up on the site of Hadrian's villa in 1506 and lodged in the Vatican Museum. Why is the mouth of the priest Laokoon, entoiled in mortal struggle with the two serpents, not wide

[2] *Laocoon*, trans. William A. Steel, Everyman's Library (London, 1930).

open in a shout of agony? Because, said **Winckelmann**, the Greek ideal of emotional restraint admirably forbade it. Because, says Lessing, a gaping cavity is a formal defect in a sculpture, and because the moment of the half-open mouth, short of the climax, is a highly "significant and fruitful" moment.[3] Students of antiquity had long considered the question whether or not the sculptural group was modeled upon the similar passage in the Second Book of Virgil's *Aeneid*. There were those who believed it highly probable that the "honour of the invention and first conception" belonged to Virgil. Lessing would agree with the sequence but reverse the honors. Why does Virgil's description of the incident differ in several important respects from the sculpture? Because, says Lessing, the sculptors, coming after Virgil, saw fit to improve upon him. There is no other way to explain the facts. With the sculptural model to work from, Virgil would have had no reason to deviate.[4]

Here we observe Lessing entangled (though like Laocoon uttering a half-suppressed cry of anguish) in the coils of the very critical assumption which the later chapters of his long essay so adroitly almost throw off. When he comes (Chapter XI) to consider the imbecilities of the Count Caylus, the attempts to exploit the greatness of Homer through pictures ("how much more perfect" the artist's "delineations will prove the more closely he clings to the very smallest circumstances noticed by the poet"), Lessing deals with the real critical issue, if not definitively, at least very acutely.

The difference, says Lessing in effect, between poetry and painting (Chapter XVI) is more important for criticism than the resemblance between them. He was not the first to have said something like this. In the somewhat remote past Leonardo, with an insistence on the direct and natural appeal of paint to the eye, *virtù visiva*, had drawn a clear distinction, albeit all in favor of his own art. Both the 17th and the 18th century are full of casual protests against the prevailing trend toward assimilation. "*Les mots et les couleurs ne sont choses pareilles*," says La Fontaine. "*Ni les yeux ne sont les oreilles.*" [5] Within the more immediate era of 18th-century theorizing the Abbé Du Bos had distinguished between the real imitations ("signes naturels") of painting and the arbitrary symbols ("signes artificiels") of poetry.[6] In the fifth part of his

---

[3] Chapters I–III. *Fixierte Blitz* Goethe was to call this piece of sculpture, with a slightly different emphasis on the single moment. See Margarete Bieber, *Laocoon* (New York, 1942).

[4] Chapters V–VI. The Laocoon, a composition in six pieces of stone by three Rhodian sculptors, Athenodorus, Polydorus, and Agesander, is dated by modern archeologists about 50 B.C.

[5] *Conte du Tableau*. See Atkins II, 329, for an instance of the distinction in antiquity.

[6] *Réflexions* I, xl. Cf. E. N. S. Thompson, "The Discourses of Sir Joshua Reynolds," *PMLA*, XXXII (September, 1917), 342, on Johnson, Shaftesbury, and James Harris.

Inquiry (a work which Lessing long pondered translating) Burke had taken some pains to assert that words are not pictorial substitutes for the visible world.[7] Yet Lessing is the first to write an extended argument in an accent that establishes the importance of the question. The difference between poetry and painting, he says, is a basic difference, that between a medium of time and a medium of space. A medium of space can present corporeal objects directly and vividly; the same medium can present the actions of such bodies only indirectly and through images of the bodies themselves. Conversely, a medium of time can present actions directly and vividly, but can present bodies only indirectly and through actions. Certain passages of 18th-century nature poetry (for example, a flower stanza from Von Haller's *Alpen*—a few English examples might have been found in Thomson's *Seasons*) are adduced to show the opaque effect of over-thick painting—static and minute attention to the corporeal object.[8] Poetry ought to describe not objects as such but objects in action—not the color and shape of Helen but the effect of her beauty upon the lascivious graybeards of Troy. Writing as he does in the face of the classical doctrine, and that freshly sanctioned by the new empirical aesthetics, Lessing must be credited with a keen theoretical insight. An idea of his originality and daring may be got from the retrospect of Goethe.

> One must be a youth to realize the effect exercised upon us by Lessing's *Laokoon*, which transported us from the region of miserable observation into the free fields of thought. The long misunderstood *ut pictura poesis* was at once set aside; the difference between art and poetry made clear; the peaks of both appeared separately, however near each other might be their bases. . . .[9]

Yet some reservations seem in order. A certain incompleteness of critical reorientation may perhaps be seen here and there in Lessing's argument. There is, for example, his curious recommendation that poetry should get around troublesome descriptive spots by the device of reducing them to some kind of narration. See how Homer does the shield of Achilles—an elaborate description but all conveyed in the process of the fabrication of the shield by Vulcan. See how Homer describes the bow of Pandarus, all through an account of how a goat was hunted and killed to yield the horns of which the bow was made. See how Anacreon describes the lovely boy Bathyllus—by the exquisite con-

[7] In *Spectator* No. 416, Addison expresses the contrary view—that words can call up more lively images than nature itself.

[8] Cf. *post*, Chapter 15, p. 315, the recommendation of particulars by Joseph Warton and other English critics of the mid-century.

[9] *Wahrheit und Dichtung* VIII, quoted by James Sime, *Lessing* (London, 1877), I, 304; Cf. Goethe, *Werke*, XXVII (Weimar, 1889), 164.

trivance of having his portrait made by a painter. In short, Lessing's conception of the difference between painting and poetry, when put under the pressure of a practical application, seems to amount to a distinction between still pictures and moving pictures. He offers us an urgent invitation to speculate what would have happened to his theory if his experience of artistic media had been broadened by an acquaintance with the cinema. His notion of the moving pictures that make up poetry would perhaps better correspond to the now archaic and naive phases of the modern cinematic art than to the advantages of verticality or associational depth which have been explored in more recent techniques.[1]

Lessing's theory leans all too clearly toward vividness or illusionism, the *enargeia*, the *phantasiae* of the ancient rhetoricians, though in a footnote he astutely identifies those very figures with 18th-century poetical pictures.[2] The fact that he actually countenanced this aesthetic norm, while perhaps believing that he was severe upon it, is suggested not only in *Laokoon* but in some moments of his dramatic theory. He was a pioneer German dramatic critic and a rebel against French neo-classicism. He had an ideal of intensity for poetry, and especially for drama, which he explained by starting with that distinction between natural and artificial signs which we have already cited from the Abbé Du Bos. Thus in a letter written to a friend about the reception of the *Laokoon*:

> Poetry must try to raise its arbitrary signs to natural signs: that is how it differs from prose and becomes poetry. The means by which this is accomplished are the tone of words, the position of words, measure, figures and tropes, similes, etc. All these make arbitrary signs more like natural signs, but they do not actually change them into natural signs; consequently all genres which use only these means must be looked upon as lower kinds of poetry; and the highest kind of poetry will be that which transforms the arbitrary signs completely into natural signs. That is dramatic poetry.[3]

That is to say: the directness of drama, the mimetic use of language as the speech of dramatic persons, is more poetically important than the poet's management of language, his rhythms, and his figurative imagination. A passage in the *Laokoon* which Lessing permitted himself to indulge in almost as if it were a joke gives perhaps a better clue to the power which he actually displayed as dramatic critic in his celebrated *Hamburg Dramaturgy*. In his discussion of the Homeric lines on the

[1] Cf. Sergei Eisenstein, *The Film Sense*, trans. Jay Leyda (New York, 1947), *passim*, and especially "montage," pp. 3-12, 30-6, 43-6.

[2] Chapter XXV.

[3] Letter to Nicolai, May 26, 1769, about a review of *Laokoon* by Garve, quoted by Wellek, *History*, I, 164-5, from Lessing's *Sämtliche Werke*, ed. K. Lachmann and F. Muncker (Leipzig, 1886-1924), XVII, 290-1.

sceptre of Agamemnon he seems partially at a loss to explain their power. Somewhat diffidently and apologetically, he assumes the manner of a Hellenistic grammarian—or perhaps of some future pedant-exegete— and writes the following reverie:

> It would not surprise me if I found that one of the old commentators of Homer had admired this passage as the most perfect allegory of the origin, progress, establishment, and hereditary succession of the royal power amongst mankind. True, I should smile if I were to read that Vulcan, the maker of this sceptre, as fire, as the most indispensable thing for the preservation of mankind, represented . . . the satisfaction of those wants which moved the first men to subject themselves to the rule of an individual monarch; that the first king, a son of Time (*Zeus, Kroniōn*), was an honest ancient who wished to share his power with, or wholly transfer it to, a wise and eloquent man, a Mercury . . . that the wily orator, at the time when the infant State was threatened by foreign foes, resigned his supreme power to the bravest warrior. . . . I should smile, but nevertheless should be confirmed in my esteem for the poet to whom so much meaning can be attributed.—Chapter XVI

VI

BUT *ut pictura poesis* was part of something larger, a general ground swell toward assimilating the arts which a *Laokoon* could scarcely have much success in checking. A companion movement which should be noticed here, though more briefly, was that toward unifying the arts of poetry and music, the restoration of that primitive harmony and sisterhood which had been noted with approval by Plato and illustrated by such classical figures as Orpheus and Timotheus and in the Old Testament by David. The modern separation of music and poetry was an actuality which had begun to emerge during the 16th century with the specialized development of instrumental music. But even during the same period a theoretical drive toward unifying these arts had begun with the musical academies (Baïf's *Académie de Poésie et de Musique* most notably in France and in Italy the Florentine *Camerata*).[4] This was a reaction, towards simplicity and naturalism, against the contrapuntal intricacies of polyphonic music in the medieval tradition. The movement continued and gained strength through the 17th century as part of the same humanistic yearning for emotive imitation which we have sampled

[4] See James E. Phillips, "Poetry and Music in the Seventeenth Century," in *Music & Literature in England in the Seventeenth and Eighteenth Centuries* (Los Angeles: William Andrews Clark Memorial Library, 1953), pp. 2–18.

in the theory of poetry and painting. The formula "poetry plus melody equals music" meant first, in the 16th and early 17th centuries, that music was to serve the higher, more intellectual and imitative purposes of poetry. The proposed ideal was a single melodic line closely matching the verbal line, note for syllable, quantity for quantity, and aiming even at some degree of story-telling, that is, a harmony of notes and "modes" with passions and motions, with heights and depths of verbal meaning.

> If the subject be light, you must cause your music to go in motions which carry with them a celerity or quickness of time . . . ; if it be lamentable, the note must go in slow and heavy motions. . . . Moreover, you must have a care that when your matter signifieth ascending, high heaven and such like, you make your music ascend; and . . . where your ditty speaks of descending, lowness, depth, hell and other such, you must make your music descend. For as it will be thought a great absurdity to talk of heaven and point downward to the earth: so it will be counted great incongruity if a musician upon the words *He ascended into heaven* should cause his music to descend.[5]

Thomas Campion's songs and his theoretical aim (to "couple" his "words and notes lovingly together"), Milton's *Comus* and the music of Henry Lawes [6] are examples which will readily occur to the student of English poetry.

Later, in the second half of the 17th century, the subserviency of music to poetry was reversed. Poetry came actually to be written to meet the requirements of musical setting. Witness the operas of Dryden, or the tame libretto of Tate's *Dido and Aeneas*, for the music of Purcell. The poetry, Dryden complained in his Preface to *Albion and Albanius*, 1685, must "please hearing rather than gratify understanding." "The same reasons which depress thought in an opera have a stronger effect upon the words." The trend of the times is manifest in the social and musico-dramatic forms which were increasingly popular—opera, oratorio, song, ballad, hymn, and the great Pindaric ode for music, which began in 1683 with the London Musical Society's annual performance of an ode celebrating the powers of music and paying honor to the patron saint of Christian music, St. Cecilia.[7] Dryden's two poems for St. Cecilia's Day are magnificent instances of that genre of poetry which came to be written as an invitation to an exercise of powers by the

[5] Thomas Morley, *A Plain and Easy Introduction to Practical Music*, 1597, quoted by Bertrand H. Bronson, "Some Aspects of Music and Literature in the Eighteenth Century," in *Music & Literature* . . . , p. 31.

[6] Cf. Willa M. Evans, *Henry Lawes, Musician and Friend of Poets* (New York, 1941), pp. 90–109.

[7] Cf. Robert M. Myers, "Neo-Classical Criticism of the Ode for Music," *PMLA*, LXII (June, 1947), 399–421.

musical composer. A series of stanzas from the first of these poems, the
"Song for St. Cecilia's Day, 1687," will illustrate the poetic range.

III

> The trumpet's loud clangor
>   Excites us to arms
> With shrill notes of anger
>   And mortal alarms.
> The double double double beat
>   Of the thundering drum
> Cries: "Hark! the foes come;
> Charge, charge, 'tis too late to retreat."

IV

> The soft complaining flute
> In dying notes discovers
> The woes of hopeless lovers,
> Whose dirge is whisper'd by the warbling lute.

V

> Sharp violins proclaim
> Their jealous pangs, and desperation,
> Fury, frantic indignation,
> Depth of pains, and height of passion,
>   For the fair, disdainful dame.

On the side of the music, it may be observed that Handel's setting of
this Song, for Soprano and Tenor, Chorus and Orchestra, 1739, is "about
fifteen times" longer than a plain reading of the words. The word "warbling," for instance, is extended over six bars of vocalization, with "lute-
like 'warbling' in the bass accompaniment." [8] In this baroque elaboration, all those gains of the 16th-century humanists against medieval poly-
phony were sadly voided—as John Wesley would complain in a pamphlet
entitled *Thoughts on the Power of Music* and Dr. John Brown (1763)
in his *Dissertation on the Rise, Union, and Power, the Progressions, and
Corruptions, of Poetry and Music*.[9]

The effort on the side of poetry was carried into the 18th century
with less success by Pope [1] and petered out in poems like Collins' *The*

---

[8] Bertrand H. Bronson, "Some Aspects of Music and Literature in the Eighteenth Century," in *Music & Literature*, pp. 32, 38, 40.

[9] Bronson, *loc. cit.*, p. 47, Wesley; Phillips, *loc. cit.*, p. 19, Brown.

[1] *Ode for Music on St. Cecilia's Day*, 1713. At a later date (*Dunciad* I, 40) Pope
would allude to "soft sing-song on Cecilia's day." His *Epistle to Augustus* and his
Fourth *Dunciad* express the Aristotelian and intellectualist contempt of a literary
man for the merely acoustic and emotive tendencies of Italian opera and for the
concurrent optical excess or spectacularism of the stage.

Passions: An Ode for Music (1747) and Gray's *Ode for Music, Irregular* (1768). The end was indicated by the burlesque *Cantata* of Swift and Bonnell Thornton's *An Ode on St. Cecilia's Day, Adapted to the Ancient British Music, viz. the Salt-Box, the Jew's Harp, the Marrow-bones and Cleavers, the Humstrung or Hurdy-gurdy* (1749).[2] The serious odes show us the painting of the passions in all the virtuosity of "vivid"[3] allegorical image and metrical representation of movement. Dryden's second poem, *Alexander's Feast*, so highly esteemed by himself and by several succeeding generations of critics, is without question the most flamboyantly successful demonstration of the technique. Its rapidly shifting succession of passionate announcements and appropriate rhythmical variations surely go far to justify the place it has long held in the repertoire of school declamations.

By the mid-18th century, English theorists were a highly vocal chorus, though today quite obscurely known—Avison, Mason, Jones, Beattie, Brown, Webb, Harris, and others. They picked up and carried along the theme of poetry and music at about the time when *ut pictura poesis* was beginning to falter—and when the norm of classical imitation, in literary art at least, was beginning to shift toward that of romantic emotion and expression. This school of theorists contrived to recognize three main kinds of resemblance between music and poetry:

1. Technical and formal. (The verbal "matter" of poetry was said to correspond to the harmony of music; the subject or story, to the melody; the meter, to the measure.)
2. Imitative. (In the choral works of Bach and Handel, the voices rise, with the mention of hills, descend with the valleys. Bach's "Clavier-piece" imitates a post-horn and in Mozart's *Marriage of Figaro* horns express cuckoldry.)
3. Expressive. (Music expresses classes of passions—joy, grief, love. "To imitate the passions was to describe them in music; the pleasure of music was the pleasure of the passions themselves.")[4]

Correspondences of the second kind, the most distinctly recognizable, were looked on with some suspicion by the critics and were called

[2] Robert M. Myers, *loc. cit.*, pp. 410–11; A. D. McKillop, "Bonnell Thornton's Burlesque Ode," *Notes and Queries*, CXCIV (July 23, 1949), 321–4.

[3] Cf. Earl Wasserman, "The Inherent Values of Eighteenth-Century Personification," *PMLA*, LXV (June, 1950), 444–8.

[4] See the valuable articles by Herbert M. Schueller, "Literature and Music as Sister Arts: An Aspect of Aesthetic Theory in Eighteenth-Century Britain," *PQ*, XXVI (July, 1947), 193–205; " 'Imitation' and 'Expression' in British Music Criticism in the Eighteenth Century," *Musical Quarterly*, XXXIV (October, 1948), 544–66; "The Pleasures of Music: Speculation in British Music Criticism, 1750–1800," *JAAC*, VIII (March, 1950), 155–171; "The Use and Decorum of Music as Described in British Literature, 1700 to 1780," *JHI*, XIII (January, 1952), 73–93; "Correspondences Between Music and the Sister Arts, According to 18th Century Aesthetic Theory," *JAAC*, XI (June, 1953), 334–59.

musical "puns." Comparative theorists of the day considered poetry to be the highest art, because it could say things. Painting was second. Music, third. Vocal music was preferred to instrumental. That is, the norm of imitation was (so far as formal commitments went) preferred to norms of sensory pleasure, of the geometric or formal, or even of direct emotive expression. The genres of opera, oratorio, and song were hailed as steps toward an ideal reunion of poetry and music, a restoration of music to its primitive and correct status as the handmaid of poetry. There were some Aristotelian echoes in this discussion (as in Thomas Twining's notable edition of the *Poetics,* 1789) and doubtless a faintly quadrivial strain, some sound across the centuries from the Pythagorean, Platonic, and medieval aesthetic of harmonious numbers.

VII

BECAUSE of its basic assumption that the aim of the arts is a direct imitation of nature, 18th-century theory was in the curious position of seeing literature as the contentual norm of painting and music, and at the same time of seeing either painting or music as the technical norm of literature. For literature was clearly in possession of objects for imitation but was handicapped by having really no paint (no natural sensory signs) or none to speak of; painting itself was in a favorable middle position, having both definable objects and natural signs; while music (when pure and not allied to vocal art) was in the odd position of having a persuasively direct sensory medium but no controllable correspondence between the medium and any definite objects.[5]

Despite the analytic glance of a Lessing here and there, the tide of theory and taste moved toward a synthesis, inevitably to be made easier by the metaphysical ascendancy of idea over material in the romantic era. In the mid-18th century occur such phenomena as the Abbé Castel's Clavecin de Couleurs and speculations such as Diderot's on transfer of sense experience,[6] and in the early 19th century the references of German literary philosophers to architecture as frozen music, to poetry as music for the inner ear and painting for the inner eye. The verbal synaesthesis which is epidemic in romantic poetry and is advertised later, quite self-consciously, in such doctrinaire poems as those of Baudelaire

[5] The lesson of Professor Calvin Brown's *Music and Literature, a Comparison of the Arts* (Athens, Georgia, 1948) would seem to be that music owes more to literature than it is able to repay.

[6] See Irving Babbitt, *The New Laokoon* (Boston, 1910). The story of the man born blind who identified the color scarlet by the sound of a trumpet, first published in Locke's *Essay* (from the communication of the Irish philosopher Molyneux), reverberated through the century. Cf. Marjorie Nicolson, *Newton Demands the Muse* (Princeton, 1946), pp. 83–5.

and Rimbaud on "correspondences," the Pre-Raphaelite experiment,[7] the Wagnerian *Gesamtkunstwerk*, the birth of ballet, the hero of Huysmans' *A Rebours* playing his fugues on a taste organ of spigots inserted in kegs of liqueurs, all these are typical of a trend (a mélange and confusion of the arts) which as late as 1910 provoked the Harvard humanist Irving Babbitt to write his summation and alarm entitled *The New Laokoon*. The vogue during recent centuries of what Tolstoy in a reactionary treatise characterizes as upper-class voluptuary art has been a vogue of sensory pleasures analogized and merged, and it has moved climactically away from objects of imitation toward media and hence toward the imitation of media by one another.

> When the center of life disappears, the arts of poetry become the art of poetry. And in an advanced stage of the evil, in the nineteenth century and today, we get the *mélange des genres*, one art living off another, that the late Irving Babbitt so valiantly combated without having understood the influences that had brought it about. Painting tries to be music; poetry leans upon painting; all the arts "strive toward the condition of music"; till at last seeing the mathematical structure of music, the arts become geometrical and abstract, and destroy themselves.[8]

VIII

The Abbé Charles Batteux had, as we have seen, reduced all the arts to a single principle, and his unified view of the fine arts taken up by Diderot and D'Alembert in the *Encyclopédie*, proved widely influential during the second half of the century. Batteux's single "principle" was the classical principle of "imitation." But no matter what the principle, the unification of the arts was a fertile ground for subsequent attempts at more or less scientific division and subdivision. Where Lessing was concerned only with the modest project of separating poetry from painting (time from space), his contemporary and critic J. G. Herder distinguished painting (the art of the eye), music (the art of the ear), and sculpture (the art of touch). And from these arts poetry differed yet

[7] Compare, for instance, D. G. Rossetti's painting *The Blessed Damozel* with his poem of the same title. "Whether this interpenetration of poetry and painting is of advantage to either, may admit of question. . . . The sonnets of 'The House of Life' have appeared to many readers obscure and artificial, the working out in language of conceptions more easily expressible by some other art. . . . Such readers are apt to imagine that Rossetti suffers from a hesitation between poetry and painting. . . . The method proper to one art intrudes onto the other; everything the artist does has the air of an experiment; he paints poems and writes pictures" (Henry A. Beers, *A History of English Romanticism in the Nineteenth Century*, New York, 1901, p. 307).

[8] Allen Tate, *Reactionary Essays* (New York, 1936), p. 55.

again. It was the only immediate art of the soul, the music of the soul—
not work, but energy.[9] J. G. Sulzer's *Allgemeine Theorie der Schönen
Künste*, 1771–1774, an alphabetically arranged encyclopedia, divided the
fine arts somewhat simply by media: color, body, tone, words. In his
aesthetic entitled *The Critique of Judgment*, 1790, Kant arrived at a
three-fold basic division of the arts corresponding to three characters
of spoken communication, word, gesture, and tone: 1. arts of speech
(*redende Künste*), poetry and rhetoric; 2. arts of shaping (*bildende
Künste*), architecture, sculpture, painting; 3. arts of beautiful sensory
pattern (*Künste des schönen Spiels der Empfindungen*), music and color
design.[1] This became an important landmark. Still it was but a limited
model for the brilliant efflorescence of "systems" which marks the subsequent history of general aesthetics—in the work of Hegel and a host
of other 19th- and 20th-century continental writers. The system of the
English aesthetician Sidney Colvin may be consulted in his article "Fine
Arts" in the *Encyclopedia Britannica*, 11th edition, 1910. The most recent system to appear is perhaps that of Etienne Souriau in his *La
Correspondance des Arts*, 1947.[2]

The modern activity of classifying the arts has been an attempt to
put certain traditionally distinguished arts into more or less neatly
bounded areas in a pattern having two basic dimensions. These dimensions are, unavoidably: (1) the dimension of physical medium—under
the aspects of time and space; and (2) the dimension of intellectual
reference—positive and negative, that is, symbolic and non-symbolic.
Attempts to add other basic dimensions [3] or to refine too far on the sub-
divisions of these two have produced overlapping or have created areas
of unoccupied abstraction. Such attempts have only accentuated the ir-
reducibly concrete character of works of art. In the symbolic dimension a useful division seems to be that (defined so early by the Abbé
Du Bos) between more or less natural symbols (pictures) and more or
less artificial symbols (words). But a great obstacle to tidiness in the
whole system arises from the fact that in the physical dimension so
radical a thing as movement appears in both space and time—so that arts
of movement in space (dancing, drama, opera) are inevitably also time

[9] Robert T. Clark, Jr., "Herder's Conception of 'Kraft,'" *PMLA*, LVII (1942),
737–52. Herder's distinctions appeared in his *Plastik*, 1778.

[1] Kristeller, *loc. cit.*, XIII, 43 n., 278, explains Kant's *Farbenkunst* (mentioned
also by Herder and by Mendelssohn) with reference to the Abbé Castel's color piano.
For the moment we are not concerned with Kant's more radical preliminary distinctions between science and skill, between mercenary art (*Lohnkunst, Handwerk*)
and free art, between the merely pleasing (*angenehm*) and the beautiful (*schön*).
Cf. *post* Chapter 17, p. 371.

[2] See the excellent survey in Thomas Munro's *The Arts and Their Interrelations* (New York, 1949), Chap. V.

[3] As: utilitarian and non-utilitarian (table utensils, sculpture); made with or
without tools (sculpture, dancing).

arts, though not the only time arts. There are also time arts of pure sound (either symbolic or non-symbolic—poetry or music). The element of symbol (natural, artificial, or combined) may obviously be joined with the elements of space, time and movement in a variety of complexes, from the simplicity of song to the hetereogeneity of opera. It is, in short, impossible to construct a classification both basic and abstract and yet precise enough to isolate the several arts as they are traditionally and concretely marked off from one another.[4]

Our own effort to construct such a classification produces a table of the following sort.

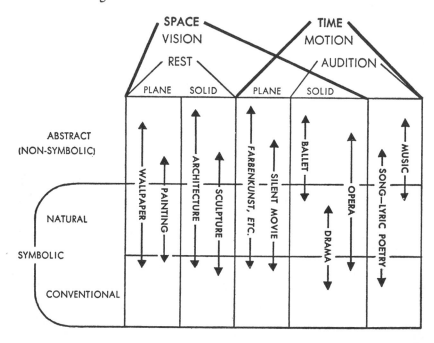

The construction or the perusal of a table like this has no very immediate relation to literary criticism. The exercise may, however, have some merit. It may have the merit of persuading us that some differences are more basic than others—as that between symbolic and non-symbolic, that between space and time, or that between natural resemblance and conventional sign. It may further remind us that art works are always concrete, that classifications are abstract, and that there are

---

[4] Etienne Souriau attempts to avoid the difficulty by making symbolic and non-symbolic his only two-fold division and multiplying across that the enumeration of the several media in one spectrum. Thus to the visual media of line, color, and volume he adds "luminosity." In the symbolic zone of his wheel he has a space for cinema, but in order to fill the corresponding non-symbolic space he has to make use of "luminous projections"; in the non-symbolic space corresponding to literature he has to introduce "pure prosody."

differences between the concrete arts which are better bridged metaphorically than literally. A theorist of poetry, being inevitably a person
who subscribes to metaphoric and analogical ways of thinking, is in a
good position to avoid both the fault of running the arts confusedly together by metaphors which become literal and the opposite fault of cut-
ting the arts off from one another too completely by the denial of all
such relations. There are poetic dimensions which can never be described
except metaphorically, and to keep open, if only tentatively, the time-
honored metaphoric avenues may do something to prevent theoretical
discussion from declining into the literalism of a quasi-scientific semantics.

SUPPLEMENT

On the Camera Obscura

Yield *Raphael*, Titian yield, whose mimic strife
Would warm th' unwilling Canvas into life;
Colours more true shall in my Landskip glow,
If equal to my Theme my Numbers flow;
The Cloud-topt Summit, or enamel'd Lawn,
Woods, Rivers, Seas, by Nature's Pencil drawn;
By Art contracted shall Assistance bring,
And from their blended Charms a fair Creation spring.
Thro' the small Portal, see a gath'ring Ray,
To the dark Room transmit a doubtful Day!
Spontaneous Beauties fill th' extended Scroll,
Reflected Streams with silent Motion roll.

—from *The Museum*, published by Robert Dodsley, No. 13, September
12, 1746, pp. 492–3

When taken out, the plate [of the Daguerreotype] does not at first appear to
have received a definite impression—some short processes, however, develop
it in the most miraculous beauty. All language must fall short of conveying
any just idea of the truth, and this will not appear so wonderful when we
reflect that the source of vision itself has been, in this instance, the designer.
Perhaps, if we imagine the distinctness with which an object is reflected in a
positively perfect mirror, we come as near the reality as by any other means.
For, in truth, the Daguerreotyped plate is infinitely (we use the term
advisedly) is *infinitely* more accurate in its representation than any painting
by human hands. If we examine a work of ordinary art, by means of a powerful microscope, all traces of resemblance to nature will disappear—but the

closest scrutiny of the photographic drawing discloses only a more absolute truth, a more perfect identity of aspect with the thing represented. The variations of shade, the gradations of both linear and aerial perspective are those of truth itself in the supremeness of its perfection.

> —*Alexander's Weekly Messenger*, Philadelphia, December 15, 1840, reprinted by Clarence S. Brigham, *Edgar Allan Poe's Contributions to Alexander's Weekly Messenger* (Worcester, Mass., 1943), p. 21. Poe's authorship seems likely.

The analogy anciently suggested in the phrase ut pictura poesis *is a very hard one to keep down; it is revived with a varied accent according to the bent of each age. Mr. Allen Tate, in the essay from which we have quoted above, draws an interesting parallel between the poetry of John Peale Bishop and some features of 20th-century surrealism in painting.*

PERSPECTIVES ARE PRECIPICES

Sister Anne, Sister Anne,
Do you see anybody coming?

 I see a distance of black yews
 Long as the history of the Jews.

 I see a road sunned with white sand
 Wide plains surrounding silence. And

 Far off, a broken colonnade
 That overthrows the sun in shade.

Sister Anne, Sister Anne,
Do you see nobody coming?

                          A man
 Upon that road a man who goes
 Dragging a shadow by its toes.

 Diminishing he goes, head bare
 Of any covering even hair.

 A pitcher depending from one hand
 Goes mouth down. And dry is sand

Sister Anne, Sister Anne,
What do you see?

 His dwindling stride. And he seems blind
 Or worse to the prone man behind.

Sister Anne! Sister Anne!

· · ·

> I see a road. Beyond nowhere
> Defined by cirrus and blue air.
>
> I saw a man but he is gone
> His shadow into the sun.

From *Now with His Love* by John Peale Bishop; copyright 1933 by Charles Scribner's Sons and used with their permission.

As Bishop himself was to suggest in a lecture delivered partly as a response to Tate's essay,[5] a painting may do more than merely refer to time in the way it does when it shows a season or a time of day, a calendar or a clock. A painting may achieve something more like a direct presentation of the experience of time. This it can do by the use of perspective (a technique not merely of versimilitude but of temporal metaphor),[6] and by the use of successively placed and postured figures, as in a battle scene of raised, falling, and thrusting lances or swords, or in a Fall of Manna. Or fantastically, as in certain Siennese narrative paintings showing the same person simultaneously at different points on a road.[7] By a technique approximately the counterpart of this, that is, by patterns of repetition and diminishment (the refrain of Bishop's Perspectives), by a degree of overt reference to spatial features, and by certain associations with a style of painting, that of Salvador Dali in the present instance, the poet may achieve something curiously like a realization of space in the time art of words.

Although each art has . . . its own specific order of impressions, and an untranslatable charm, while a just apprehension of the ultimate differences of the arts is the beginning of aesthetic criticism; yet it is noticeable that, in its special mode of handling its given material, each art may be observed to pass into the condition of some other art, by what German critics term an *Andersstreben*—a partial alienation from its own limitations, through which the arts are able, not indeed to supply the place of each other, but reciprocally to lend each other new forces.

Thus some of the most delightful music seems to be always approaching to figure, to pictorial definition. Architecture, again, though it has its own laws—laws esoteric enough, as the true architect knows only too well—yet sometimes aims at fulfilling the conditions of a picture, as in the *Arena* chapel; or of sculpture, as in the flawless unity of Giotto's tower at Florence; and often finds a true poetry, as in those strangely twisted staircases of the *chateaux* of the country of the Loire, as if it were intended that among their

[5] "Poetry and Painting," *The Sewanee Review*, LIII (Spring, 1945), 247–58.

[6] "The conquest of perspective by the great Western painters was no mere display of erudition or of virtuosity in imitation. It was what Oswald Spengler calls it, the creation of a spiritual space, 'wide and eternal,' which responds to the imperious need of Western man for a symbol of distance and the infinite" (Melvin Rader, *A Source Book of Modern Aesthetics*, Introduction, p. xii).

[7] Lessing refers to such pictures with disapproval. He is dealing with essentially the same problem as the 17th-century theorists of stage unity when they were confronted with the Italian perspective stage and the French medieval *maisons*. The question of what constitutes a true unity in painting—harmony of line and color, coherence of story, continuity of background, consistency of perspective, or mere adjacency of lines and colors—is one which we leave for the theorist of painting.

odd turnings the actors in a theatrical mode of life might pass each other un-
seen; there being a poetry also of memory and of the mere effect of time, by
which architecture often profits greatly. Thus, again, sculpture aspires out of
the hard limitation of pure form towards color, or its equivalent; poetry also,
in many ways, finding guidance from the other arts, the analogy between a
Greek tragedy and a work of Greek sculpture, between a sonnet and a relief,
of French poetry generally with the art of engraving, being more than mere
figures of speech; and all the arts in common aspiring towards the principle
of music; music being the typical, or ideally consummate art, the object of
the great *Anders-streben* of all art, of all that is artistic, or partakes of artistic
qualities.

All art constantly aspires towards the condition of music. For while in
all other kinds of art it is possible to distinguish the matter from the form, and
the understanding can always make this distinction, yet it is the constant effort
of art to obliterate it. That the mere matter of a poem, for instance, its subject,
namely, its given incidents or situation—that the mere matter of a picture, the
actual circumstances of an event, the actual topography of a landscape—should
be nothing without the form, the spirit, of the handling, that this form, this
mode of handling, should become an end in itself, should penetrate every
part of the matter: this is what all art constantly strives after, and achieves in
different degrees.

—Walter Pater, "The School of Giorgione," in *The Renaissance* (Modern
Library edition), pp. 110–11

CHAPTER 14

GENIUS, EMOTION, AND ASSOCIATION

§ *resumé of "dissociation"—II. inspirationalism, neo-Longinianism, Boileau, the sublime in England, external grandeur, Dennis and Addison, Gothic irregularity, Pope, untrammeled genius vs. correctness, Addison, Reynolds, Ruskin, Macaulay's objection—III. originality, Edward Young, "imitation" damned, "pleasures of the pen," Johnson on Homer and Virgil, athletes who died young—IV. "ecstasis," Dennis, "enthusiastick emotion," Aristotelian catharsis, as purgation, as sublimation, as moderation (1) Stoic, (2) sentimental, Rapin, Dryden, Dennis, Steele, Addison, Johnson—V. pleasures of painful emotion, mimetic and didactic explanations, affective explanations: safety and self-congratulation, Hobbes and Lucretius, the unselfish alternative, Descartes, merger with sentimental catharsis—VI. "sympathy," Sterne and Adam Smith, Kames, Blair, Cowper to a young lady, illusionism, everyday life, simplicity, George Campbell, Coleridge—VII. genealogy of the Man of Feeling, tearful literature, reputation of Pope's Elegy, pure emotion dark, opposition between wit and passion, Dennis, Hume, Johnson, Warton on Pope, "sublime and pathetic" poets, "ethical" poets—VIII. Burke again, physiological and affective theory of beauty, the problem of verbal art, picture or passion, "expression," —IX. the Lockean special sense of association, the Humean and Hartleyan general sense, flattening of a distinction—X. kinds of application: the garrulous dramatic, the Shandean whimsical, the synecdochic, pregnant particulars, "associational response," putting the world back together again, "imagination," Adam Ferguson, "coalescence," Abraham Tucker—XI. association of values, Alison, Hazlitt, Coleridge, Hobbes, Gerard and Tucker. Coleridge on Hartley, "gift of spreading the tone," Hazlitt, J. S. Mill's essays on poetry, 1833 §*

W E HAVE NOTED THAT A CERTAIN MISTRUST OF THE MEANINGS CON-
veyed by poems, especially by witty or imaginative poems, had
grown during the later 17th century with the growth of
scientific philosophy. The epistemological charter of the new philosophy,
the Hobbesian and Lockean sensationalism, had inspired its own kind of
substitute for the moral, political, and religious values which the older
defences of poetry had been likely to rely upon. In the place of Sidney's
"feigning notable images of virtues [and] vices," appeared Addison's
ocular pleasures, the "beautiful," the "grand," and the "novel." Here was
a tendency to assign to poetry a new and simpler province, less pre-
tentious, more soothing, and more easily amusing. This at least had the
advantage of suggesting that poetry was something by itself, an innocent
pleasure set aside from both the sterner prerogatives and the heavy responsibilities which the didactic view would confer upon it. We shall
have occasion in a later chapter to notice these ideas from the retrospective advantage of the 19th-century doctrine of autonomous or gratuitous
aesthetic value—*l'art pour l'art.* Meanwhile we may observe certain other
ways in which the apology for poetry during the age of reason retreated
from the area of rational truth claimed by the scientific and rationalist
forces. These ways may be broadly described as retreats into the area of
feeling and emotion, or into an area of feeling and emotion conceived
as pure and prior to, or separate from, the objects of knowledge which
had previously been considered their grounds. The term "dissociation of
sensibility," to which we have referred already, at the start of our last
chapter, is a coinage which aptly suggests that situation—a dissociation
of the feeling and responding side of human consciousness from the side
of knowing and rational valuing. There were two emotive directions in
which the dissociation could work—toward the inspirations of the author
of poetry, and toward the responses of his audience.

I I

The inspiration of the poet had been since early classical times a
main reliance of those who would account for the element of the mysterious in poetry. The muse invoked by Homer or Hesiod personified
the magnetic frenzy ironically ascribed by Socrates both to the un-
scientific bard and his enraptured critic. In later antiquity the treatise of
"Longinus" *On The Sublime* centered these ideas less in the divine inspiration than in the great soul—the great thoughts and emotions—of
the poet himself. And the modern career of Longinus, which began with
the first edition by Robortello in 1554 and reached its influential phase
with the translation of Boileau, *Du Sublime,* in 1674, was a strain of

classicism very well qualified to promote a subjective and inspirationalist
trend in contemporary poetics. Such a trend was in part to be expected
from the introspective implications of the available new psychology, in
the tradition of Descartes' *Treatise on the Passions of the Soul,* and also,
as we have been saying, from the mere pressure of the rationalist objections to the traditionally cognitive or "imitative" premises of criticism.
But inspirationalism as it appears in actual literary theory at this period
takes a strong local coloration from Longinianism. Criticism was still
nominally under the authority of the classics; it was a great point in favor
of a literary thesis to have classical countenance or to be able to assume
a classical form. By a slight oversimplification, we may think of Longinus
as the Trojan horse in the camp of neo-classicism.

The term "sublime" in French criticism, shortly before the work of
Boileau, had been applied to diction and had meant something like *préciosité* or a metaphysical affectation of nicety. And Boileau's main point
in his classic Preface (the effort which established the modern term "sublime" for French and English criticism) was that the sublime so well
described by Longinus resided not in nicety of terms but in grandeur of
conception—a grandeur which had to be expressed, not preciously, but
strongly, and which was capable of being expressed in only a few simple
words. The example cited by Longinus from the opening of the "Hebrew
Lawgiver's" *Genesis* lent itself most impressively to Boileau's new conception.

> By the "sublime" Longinus did not mean what orators call "the
> sublime style;" he meant the element of the extraordinary in
> discourse, the marvellous, the striking, that in virtue of which a
> work exalts, ravishes, transports. The sublime *style* needs lofty
> language; but the *sublime* may appear in a single thought, a fig-
> ure, a phrase . . . *Le souverain arbitre de la nature d'une seule
> parole forma la lumière*: there is the sublime *style* for you. . . .
> But, *Dieu dit: Que la lumière se fasse; et la lumière se fit.* This
> extraordinary expression . . . is genuinely sublime; it has some-
> thing divine about it.[1]

[1] *Oeuvres Complètes,* ed. Daunou (Paris, 1839), II, 311–12. Cf. A. F. B. Clark,
Boileau and French Classical Critics in England (Paris, 1925), pp. 371–9; Samuel
Monk, *The Sublime* (New York, 1935), pp. 30–1. An accent on simplicity of diction
can be derived not so much from the words of Boileau himself as from his Biblical
example and the interpretation of that by French and English readers. See Monk,
p. 33, the protest of Huet that the style was too simple, and the following from Robert South, Sermon XVI, "A Discourse against Long and Extempore Prayers," first
published in 1694 (*Sermons,* Oxford, 1842, I, 335): "Was it [this way of speaking]
not authorized and ennobled by God himself in his making of the world? Was not
the work of all the six days transacted in so many words? There was no circum-
locution or amplification in the case; which makes the rhetorician Longinus, in his
book of the Loftiness of Speech, so much admire the height and grandeur of Moses's
style in the first chapter of Genesis."

Boileau was later somewhat hard pressed by French critical opponents, and in

In England the importance of Boileau's sublime was the launching of a term and a text rather than of a single clearly defined idea. English critics made mainly two things of the sublime, and each of these was an exaggeration of hints contained in memorable Longinian passages which we have quoted in an earlier chapter. For one thing, looking chiefly at the passage in Chapter XXXV of Longinus, on the Nile, the Danube, the Rhine, the Ocean, the celestial fires, the craters of Etna ("whose eruptions throw up stones from its depths and great masses of rock, and at times pour forth rivers of . . . pure and unmixed subterranean fire"), the critics erected a theory of the external objects which are sublime—namely, the big, the irregular, the surprising, and frightening. In our last chapter we have touched on this topic apropos of the 18th-century preoccupation with the externally definable sensational stimulus.[2] But certain features of the external sublime deserve to be specially noted in the present context. One of these was what might be summed up in the phrase "dangerous bigness." This was a bigness especially of landscape objects, the Alps, for instance, over which Dennis made a journey in 1688 and was impressed with "a delightful Horrour, a terrible Joy." Addison later made a similar journey with similar feelings,[3] and in a *Spectator* he wrote:

> . . . of all Objects that I have ever seen, there is none which affects my Imagination so much as the Sea or Ocean. I cannot see the Heavings of this prodigious Bulk of Waters, even in a calm, without a very pleasing Astonishment. But when it is worked up in a Tempest, so that the Horizon on every side is nothing but foaming Billows and floating Mountains, it is impossible to describe the agreeable Horrour that rises from such a Prospect.[4]

a series of twelve *Réflexions sur Longin,* the last three published posthumously, he arrived at the modified view that the sublime could in effect be a medley of all five of the Longinian sources—great thought and passion and (on the side of technique or rhetoric) words, figures, and harmonious composition.

[2] Cf. *ante* p. 255.

[3] C. D. Thorpe, "Two Augustans Cross the Alps: Dennis and Addison on Mountain Scenery," *SP,* XXXII (1935), 463–82.

[4] No. 489. In another *Spectator* (No. 592) Addison gives a humorous report on this kind of sublime as artificially arranged in the theater. "I look upon the Playhouse as a World within itself. They have lately furnished the Middle Region of it with a new Sett of Meteors, in order to give the Sublime to many modern Tragedies. I was there last Winter at the first Rehearsal of the new Thunder, which is much more deep and sonorous than any hitherto made use of. . . . They are also provided with above a Dozen Showers of Snow, which, as I am informed, are the Plays of many unsuccessful Poets artificially cut and shredded for that Use."

Another passage worth consulting here is that in which Samuel Johnson gives his estimate of the lines describing Dover Cliff in *King Lear* (Boswell, *Life,* 16 October, 1769). "No, Sir; it should be all precipice—all vacuum. The crows impede your fall. The diminished appearance of the boats, and other circumstances . . . do not impress the mind at once with the horrible idea of immense height."

Here was an aspect of the sublime which seems to have blended very readily with ideas of grandeur such as we shall discuss mainly under the head of neo-Platonic universality in our next chapter. A second main feature of the external sublime, relating obviously to bigness and danger, was that of wildness, shagginess, or Gothic irregularity. And this was a landscape feature which more easily even than bigness became a companion and external counterpart of the great and original soul of the poet. Thus Pope, in a liberalizing part of his *Essay on Criticism*:

> In prospects thus, some objects please our eyes,
> Which out of nature's common order rise,
> The shapeless rock, or hanging precipice.
> Great Wits sometimes may gloriously offend,
> And rise to faults true Critics dare not mend.
> —ll. 156–60

And with this we have, in fact, the second of the two main things which English criticism made of the Longinian sublime—a philosophy of untrammeled great "genius." Longinus himself, we may recall, had gone rather far in conferring upon such ideas as "perfection," "precision," and "regularity" a pejorative cast and in setting these against the idea of poetic genius. Addison in several of his *Spectators* was able to make the doctrine more precise and naive.

> At the same time that we allow a greater and more daring Genius to the Ancients, we must own that the greatest of them very much failed in, or, if you will, that they were very much above the Nicety and Correctness of the Moderns.—No. 160

> I must . . . observe with Longinus, that the Productions of a great Genius, with many Lapses and Inadvertencies, are infinitely preferable to the Works of an inferior kind of Author, which are scrupulously exact and conformable to all the Rules of correct Writing.—No. 291

> There is sometimes a greater Judgment shown in deviating from the Rules of Art, than in adhering to them; and . . . there is more Beauty in the Works of a great Genius who is ignorant of all the Rules of Art, than in the Works of a little Genius, who not only knows, but scrupulously observes them.
> —No. 592

Later in the century Reynolds was to report:

> So far, indeed, is the presence of genius from implying an absence of faults, that they are considered by many as its inseparable companions.[5]

[5] *Discourses Delivered to the Students of the Royal Academy*. The Eleventh Discourse, 1782, par. 2. Cf. *ante* Chapter 6, pp. 105–6; Chapter 11, p. 202, the similar theme of "imitative form."

This was the bizarre critical doctrine (according to which poetic form consists in imperfection) inherited with distaste by Macaulay in his review of Moore's *Byron,* and with an anachronistic gusto by Ruskin in the chapter of his *Stones of Venice* (II, 6) where the handwrought irregularity of Gothic architecture is praised in contrast to the machine-made "perfection" of modern glass beads. Macaulay's views are perhaps an adequate summation of the issue:

> Wherein especially does the poetry of our times differ from that of the last century? Ninety-nine persons out of a hundred would answer that the poetry of the last century was correct, but cold and mechanical, and that the poetry of our time, though wild and irregular, presented far more vivid images and excited the passions far more strongly than that of Parnell, of Addison, or of Pope. In the same manner we constantly hear it said that the poets of the age of Elizabeth had far more genius, but far less correctness, than those of the age of Anne. It seems to be taken for granted that there is some incompatibility, some antithesis, between correctness and creative power. We rather suspect that this notion arises merely from an abuse of words, and that it has been the parent of many of the fallacies which perplex the science of criticism.
>
> What is meant by correctness in poetry? If by correctness be meant the conforming to rules which have their foundation in truth and in the principles of human nature, then correctness is only another name for excellence. If by correctness be meant the conforming to rules purely arbitrary, correctness may be another name for dulness and absurdity.[6]

III

THE most quotable expression of the Longinian philosophy of original genius to appear in 18th-century England was the essay entitled *Conjectures upon Original Composition* published in 1759 by the aged poet of melancholy *Night Thoughts,* Edward Young.

> A *genius* differs from a *good understanding,* as a magician from a good architect; . . . Hence genius has ever been supposed to

[6] Alden, p. 346. Macaulay's bullseye appeared in the *Edinburgh Review* for June, 1831. Cf. A. W. Schlegel, *Lectures on Dramatic Literature* (1809–11), XXIII (Bate, p. 423): "If the formation of a work throughout, even in its minutest parts, in conformity with a leading idea; if the domination of one animating spirit over all the means of execution, deserves the name of correctness (and this, excepting in matters of grammar, is the only proper sense of the term); we shall then, after allowing to Shakespeare all the higher qualities which demand our admiration, be also compelled, in most cases, to concede to him the title of a correct poet."

partake of something divine. *Nemo unquam vir magnus fuit, sine aliquo afflatu divino.*[7]

While he adopts and magnifies the Longinian notion that true poetic imitation is the intercourse of the aspiring poet's mind with the master spirits of the past,[8] Young flatly rejects the doctrine that it is a good thing to study the classic models. His essay is a vigorous recommendation of the *cacoethes scribendi*, a sustained celebration of the "pleasures of the pen," the "sweet refuge" of original composition. "The more composition," he says, "the better." "How independent of the world is he, who can daily find new acquaintance . . . in the little world, the minute but fruitful creation, of his own mind?"[9] In bold strokes Young lays down the poetic criteria of chronological novelty and loyalty to the self's own productions—no matter what their quality.

> We read *Imitation* with somewhat of his languor, who listens to a twice-told tale: Our spirits rouze at an *Original;* and all throng to learn what news from a foreign land: . . . tho' it comes, like an *Indian* prince, adorned with feathers only, having little weight.[1]

The study of great models is not only *not* helpful but actually baneful, because:

> They *engross* our attention, and so prevent a due inspection of ourselves; they *prejudice* our judgment in favor of their abilities, and so lessen the sense of our own; and they intimidate us with this splendor of their renown.[2]

It is a paradoxical fact that the ancients themselves "had no merit in being *Originals*." In those days it was impossible to be otherwise. "They could *not* be *Imitators*."[3] Young is presumably here thinking back to the really first, but now altogether forgotten, ancients. The actually known ancients may very well be holding their honors only through our own ignorance.

> . . . they tho' not *real*, are *accidental Originals;* the works they imitated, few excepted, are lost.[4]

If we suppose Young's manifesto to be representative of a thickening climate of literary opinion, we shall not be surprised when, about twenty years later, that far more severe critical thinker, Samuel Johnson, lets fall the following *obiter dictum.*

[7] *Conjectures*, ed. Edith Morley (Manchester, 1918), p. 13. See Gilbert and Kuhn, p. 342, n. 45, on 20th-century studies of the *Geniebegriff*.

[8] Cf. Elizabeth Nitchie, "Longinus and the Theory of Poetic Imitation in Seventeenth and Eighteenth Century England," *SP*, XXXII (1915), 580–97.

[9] *Conjectures*, pp. 4–5.

[1] *Conjectures*, p. 7.

[2] *Conjectures*, p. 9.

[3] *Conjectures*, p. 10.

[4] *Conjectures*, p. 8.

'We must consider (said he) whether Homer was not the greatest poet, though Virgil may have produced the finest poem.
Virgil was indebted to Homer for the whole invention of the
structure of an epick poem, and for many of his beauties.' [5]

Dryden, in his elegantly blunt way, had once said of the Elizabethan
writers:

> Fame then was cheap, and the first comer sped;
> And they have kept it since, by being dead.

This gross mistake had at least the merit of proceeding on the assumption that literary worth was something that might suffer by comparison
with superior worth. On the new theory, of genius and originality, the
only way to be sure of having any worth (a kind of inescapable and
hence unmeritorious worth) was to be in on the threshold of literary
history, to get there first, even if with the least. For all improvements on
the beginning would inescapably suffer the handicap of not being first.
Thus literary creators were accorded in effect that variety of honor, in
most cases necessarily sentimental and archaic, which the world can afford
for its inventors—an Archimedes, a Fulton, a Watt, the brothers Wright
—athletes who died in good time, runners whom renown did not outrun. Why would not Homer's poems, on Edward Young's view, be
subject to the same discount in value as the first steamboat or the first
airplane if put into competition with the machines of 1950? Simply because of the peculiar fiat, the confusion in critical thinking between
poet and poem, by which during this period in critical history the first
became equivalent with the best.

IV

THE neo-Longinian great soul was never far from an attendant concept,
that of emotion. Yet emotion is a thing more externally manifest than the
secret inspiration of poetry, and it is better observed in the audience
than in the poet. In the neo-classic era, as in the ancient, emotion characteristically attaches itself to the audience; it is discussed under the head
of the results or aims of poetry. The affective side of ancient Longinianism, the emotion of the sublime, had been called "transport" (*ekstasis*).
The affective side of neo-Longinianism was "enthusiasm" or "passion,"
a kind of emotion raised by reason above pettiness to the grandeur of a

[5] Quoted by Boswell in *Life of Johnson*, 22 September, 1777.
Even Dryden had been guilty of this sort of thinking on the Homer-Virgil
question. See his Preface to *Fables*, 1700 (*Essays*, ed. Ker, II, 251–4). He furthermore
gave great credit to Chaucer for inventing the *Wife of Bath's Tale* and the *Nun's
Priest's Tale* (p. 255).

religious experience. "Vulgar Passion," according to John Dennis, is aroused by external "Objects;" "Enthusiastick emotion," by "Ideas in Contemplation." [6] This was a kind of thinking that later might easily be turned to the account of the wild genius of the poet himself. Yet in this earlier phase of neo-Longinianism the emphasis was not actually there. Dennis is a classically oriented critic; he holds the exalted and religious emotion up for some scrutiny and stresses its rational transcendence in a way that clearly concerns the semi-public realm of the collective reader's bosom.

In another place—in the diluted strain of Aristotelianism that continued during the later 17th and the 18th centuries—one finds a kind of affectivism appearing more clearly under a classic sanction. As far back as Dryden's heroic and French classical period—or even in the earlier Preface by Milton to his classical drama *Samson Agonistes*—we can detect a softer tone in the English account of catharsis than would be familiar to a person who had read only the documents of antiquity. Catharsis, we may remember, in the Aristotelian construction *tēn tōn toioutōn pathēmatōn katharsin*, referred in a very practical, downright and medical way to a supposed capacity of tragic drama to cleanse our minds of painful and unhealthy emotions. Yet through religious and lustratory metaphoric interpretation the notion was susceptible of being sublimed to mean something like a purifying and exalting of the emotions themselves. This interpretation seems to have appeared even during later antiquity, in neo-Platonic thought. But its hyper-development, to the eclipse of purgative Aristotelianism, was a modern accomplishment. The first step in a fairly plausible evolution was to say—as we may notice, for instance, the Dutch critic Daniel Heinsius saying, and later Milton—that purging the emotions meant tempering or moderating them, to a just proportion in our temperamental equilibrium. From there a later step would be the extreme already mentioned, the exaltation of pity and fear to the heights of unselfish contemplation, a zenith reached in the post-romantic 19th century. Or, by a kind of sidestep, the theory might arrive—and did even during the 17th century arrive—at the position of saying that the emotions of pity and fear aroused by tragedy were beneficent because they neutralized *other* and dangerous passions —such as anger, ambition, or greed.

These are plausible variations on the cathartic theme. Yet a great significance lies in the matter of *what* emotions "catharsis" is thought to moderate. The homeopathic moderation of pity and fear (like the Aristotelian purgation) is anti-emotional. In its 17th-century form it was

[6] John Dennis, *The Grounds of Criticism in Poetry*, 1704, in *Works*, ed. E. N. Hooker, I, 338–9. Cf. the excellent statement by Norman Maclean concerning Dennis and other writers in the same vein, e.g., Bishop Lowth in his *De Sacra Poesi Hebraeorum*, 1753 ("From Action to Image: Theories of the Lyric in the Eighteenth Century," in *Critics and Criticism Ancient and Modern*, ed. R. S. Crane, pp. 438–9).

neo-Stoic and allied to the sort of severe statement exemplified in Spinoza's *Ethics*, where passion is "Human Bondage."

> Pity, in a man who lives under the guidance of reason, is in itself bad. The good effect which follows, namely our endeavour to free the object of our pity from misery, is an action which we desire to do solely at the dictation of reason; only at the dictation of reason are we able to perform any action, which we know for certain to be good; thus, in a man who lives under the influence of reason, pity in itself is useless and bad.[7]

On the other hand, the allopathic theory that pity and fear moderate *other* less desirable passions was on the side of emotional development and would run quite naturally into 18th-century sentimentalism. By a partial suppression of Rapin's view in his *Réflexions sur la Poétique d'Aristote* (1674), Dryden in his Preface to *Troilus and Cressida* (1679) arrived at an early English statement:

> Rapin, a judicious critic, has observed from Aristotle, that pride and want of commiseration are the most predominant vices in mankind; therefore, to cure us of these two, the inventors of Tragedy have chosen to work upon two other passions, which are, fear and pity. . . . When we see that the most virtuous, as well as the greatest, are not exempt from [such] . . . misfortunes, that consideration moves pity in us, and insensibly works us to be helpful to, and tender over, the distressed; which is the noblest and most godlike of moral virtues.[8]

The triumphant progress of the argument may be illustrated at pleasure from the aestheticians and essayists of the next hundred years: from Dennis, for instance ("Tragedy . . . has been always found sufficient to soften the most obdurate Heart"); from Steele ("The contemplation of distresses . . . softens the mind, and makes the heart better. It extinguishes the seed of envy and ill will . . . corrects the pride of prosperity"); from Addison ("Diversions of this kind . . . soften insolence, sooth affliction, and subdue the mind to the dispensations of providence").[9] The casually axiomatic status of the doctrine, and a version of it which tries to include Stoic moderation, may be shown by quoting another of Samuel Johnson's off-the-cuff pronouncements:

[7] *Ethics, Chief Works*, trans. R. H. Elwes (London, 1887), II, 221, quoted by Baxter Hathaway, "John Dryden and the Function of Tragedy," *PMLA*, LVII (September, 1943), 668.

[8] Ker I, 210. Rapin had argued that the play not only increases sensibility in those who are deficient in it, but moderates it in those who have too much (Hathaway, p. 668).

[9] *The Critical Works of John Dennis*, ed. E. N. Hooker (Baltimore, 1939), I, 164; Steele, *Tatler* No. 82; Addison, *Spectator* No. 39. See Hathaway, pp. 666–7 for more complete quotations and further authorities.

'But how are the passions to be purged by terrour and pity?' (said I, with an assumed air of ignorance, to incite him to talk . . .). Johnson, 'Why, Sir, . . . The passions are the great movers of human actions; but they are mixed with such impurities, that it is necessary they should be purged or refined by means of terrour and pity. For instance, ambition is a noble passion; but by seeing upon the stage, that a man who is so excessively ambitious as to raise himself by injustice, is punished, we are terrified at the fatal consequences of such a passion. In the same manner a certain degree of resentment is necessary; but if we see that a man carries it too far, we pity the object of it, and are taught to moderate that passion.'[1]

V

SUCH reasonings pertained to the moral effects of tragedy and were aimed at an emotive moral justification. They could be more or less closely tied in with a more cognitive and a more aesthetic kind of argument which we have touched upon in an earlier chapter, the didactically aesthetic plea that our pleasure in witnessing the painful events of a tragedy arises from our use of the mind in learning, as well as our use of the will in approving, a moral pattern of actions and sanctions, a pattern of "poetic justice."[2] But the aesthetic justification of tragedy was on the whole more difficult than the moral. How can it be that the human mind actually takes pleasure in the contemplation of suffering, the evocation of painful emotions? Another classical answer was the mimetic:—that our pleasure in the imitation of a disagreeable or a painful object (a dunghill[3] or a murder) arises just from the skill of the imitation and the exercise of our minds in seeing the likeness. Both these types of explanation, the ethical and the simply mimetic, had been developed from hints in Aristotle by the Italian writers of the 16th century, were handed on by Corneille and other French writers of the 17th century, and during the 18th century in England were still more or less available.

Meanwhile, however, certain explanations of a different sort had originated in 17th-century psychology and had made some headway. One of these was a theory of safe feelings and self-congratulation on the part of the spectator as he realized the merely mimetic and playful character of the drama and his own detachment from the sufferings portrayed. "We consider tragedy at the same time as Dreadful and Harmless," said Addison.—"The Pleasure we receive [is] from the sense of our

---

[1] Boswell, *Life of Johnson*, April 12, 1776.
[2] See *ante* Chapter 11, pp. 204–6.
[3] Addison's example in *Spectator* No. 414; see *ante* Chapter 13, p. 255.

own safety." [4] "The movement of our melancholy passions is pleasant," said Edward Young, "when ourselves are safe: We love to be at once, miserable, and unhurt." [5] This had a root in the self-regarding philosophy of Hobbes and was an analogue to the idea of self-enhancement which appears in the Platonic and Hobbesian theory of laughter and to that increase of self-confidence and expansion of soul in the presence of the "sublime" described by Addison and Burke and later refined theologically in the "Dynamic sublime" of Kant.[6] The theory also had an antique source in a passage by Lucretius which was often quoted by the literary theorists.

> There is a pleasure in looking out over the great ocean when a storm rages across it and seeing some vessel in distress, not because we are glad that somebody else is suffering, but because we have our own feet safely on the shore. There is a pleasure in watching the struggle of armies upon a battlefield—so long as we ourselves are standing out of danger.[7]

But a second affective explanation of tragic pleasure which had arisen during the 17th century was a less clearly selfish one, and during an era so consciously goodhearted as the 18th century, this was bound to engulf the selfish Hobbesian. According to Descartes, sensory pain is something that presses inward on our vital spirits, but emotion is an outward motion, a form of responsory exercise and assertion, in itself pleasurable, healthy, and in general good (the opposite of lethargy)— so long as painful impressions are not so strong as to overwhelm us, and so long as our inner state of soul is positive and strong enough to launch the vigorous response.[8] The mimetic character of drama tended of course to accomplish the necessary softening of the painful impression; and the ethical nature of tragedy was friendly to the inner calm and strength. The Cartesian theory of the emotional workout had from the start the

---

[4] *Spectator* No. 418.

[5] *Conjectures*, ed. Morley, p. 41.

[6] Cf. *post* Chapter 17, p. 371, the Kantian sublime; and Chapter 25, psychological theories of laughter.

[7] *Suave, mari magno turbantibus aequora ventis,*
e terra magnum alterius spectare laborem;
non quia vexari quem quamst jucunda voluptas,
sed quibus ipse malis careas quia cernere suave est.
suave etiam belli certamina magna tueri
per campos instructa tua sine parte pericli.
Lucretius, *De rerum natura*, II, 1–6. Cf. Baxter Hathaway, "The Lucretian 'Return upon Ourselves' in Eighteenth-Century Theories of Tragedy," *PMLA*, LXII (September, 1947), 672–89.

[8] Earl R. Wasserman, "The Pleasures of Tragedy," *ELH*, XIV (December, 1947), 283–307. The present treatment of 18th-century tragic theory is substantially indebted to Professor Wasserman's essay, which may be consulted for copious illustration of nearly all the points made here. See also A. O. Aldridge, "The Pleasures of Pity," *ELH*, XVI (March, 1949), 76–87.

strongest affinity for the sentimental version of Aristotelian "catharsis" which we have already described. The latter was a theory of the moral function of tragedy; the former a theory of tragic pleasure; but they were natural complements. They may be seen, for instance, early in the 18th century, coming together in the words of Shaftesbury's *Inquiry Concerning Virtue or Merit:* ". . . the moving our passions in this mournful way, the engaging them in behalf of merit and worth, and the exerting whatever we have of social affection, and human sympathy, is of the highest delight." [9]

VI

Both in hard ethical theory and in literary art—in *The Theory of Moral Sentiments* by Adam Smith and in *A Sentimental Journey* by Laurence Sterne [1]—the finest thing in the world during the age of reason was "sympathy." For sympathy was not selfish, it was both Cartesian emotive self-development, and moreover it was ethical but not in a cold reflective sense; it was a spontaneous overflow of our best, our softest, warmest, most benevolent feelings, the loving and social impulses never so fully elicited as at the intuition of our fellow beings in distress. It was a good thing for us that they *were* in distress. It was good for us to go out of ourselves in this way, and to be aware of the fact. And it was pleasant. The pleasure of tragedy, said Lord Kames, arises from "an appetite after pain," "an inclination to render one's self miserable." [2] The pleasure of tragedy, said another Scotch theorist, Hugh Blair, is a "luxury of woe." [3] A young lady who had uttered a "Prayer for Indifference" was rebuked by the poet Cowper in the following definitive stanzas.

> 'Tis woven in the world's great plan,
> And fixed by Heaven's decree,
> That all the true delights of man
> Should spring from Sympathy.

. . .

[9] *Characteristics*, ed. J. M. Robertson (London, 1900), I, 297-8, quoted by Hathaway, p. 666. We may note also the theory of Hume (*Of Tragedy*, 1757): Any passion (even a contrary passion, provided it be not too strong) will strengthen another. The secret of tragic pleasure, therefore, is that our admiration for the mimetic art of the representation is buoyed and enhanced by the surge of more painful emotions—as flowery essences in a perfume, one might say, are embodied more effectively in musk. See Hume, *Essays and Treatises* (Edinburgh, 1804), I, 236. Cf. J. Frederick Doering, "Hume and the Theory of Tragedy," *PMLA*, LII (December, 1937), 1130-4. Cf. Burke, *Inquiry* (1757), I, xv.

[1] Kenneth MacLean, "Imagination and Sympathy: Sterne and Adam Smith," *JHI*, X (June, 1949), 399-410.

[2] *Essays on the Principles of Morality and Natural Religion* (Edinburgh, 1751), p. 14.

[3] *Lectures on Rhetoric and Belles Lettres* (Philadelphia, 1829), p. 515. The *Lectures* were first published in 1783.

'Tis Nature bids, and whilst the laws
Of Nature we retain,
Our self-approving bosom draws
A pleasure from its pain.

Thus grief itself has comforts dear
The sordid never know;
And ecstasy attends the tear
When virtue bids it flow.

For when it streams from that pure source
No bribes the heart can win,
To check, or alter from its course,
The luxury within.[4]

The earlier stages of sentimental theory had remained more or less compatible with classicism. But full-grown "sympathy" was strongly anti-classical. Sympathy allied readily with the neo-Longinian free genius soaring above the trammels of the rules, and hence sympathy worked against the Aristotelian conception of mimetic decorum. Sympathy pleaded persuasively for a kind of illusionistic naturalism. A really tragic happening, argued Burke,[5] for instance a public execution of a criminal, is more moving than the most horrible figment of the stage. And so sympathy worked also against the Aristotelian person of high estate and in favor of every-day life, the shopkeeper protagonist of bourgeois drama. At the same time, sympathy was too simple to accommodate the Aristotelian tension of pity and fear. The "mixture of good and odious qualities" in a protagonist, said yet another Scotch theorist, the rhetorician George Campbell, tears the mind "opposite ways at once, by passions which, instead of uniting, repel one another." Such a mixture is "shocking and disgustful." [6] The tragedy of sympathy was a tragedy of simple pity, without fear, a tragedy of "innocent misfortune," without moral, without "poetic justice." It was an illusionistic tearjerker, the Kotzebuian tragedy with which Coleridge was to be so much disgusted.[7] In the year of the *Lyrical Ballads*, a minor theorist achieved the following happy summary of both the genetic and affective sides of the sympathetic complex.

[4] *Addressed to Miss Macartney on Reading the Prayer for Indifference* (1762), ll. 45–60.

[5] *Inquiry* I, xv. The announcement that a great criminal was about to be executed in a neighboring square would immediately empty any theater in which even the most sublime of tragedies was being performed. Boswell will bear Burke witness.

[6] *The Philosophy of Rhetoric* (1776), I, 327.

[7] *Biographia Literaria*, ed. Shawcross, II, 159. It works on our "sluggish sympathies by a pathos not a whit more respectable than the maudlin tears of drunkenness."

An untutored genius, having strong conceptions, a heart that can enter into the feelings of a fellow heart, quick in catching the most striking features of distress, judgment to select a happy tale of virtuous suffering, and simplicity to follow nature in her plain walk, will in the fabrication of tragedy reach its highest excellence.[8]

VII

THE Man of Feeling and his "genealogy," [9] the sympathetic and tearful tendencies in the literature of the later 17th and the 18th centuries—especially in novels and in the kind of ethical comedy that replaced the immodest satire of manners—these constitute a phase of literary history which was both a record and a cause of a deep turn in the minds of our ancestors, towards an attitude which we today are likely to betray in some of our most spontaneous habits of speech—as when we say that we "feel" a thing to be so rather than "think" it, or when we speak of a "sensitive" rather than a "perceptive" person or mind. Feeling, sad feeling, melancholy musing, pensive meditation, were among the most pervasive strains of the 18th-century music and of the thinking about it. The classically generic term "pathetic" (meaning what arouses *any* kind of emotion) gradually assumed during this period the more special modern English meaning of the tenderly moving and pitiful. Not long after Pope's death it became possible to say that among the poems on which his reputation would principally depend was his early exercise in the "pathetic" mode *Eloisa to Abelard*.[1] Even so tough-minded a person as the philosopher David Hume knew Pope's *Elegy to the Memory of an Unfortunate Lady* by heart, and so did many others.[2] The pleasures of melancholy, the pleasures of pity, the pleasures of tragedy, the pleasures of the painful, the pleasures of the unpleasant—these, as we have been seeing, were the reiterated paradoxes of 18th-century aesthetic theory. And this is a matter of some general theoretical interest.

When emotion is attached to extremely simplified motives or when it is cut away from concrete motives altogether, it becomes emotion of great purity and intensity; it is likely to be dark rather than light, it is likely to be painful even if at the same time pleasurable. It is the "ro-

[8] George Walker, "On Tragedy and the Interest in Tragical Representations," *Memoirs of the Literary and Philosophical Society of Manchester*, V (1798), 332-3, quoted by Wasserman, p. 306.
[9] Cf. R. S. Crane, "Suggestions toward a Genealogy of 'The Man of Feeling,'" *ELH*, I (1934), 205-30.
[1] Joseph Warton, *An Essay on the Genius and Writings of Pope* (London, 1806), I, 330.
[2] Cf. Geoffrey Tillotson, ed. *The Rape of the Lock and Other Poems* (London 1940), p. 336.

mantic agony." Again, joy does not feed on joy, as melancholy feeds on melancholy. And melancholy, as a romantic inheritor of the tradition would write, may feed on both. "Ay, in the very temple of delight Veil'd Melancholy holds her sovran shrine." It is perhaps a truth of 20th-century psychology, perhaps only a truism, to say that melancholy tends to be automatic and morbid. Dark emotions drive toward purity.

On the other hand, cheer and wit go handily together. Cheer is sociable and extrovert: 18th-century theorists recognized this principle when they removed the "man of wit," the poet of social poetry, from the ranks of genius. Back in 1679 Dryden had said that "no man is at leisure to make sentences and similes, when his soul is in an agony." [3] And Dennis a little later had asserted that the production of similes was an exercise of the mind "utterly inconsistent" with intense grief.[4] Hume in his essay "Of Simplicity and Refinement in Writing" found wit and passion "entirely incompatible." [5] Johnson's classic objection to Milton's *Lycidas* was that it "is not to be regarded as the effusion of real passion; for passion runs not after remote allusions and obscure opinions." [6] The most sustained insistence on the theme occurs no doubt in the two volumes of Joseph Warton's *Essay on Pope* published, with so long an interval for meditation between them, in 1756 and 1782. In the Dedication of the first volume, to Edward Young, Warton not only divides real poets from mere "men of wit" and "mere versifiers," but with equal decision elevates a class of "sublime and pathetic" poets (Spenser, Shakespeare, Milton—"at proper intervals" Otway and Lee) above a second class of more moderately gifted ("ethical") poets (Dryden, for instance, Donne, Denham, Cowley, Congreve).[7] The main argument of Warton's *Essay*, culminating at the end of the second volume, is that Pope is "the great poet of Reason, the First of Ethical authors in verse." He has written "nothing in a strain so truly sublime, as the *Bard* of Gray." [8] In one of his most pointed passages, Warton asserts that "WIT and SATIRE are transitory and perishable, but NATURE and PASSION are eternal." [9] Pope, he asserts, "stuck to describing *modern manners;* but

---

[3] Preface to *Troilus and Cressida*, in *Essays*, ed. Ker, I, 223.

[4] Preface to *The Passion of Byblis*, 1692, in *Works*, ed. E. N. Hooker, I, 2, 424.

[5] *Essays Moral, Political, and Literary*, ed. T. H. Green and T. H. Grose (London, 1898), I, 242: "It is a certain rule, that wit and passion are entirely incompatible. When the affections are moved, there is no place for the imagination."

[6] Johnson, *Lives of the Poets*, ed. G. B. Hill, I, 163. Cf. J. H. Hagstrum, *Samuel Johnson's Literary Criticism* (Minneapolis, 1953), pp. 45–6.

[7] Otway, Lee, and Congreve were dropped from the listing in the edition of 1782, and Donne was demoted to a mere man of wit. Hoyt Trowbridge, "Joseph Warton's Classification of English Poets," *MLN*, LI (December, 1936), 515–18.

[8] *Essay on the Genius and Writings of Pope* (London, 1806), II, 403–5. In Warton's satire *Ranelagh House*, 1744, Pope in the Elysian fields is found not among the poets but among the philosophers.

[9] *Essay*, 1806, I, 330.

those *manners*, because they are *familiar, uniform, artificial,* and *polished,* are, in their very nature, unfit for any lofty effort of the Muse." [1]

VIII

IN OUR last chapter we have noticed that according to the philosophical view of Edmund Burke "beauty is, for the greater part, some quality in bodies acting mechanically upon the human mind by the intervention of the senses" (III, xii). "Beauty," he said, "acts by relaxing the solids of the whole system" (IV, xix). And the external symptoms of this relaxation were to be described with considerable precision.

> When we have before us such objects as excite love and complacency, the body is affected, so far as I could observe, much in the following manner: The head reclines something on one side, the eyelids are more closed than usual, and the eyes roll gently with an inclination to the object; the mouth is a little opened, and the breath drawn slowly, with now and then a low sigh; the whole body is composed, and the hands fall idly to the sides. All this is accompanied with an inward sense of melting and languor.—IV, xix [2]

In the fifth part of his *Philosophical Inquiry* Burke turns directly to the problem of verbal art and states the alternatives which lay before an age of anti-metaphysics. In effect: *Aut pictura poesis, aut passio.* He is mistrustful of the first alternative, the Addisonian, for he feels certain that words do not really excite very good pictures, neither words like "honour," "justice," "liberty," nor even words like "blue," "hot," "man," or "horse." So there is no other choice than *passio.*

> Poetry and rhetoric do not succeed in exact description, so well as painting does: their business is, to effect rather by sympathy than imitation; to display rather the effect of things on the mind of the speaker, or of others, than to present a clear idea of the things themselves.—V, v

Our "Passions are affected by words from whence" we "have no ideas." Our highest range of words, "compound" abstractions like "virtue," "liberty," "honour," are:

> in reality but mere sounds; but they are sounds, which being used on particular occasions, wherein we receive some good or suffer some evil . . . produce in the mind whenever they are afterwards mentioned, effects similar to those of their occasions.
>
> —V, ii

---

[1] *Essay,* 1806, II, 402.   [2] Cf. *ante* Chapter 13, p. 265.

We arrive thus at the idea that a poetry of emotion "cannot with strict propriety be called an art of imitation." As other writers of the time were putting it, poetry, along with music, is a kind of passionate "expression." [3] We arrive also at another idea, one which, along with "sensation" and "emotion," played a persuasive role in the new aesthetic thinking of the age. That is, "association." "Association," we may observe provisionally, was for the age of reason something which acted as a kind of intermediate justification of emotions—a form of mechanical operation softened and subtilized to shade off into what had once been conceived of as thinking.

IX

THE first main sense attached to the term "association of ideas" when it was launched by John Locke in the fourth edition of his Essay, 1700, was very much like that which the word now has for the ordinary user. It meant a connection between ideas which has occurred a number of times or some one memorable time, yet is not thought of, or should not be thought of, as always or necessarily occurring. A boy eats a surfeit of mince pie and gets sick. Twenty years later the man associates mince pie with a feeling of nausea. A man meets a girl several times at a certain restaurant, and after that he never goes there without thinking of her. She used a certain perfume; the smell of it later on will remind him of her. This way of connecting things seemed to Locke unsound in principle. He contrasted it to the way of thinking which seeks out the underlying and reliable connections between things—i.e., the laws of nature.

Locke himself, however, by his insistence on the phenomenal (rather than the real or substantial) character of much of our experience, did a great deal to develop the Hobbesian "train of ideas" toward the full doctrine of association announced by Hume in his *Treatise* of 1739 (the source of his later and more influential works) and by David Hartley in his *Observations on Man*, 1749. This kind of association was in effect an extension of the other until it covered the whole field of our knowledge; association was on this view not an accidental and occasional way of connecting things, but the basic principle of all connections—a "transcendental"—the principle by which our sensations, all of them, happen to occur in certain bundles and establish in our minds certain patterns of expectancy. I have a more or less casual and infirm association of a cer-

---

[3] See Wellek, *Rise*, pp. 51-2, citing James Harris *Three Treatises*, 1733; Charles Avison, *Essay on Musical Expression*, 1752; James Beattie, *Essays on Poetry and Music*, 1776; and Sir William Jones, "Essay on the Arts Commonly Called Imitative" (1772) in his *Poems Consisting Chiefly of Translations from the Asiatick Languages* (2d ed., London 1777), p. 207. Music and poetry are "expressive of the passions and operate on our mind by sympathy."

tain person with a certain place or a certain old hat, and only a somewhat firmer association of his head with his shoulders, of the sun with light and heat, of summer time with the ripening of fruit, and so on. The several Aristotelian principles of association—that is, likeness and difference, cause and effect, contiguity in space and time—with which Hume began his discussion (cf. *Treatise* I, i, iv.)—were at a stroke reduced by Hartley to a single mechanical principle of contiguity in time (either "synchronous" or "successive"). Hartley made that contiguity a character not of things as known by the human subject but of sensory vibrations and of their "miniature" reproductions (vibratiuncles) in the "medullary" substance of the brain. For each unit or simple item of experience, a vibration of a certain sort and a vestigial remainder of it. If several of these experiences happened to occur together often enough, the recurrence of a single one of the group stimulated from outside would set up a reminiscential jangle of the others.[4] Hume, by a subtler technique of introspection (without Hartley's externalizing clatter of mechanization), pushed the principle of mere association to its ultimate, reducing all real knowledge to unitary discrete phenomenal moments and thus exploding not only external substances and causes but the internal substance or self which we usually think of as the receptacle of knowledge or as the knowing agent. As his argument might be rephrased by a modern positivist: The Cartesian "cogito, ergo sum" takes too much for granted. "Descartes is only the name of a series of mental phenomena."

The new concepts of "association," the Humean and Hartleyan, in effect washed out the earlier Lockean kind of "association" by making it no different from any other connection between things. If fire and cooking, heart and blood, sunlight and leaves, are only associations,

---

[4] Hartley, *Observations*, 1749, Part I, Chapter I, Section ii, Propositions 9–10, pp. 58–66. The human body was viewed as "a kind of barrel-organ . . . set in motion by the external forces of the world" (Leslie Stephen, *English Thought in the Eighteenth Century*, 1927, II, 64). The physiological aspect of this theory of association is anticipated in Descartes' flow of "animal spirits" into traces in the brain—with wider and easier traces worn for pleasure than for pain. Cf. Addison, *Spectator* No. 417. As Coleridge would later point out, the physiological elaboration is irrelevant to the psychological and aesthetic problem. "The wise Stagyrite speaks of no successive particles propagating motion like billiard balls (as Hobbs); nor of nervous or animal spirits, where inanimate and irrational solids are thawed down, and distilled, or filtrated by ascension, into living and intelligent fluids, that etch and reetch engravings on the brain, (as followers of Des Cartes, and the humoral pathologists in general); nor of an oscillating ether which was to effect the same service for the nerves of the brain considered as solid fibres, as the animal spirits perform for them under the notion of hollow tubes (as Hartley teaches)—nor finally (with yet more recent dreamers) of chemical compositions by elective affinity, or of an electric light at once the immediate object and the ultimate organ of inward vision, which rises to the brain like an Aurora Borealis, and there disporting in various shapes (as the balance of plus and minus, or negative and positive, is destroyed or re-established) images out both past and present" (*Biographia Literaria*, Chapter V, ed. Shawcross, I, 71–2).

then association in the sense of a kind of accidentally pertinacious cohesion of ideas is no longer distinguishable. By the subsumption of a special into a more generic sense, a distinction has been levelled off; a certain flattening of experience and vocabulary has been at least attempted. The difficulty with the attempt is to some extent indicated by the fact that "association" as it survives in usual discourse today still has the sense of the Lockean coinage. We associate persons with places, but not their heads with their shoulders.

During the 18th century, however, "association" was in the air. It was a smart term in the vocabulary of moral and aesthetic theorists and litterateurs. It was a system of gently persuasive laws of connection between our ideas (analogous to Newton's more exact but equally pervasive physical laws) by which Hume hoped to advance moral philosophy to the stage where some century earlier physical science had moved ahead of it. A number of variations would be played on the two main senses we have defined, the sense of accidental connection, and the sense of the principle behind all connections. The history of association in 18th-century literary theory is a history of such variations and of several merging relations between the two radical senses.

X

In a quite simple form, for instance, Shakespearian criticism might invoke the phenomenon of superficial or accidental association to explain how faithfully the speech of certain characters—Dame Quickly or Juliet's nurse—imitates the incoherent reality of garrulous and rambling conversation, or of partially irrelevant retort. Association was thus subsumed under the principle of dramatic interpretation.

> Falstaff: What is the gross sum that I owe thee?
> Dame Quickly: Thyself and thy money too.[5]

A similar meaning of association—perhaps better exploited by creative writers than by theorists—might be synopsized as a thesis that the sequences of ideas which pass through our minds are not so rigorously determined by laws of logic or the structure of external nature as we

[5] Walter Jackson Bate, *From Classic to Romantic* (Cambridge, Mass., 1946), pp. 96, 105, 123, citing Lord Kames, *Elements of Criticism* (Edinburgh, 1762), and Alexander Gerard, *Essay on Genius* (1774). The present account of association is substantially indebted to Bate's chapter on the subject. See too Gordon McKenzie, *Critical Responsiveness* (Berkeley, 1949)—p. 139 concerns Falstaff's Hostess; Martin Kallich, "The Association of Ideas and Critical Theory: Hobbes, Locke, and Addison," *ELH*, XII (1945), 290–315; "The Associationist Criticism of Francis Hutcheson and David Hume," *SP*, XLIII (October, 1946), 644–67; and Walter J. Ong, "Psyche and the Geometers: Aspects of Associationist Critical Theory," *MP*, XLIX (August, 1951), 16–27.

might hope, but are nevertheless determined in ways that make curious sense and may be studied with profit. We may learn many unsuspected things about the human being and his world if we study his habits of "association." One of the most subtly sustained 18th-century illustrations of this principle is the pedantically talkative and humorous novel *Tristram Shandy*, in which the hero is not born until the third volume and disappears from the story after the sixth of the total nine. Various absurdities and accidents of his pre-nativity and early infancy are affectionately developed as critical or nearly critical events in the shaping of a character and career—the fact that his mother a few moments before he was conceived remembered to ask his father whether he had wound the clock, the bungle of a servant girl at his christening by which the name Tristram was made out of Trismegistus, the later carelessness of the same girl in holding the child under a window sash from which the leaden weights happened to have been removed to make toy cannon for his Uncle Toby. Sterne was whimsical. By a technique of apparently disordered and meandering fancy, he was concerned to build a comic contrast between associational causes and the more reliable patterns of deliberation and predictability which we usually suppose to hold our world together. He was thus antimetaphysical while escaping the embarrassment of being too seriously and scientifically associational.[6]

The 18th-century theorist, however, was on the whole working very seriously. He was less concerned with whimsy or with intuitive flashes of mind-reading than with the achievement of a grammarian's or a mechanist's reliable map of the whole of our thinking. One such application of associationism proceeded upon what in ancient times might have been called the principle of "synecdoche," or part for whole. The 18th century saw a growing theoretical concern—especially on the part of critics like Joseph Warton who relished nature description in poetry and on the part of certain Scottish rhetoricians—for the concrete particular, the kind of thing to be found in the drama of Shakespeare, or in the Bible, or in the seasonal paintings of Thomson, as distinguished from the supposed generalizations of Pope's ethical *Essays*.[7] The associational way of explaining the force of skilfully chosen particulars in description was to say that certain particulars were extremely potent in evoking a cloud of further particulars in the imagination of a reader. As Addison had put it in *Spectator* No. 417:

[6] Cf. D. W. Jefferson, "*Tristram Shandy* and the Tradition of Learned Wit," *Essays in Criticism*, I (July, 1951), 239, 244–5; Kenneth MacLean, *John Locke and English Literature of the Eighteenth Century* (New Haven, 1936); *Tristram Shandy*, ed. James A. Work (New York, 1940), Introduction, pp. xlix–li.

[7] See *ante* Chapter 13, p. 264, the relation of this interest to the parallel between poetry and painting, and *post* Chapter 15, p. 316, the conflict with the neoclassic universal.

. . . any single Circumstance of what we have formerly seen often raises up a whole Scene of Imagery, and awakens numberless Ideas that before slept in the Imagination; such a particular Smell or Colour is able to fill the Mind, on a sudden, with the Picture of the Fields or Gardens, where we first met with it, and to bring up into View all the Variety of Images that once attended it. Our Imagination takes the Hint, and leads us unexpectedly into Cities or Theatres, Plains or Meadows.

Happy powers of association! A striking complement to all this was the principle that the particular gets all of its significance or at least most of it from the other particulars that cluster around it in our memories (helping us to co-ordinate and interpret it),[8] and further that the significance of any particular for a given person will depend on the other particulars which that given person happens to associate with it. The name for this interpretation and valuing of particulars was "associational response." The fruits of an individual's past experience constitute his readiness or power of associational response.[9] And "objects stand in order when their situation corresponds with that of our ideas."[1]

At the same time a different emphasis (complementary to the subjective concept of "response") was possible, and toward the end of the century this began to emerge as one of the main lessons of associationism. By a kind of inversion of the synecdochal viewpoint, one might observe that, after all, association was a potent faculty for making combinations, for seeing objects, not thin and meager as they are rendered by abstraction, but in the whole richness of their concrete significance or of some particular significance they may have in a given situation. Association under this aspect might be a way of putting back together the world which had been fragmented into atoms or moments of discrete experience by the Humean *dis*sociation. It might be that we ought to set less store by reason and logic, our rationalist abstractive powers, and a great deal more by our entire mental and emotional workings, our total minds, even our instincts. These might give us a world of solid and extremely valuable reality. Under this aspect the name "association" gave way to the name "imagination." Imagination, said the common-sense moral philosopher Adam Ferguson, conceives a thing

with all its qualities and circumstances . . . in respect to all their relations of similitude, analogy, or opposition; whereas, in ab-

[8] Abraham Tucker, *The Light of Nature Pursued* (1768–1778), II, 18, observes that little children are uneasy when hungry but are not experienced enough to know what they want; they push the food away from them (Bate, *Classic to Romantic*, p. 111).

[9] Bate, *Classic to Romantic*, p. 112, citing Hume and also Priestley's Introduction to an edition of Hartley's *Theory of the Human Mind*, 1775.

[1] Bate, *Classic to Romantic*, p. 103, quoting Abraham Tucker.

stractions, we should consider subjects, or *parts* of subjects, in some *limited* point of view, to which our reasoning or thought in that instance is directed.[2]

A related emphasis was that on "coalescence," an aspect of the associative imagination which today we discuss under such names as "synthesis," "fusion," or "integration." Wordsworth and J. S. Mill would use the term "mental chemistry." The English associationist Abraham Tucker in his *Light of Nature Pursued*, 1768, was the first to stress the uniqueness of the object produced by the associational coalescence. Not an addition or juxtaposition of simple qualities in complex ideas, as in the Lockean epistemology, but a fusion into a special and irreducible whole—this is the process by which we know syllables composed of letters, words composed of syllables, and a lump of sugar as a white, sweet, hard, and angular somewhat.[3]

XI

But let us return to the theme of emotion and value—or of value explained by emotion—from which our account of association began and with which, if we are to be faithful to the subtlest and most persistent meaning of association for aesthetic theory, we ought to conclude. If our power of combining and of enjoying ideas was in any event a free, plastic, fluent, even whimsical power of "association," what might this power not be capable of when loosened and encouraged by the genial heat of emotion?

One fairly simple way in which association dealt with value was the attempt to explain our pain or pleasure in some things by shoving these things back on their associations with other things, which might or might not be more basic. Why do we consider such colors as bright blue and gold beautiful? Because, said the Scotch aesthetician Archibald Alison, we associate these with the clothes and furniture of the opulent, comfortable, and titled persons who wear blue coats with gold braid. And on the contrary the colors "of the Earth, of Stone, of Wood, etc. have no kind of Beauty, and are never mentioned as such. . . . The colours in the same manner, which distinguish the ordinary dress of the common people, are never considered as Beautiful." [4] Why do we enjoy

---

[2] *Principles of Moral and Political Science* (Edinburgh, 1792), I, 104, "Imagination"; cf. Dugald Stewart, *Elements of the Philosophy of the Human Mind* (Edinburgh, 1792), 477–8, "Of Imagination" (Bate, *Classic to Romantic*, pp. 113–17). Cf. Bate, "The Sympathetic Imagination in Eighteenth-Century English Criticism," *ELH*, XII (June, 1945), 144–64.

[3] Cf. Bate, *Classic to Romantic*, pp. 118–20.

[4] Archibald Alison, *Essay on The Nature and Principles of Taste*, 1790, quoted by J. H. Muirhead, *Coleridge as Philosopher* (New York, 1930), p. 196. For a helpful account of Alison, see Martin Kallich, "The Meaning of Archibald Alison's *Essays on Taste*," *PQ*, XXVII (October, 1948), 314–24.

ourselves when out for a day in the country? Because, explained a later essay by Hazlitt, we had a good time sporting in the country as children, and on returning to the country we still invest it with these pleasures by association.[5] As homesick poet, and even at moments as metaphysician, Coleridge would subscribe to the same view:

> I had found
> That grandest scenes have but imperfect charms
> Where the eye vainly wanders, nor beholds
> One spot with which the heart associates
> Holy remembrances of child or friend.
> —*Lines Written at Elbingerode in 1799*

This kind of value association had been invoked earlier in the 18th century, by Francis Hutcheson and others, to explain individual aberrations from the true standard of taste. The main 18th-century drift, however, was toward giving it the full sanction of theoretic approval.

The desires and interests of a human being, his *patterns* of response to the objects of his experience, one might easily enough reflect, have a great deal to do with determining the pattern of his associations so far as these may differ from what might be considered the stereotyped or merely normal, the logically or scientifically directed. It was just this thought which occurred with special force to Scottish "Common-Sense" theorists and others in the later 18th century. The aesthetic and ethic of feeling, the Shaftesburyan "moral sense," appeared as if specially designed to complete the doctrine of association and bring out happily all its implications. Emotions, or more broadly feelings, were precisely the norm by which association in ethics and in aesthetics could be distinguished from association in physical science.[6] Toward the end of the century and in the early nineteenth, the union was firmly and contentedly established—"as the rose blendeth its odor with the violet, —solution sweet."

Back in 1651 Hobbes had been of the opinion that "wit" is a "swift succession" of thoughts to "some approved end," and that the reason why some men are more quickwitted than others lies in "the difference of men's passions; that love and dislike, some one thing, some another" (*Leviathan*, I, viii). In 1774 Alexander Gerard's *Essay on Genius* makes the common-sensical observation that our passions tend to keep our minds running in certain directions. For instance, a man who is extremely angry about something

> can scarce avoid thinking of the person who has offended him, and of the injury he has done him, recollecting everything he

[5] *On the Love of the Country.*

[6] Associationism as an all-inclusive basis not only for psychology but for ethics was first formally proposed in 1731 by John Gay, the cousin of the poet (Bate, *Classic to Romantic*, p. 100). It was of course a part of Hartley's system.

can dishonourable to that person, . . . and in a word dwelling
on everything immediately relating to his anger.[7]

A passion, said Gerard, "preserves us from attending to foreign ideas,
which would confound our thoughts and retard our progress." Passion
promotes unity of thinking. And not only "passions" in the sense of
strong excitement but all the quieter kinds of feeling and interest. In his
Light of Nature Pursued Tucker meditates on how a person going to
market to buy oats for his horse meets a wagon on the way and is re-
minded, not of turnpikes, roads, or commerce, but of the fact that the
owner of the wagon is a farmer who might have some oats for sale more
cheaply than at the market.[8] Such is the magnet-like power of our
imagination when informed by a desire for some satisfaction.

　　These pronouncements of the philosophers went a long way, if
not all the way, in anticipating the things that both German philosophers
and the great English romantic poets were later on to say about emotion
in the high tide of their revulsion from the mechanistic phases of association theory. "Hartley's system totters," wrote Coleridge to Southey
in 1803. Why did Hartley's system totter? Because "association depends
in a much greater degree on the recurrence of resembling states of feeling than trains of ideas."

> I almost think that ideas never recall ideas, as far as they are
> ideas, any more than leaves in a forest create each other's mo-
> tion. The breeze it is runs thro' them—it is the soul or state of
> feeling.[9]

And this was not only a doctrine that concerned the emotions but one
which appealed *to* them. "A metaphysical solution [like Hartley's] that
does not instantly tell you something in the heart is grievously to be
suspected." The literary theory of both Coleridge and his friend Wordsworth, a theme to which we shall return in later chapters, is marked
by frequent and notable utterances about such topics as "predominant
passion" in poetry, the "union of deep feeling with profound thought,"
the "gift of spreading the tone," "emotion recollected in tranquillity." [1]
The bearing of this associationist victory for feeling and emotion on the
metaphysical point of reference, from which theory had been moving
so steadily away, may be handily consulted in an essay by Hazlitt on
"Wit and Humour," the introduction to his *English Comic Writers*

　　[7] Alexander Gerard, *Essay on Genius* (1774), p. 163; cf. Bate, *Classic to Romantic*, p. 124. Gerard's *Essay on Taste* first appeared in 1759.

　　[8] Abraham Tucker, *Light of Nature Pursued* (1768–1778), I, 246; cf. Bate, *Classic
to Romantic*, p. 126.

　　[9] Coleridge to Southey, August 7, 1803 (*Letters*, 1895, I, 428). Cf. Muirhead,
Coleridge as Philosopher, p. 199.

　　[1] *Biographia Literaria*, Chapters IV, XV; Preface to *Lyrical Ballads*.

of 1819. Hazlitt was a kind of Addisonian spokesman of the romantic age, a very knowledgeable educator who blurted out secret meanings in quite plain prose. As Addison had often been influenced by Locke, so Hazlitt in his theorizing about aesthetic principles was influenced by Abraham Tucker, whose *Light of Nature Pursued* he abridged and edited in 1807.[2] In his essay on "Wit and Humour" Hazlitt proposes that "wit principally aims at finding out something that seems the same, or amounts to a momentary deception where you least expected it, viz. in things totally opposite"—but that "imagination may be said to be the finding out something similar in things generally alike, or with like feelings attached to them."[3]

During the mid-19th century the prime role of emotion as a principle of association or of artistic unification is not so much a discovery or matter of argument as an assumption that may be reproclaimed with more or less éclat. The statements in J. S. Mill's *Autobiography* and in his two essays on poetry published in the year 1833 represent a memorable dramatization of the problem and of the sentimental associationalist resolution. As a young man Mill passed through the stages of the 18th-century association philosophy; he "entered the whirlpool."

> The very excellence of analysis (I argued) is that it tends to weaken and undermine whatever is the result of prejudice: that it enables us mentally to separate ideas which have only casually clung together; and no associations whatever could ultimately resist this dissolving force, were it not that we owe to analysis our clearest knowledge of the permanent sequences in nature; the real connexions between Things, not dependent on our will and feelings; . . . . Analytic habits may thus even strengthen the associations between causes and effects, means and ends, but tend altogether to weaken those which are, to speak familiarly, a *mere* matter of feeling.[4]

What then of poetry? Poetry is clearly not analysis and on the record of the past two hundred years or so seems not especially flattered by analysis. Mill's own view of analysis seems not likely to reverse the trend. By a kind of wilful flip-flop in his evaluation of one part of the analytic doctrine, he marks out the honors of poetry. "Whom, then," he asks in the second of his essays dealing precisely with the problem of poetry, "Whom, then, shall we call poets?" And he replies:

---

[2] John Bullitt, "Hazlitt and the Romantic Conception of the Imagination," *PQ*, XXIV (October, 1945), 351.

[3] *Lectures on the English Comic Writers* (Philadelphia, 1819), p. 38.

[4] *Autobiography* (New York, 1874), pp. 137–8, quoted by Walter J. Ong, "J. S. Mill's Pariah Poet," *PQ*, XXIX (July, 1950), 333–44.

Those who are so constituted, that emotions are the links of
association by which their ideas, both sensuous and spiritual,
are connected together.[5]

With these words Mill succeeded in reformulating briefly, to his own
satisfaction, a supposition which for about a hundred years had been
becoming more and more normal in critical thought, and which has
very largely continued until our own day to operate as a latent premise
in theoretical discussions of the value of poetry. It would be difficult to
find a person who has theorized to any extent about his literary pre-
ferences without at some time, under the stress of analytic objections,
having fallen back on the plea that some poem which he admires is not
constructed on a principle of logical unity, or of narrative unity, but
simply and sufficiently on one of emotional unity.[6]

SUPPLEMENT

It is likewise necessary for a Man who would form to himself a finished
Taste of good Writing, to be well versed in the Works of the best *Criticks*
both Ancient and Modern. I must confess that I could wish there were Authors of this kind, who beside the Mechanical Rules which a Man of very little
Taste may discourse upon, would enter into the very Spirit and Soul of fine
Writing, and shew us the several Sources of that Pleasure which rises in the
Mind upon the Perusal of a noble Work. Thus although in Poetry it be abso-
lutely necessary that the Unities of Time, Place and Action, with other Points
of the same Nature, should be thoroughly explained and understood; there
is still something more essential to the Art, something that elevates and aston-
ishes the Fancy, and gives a Greatness of Mind to the Reader, which few of
the Criticks besides *Longinus* have considered.

Our general Taste in *England* is for Epigram, Turns of Wit, and forced
Conceits, which have no manner of Influence, either for the bettering or enlarging the Mind of him who reads them, and have been carefully avoided by
the greatest Writers, both among the Ancients and Moderns. I have endeav-

[5] Mill's first essay on poetry, "What is Poetry?" appeared in the *Monthly Re-
pository* for January, 1833; his second essay, "The Two Kinds of Poetry," in the same
journal for October, 1833. He reprinted the two together, with slight revisions, as
"Thoughts on Poetry and Its Varieties," in his *Dissertations and Discussions: Political,
Philosophical, and Historical* (New York, 1874-82); see I, 106. And cf. Ong, *loc. cit.*,
pp. 334, 339. For some complications and qualifications in Mill's theory, see Alba
Warren, pp. 69-77.

[6] "Continuity of interest" is a less emotively committed term which psycholo-
gists in the positivist tradition have used to designate a principle of associative order
which to a large extent is taken for granted by the modern mind. G. F. Stout, *Manual
of Psychology*, 3d. ed, p. 558, quoted by Muirhead, *Coleridge as Philosopher*, p. 200.

oured in several of my Speculations to banish this *Gothic* Taste, which has taken possession among us. I entertained the Town, for a Week together, with an Essay upon Wit, in which I endeavoured to detect several of those false Kinds which have been admired in the different Ages of the World; and at the same time to shew wherein the Nature of true Wit consists. I afterwards gave an instance of the great Force which lyes in a natural Simplicity of Thought to affect the Mind of the Reader, from such vulgar Pieces as have little else besides this single Qualification to recommend them. I have likewise examined the Works of the greatest Poet which our Nation or perhaps any other has produced, and particularized most of those rational and manly Beauties which give a Value to that Divine Work. I shall next *Saturday* enter upon an Essay *on the Pleasures of the Imagination,* which, though it shall consider that Subject at large, will perhaps suggest to the Reader what it is that gives a Beauty to many Passages of the finest Writers both in Prose and Verse. As an Undertaking of this Nature is entirely new, I question not but it will be received with Candour.

—Joseph Addison, *Spectator* 409, June 19, 1712

The father of English poetry, like that of the Grecian, lived in a period little favourable to simplicity in poetry, and several meannesses occur throughout his works, which, in an age more refin'd, or more barbarous, he must have avoided. We see among the *worthie* acts of *Duke* Theseus,

> *How he took the nobil cite after,*
> *And brent the walls and tore down roof and rafter.*

And, among the horrid Images which crowd the temple of Mars,

> *The child stranglid in the cradil,*
> *The coke scaldid for alle his long ladil.*

That state of equipoise between horror and laughter, which the mind must here experience, may be rank'd among its most unpleasing sensations.

—J. Hookham Frere, in *The Microcosm* (Windsor, 1787), No. IX, January 29, 1787. The "microcosm" reflected in this periodical work was the world of Eton College. Frere was in his seventeenth year.

The *Association* of Ideas above hinted at, is one great Cause of the apparent Diversity of Fancys in the *Sense of Beauty,* as well as in the external Senses; and often makes Men have an aversion to Objects of *Beauty,* and a liking to others void of it, but under different Conceptions than those of *Beauty* and *Deformity.* And here it may not be improper to give some Instances of some of these Associations. The *Beauty* of *Trees,* their *cool Shades,* and their *Aptness* to conceal from Observation, have made *Groves* and *Woods* the usual Retreat to those who love *Solitude,* especially to the *Religious,* the *Pensive,* the *Melancholy,* and the *Amorous.* And do not we find that we have so join'd the Ideas of these Dispositions of Mind with those external Objects, that they always recur to us along with them. The Cunning of the *Heathen Priests* might make such obscure Places the Scene of the fictitious Appearances of their *Deitys;* and hence we join Ideas of something *Divine* to them. We know the like Effect in the Ideas of our Churches, from the perpetual use of them only in religious Exercises. The faint Light in Gothick Buildings has had the same Association of a very foreign Idea, which our Poet shews in his Epithet.

A Dim religious Light.

In like manner it is Known, "That often all the Circumstances of *Actions* or *Places,* or *Dresses* of Persons, or *Voice,* or *Song,* which have occur'd at any time together, when we were strongly affected by any Passion, will be so connected that any one of these will make all the rest recur." And this is often the occasion both of great Pleasure and Pain, Delight and Aversion to many Objects, which of themselves might have been perfectly indifferent to us: but these *Approbations,* or *Distastes* are remote from the Ideas of *Beauty,* being plainly different Ideas.

—Francis Hutcheson, *An Inquiry into the Original of Our Ideas of Beauty and Virtue* (London, 1725), pp. 76–77 (Sec. 6, par. 11)

In Collins' *Ode to Evening* we find a melancholy which at moments, as in the description of the bat, verges on disorder, and which at all times is far too profound to arise from an evening landscape alone. . . . Collins' bat is not mad nor a sufficient motive for madness, but it is used to express a state of mind irrelevant to him. It is as if a man should murder his mother, and then, to express his feelings, write an *Ode to Thunder.* Or rather, it is as if a man should murder his mother with no consciousness of the act, but with all of the consequent suffering, and should then so express himself. A symbol is used to embody a feeling neither relevant to the symbol nor relevant to anything else of which the poet is conscious: the poet expresses his feeling as best he is able without understanding it. . . . Shelley's *Ode to the West Wind,* and in a measure Keats' *Ode to the Nightingale,* are examples of the same procedure; namely, of expressing a feeling, not as among the traditional poets in terms of its motive, but in terms of something irrelevant or largely so, commonly landscape. No landscape, in itself, is an adequate motive for the feelings expressed in such poems as these; an appropriate landscape merely brings to mind certain feelings and is used as a symbol for their communication. The procedure can be defended on the grounds that the feeling may be universal and that the individual reader is at liberty to supply his own motive; but the procedure nevertheless does not make for so concentrated a poetry as the earlier method, and as an act of moral contemplation the poem is incomplete and may even be misleading and dangerous.

—Yvor Winters, *Primitivism and Decadence* (New York, 1937), pp. 36–7. Reprinted from *In Defense of Reason* (pp. 50–1) by Yvor Winters by permission of the publisher, Alan Swallow. Copyright 1937 and 1947 by Yvor Winters.

· · ·

LADY BLUEBOTTLE: Well, now we break up;
   But remember Miss Diddle invites us to sup.
INKEL: Then at two hours past midnight we all meet again,
   For the sciences, sandwiches, hock, and champagne!
TRACY: And the sweet lobster salad!
BOTH: I honour that meal;
   For 'tis then that our feelings most genuinely—feel.

—Lord Byron, *The Blues, Eclogue the Second*, ll. 154–9

CHAPTER 15

THE NEO-CLASSIC UNIVERSAL: SAMUEL JOHNSON

§ *enargeia, particularity, Longinus, Quintilian, Pope,
Spence, Joseph Warton on Thomson, Kames, George
Campbell—II.* ut pictura poesis *again, ideal form, Dryden's
Du Fresnoy,* Pope's Essay on Criticism, *neo-classic senses
of "nature," Lovejoy, the universal, Cartesian and Newtonian reason, authority of the ancients, "Nature methodized," literary genres, decorum, character types,* Peri
Bathous, *the social accent, the unnatural, outdoor nature,
Samuel Johnson and Fleet Street, Wordsworth—III. Johnson on species and grandeur:* Rasselas, Preface to Shakespeare, Life of Cowley, Rambler 36; *Sir Joshua Reynolds:*
Idlers, Discourses, *passage like Bacon; complexity and
inconsistency of Johnson's views—IV. Johnson on genius,
catharsis, the pathetic, the sublime, poetry and religion,
the beautiful, the vast and the general, Longinus* vs.
*Quintilian, Johnson's rationalism and empiricism, classical
and anti-classical details of his criticism: couplet verse,
dramatic structure, pastoral conventions, tragi-comedy,
unities, his affectivism, regard for the audience, distinction
between laws of nature and convention—V. Johnson on
plagiarism and models, on genius as general capacity,
scope of his writing, "the common voice of the multitude,"
specialized diction* vs. *general (synopsis of Renaissance
theory and Augustan), Johnson on particular detail, personal morality and introspection* vs. *social philosophy and
history, the life-and-letters method, uniformity of the
state of man, truth of fact, distrust of "imagination," scepticism about "representative" verse—VI. nine meanings
of the "universal"—VII. classic and neo-classic preoccupation with* art *and* nature: *anthology of short passages* §

VIVIDNESS (ENARGEIA) APPEARS IN CLASSICAL TREATISES AS A QUASI-cognitive figure, a rhetorical merit which tends to be definable best in terms of the imaginative excitement which it is said to induce in an audience. In the treatise of Longinus, the conception is treated under the head of images (*phantasiai*).

> At the present day the word [*phantasia*] is predominantly used in cases where, carried away by enthusiasm and passion, you think you see what you describe, and you place it before the eyes of your hearers.—XV

Aristotle (*Rhetoric*, III, xi) had suggested that vividness is likely to appear along with such more definable figures as metaphor, antithesis, and parallel. The most extended classical attempt to give the figure a cognitive basis is that of Quintilian in Book VIII, Chapter 3 of his *Institute*, where he dwells on the merit of multiplying descriptive particulars.

> The mere statement that the town was stormed, while no doubt it embraces all that such a calamity involves, has all the curtness of a dispatch, and fails to penetrate to the emotions of the hearer. But if we expand all that the one word "stormed" includes, we shall see the flames pouring from house and temple, and hear the crash of falling roofs and one confused clamour blent of many cries; we shall behold some in doubt whither to fly, others clinging to their nearest and dearest in one last embrace, while the wailing of women and children and the laments of old men that the cruelty of fate should have spared them to see that day will strike upon our ears. Then will come the pillage of treasure sacred and profane, the hurrying to and fro of the plunderers as they carry off their booty or return to seek for more, the prisoners driven each before his own inhuman captor, the mother struggling to keep her child, and the victors fighting over the richest of the spoil.[1]

Such testimonies were to be quite convenient to English theory of the 18th century. Alexander Pope, citing Longinus in a footnote to his translation of the *Iliad*, pointed out that Homer deals not only in the "great and noble" but in the minutely observed detail.[2] Pope's friend Spence, in an *Essay on Pope's Odyssey* (1726–1727), invoked the state-

[1] Reprinted by permission of the publishers from Quintilian, *Institutio Oratoria*, III, 249, translated by H. E. Butler, Loeb Classical Library, Cambridge, Mass.: Harvard University Press, 1943.

[2] George Sherburn, "The *Dunciad*, Book IV," in *Studies in English . . . The University of Texas, 1944* (Austin, 1945), p. 184, quoting Pope's note to *Iliad* VI, 595.

ment by Quintilian as a classical sanction for the same thing.[3] And so too did Joseph Warton in his *Essay on the Genius and Writings of Pope*,[4] though here the general argument was at the expense of Pope's *Pastorals* and in favor of the more minutely descriptive poetry of Thomson's *Seasons*.

> Thomson was blessed with a strong and copious fancy; he hath enriched poetry with a variety of new and original images, which he painted from nature itself, and from his own actual observations: his descriptions have, therefore, a distinctness and truth, which are utterly wanting to those poets who have only copied from each other, and have never looked abroad on the objects themselves. . . . Innumerable are the little circumstances in his descriptions, totally unobserved by all his predecessors.—I, 40–2

> The judicious addition of circumstances and adjuncts is what renders poesy a more lively imitation of nature than prose.
> —I, 11

> A minute and particular enumeration of circumstances judiciously selected, is what chiefly discriminates poetry from history, and renders the former, for that reason, a more close and faithful representation of nature than the latter.—I, 47

Warton thought that contemporary literature showed many symptoms of "departing from these *true* and lively and *minute* representations of Nature, and of *dwelling in generalities.*" [5]

The doctrine of particularity became something like a rhetorical standard during the latter half of the 18th century, especially in the work of Scottish rhetoricians and associational aestheticians. Thus Lord Kames in his *Elements of Criticism:*

> . . . avoid as much as possible abstract and general terms. . . . images, which are the life of poetry, cannot be raised in any perfection but by introducing particular objects.[6]

And George Campbell in his *Philosophy of Rhetoric* (1776):

> . . . the more general any name is as it comprehends the more individuals under it, and consequently requires the more ex-

---

[3] *An Essay on Pope's Odyssey*, Part II (Oxford, 1727), "Evening the Fourth," p. 122. "There is a *Poetical Falsity*, if a strong Idea of each particular be not imprinted on the Mind; and an *Historical*, if some things are passed over only with a general mark of Infamy or Dislike. It was in *Quintilian* I first met with this Observation. . . ."

[4] Edition of 1806, II, 168.

[5] II, 168.

[6] *Elements of Criticism*, 2d. ed. (Edinburgh, 1763), I, 307, Ch. 4.

tensive knowledge in the mind that would rightly apprehend it, the more it must have of indistinctness and obscurity.[7]

> Nothing can contribute more to enliven the expression, than that all the words employed be as particular and determinate in their signification, as will suit with the nature and the scope of the discourse. The more general the terms are, the picture is the fainter; the more special they are, it is the brighter.[8]

The rule of thumb concerning particular descriptive writing is so well established in the textbook code of our own century in America and England that it scarcely needs illustration for anybody who has ever been either a pupil or a teacher in a high school or college freshman course in composition. The descent of the rule from the 18th century through such 19th-century rhetoricians as Archbishop Whately and the Scottish logician and moralist Alexander Bain is not a part of the story which this book aspires to tell.

Particularity was part of an 18th-century reaction against the neo-Platonic classical tradition. The aim of our chapter is to describe the terminus and the last enfeebled exaggeration of that theoretically anti-particularist tradition.

II

ONE feature of the doctrine of ideal form was its great readiness to embrace both the arts of language and those of picturing. This was part of the parallelism *ut pictura poesis* and illustrated most of the general weaknesses of the parallel. There is scarcely any general theory of literary value (unless the opposite theory of particularization) which will translate so easily into painters' terms. The climax of the tradition and its grandest claim appeared, as we shall see, in the shoulder-to-shoulder pronouncements of the giant litterateur Samuel Johnson and his friend the portrait painter Sir Joshua Reynolds. One of the earliest strong statements in English was that by Dryden in the Preface to his translation (1695) of the French painter Du Fresnoy's *Art of Painting*. In part Dryden quoted from the Italian neo-Platonist Bellori.

> Nature always intends a consummate beauty in her productions, yet through the inequality of the Matter, the Forms are altered.

[7] *Philosophy of Rhetoric*, 2d. ed. (London, 1801), II, 103, Bk. II, Ch. 7.
[8] II, 136. Cf. Scott Elledge, "The Background and Development in English Criticism of the Theories of Generality and Particularity," *PMLA*, LXII (March, 1947), esp. 176–81; and Houghton W. Taylor, "Particular Character": an Early Phase of a Literary Evolution," *PMLA*, LX (March, 1945), 161–74.

. . . For which Reason, the artful Painter, and the Sculptor, imitating the Divine Maker, form to themselves, as well as they are able, a Model of the Superior Beauties.[9]

Pope in his *Essay on Criticism* stated the thesis in the literary context:

> Unerring Nature, still divinely bright,
> One clear, unchang'd, and universal light,
> Life, force, and beauty, must to all impart,
> At once the source, and end, and test of Art.
>
> —I, 68–73
>
> In some fair body thus th' informing soul
> With spirit feeds, with vigour fills the whole.
>
> —I, 76–7

One ingratiating feature of this doctrine of the universal-ideal as found in Dryden and Pope, a derivative amalgam of Platonic, Aristotelian and Roman Stoic ideas, was its accommodating vagueness. Recent students of the history of ideas, in a somewhat overanalytic enthusiasm, have found themsleves able to distinguish an indeterminate number of senses or "uses" of the term "nature" as it appears during the neo-classic age in English and continental writers. Yet the senses thus distinguished are not all strictly co-ordinate. They are not on the same footing and do not actually make the problem as unmanageable as one might fear. In Professor Lovejoy's early article on the subject, "Nature as Aesthetic Norm" (1927),[1] some of the 37 senses which he distinguished refer to the external world of nature, some to the artistic imitation, some to the artist's genius, some to the responses of the audience. Of those which refer to the external world, some refer to separate objects in that world, some to rules or principles, and some to the whole world order, the total embodiment of the principles. We have in short a set of complementary and analogical senses intrinsic to the subject-object relation of human knowledge and to the process of abstracting principles from concreteness. The main neo-classic emphasis was on the idea that there is a world order, both as a total embodiment,[2] as a set of principles, and as a realm of more or less knowable and predictable objects of various classes. Among these classes of objects the most important for

---

[9] *Art of Painting* (London, 1795), p. v. Cf. L. I. Bredvold, "The Tendency toward Platonism in Neo-Classical Esthetics," *ELH*, I (September, 1934), 91–119.

[1] A. O. Lovejoy, "Nature as Aesthetic Norm," *MLN*, XLII (November, 1927), 444–50. The same writer in "The Parallelism of Deism and Classicism," *MP*, XXIX (February, 1932), 283 ff., refers to 60 odd senses or uses; and Harold S. Wilson, "Some Meanings of 'Nature' in Renaissance Literary Theory," *JHI*, II (1941), 430–48, refers to 35.

[2] The plenitude, continuity, and gradations of the Great Chain of Being, as A. O. Lovejoy points out, constituted a system rife with implications of fecundity, variation, and romantic diversification.

the artist's study were human beings themselves, in their several sub-classes, and in their institutions and productions. Lovejoy's sense I. E 17, "the universal and immutable in thought, feeling, and taste," is referred by him to the artist's public, but it referred equally and reflexively in the Augustan mind to the most important objects of the artist's imitation.

As the classical idea of nature worked its way out in the aesthetic speculations of Pope and his contemporaries, it took on certain highly significant local colorations. For one thing, the idea of the uniformity and universality of nature appeared now strongly re-enforced by Cartesian and geometric standards of clear reason, and by Newtonian concepts of a mechanically ordered universe.

We have alluded in an earlier chapter to the geometric spirit which flourished among French critics. At the same time, the most agile literary men of the age were able to reconcile this new scientism and modern spirit of "reason" with the older principle of authority or reverence for the ancient models. The literary rules were said not to supplant, but to methodize nature. And as the central concept was that of a universal truth, the reconciliation of reasonable rules and ancient authorities was not in fact so difficult. What is permanent is bound to have been known to the ancients, and vice versa. "These rules of old discovered, not devised, Are Nature still, but Nature methodized."

> When first young Maro in his boundless mind
> A work t' outlast immortal Rome design'd,
> Perhaps he seem'd above the Critic's law,
> And but from Nature's fountains scorn'd to draw:
> But when t' examine ev'ry part he came,
> Nature and Homer were, he found, the same.
> —*Essay on Criticism*, I, 130–5

As once long before, in the age of Cicero and Horace, so now again the idea of the universal made its practical literary appearance in close association with the implemental ideas of literary genre and of decorum for various kinds of detail, notably for character-drawing. Pope's theoretical assumptions about character types, for instance, are clearly seen in the irony of the following passage from his *Peri Bathous*, a recital upside-down of a classical code which includes not only Longinian but Horatian and Aristotelian clauses.

> Since the great Art of all Poetry is to mix Truth with Fiction, in order to join the *Credible* with the *Surprising*; our author shall produce the Credible, by painting nature in her lowest simplicity; the Surprising, by contradicting common opinion. In the very Manners he will affect the *Marvelous*; he will draw

Achilles with the patience of Job; a Prince talking like a
Jack-pudding; a Maid of honour selling bargains; a footman
speaking like a philosopher; and a fine gentleman like a
scholar. . . .

Nothing seemed more plain to our great authors, than that
the world had long been weary of *natural things.*—Ch. V

We have already suggested that the Augustan concept of "nature"
had a strongly social cast. It was a nature of man's creations, his civilization, cities, estates, temples, palaces, drawing rooms, boudoirs, theaters,
debates, conversations, and literature. It included, but it was not centered in, the kind of "nature" which nowadays we mostly mean by the
term "nature" and which we experience chiefly on picnics—the Rous-
seauistic and Wordsworthian nature of the outdoors and of the unspoiled,
spontaneous and primitive man who might be supposed to inhabit
the outdoors. The *un*natural for Pope was a deviation from a norm;
for romantic naturalists the unnatural would actually be the restraint imposed by a norm [3] (a meaning, incidentally, that grew plausibly enough
out of the 17th-century trend in favor of reason, "good sense" (*le bon
sens*), or "common sense," as opposed to mere authority).[4] One fled
from authority to the outdoors. It is not difficult to illustrate the antithesis, especially in its indoor-outdoor, city-country, aspect, from statements
by the leading English men of letters. It is standard procedure to quote
Samuel Johnson's preference for the vista of Fleet Street over any
rural landscape or his meditation at Anoch in the Western Islands:

> I sat down on a bank, such as any writer of romance might have
> delighted to feign. I had indeed no trees to whisper over my
> head, but a clear rivulet streamed at my feet. The day was
> calm, the air soft, and all was rudeness, silence, and solitude.
> Before me, and on either side, were high hills, which, by hinder-
> ing the eye from ranging, forced the mind to find entertainment
> for itself.

And by contrast, Wordsworth's avowal: "One impulse from a vernal
wood May teach you more of man, Of moral evil and of good, Than all
the sages can." Or Byron's "High mountains are a feeling, but the hum
Of human cities torture." It is a fairly easy matter to connect this shift
in appreciation with the neo-Longinian vast and irregular, and with the

---

[3] This romantic idea is of course to be found in Pope too. "The great secret
how to write well, is to know thoroughly what one writes about, and not to be
affected . . . to write naturally." "Arts are taken from nature; and after a thousand
vain efforts for improvements are best when they return to their first simplicity."
Joseph Spence, *Anecdotes,* ed. S. W. Singer (London, 1820), pp. 11–12, 291.

[4] Cf. Austin Warren, *Alexander Pope as Critic and Humanist* (Princeton,
1929), pp. 17–18.

taste in painting, in landscape gardening, and in loco-descriptive poetry which we have earlier noted.

III

BUT our present theme is rather the natural as the universal. And here the critics of the last classical generation, the Johnsonian, offer us a definition that has both the advantage for the historian and the disadvantage to itself of being somewhat over-formally drawn. Three of Samuel Johnson's least escapable statements on the theme are the often-quoted tulip passage in the discourse of the philosopher Imlac in *Rasselas* (1759), that on character in his *Preface to Shakespeare* (1765), and that on metaphysical wit in his *Life of Cowley* (1781).

> The business of the poet . . . is to examine, not the individual, but the species; to remark general properties and large appearances; he does not number the streaks of the tulip, or describe the different shades in the verdure of the forest. He is to exhibit in his portraits of nature such prominent and striking features, as recall the original to every mind; and must neglect the minuter discriminations, which one may have remarked, and another have neglected, for those characteristics which are alike obvious to vigilance and carelessness. . . . He must divest himself of the prejudices of his age or country; he must consider right and wrong in their abstracted and invariable state; he must disregard present laws and opinions, and rise to general and transcendental truths, which will always be the same.—*Rasselas*, Ch. X

> [Shakespeare's] characters are not modified by the customs of particular places, unpractised by the rest of the world; by the peculiarities of studies or professions, which can operate but upon small numbers; or by the accidents of transient fashions or temporary opinions: they are the genuine progeny of common humanity, such as the world will always supply, and observation will always find. His persons act and speak by the influence of those general passions and principles by which all minds are agitated, and the whole system of life is continued in motion. In the writings of other poets a character is too often an individual; in those of Shakespeare it is commonly a species.
> *Preface to Shakespeare* [5]

Great thoughts are always general, and consist in positions not

[5] Cf. Fielding's statement about his own comic characters the lawyer and Mrs. Slipslop, in *Joseph Andrews*, Part III, chapter 1.

limited by exceptions, and in descriptions not descending to minuteness.

> The fault of Cowley, and perhaps of all the writers of the metaphysical race, is that of pursuing his thoughts to their last ramifications, by which he loses the grandeur of generality; . . . all the power of description is destroyed by a scrupulous enumeration.—*Life of Cowley*, paragraphs 58, 133 [6]

Let us add to this gallery some of the statements made by Johnson's friend and pupil in aesthetic discourse, Sir Joshua Reynolds. First some samples from three essays which he contributed to Johnson's periodical series of 1759, *The Idler*.

> The *Italian* attends only to the invariable, the great and general ideas which are fixed and inherent in universal nature; the *Dutch*, on the contrary, to literal truth and a minute exactness of detail, as I may say, of nature modified by accident. The attention to these petty peculiarities is the very cause of this naturalness so much admired in the *Dutch* pictures, which, if we suppose it to be a beauty, is certainly of a lower order.—No. 79

> In consequence of having seen many [individuals of the same species] the power is acquired . . . of distinguishing between accidental blemishes and excrescences which are continually varying the surface of nature's works, and the invariable general form which nature most frequently produces, and always seems to intend in her productions. . . . Every species of the animal as well as the vegetable creation may be said to have a fixed or determinate form towards which nature is continually inclining . . . . perfect beauty is oftener produced by nature than deformity; I do not mean than deformity in general, but than any one kind of deformity.—No. 82

Then from his annual *Discourses* (1769–1790) as President of the Royal Academy, these rules for the serious painter:

[6] *Rambler* No. 36 includes in the following succinct statement the two important words "species" and "grandeur." "Poetry cannot dwell upon the minuter distinctions, by which one species differs from another, without departing from that simplicity of grandeur which fills the imagination; nor dissect the latent qualities of things, without losing its general power of gratifying every mind by recalling its conceptions." In his last *Rambler*, Johnson states what he believes to be the relation of the theory to his own practice as a prose essayist. "I have never complied with temporary curiosity, nor enabled my readers to discuss the topick of the day; I have rarely exemplified my assertions by living characters; in my papers, no man could look for censures of his enemies, or praises of himself; and they only were expected to peruse them, whose passions left them leisure for abstracted truth, and whom virtue could please by its naked dignity."

The sentences quoted above from the *Life of Cowley* are closely associated in their context with a neo-Longinian notion of the sublimely vast. Cf. *post*, p. 324.

He will leave the meaner Artist servilely to suppose that those are the best pictures which are most likely to deceive the spectator. He will permit the lower painter, like the florist or collector of shells, to exhibit the minute discriminations, which distinguish one object of the same species from another; while he, like the philosopher, will consider Nature in the abstract, and represent in every one of his figures the character of its species.

—*Discourse* III [7]

In the same manner as the historical Painter never enters into the detail of colours, so neither does he debase his conceptions with minute attention to the discriminations of drapery. It is the inferior style that marks the variety of stuffs. With him the clothing is neither woollen, nor linen, nor silk, satin, or velvet; it is drapery; it is nothing more.—*Discourse* IV

It is of course possible to show that both Johnson and Reynolds uttered a variety of other critical statements and even at times contradicted or came close to contradicting the emphatic rule of the universal. Thus in one of his latest *Discourses*, Reynolds, having apparently read Bacon's well-turned compliment to the poetic imagination in the *Proficience and Advancement of Learning*,[8] introduces the following variation upon his own basic distinction between naturalistic detail and the grandeur of generality.

Apply to that reason only which informs us not what imitation is—a natural representation of a given object—but what it is natural for the imagination to be delighted with.

It is allowed on all hands, that facts and events, however they may bind the historian, have no dominion over the poet or the painter. With us, history is made to bend and conform to this

[7] A person concerned to drive home the difficulties involved in taking the species as aesthetic norm could do no better than quote certain other passages of this *Discourse*. "In the human figure . . . the beauty of the Hercules is one [beauty], of the Gladiator another, of the Apollo another; which makes so many different ideas of beauty. It is true, indeed, that these figures are each perfect in their kind, though of different characters and proportions; but still none of them is the representation of an individual but of a class." "I should be sorry, if what is here recommended should be at all understood to countenance a careless or undetermined manner of painting. For though the painter is to overlook the accidental discriminations of Nature, he is to exhibit distinctly, and with precision, the general forms of things."

The marginalia which about 1808 William Blake wrote in a copy of Reynolds' *Discourses* include the following pungent comments: "Real effect is making out of Parts, and it is Nothing Else but that." "Sacrifice the Parts: What becomes of the whole?" "Minute Discrimination is not accidental. All Sublimity is founded on Minute Discrimination." "Distinct General Form cannot exist. Distinctness is Particular, Not General." "To Generalize is to be an Idiot." "This Man was Hired to Depress Art."

[8] See *ante* Chapter 9, p. 171.

great idea of art. And why? Because these arts, in their highest province, are not addressed to the gross senses; but to the desires of the mind, to that spark of divinity which we have within, impatient of being circumscribed and pent up by the world which is about us.—*Discourse* XIII

As for Samuel Johnson, he is the Great Cham of 18th-century English literary criticism, a mammoth personality who was more capacious than any abstract dimension of critical theory. We surround him here with the atmosphere of the classic universal because his championship of that view is a late climax in its history and appears to be his distinctive contribution to 18th-century English criticism. As a late classical giant, however, he is even more interesting for the complexity and sometimes inconsistent detail of his views. Near the close of our discussion of neoclassicism, it will be appropriate to dwell for a few pages on this curiously rounded, or squared out, figure.

IV

JOHNSON participated heavily in the rationalistic and psychological trends which we have described in our last chapter. We have already seen, for example, his acquiescence in the doctrine of genius and originality. (If Homer did not write as good a poem as Virgil, he was yet a better poet, because he came first.) [9] We have seen his off-the-cuff sentimental answer to the ancient question about catharsis. He thought of Shakespeare as a pathetic, tender, and domestic poet, and his devotion to the pathetic differed from the prevailing attitude of his age mainly in that he refused to merge the pathetic with that other emotive keynote, the sublime. Johnson's surrender to the sublime itself was limited by his shrewd and orthodox realization that it was in effect a new form of religion—rhapsodic and worshipful of outdoor nature. He lived at a time when in fact it was impossible for poetry and religion to come together without the dilution of one or the other. His response was an attitude of contempt for the services of poetry in the cause of religion. "Devotional poetry" was simply "unsatisfactory."

> The paucity of its topics enforces perpetual repetition, and the sanctity of the matter rejects the ornaments of figurative diction. It is sufficient for Watts to have done better than others what no man has done well.

"The good and evil of Eternity," he said, summing up the limitations of *Paradise Lost*, "are too ponderous for the wings of wit."

Yet Johnson was at one with his age in recognizing the sublime as a

[9] Cf. *Rambler* No. 121, on the evils of imitating.

category distinct from the beautiful. (The beautiful for Johnson was something close to the rhetorically elegant. Milton was sublime, Pope beautiful.) [1] The sublime plays a pronounced, if somewhat disguised, role in Johnson's thought as an adjunct or ambiguous equivalent of the universal. The grandeur of generality is something inclusive, not only in the sense of being universally valid or true, but in that of being big, reaching out and taking in all. Thus, in his remarks on the metaphysical poets:

> Nor was the sublime within their reach . . . ; for they never attempted that comprehension and expanse of thought which at once fills the whole mind, and of which the first effect is sudden astonishment, and the second rational admiration. Sublimity is produced by aggregation, and littleness by dispersion. Great thoughts are always general.[2]

The ancestry of this alliance between the vast and the general becomes clearer if we revert now to a difference between the two ancient critics Quintilian and Longinus on the rhetorical merit of vividness (*enargeia*). Both believe in it. But whereas Quintilian, as we have seen, recommends in its support the meticulous description, Longinus notes the danger of falling into meanness.

> When Theopompus had dressed out in marvelous fashion the descent of the Persian king upon Egypt, he spoilt the whole by some petty words. . . . With his wonderful description of the whole outfit he mixes bags and condiments and sacks, and conveys the impression of a confectioner's shop. . . . He might have described the scene in broad outline . . . and with regard to the preparations generally have spoken of 'waggons and camels and the multitude of beasts of burden carrying everything that ministers to the luxury and enjoyment of the table.'—XLIII

We have observed that the classicism of the later 17th and the 18th centuries was supported by strains of scientific rationalism which in the end undercut the authoritarian element in classicism and placed new and disastrously heavy stresses upon its claims to being reasonable. Johnson was a resolutely reasonable classicist—not in the *a priori* mood of the French *géomètres* but with the experimental resolution of the English Baconians. The amateur empiricism which Johnson practised with chemical retorts and in such simple experiments as the plucking of his own hairs to see how long they would take to grow back [3] was matched in literary criticism by his constant appeals from literary convention to a

---

[1] See J. H. Hagstrum, "Johnson's Conception of the Beautiful, the Pathetic and the Sublime," *PMLA*, LXIV (March, 1949), 134–157, reprinted in his *Samuel Johnson's Literary Criticism* (Minneapolis, 1952), ch. VII, pp. 129–52.

[2] *Life of Cowley*, par. 58.

[3] Boswell, *Life of Johnson*, ed. Hill-Powell. III, 398, n. 3.

general knowledge of life and literature. "Reason," he says, "wants not Horace to support it."[4] And, "There is always an appeal open from criticism to nature."[5] Johnson's theory of literary criticism was something analogous to deism in contemporary theology.

It is true that he had rather rigorous ideas about metrical accuracy (His ear seems to have been open only to the couplet), and there is a pair of *Ramblers* in which he talks harshly about *Samson Agonistes* on the Aristotelian grounds that it has a beginning and end but no middle. But Johnson was not at heart a critic according to the neo-classic species. He never wrote anything approximating Addison's series of *Spectators* appraising *Paradise Lost* according to the categories laid down by neo-Aristotelianism. His notorious disgust at *Lycidas* was part of a pre-romantic preference for nature over the formal species and the conventions of the pastoral. In his Shakespeare *Preface* he not only defended the "mingled" genre of tragicomedy, but in a passage which we have quoted in an earlier chapter he gave memorably vigorous expression to that rejection of the unities of time and place (as no true illusions) which had been under way in English criticism since early in Dryden's day.[6]

The appeal to nature and reason has with Johnson a strong equalitarian orientation, toward the common audience and their spontaneous vote. Though he believes that "reason and nature are uniform and inflexible," such uniformity as he in fact discovers is often in the psychology of the persons whom the poet addresses, rather than in any norm beyond and superior to themselves. Johnson's anti-classic revolt erupts with some energy rather early in his critical career, in three of his *Ramblers*, Nos. 125, 156, and 158, devoted to an inquiry into the binding force of the literary rules.

> Definitions have been no less difficult or uncertain in criticism than in law. Imagination, a licentious and vagrant faculty, unsusceptible of limitations, and impatient of restraint, has always endeavoured to baffle the logician, to perplex the confines of distinction, and burst the enclosures of regularity. There is therefore scarcely any species of writing of which we can tell what is its essence, and what are its constituents; every new genius produces some innovation, which when invented and approved, subverts the rules which the practice of foregoing authors had established.—No. 125

Both the tone of lament and that of applause seem rather studiously absent from this passage. It is a hard-headed report on the facts. But the

---

[4] *Preface to Shakespeare, Works* (1787), IX, 248.
[5] *Life of Dryden, Lives of the Poets*, ed. G. B. Hill (Oxford, 1905) I, 423.
[6] T. M. Raysor, "The Downfall of the Three Unities," *MLN*, XLII (1927), 1–9. Cf. *ante* Chapter 10, p. 189.

writer's sympathy becomes clear enough before he is done. He is in the course of launching a fully committed attack on the "arbitrary edicts of legislators" (No. 158), the hardening into law of rules derived from over-rated classic models, and the general failure of critics to distinguish between laws of nature and mere conventions.[7]

> Some [laws] are to be considered as fundamental and indispensa-ble, others only as useful and convenient; some as dictated by reason and necessity, others as enacted by despotick antiquity; some as invincibly supported by their conformity to the order of nature and operations of the intellect; others as formed by accident, or instituted by example, and therefore always liable to dispute and alteration.—No. 156

Among the more fixed and obligatory rules of drama, Johnson recog-nizes the unity of action and the single hero. Among the more obviously legitimate targets for dissent are the unity of time, the rule against tragi-comedy, the rule of five acts, and the limit of three persons together on the stage. The superior rule by which Johnson would test all such accidents of custom and prejudice is, as we have suggested, a principle graded through "reason," "nature," and "experience" in such a way as to termi-nate rather candidly now and then in an appeal to the pleasures of the voting audience.

> . . . any man's reflections will inform him, that every dramatick composition which raises mirth, is comick. . . . If the two kinds of dramatick poetry had been defined only by their effects upon the mind, some absurdities might have been prevented.
> —No. 125

The affectivism of such remarks is, however, a relatively casual com-mitment with Johnson, the consequences of which he seems scarcely to entertain.[8]

V

BUT to turn back toward the main line of our dealing with Johnson: the principle of the neo-classic universal is something which works its way through his objective theorizing with great consistency. The titles of two of his essays, *Rambler* No. 143, "The Criterions of Plagiarism,"

[7] Cf. Joseph E. Brown, *The Critical Opinions of Samuel Johnson* (Princeton, 1921), pp. 221–6, "Rules."

[8] The "absurdities" which he has in mind in the above passage, for example, are those committed, not by critics, but by poets (like Dryden in *Don Sebastian*) when they mix the heroic with "unseasonable levity." The argument quickly leads into a plea for classical decorum which may not fit so well with Johnson's state-ments elsewhere in favor of the tragi-comic license.

and *Adventurer* No. 95, "Apology for Apparent Plagiarism, Sources of Literary Variety," go far to suggest the degree of Johnson's fidelity to the classical canon of model objectivity which we have examined some chapters back in its Jacobean phase. For a man with Johnson's advanced conception of the universal, plagiarism was something which a good poet could scarcely avoid. *Rambler* No. 36, on pastoral, offers the following concrete illustration.

> The range of pastoral is indeed narrow, for though nature it-self, philosophically [i.e. scientifically] considered, be inexhausti-ble, yet its general effects on the eye and on the ear are uniform, and incapable of much variety of description. . . . However, as each age makes some discoveries, and those discoveries are by degrees generally known, as new plants or modes of culture are introduced, and by little and little become common, pastoral might receive, from time to time, small augmentations, and ex-hibit once in a century a scene somewhat varied.[9]

This emphasis was logically compatible with the large credit which we have seen Johnson conceding to the Homeric original genius, though it was far from compatible with that mania for continuing original genius in which Edward Young's *Conjectures* were more characteristic of the age. Johnson had a view of "genius" itself which, in a way related to the Lockean *tabula rasa*, was quite consistent with his respect for the ab-stract universal. Genius was a general sort of mental superiority, a power of invention capable of being turned in any direction.[1] "I am persuaded," said Johnson in one of his moments of more advanced self-complacency, "that, had Sir Isaac Newton applied to poetry, he would have made a very fine epic poem. I could as easily apply to law as to tragic poetry."[2] He would undertake to write a preface or dedication for a book of any kind—Percy's *Reliques*, Rolt's *Commercial Dictionary*, John Payne's *Tables of Interest*, William Payne's *Elements of Trigonometry*.

We have commented on the affective side of Johnson's respect for the general opinion—the "common voice of the multitude, uninstructed by precept and unprejudiced by authority" (*Rambler* No. 52). The ap-parently comfortable relation of this concept to the doctrine of the uni-versal is no less to be noted. "About things on which the public thinks long it commonly attains to think right."[3] "In the character of his

---

[9] Compare Warton, *Essay on Pope* (1806), I, 86–7: "The Works of those who profess an art, whose essence is imitation, must needs be stamped with close resem-blance to each other. . . . Descriptions, therefore, that are faithful and just, MUST BE UNIFORM AND ALIKE." Cf. Hurd, "A Discourse on Poetical Imitation," in his edition of Horace's *Epistola ad Augustum* (London 1751), pp. 133–4.

[1] See *Idler* No. 40; *Life of Cowley*, in *Lives of the Poets*, ed. G. B. Hill, I, 2; Joseph E. Brown, *The Critical Opinions*, pp. 118–23, "Genius."

[2] Boswell, *Journal of a Tour to the Hebrides*, 15 August, 1773.

[3] *Life of Addison*, in *Lives*, ed. G. B. Hill, II, 132.

Elegy I rejoice to concur with the common reader." [4] "That cannot be unpoetical with which all are pleased." [5] Everybody could recognize a tulip. And the species tulip we must suppose was precisely something which everybody could recognize.

One of the most practical operations of the universal was in the area of diction. In the high Renaissance the taste had been in favor of the local color and baroque individuality of specialist vocabularies. Terms of mining, founding, and gold working, of marine, hunting, and falconry, Ronsard had especially recommended. The time was to come, beginning perhaps about the date of Falconer's *Shipwreck* (1762), and running through the whole 19th century and our own, when localization was again the norm. But Johnson was a late spokesman for an era in which the specialized or technical vocabulary was an accidental, bastard, and vulgar lingo. Addison censured Milton for using "larboard," "Doric," "pilasters," "cornice," "ecliptic," "eccentric" (*Spectator* No. 297). The minor critics of the time may almost all be quoted to the same effect. Boileau was 46 years old but spoke of himself in a poem as 40, and Dennis commended him, "for poetry admits of no odd Numbers above Nine." [6] Both Pope [7] and Johnson objected to Dryden's parade of special knowledge in *Annus Mirabilis*.

> Some the *gall'd* ropes with dawby *marling* bind,
> Or sear-cloth masts with strong *tarpawling* coats.

"I suppose," says Johnson, "here is not one term which every reader does not wish away."

> It is a general rule in poetry that all appropriated terms of art should be sunk in *general* expressions, because poetry is to speak an universal language. [8]

The norm of style which Johnson was expounding was close to the metaphysics and the science of his age. It was recommended by the French naturalist Buffon as a "care in naming things only in the most

---

[4] *Life of Gray, Lives* III, 441.

[5] *Life of Milton, Lives* I, 175. Hume's appeal to the verdict of time in questions of art ("Of the Standard of Taste") was a contemporary parallel to Johnson's view. Longinus and Castelvetro are two earlier critics who entertain a clear respect for the universal suffrage. In the next century Tolstoy's peasant standard is the *reductio ad absurdum*.

[6] Dennis, *Miscellanies in Prose and Verse*, 1693, p. 50. See Spingarn, *Essays*, II, 333.

[7] Letter 23 in *Works*, ed. W. Elwin and W. C. Courthope, VI, 107. In the second volume of his *Essay on Pope*, 1782 (1806, II, 170), Joseph Warton writes in the new spirit, defending familiar words like "market-place," "alms-house," "seats," "spire." But in the Dedication of his *Virgil*, 1753, he had regretted the georgic necessity of using such coarse and common words as "plough," "sow," "wheat," "dung," "ashes," "horse," "cows." These would disgust "many a delicate reader."

[8] *Lives* I, 433-4.

general terms." With that and a delicate taste, one achieved "nobility" of style.

It may be with some dismay—yet it should be also with an improved sense of the difficult problem which 18th-century neo-classicism was trying to solve—that one comes upon Johnson's frequent statements in favor of something like literary particularity. Some of these are miscellaneous and casual. He did not like the "general and undefined" drawing of human nature in the plays of Nicholas Rowe.[9] No more did he like a "general" and "indefinite" encomium in epitaphs. And he said of these: "There are no rules to be observed which do not equally relate to other compositions." [1] He thought that as Pope had never seen America, he did well by not writing his projected American pastorals.[2] Toward the end of his life it is possible that Johnson shows the influence of the Wartonian doctrine of particulars. The *Life of Thomson*, 1781, might be expected to reflect Warton's *Essay on Pope*, and perhaps it does, with a certain dipping of the standard in recognition of Thomson's nature pencilling.

But there is a deeper strain of particularism which is with Johnson both early and late and tied in closely with one of his most basic inclinations, that toward introspection and personal morality rather than social philosophy or the history of princes. This particularism is part of his interest in biography, in the "life and letters" method, of which William Mason's *Gray* in 1777 was the first classic example, and Johnson's *Lives* and Boswell's *Life of Johnson* greater examples, and for which Johnson and his friends in their conversations and journals were continually and consciously at work producing materials. "I esteem biography," said Johnson, "as giving us what comes near to ourselves, what we can turn to use." [3] He wrote two essays, *Rambler* No. 60 and *Idler* No. 84, in development of the theme.[4]

> The general and rapid narratives of history, which involve a thousand fortunes in the business of a day, and complicate innumerable incidents in one great transaction, afford few lessons applicable to private life, which derives its comforts and its wretchedness from the right or wrong management of things, which nothing but their frequency makes considerable.—*Rambler* No. 60

Johnson conceives that his preference here is related consistently enough to the master principle of the universal—"there is such an uniformity in

[9] *Lives* II, 76.
[1] *Works* (1787), IX, 443.
[2] *Works* (Oxford, 1825), VI, 39–40, 42.
[3] Boswell, *Journal of a Tour to the Hebrides*, 21 August, 1773.
[4] Cf. Bergen Evans, "Dr. Johnson's Theory of Biography," *RES*, X (1934), 301–10.

the state of man, considered apart from adventitious and separable decorations and disguises." But the passage might stand very well as epigraph to a treatise on the anti-Aristotelian, anti-aristocratic poetic theory of the 18th-century drama. That theory, as we have seen, was a lover not only of sentiment but of naturalistic detail. The more true to life a story was, the better, the more convincing, the more sympathetic. Such connections undoubtedly lie behind Johnson's well-known and somewhat scandalous dedication to truth of fact.

> A story . . . should be a specimen of life and manners, but if the surrounding circumstances are false, as it is no more a representation of reality, it is no longer worthy our attention.[5]

> The value of every story depends on its being true. A story is a picture of either an individual or of human nature in general: if it be false, it is a picture of nothing.[6]

As a 20th-century neo-humanist has observed, such passages would seem to cut the Johnsonian grandeur of generality off from any commerce with fiction. It is difficult to see where poetry can come in. In dealing with poetry Johnson frequently enough paid his respects to the power of make-believe or fantasy—a power which he called "invention." But the term "imagination" meant for Johnson characteristically either (1) the normal 18th-century power of vivid picturing (or perhaps combining pictures—*Idler* 44), or (2) on the other hand, something verging on the pathological, a tendency to vagrant invention, seductive reverie, castles in Spain, day-dreaming. He speaks of the "Luxury of Vain Imagination" (*Rambler* 89), the "seducements of imagination" (*Rambler* 134), the "Dangerous Prevalence of the Imagination" (*Rasselas*, Chapter 44).[7] He resolves for his own part "to reclaim imagination" (*Prayers and Meditations*, September 18, 1760). In a *Rambler* which we have already quoted (No. 25), the same sort of derogatory phrasing seems to apply specifically to the faculty of poetic invention. "Imagination, a licentious and vagrant faculty . . . has always endeavoured to baffle the logician, to perplex the confines of distinction." We confront here in part of course a matter of semantics. The word "imagination" bore for Johnson a different burden from that which it has borne for the post-Coleridgean world. But in part also, and in large part, we are involved with the fact that in the Johnsonian world there was small place for that later burden.[8]

---

[5] Hester Lynch Piozzi, *Anecdotes* (2d. ed., 1786), p. 18.
[6] Boswell, *Life of Johnson*, 16 March, 1776.
[7] Cf. Irving Babbitt, "Dr. Johnson and Imagination," *On Being Creative*, Boston, 1932; R. D. Havens, "Johnson's Distrust of the Imagination," *ELH*, X (September, 1939), 243–55.
[8] There have been some efforts lately to attribute to Johnson an almost Coleridgean view of imagination as reconciliation and transvaluation, the combination of the familiar and the unfamiliar, the *discordia concors*. See J. H. Hagstrum, *Samuel*

In an earlier chapter we have noticed the reduced and uncertain status enjoyed by the term "wit" as it was used by Johnson and his contemporaries, the degraded condition of metaphor, and the general ornamentalism of stylistic theory. In recent years Johnson has earned a dry rebuke for his failure of response to Denham's metaphysical comparison between the flow of the Thames and that of poetic discourse.[9] A certain myopic literalism was undoubtedly one of the limitations of his critical theory and practice. His scepticism about the "representative" or directly imitative powers of verse (*Ramblers* 92, 94) is another case in point. This was shrewd, and within limits Johnson argued on a sound principle, that verse directly imitates very little. But a stubborn lack of interest in presentational analogy seems to prevent Johnson from hearing the fact that Pope had written one hexameter slow ("That like a wounded snake drags its slow length along") and one hexameter fast ("Flies o'er th' unbending corn and skims along the main").

VI

WHAT then of the grandeur of generality? In Johnson the literary theorist we confront a system of ideas (in part rigidly consistent, in part rather manifestly inconsistent, in part at least paradoxical) which constitutes a massive summary of the neo-Platonic drive in literary theory and of its difficulties. Johnson's occasional downright contradictions do not make him a worse theorist than many another; they do make him an exceptionally revealing one. It would be difficult to say exactly what neo-classic theory as a whole, or what any particular neo-classic theorist, meant by the standard of universality. Let us move toward a conclusion of our account of the neo-classic era by looking at several things which the theory might or could mean. The nine meanings which follow are related to one another not so much by semantic or dictionary fact (which is not always the most important) but by a logic of resemblances, analogies and relations. We should say that:

1. An idea is general (or universal) when it is viable from one mind to another. Even a strictly singular idea—*Socrates*, for instance—is general in this way. (And even the most highly individual and personal romantic poem has to be general in this sense. It has to be intelligible and negotiable.)

2. An idea is general in a more special way if it is viable for a great many persons, or for the average person, or for a natural person un-

---

Johnson's Literary Criticism (Minneapolis, 1952), Chapter VIII, and W. B. C. Watkins, "Dr. Johnson on the Imagination: a Note," *RES*, XXII (April, 1946), 131-4.

[9] Allen Tate, "Johnson on the Metaphysical Poets," *The Forlorn Demon* (Chicago, 1953), pp. 114-15.

corrupted by civilized sophistications. Such an idea seems to be most often conceived by the theorist as being *very* simple. We have noted Samuel Johnson's participation in this form of primitivism.

3. An idea is general when it is applicable to several individuals. The idea expressed by any common noun is general, for example, *philosopher*.

4. An idea is general, again in a more special way, if it is *more* general (or generic) as opposed to more limited or specific. *Man* is more general than *philosopher*, and *animal* is more general than *man*. The more general an idea is in this sense the more "abstract" it may also be said to be. The more ready it is, at least, to be turned into a second-stage abstraction—e.g., *animality*.

5. An idea is general if it refers to objects which generally exist, i.e., which are statistically common. A high degree of such generality does not necessarily go along with a high degree of that just described under 4., though much neo-classic discussion seems to assume that it does. There are more bald-headed philosophers wearing spectacles than there are philosophers with green hair—but the latter idea is the less specific of the two. This distinction may be put in terms of neo-classic literature as follows: There is fantasy and there is realism, and either form can be more specific or less specific. There is *Gulliver's Travels,* and there is *Rasselas.* There is Defoe's *Journal of the Plague Year,* and there is the *Rambler.*

6. An idea is general if it is at the specific or substantive level conceived by Aristotle and the schoolmen. This is the Aristotelian species, the medieval *propria idea*, the essential answer to the question: What is it? "When we ask what it is," says Aristotle, "we do not say white or hot, or four cubits long, but a man or a god." "The essence of Socrates," says Aquinas, "is the essence of man." Post-Lockean logic runs against it, but this concept is actually implicit in almost all ordinary discourse, and it may be necessary to the very idea that there are individual subsistent things, distinct from one another. Quiddity is something like a limit of change beyond which a thing becomes a different thing. It is the highest level [1] of stable differentiation between classes of things. The history of the neo-classic universal suggests a close connection with this Aristotelian quiddity—though it was often idealized into a kind of Platonic unreality. Johnson and Reynolds often employ the word *species*. One thing, however, which must be obvious is that neither poetry nor painting is confined either, in detail, to alluding to species (tulips rather than streaks) or, in whole works, to presenting a species or any subspecies (essential man, or essential gladiator). If the species or the subspecies were the norm, then all paintings of human beings, or all

---

[1] Cf. Mortimer Adler, "The Hierarchy of Essences," *The Review of Metaphysics,* VI (September, 1952), 3–30.

paintings of certain classes of human beings, would have the same aesthetic value. This seems a sure enough principle, even though it solves no critical problem. Ruskin's critique of Reynolds in a chapter of *Modern Painters* (III, i) touches a fundamental truth about poetry in the observations:

> Instead of finding . . . the poetry distinguished from the history by the omission of details, we find it consist entirely in the *addition* of details. . . . yet it cannot be simply that addition which turns the history into poetry. For it is perfectly possible to add any number of details to a historical statement, and to make it more prosaic with every added word.

7. An idea is general if it is large and inclusive—if it contains, for instance, the whole universe. Platonism has always tended to promote the generically universal to the status of the inclusive universal. *Being*, for instance, is a term which covers both ideas. Platonism has always tended to the sublime—the big, the overwhelming, the awesome. Despite Johnson's religious misgivings about the secular sublime, his version of the grandeur of generality was, as we have seen, an ambiguous junction of neo-Platonic largeness with the Aristotelian species.

8. An idea is general if it represents what is necessary—either *a priori*, like the Pythagorean theorem, or *a posteriori* (which shades off into the probable), like the law of gravity or the fact that every living man must have a head. This kind of generality may be considered as a development of 5. or 6. above, and as preparing the way for 9.

9. An idea is general if it represents what is perfect, or ideal, and hence, in the direction of structure and purpose, most real—that which tends to fulfil a possibility, capability, or potentiality of some being. A man who is a philosopher or who has profound religious experience may be statistically less common than his opposite, but there is a sense in which he is more completely a man. The Aristotelian *to beltion* comes in here, and the kind of idealism reflected in the passage from Reynolds' Thirteenth *Discourse* quoted earlier in this chapter.

None of these senses of the general or the universal will completely explain or justify the neo-classic theory. None of these is by itself a sufficient account of poetry. By and large the neo-classic universal centered too simply in the area of 3., 4., and 5. (the logical and scientific universals). These concepts were too literally taken as sufficient, and they were confused with one another. In the opinion of the present writers, 8. and 9. (the universals of structure and coherence) look more directly toward poetry and suggest a circuit of ideas which will include 1.—the intelligible and negotiable individual.

VII

THE neo-classic theory of general truth was an attempt to say what kind of reality is given in art, an attempt to relate and even to identify the real and the ideal. Yet the human ideal must be always in some sense fictitious. And fiction stretches out to embrace fable. Art, in the classic tradition, professed to render reality through a trick of presenting something either better or more significant than reality. But the trick obviously and quite often involved the unreal. Four antitheses: realism *vs.* fantasy, history *vs.* fiction, particular *vs.* universal, real *vs.* ideal, were subsumed in a medley of ways by the classic tradition under the basic antithesis nature *vs.* art. We have noticed how some of these antitheses clustered in the critical thinking of Samuel Johnson. And in our enumeration of senses for the term "general" we have suggested some of the logical dangers inherent in the whole situation. We may perhaps fittingly close not only this chapter but our narrative of neo-classicism with a brief anthology of passages touching with various accents on the most persistent preoccupation of all classic and neo-classic criticism, the puzzling relation between nature and art.

Do you mean that a rhapsode will know better than the pilot what the ruler of a sea-tossed vessel ought to say?—Plato, *Ion* 540

Not to know that a hind has no horns is a less serious matter than to paint it inartistically.—Aristotle, *Poetics* XXV

And he tells lies and mixes true and false in such a way that the middle is consistent with the beginning and the end with the middle.—Horace, *Ars Poetica*, ll. 151-2

For (as I never cease to say) the deeds and passions which verge on transport are a sufficient lenitive and remedy for every audacity of speech.—Longinus, *On the Sublime*, XXXVIII

The poet is not a recorder of facts in verse; historians take care of facts much better. The poet's job is, by a technique of mystery, by invocations of the supernatural, by a boldly fictive elaboration of ideas, to release the free spirit of poesy—so that what he writes sounds like the prophetic utterance of a soul aflame, not like a scrupulous statement of fact testified to by witnesses.—Petronius, *Satyricon*, 118

We have known of festivals without pipes and dances; but never of a poem without its fabulous or fictitious element.
—Plutarch, *How to Study Poetry* 16c

The arts are not to be slighted on the ground that they create by imitation of natural objects; for, to begin with, these natural objects are themselves imitations; then, we must recognize that they give no bare reproductions of the thing seen but go back to the Ideas from which Nature itself derives.

—Plotinus, *Ennead* V, viii

He goeth hand in hand with nature, not enclosed within the narrow warrant of her gifts, but freely ranging within the zodiac of his own wit.

—Philip Sidney, *Apologie for Poetrie*, c. 1580–4

When Aristotle said in the beginning of the *Poetics* that all the species of poetry were imitative, he meant that imitation which has for its object the image that springs entirely from human artifice. . . . Plato in the *Sophist* has left a statement that imitation is of two sorts. One of these he has named icastic; it represents things that are truly derived from some work already existing. . . . The other, which he called phantastic, is exemplified in pictures that are made by the caprice of the artist.

—Jacopo Mazzoni, *On the Defense of the Comedy*, 1587, Introduction

Poesie was ever thought to have some participation of divinesse, because it doth raise and erect the Minde, by submitting the shewes of things to the desires of the Mind, whereas reason doth buckle and bowe the Mind unto the Nature of things.

—Francis Bacon, *Advancement of Learning*, 1605

For he knows poet never credit gained
By writing truths, but things like truths, well feigned.

—Ben Jonson, Prologue to *Epicoene*, 1609

We shall tolerate flying Horses, black Swans, Hydra's, Centaur's, Harpies and Satyrs; for these are monstrosities, rarities, or else Poetical fancies, whose shadowed moralities requite their substantial falsities.

—Sir Thomas Browne, *Pseudodoxia Epidemica* (1646), V, 19

If I am not deceived, a play is supposed to be the work of the poet, imitating or representing the conversation of several persons.

—John Dryden, *A Defence of an Essay of Dramatic Poesy*, 1668

An heroic poet is not tied to a bare representation of what is true . . . but . . . he may let himself loose to visionary objects, and to the representation of such things as depending not on sense, and therefore not to be comprehended by knowledge, may give him a freer scope for imagination.

—John Dryden, *Of Heroic Plays*, 1673

The Poetic World is nothing but Fiction; Pernassus, Pegasus, and the Muses, pure imagination and Chimaera. But being, however, a system universally agreed on, all that shall be contriv'd or invented upon this Foundation according to Nature shall be reputed as truth: But what so ever shall diminish from, or exceed, the just proportions of Nature, shall be rejected as False, and pass for extravagance, as Dwarfs and Gyants for Monsters.

—George Granville, *An Essay upon Unnatural Flights in Poetry*, 1701

As no Thought can be justly said to be fine, unless it be true, I have all along had a regard for Truth; except only in Passages that are purely Satirical, where some Allowance must be given: For Satire may be fine, and true Satire, tho' it be not directly and according to the Letter, true: 'tis enough that it carry with it a Probability or Semblance of Truth.

—Edward Bysshe, *The Art of Poetry*, 1702, Preface

A strict Verisimilitude . . . [is] not requir'd in the Descriptions of this visionary and allegorical kind of Poetry, which admits of every wild Object that Fancy may present in a Dream, and where it is Sufficient if the moral meaning atone for the Improbability.—Alexander Pope, *The Temple of Fame*, 1715

The task of an author is, either to teach what is not known, or to recommend known truths by his manner of adorning them.

—Samuel Johnson, *Rambler* 3, 1750

The muses wove, in the loom of *Pallas*, a loose and changeable robe, like that in which *Falsehood* captivated her admirers; with this they invested *Truth*, and named her *Fiction*.

—Samuel Johnson, *Rambler* 96, 1751

Poetry is the art of uniting pleasure with truth, by calling imagination to the help of reason.

—Samuel Johnson, *Life of Milton*, 1779 (*Lives*, I, 170)